A Concise History of
U.S. Foreign Policy

A Concise History of U.S. Foreign Policy

Fifth Edition

Joyce P. Kaufman

ROWMAN & LITTLEFIELD
Lanham • Boulder • New York • London

Published by Rowman & Littlefield
An imprint of The Rowman & Littlefield Publishing Group, Inc.
4501 Forbes Boulevard, Suite 200, Lanham, Maryland 20706
www.rowman.com

86-90 Paul Street, London EC2A 4NE, United Kingdom

British Library Cataloguing in Publication Information Available

Library of Congress Cataloging-in-Publication Data

Names: Kaufman, Joyce P., author.
Title: A concise history of U.S. foreign policy / Joyce P. Kaufman.
Other titles: Concise history of United States foreign policy
Description: Fifth edition. | Lanham : Rowman & Littlefield, [2021] | Includes bibliographical references and index.
Identifiers: LCCN 2021009890 (print) | LCCN 2021009891 (ebook) | ISBN 9781538151358 (cloth) | ISBN 9781538151365 (paperback) | ISBN 9781538151372 (epub)
Subjects: LCSH: United States—Foreign relations.
Classification: LCC E183.7 .K36 2021 (print) | LCC E183.7 (ebook) | DDC 327.73—dc23
LC record available at https://lccn.loc.gov/2021009890
LC ebook record available at https://lccn.loc.gov/2021009891

∞™ The paper used in this publication meets the minimum requirements of American National Standard for Information Sciences—Permanence of Paper for Printed Library Materials, ANSI/NISO Z39.48-1992.

Contents

Part III: The Cold War

Part IV: The Post–Cold War Period

Preface to the Fifth Edition

When my long-time editor and friend, Susan McEachern, asked me to revise the fourth edition of this book, I told her that I would do so only after the November 2020 presidential election. I wrote the revisions to the fourth edition primarily in the summer of 2016, when I thought that the outcome of the 2016 presidential election was obvious. I was wrong, as were many other political scientists and pundits, none of whom could imagine how Donald Trump could possibly beat Hillary Clinton. As I told Susan, I did not want to be put into the position of revising the draft on the basis of what seemed like the logical outcome in the 2020 election, Joe Biden becomes president, when nothing is preordained anymore.

Little did I know that there would be a more insidious attack on the country in 2020, as the election season was starting to heat up: coronavirus. No matter how much any country or government plans to ensure its security, virtually none was prepared for the onslaught of this global pandemic, which left no country untouched. Hence, even though I was not planning to revise the book until after the election, the combination of my retirement and the stay-at-home order gave me more time than I had expected to start working on the revisions of this book earlier than I had planned. This meant that I was also able to do a lot more reading and thinking about what I wanted to include in this revised edition than I have had the luxury of being able to do in the past.

Quite a number of books have come out since the 2016 election and the period when I last revised this book that looked at the Trump administration and what it meant for the United States and its place in the world. I have had the time to read many of them, and they helped me focus my approach to this revision. My thinking was influenced especially by the publication of a new book, *The Bomb: Presidents, Generals and the Secret History of Nuclear War* by Fred Kaplan (New York: Simon & Schuster, 2020), as well as input and feedback to the fourth edition from colleagues and friends. Here the input I got from Robert Herold was especially insightful. It was seeing the name of my old friend Franklin Miller in a review of the Kaplan book that piqued my interest in reading that book, and Frank provided some additional information that helped my thinking about U.S. Cold War policy and the longer-term impacts of those policies. The result was that I realized it would be impossible to understand U.S. foreign policy since the end of the Cold War without a greater description of U.S. foreign policy *during* the Cold War. Hence, this revised version includes more extensive background on the Cold War, which is contrasted with the attempts to make a cohesive foreign policy after the Cold War ended.

Also different in this edition, at the advice of the reviewers, is that each chapter concludes with a chronology highlighting the major events during the period of time that the chapter covers and a list of important primary source documents referenced in the chapters.

Included here is information about the Trump administration, not just to critique the policy decisions made by that administration, but because of the lessons that we can learn from studying those decisions. While it is clearly too early to know what the long-term impact of those decisions will be, it is not difficult to determine some of the short-term impacts. And here we must again bring in the coronavirus pandemic and the impact that it had on the global economy in order to understand how woefully unprepared the United States was to deal with it. And while it is too soon to know what the Biden foreign policy will be as it continues to unfold, it is possible to speculate based on speeches that Biden gave as a candidate, preliminary position papers, and the words of those he tapped to work in the administration with him.

Although in previous editions I tried to keep my own opinions from the text as much as I could, in describing the Trump administration and the plight of the United States as a result of decisions made by that administration it is hard not to judge. I have tried to keep those judgments to a minimum, as I believe that it is important that students who read this book make their own decisions and reach their own conclusions. However, as a warning, my own biases do creep in.

In chapter 8, I discuss the emerging foreign and defense policies of the Biden administration based on early transition documents but also speeches and statements given by then-candidate and President-Elect Biden. Also of critical importance here are the people whom Biden tapped to join his administration and to help formulate and carry out those policies. While events could intervene, at least the early stages of Biden's presidency suggest carefully formulated policies based on more traditional understandings of "national interest" than was seen by his predecessor.

In that concluding chapter I have also added a section on "new threats." As the coronavirus pandemic illustrated clearly, the end of the Cold War did not mean an end to threats, but simply the prominence of new threats that the United States has to address. This includes not only the spread of pandemics, but climate change, humanitarian crises as a result of civil conflicts, and migration and immigration, to name but a few. While these threats existed during the Cold War, they took a back seat to the threat posed by the Soviet Union, and so it was not until after the Cold War ended that they started to be featured more prominently in U.S. foreign policy, either proactively, as in the desire to confront global warming and climate change, or reactively, as was the case with the various epidemics/pandemics, such as Ebola, SARS, and more recently coronavirus. I want to thank Dan Caldwell for sharing some of his writings with me about the spread of diseases as well as his feedback on earlier editions of this book.

As I do the reframing of this edition while sequestered at home through much of 2020 and into 2021, I also have to reflect on how fortunate I am to be in one of the most wonderful places possible. When we retired at the end of the 2018–2019 academic year, it was to move from the Los Angeles area to our home in June Lake in the Eastern Sierra, a place where "social distancing" is almost a way of life. I was fortunate during the difficult times due to the pandemic to have a small group of women friends, especially Nancy, Linda, and Jeanne, to play tennis with at least weekly, keeping appropriate distance at all times of course. They represented a welcome diversion as well as a sounding board for some of my ideas. Russ, my apparently permanent tennis coach, has also been important to my tennis game, as well as my mental health. Similarly, my golf pals, especially Deborah, Barb, Alicia (Whittier College '09), and of course Chuck also helped me keep things in perspective. And Francesca has her own special place for the friendship and support she provides. I also want to thank my old friend Julia Risser for raising interesting questions and provocative ideas about foreign policy that always made me think.

The comments and feedback provided by the reviewers solicited by Rowman & Littlefield as well as those friends and colleagues who have already offered their thoughts on earlier editions helped provide insight that I hope has strengthened this edition. Once again, I imposed on my dear friend and former colleague Irene Carlyle to read various parts of this draft, especially chapter 7. Her insights and feedback are much appreciated. I also want to thank former student Grace Creelman (Whittier College, '18) who had taken my foreign policy class at Whittier and who reviewed my outline for this revision and especially the changes that I proposed for this edition. I find it is always helpful to get input from students, as they are the intended audience for this text. However, any errors are my responsibility alone.

Of course, I owe a great deal to Susan McEachern, editor and friend, for her ongoing support and encouragement. Even when I was not ready to revise this book, it was she who convinced me that it was time, and she was right. As always, her team at Rowman & Littlefield, including assistant editor Katelyn Turner and production editor Alden Perkins, responded to all my questions and concerns quickly and patiently.

My husband, Robert Marks, has been an ongoing source of love and support, as well as great food. I could not do—or have done—all that I did without him. He, more than anyone else, understands what is necessary to write or revise a book, and the needed balance between solitude and companionship. And of course I owe a great deal to Seger, our very energetic Black Lab. Especially during the coronavirus pandemic, Seger became a good reason for many walks each day, often at the shores of Mono Lake, one of the most spectacular places in the United States if not the world. I am very fortunate indeed.

Joyce P. Kaufman

I

THE FRAMEWORK

1

Setting the Stage

The period between the election of Donald J. Trump as president in November 2016 and the presidential transition in January 2021 was a time of turmoil for the United States and for the rest of the international system. The apparently erratic decisions made by the Trump administration during its four years in office upended what had been the generally orderly process of making foreign policy. Trump's refusal to concede to Joe Biden made the transition period even more fraught, although Biden and his team moved forward, looking to the time when they would officially take office. Even though the United States had fairly elected a new president, Trump's allegations that the election was stolen raised questions about the state of American democracy. Even foreign leaders, who were used to seeing the United States as the most stable of democracies, could not help but wonder about the future of the American political system.

As we will see throughout this book, the making of U.S. foreign policy is generally premised on some basic assumptions: that foreign policy will be made in the national interest (which is commonly understood); that it will be continuous, in other words, that policies are based on previous policies; that it is often reactive (that is, made in response to events) rather than proactive; and that the highest priority is always to ensure the security of the country and the people within it. Even when there is a change in leadership from the president of one party to another, the assumption is that the transition will be orderly and that some of the basic priorities—national interest, security, and commitment to alliances—will not change dramatically. The ascension of Donald Trump and the Trump administration and then the chaotic transition to Biden threw those assumptions into disarray.

The end of the Cold War and the period that followed was a time of intense disruption to U.S. foreign policy. While the Cold War provided a clear framework for U.S. foreign policy and for the role of the United States globally, following the fall of the Soviet Union in 1991 the United States floundered to find its place internationally. It was still the unchallenged dominant global power, and other countries, both friends and foes, looked to this country to help define a new framework. In some cases this was relatively successful, such as Bill Clinton's emphasis on globalization that, for the most part, redefined the global economic order through the creation and use of international organizations. However, it was far less successful in other cases, such as the U.S. role in civil conflicts and its involvement in so-called nation-building in Haiti, Somalia, Iraq, and Afghanistan, the latter resulting in the longest war in U.S. history, one without any real conclusion as of this writing.

The absence of a clear foreign policy framework with the attendant dangers that lacuna brought with it must be coupled with the emergence of new threats such as climate change, immigration and migration, the rise of "the rest" such as China,[1] and, as made apparent recently, the global spread of diseases, most notably the coronavirus pandemic. U.S. foreign policy was so focused on traditional security threats from the time of the Cold War, that it was woefully unprepared either structurally or in terms of policy to address these new challenges. And Trump, as president, was unwilling to have his administration take the lead on any international response to these threats, especially the pandemic. Yet, as will be made clear in this book, if not foreign policy issues per se, they all have foreign policy implications, and the default was for countries to look to the United States for leadership.

This can be seen during the period following the outbreak of the coronavirus/COVID-19 pandemic in January 2020. Countless articles were published in the popular press at the time excoriating the United States for its abrogation of global leadership.[2] In *Foreign Affairs*, Nicholas Burns, currently a professor at Harvard's Kennedy School of Government and before that a U.S. ambassador and policy-maker, writes that during a time of crisis like we are seeing now with COVID-19, "under all prior U.S. presidents since World War II, the institutions of U.S. foreign policy mobilize for leadership. They call nations to action. They set the agenda for what needs to be done. They chart a path beyond the point of crisis." Yet, as Burns notes, that has not been the case now due, in part, because the Trump administration "has spent the last three years demeaning and degrading these very institutions and denigrating the kind of U.S. leadership and global collective action they promote."[3] The result has been a lack of international leadership that could have mobilized countries and institutions to work *together* to arrive at a collective response to the crisis. One can ponder why the Trump administration chose the path it did, and it might be years or even decades before the full story emerges. However, what is clear in the short term is that the global position of the United States has changed significantly during the four years of the Trump administration, and there are profound implications for the United States and for the world.

In January 2021, as the United States adjusts to a new administration, the country and its leaders have to face a number of important questions: Should the United States be more involved in the world or not? Is it the responsibility of the United States to help spread or foster democracy? When, and under what set of circumstances, should the United States intervene in the affairs of other countries? And, facing the new political realities, if the United States has lost its place as global leader, should it try to regain that position? If so, how? These are not new questions, although the answers keep changing as times, circumstances, and the priorities of presidents and other political leaders change.

This book on American foreign policy draws on basic political science approaches and theories. However, it is difficult to arrive at a practical understanding of U.S. foreign policy and the decisions that have been made without grounding them in history. To integrate the approaches put forward here, we will use a historical framework to put the major themes and concepts of U.S. foreign policy into the context of the time at which they were formulated. This requires looking at the various domestic political priorities as well as the international context that helped frame the decisions made, for the two go hand in hand in the making of foreign policy. In addition, this text relies heavily on primary documents in order to explore the ideas as fully as possible, using the words of the authors of those policies. Using primary sources is important since doing so will provide a broader context for understanding the particular policies as they were defined and implemented *at that particular time in U.S. history.* The time and context might change, but each policy set the stage for what followed and therefore must be examined carefully. In an era of internet technology, finding these documents is relatively easy and provides an accompaniment to this text.[4]

As we begin our historical journey through American foreign policy, it is also important to recognize that even the Trump administration, which seemed to run counter to much of what we know about the making of foreign policy, did not emerge suddenly. Rather, the roots of those policies and even the emergence of Trump himself can be seen decades earlier, as explored in more detail in chapter 7. In many ways, the divisions that contributed to Trump's election, did not arise out of whole cloth, but the seeds of them were present earlier.[5] Again, this reinforces the importance of looking at foreign policy historically.

It is important to add a caveat here: many of the references are to the words of the presidents who were the ones charged with making foreign policy, especially in the past. As both the head of state and head of government, the president defined the direction for the United States as well as serving as the embodiment of the country. In charting the direction and course of U.S. foreign policy there are few better examples than the words of the president to set the context for the policy at the time.

Why is it important to learn about American foreign policy? In other words, who cares? Generally, Americans do not give much thought to foreign policy. They don't make decisions about candidates for office based on the candidates' foreign policy positions unless the country is at war or in a conflict where Americans are dying. In fact, many Americans pay attention to foreign policy only in terms of the value of the dollar against another currency—such as the euro, the yen, or the pound—if they are planning to travel abroad. Some want to know whether a Japanese car is going to cost more or less than it did the last time they bought one or whether there will be a line of cars at the border when they cross into Mexico or Canada.

In fact, most Americans pay little attention to foreign policy unless it appears to affect them directly. But foreign policy *does* affect everyone, not only because of threats of terrorist attacks or the danger of war, but for far more mundane reasons. Look at the label on the last article of clothing that you bought. Where was it manufactured? In China? Bangladesh? What about your computer—where was it made? When you called the technology help line because you had a problem with a product, where was that person sitting? Was it in the United States or in India? All of this is possible because of trade, and trade is foreign policy.

Let's look at this another way. Do you know anyone who is out of work because his or her factory closed and the product is now made overseas? Allowing American companies to be based in another country is a foreign policy decision. Do you know someone who came to this country to get an education and then decided to stay because he or she could get a better job here than would be possible back home? The decision about who can enter the country is a foreign policy decision. Do you now have to pay more for a product made in China than you used to because of the tariffs imposed as a result of the Trump administration trade war? That was a foreign policy decision that had an impact directly on you. In other words, foreign policy is not remote, nor is it important only for diplomats or bureaucrats. Foreign policy can affect everyone. The main thing is to be aware of it.

Most of these foreign policy decisions—what countries to trade with, how many people to allow into the country and from where, whether to allow companies to relocate or outsource—are relatively routine. They become more political, and therefore get more attention, in election years or when something extraordinary happens. We certainly could see that in the run-up to the 2016 presidential elections when the candidates of the two major parties had very different visions for the United States, its role in the world, and even the people within its borders. Many of the same themes highlighted during his 2016 run for president were reprised by then incumbent Donald Trump in his reelection campaign in 2020. However, then candidate and now current president Biden saw the world very differently. To him, the United States needed to reclaim its leadership role in the world, and that included working collaboratively with other countries and welcoming immigrants for the strengths they bring. We will return to these themes in later chapters (especially 7 and 8) with the discussion of U.S. foreign policy today and what the election tells us about the future direction of U.S. foreign policy. The foreign policy decisions that most people know about and follow closely are those that are extraordinary because the stakes appear to be so high. Yet the reality is that many "routine" foreign policy decisions can have a very direct and immediate effect on individual lives.

One could argue that there is little the ordinary citizen can do about foreign policy so why bother to worry about it? Why not simply take the decision-makers' word when they state that U.S. "national interest" is best served by a particular foreign policy decision? As educated citizens, we need to ask what is in *our* national interest. We need to ask *whose* interests are being represented when "national interest" is given as a justification for particular decisions. Before casting a vote on Election Day, everyone should know how to evaluate critically the promises of a politician running for office who claims that she or he will act in the country's "best interest."

Citizens in the world today need to understand that countries are interrelated and that decisions made by one country have implications for decisions made by another. The so-called Brexit vote by the United Kingdom in June 2016 to leave the European Union is a case in point. The results of that vote, which was focused on one country's decision, sent shock waves through the international economic system, affecting the stock market in the United States and even raising questions about what it might mean for U.S. security. You cannot ask meaningful questions or make rational decisions unless you know what foreign policy is and what the related concept of *national interest* means. Not everyone will arrive at the same answers and this is a basis for legitimate intellectual debate. Since the results of foreign policy decisions affect each of us, we all have a right—and a responsibility—to ask these questions.

Make no mistake: this is not an easy process. Understanding foreign policy is an inexact science, often with no clear-cut right or wrong answers. Rather, approaching it requires putting many pieces together, looking at the outputs or the decisions that were made, and then trying to understand the various pieces or factors that went into making the decisions and why.

This book will not provide all the answers to understanding U.S. foreign policy. What it will do is provide insights into the components of foreign policy–making that can inform the questions to ask. It will also help point the reader to ways to determine answers to those questions.

INTRODUCTION TO U.S. FOREIGN POLICY

In general, Americans are ahistorical. Most have little knowledge of or concern with the lessons of history.[6] Yet it is impossible to really understand American foreign policy without putting it into historical context. To do otherwise means that each generation will have to relearn (and often repeat) the lessons of the past. The point here is that little in American foreign policy really is "new." In most cases the formulation of foreign policy is an ongoing process of assessing and evaluating previous or existing policy in light of changing circumstances. An understanding of why and how certain policies were formulated in the past should help you better understand the consequences of current foreign policy decisions for the United States, for other countries, and even for you personally.

Most students of American foreign policy and even many decision-makers tend to look at foreign policy decisions as falling into broad general categories; for example, should the United States be engaged in the world (*internationalism* or *engagement*), or should it remain aloof from the rest of the world (*isolationism* or *unilateralism*)?[7] Should U.S. foreign policy be guided by a single overarching adversary, as it was during the Cold War, or should it be based on a broader and less defined set of goals, such as fighting terrorism, as it is today? Was the "war on terror" really different from the fight against communism? Or are they both examples of a conflict against an idea rather than a single country, which is what made each so difficult to fight? Is it time to stop thinking in terms of a single "threat" and to start thinking about broader threats coming from a global pandemic, for example, or the dangers posed by a depleted environment (what have become known as issues of human security)? Foreign policy decisions are not made in a vacuum but are the result of a number of factors, both domestic and international, that are taken into account. Moreover, not all factors weigh equally all the time—to be effective, foreign policy must assign different weights to each and reflect changing priorities as well as the context within which they are made.

Changes in foreign policy, at least in theory, should reflect the current needs of the country. Often a country's success in a particular area depends on its abilities to work with actors—other countries, non-state actors, international organizations, and others—outside its borders. The United States, for all its power internationally, is no different. Therefore, we can ask what are the best ways for the United States to engage with these actors to help the country further its national interest? As we saw with the Trump administration, is the U.S. national interest best served by reaching out to former adversaries, such as Russia's Putin and North Korea's Kim Jong-un, and minimizing the role of traditional allies? How have these policies changed to reflect a new or different understanding of how best to achieve that national interest? And how has the importance of these actors changed as each has affected the development of U.S. foreign policy?

This approach to foreign policy is not unique to the United States. In fact, each country's foreign policy decisions should be premised on its own priorities and the ways in which actors outside its national border will help it achieve its goals. In the case of the United States, the student of foreign policy can track and document changes in priorities that will provide important insights into the reasons particular foreign policy decisions were made.

In order to really understand any aspect of American foreign policy and the related changing concept of security from the founding of this country through the twenty-first century, the policy must be placed within the framework of both the international situation and domestic priorities. *Foreign policy encompasses decisions a country makes that affect actors beyond its own borders.* Similarly, the decisions and policies made by other external actors (whether nations, corporations, multinational organizations, etc.) have a direct impact on the United States. Both these components, domestic and international, provide the framework that helps define the context for making foreign policy decisions.

Foreign policy decisions cannot ignore domestic factors that can involve a range of issues, including the economic situation of the country, the "mood" of the people, and the cycle of the political process (i.e., whether or not it is an election year). In fact, foreign policy decisions sometimes appear to be made to distract people from problems within the country. These two components, domestic and international, *both* feed into and affect the foreign policy decisions a country makes. This makes understanding America's foreign policy decisions over time a complex undertaking.

Grasping the broad approaches to making policy in general, along with the assumptions that go with them, are essential to understanding U.S. foreign policy. However, those approaches and assumptions are only starting points. More important to the understanding of U.S. foreign policy is the application of those approaches to the realities of the situation. For example, it is possible to look at and define the concept of "isolationism." However, doing so should also lead to questions about the prevailing view of early U.S. foreign policy, such as whether it really was "isolationist" or whether the United States was engaged in the world only in a limited and clearly defined way, which is closer to a "unilateralist" perspective. That series of questions cannot be answered without first defining the terms and then looking at when—and why—the United States adopted and then deviated from a specific foreign policy type or orientation. This exploration should lead to an understanding of why the United States adopted the policy it did and how that policy, put into the context of the time, was designed to help the United States achieve its goals as defined by its own national interest. Only then will it be possible to better understand under what set of circumstances the United States chose to break from that policy and get involved politically and militarily in world affairs. Only by exploring and addressing this range of ideas can you answer the questions posed above and then draw conclusions about the direction of U.S. foreign policy at a particular time in the country's history.

Assessing actual policy against a theoretical type is only one piece of the foreign policy puzzle. When you look at "foreign policy" what you are assessing are *policy outputs*, specifically the *results* of the policy decisions that were made within the government. Here it is important to make a distinction between the *processes* by which these decisions were made and the actual *decisions*. In most cases, foreign policy decisions are the result of a routine process involving bureaucrats in an executive department (such as State, Defense, Treasury, Commerce, etc.) who make decisions based on what has been done before. The president of the United States or the secretary of the agency sets the priorities, and the bureaucrat implements them.

However, this *implementation* process contrasts with the process of *setting the priorities* that will determine what U.S. foreign policy will be. The actual decision-making and the outputs (i.e., decisions) that result are part of the process performed by those in relatively high positions, often under circumstances of crisis or actual conflict, based on their perception of national interest as well as their own priorities and understanding of the political realities.

Here another distinction must be made, that is, the difference between those decisions that are *proactive* versus those that are *reactive*. *Proactive policies* are initiated at a high level (for example, by the president or the secretary of state or defense) and are tied to the creation of a new policy or a dramatic change from an existing one. An example of a proactive policy is the U.S. decision to invade Iraq in March 2003. Here the decision was tied directly to the goals stated in President George W. Bush's "National Security Strategy of the United States," issued in September 2002.[8] This document, which has become known as "the Bush Doctrine," puts forward a new direction for American foreign policy: "defending the United States, the American people and our interests at home and abroad by identifying and destroying the threat *before it reaches our borders*" (emphasis added). In other words, this document states that as part of the foreign policy framework for the Bush administration, the United States will be justified in going to war *preemptively* against any country or group that *potentially* threatens this country or its allies and that it will act alone if necessary. Hence, U.S. foreign policy will be proactive should the country appear to be threatened in any way.

In contrast to a proactive policy, a reactive policy is one where the president and his (or her) advisors are in a position of having to react to circumstances that were thrust upon them, regardless of what established policy might be. The Cuban Missile Crisis provides a prime example of reactive policy, as does the decision to go to war against Afghanistan in response to the attacks on September 11, 2001. In the case of the Cuban Missile Crisis, no matter how carefully President John F. Kennedy and his advisors outlined what their foreign policy priorities should be, such as fighting communism or aiding developing countries, reacting to the information about the missiles in Cuba pushed that emergency to the top of the policy agenda. It also put the United States into a position of responding to circumstances that were initiated by other countries, rather than planning for what the president hoped would happen or would like to see occur. In other words, the United States was forced to *respond* in some way.

Similarly, despite warnings about a possible terrorist attack, the government could not expect or plan for the specific events of September 11. Therefore, those events put the Bush administration into the position of deciding what policies to pursue to *respond* to that crisis. These examples stand in contrast to the decision to invade Iraq in March 2003. In that case, the United States initiated the foreign policy decision, choosing when, where, and how to act. In other words, in the case of the invasion of Iraq, the United States did not respond to events thrust upon it (reactive) but took the initiative (proactive) based on alleged evidence of weapons of mass destruction.[9] Knowing the difference between these terms is important to understanding how and why particular foreign policy decisions were and are made. In addition, these cases are examples of how circumstances dictate that decisions be made quickly, with incomplete or even incorrect information. Yet decisions must be made, and those decisions have important ramifications for future policies.

Understanding foreign policy also requires seeing the broader domestic context within which foreign policy decisions are made. For example, an understanding of the Cold War (roughly from 1947 until the collapse of the Soviet Union in 1991) would not be complete without knowledge of the role played by Senator Joseph McCarthy and the Red Scare in the 1950s here at home. The Cold War pitted the United States and its generally democratic allies against the Soviet Union and other communist countries. McCarthyism, with its desire to ferret out communists within the United States, fit well within and took advantage of the larger Cold War framework. At the same time, domestically, McCarthy fueled the fear of this ideological enemy which contributed to public support for foreign policy decisions made during that time, even though much of what he alleged was later debunked.

The role of this short text is not to examine all aspects of U.S. foreign policy decision-making; rather, it is to look at the ideological and political framework of those who made the decisions, and to see the ways in which their approach or understanding guided the decisions they made. For example, the change in U.S. foreign policy surrounding the Spanish-American War in 1898 can be attributed in part to the influence of Theodore Roosevelt and his desire to be more aggressive internationally, as well as to President William McKinley's reluctance to resist the growing pressure from the media and public to take action. Similarly, the decision to get involved in World War I in 1917 is partly the result of President Woodrow Wilson's deeply held commitment to the ideals of democracy and his belief that the war could be fought as "the war to end all wars" and "the war to make the world safe for democracy." In retrospect, we can look at these idealistic pronouncements and wonder how any leader could ever have believed them to be true. But in the context of the time, they framed the foreign policy decisions that were made, and many of the Wilsonian ideals continue to influence U.S. foreign policy today.[10] Further, at the time, they provided a rallying cry that garnered the support of the American public.

What does this tell us about what we need to know in order to understand U.S. foreign policy? First, it suggests that it is critical to understand the theoretical assumptions (for example, whether to remain unilateralist or to engage internationally) that influenced the decisions made. Second, it tells us that it is important to assess the actual decisions made against the theoretical assumptions or constructs that influenced them. And third, it indicates that it is necessary to look at the context (international and domestic) within which foreign policy decisions were made. Based on this information and a critical assessment of reality versus theory, it will be possible to draw conclusions that allow for a better understanding of U.S. foreign policy.

To start the process, we will begin by delving into the world of theory. Specifically, what is foreign policy and where does it come from?

WHAT IS FOREIGN POLICY?

"Foreign policy" refers to those decisions made within a country that are affected by and that in turn affect entities outside the country. Initially, foreign policy (and most of international relations in general) pertained to the interaction of nation-states, as those were the primary actors. Hence, foreign policy generally refers to decisions made by one country or nation-state that directly affect another. One of the major changes seen in the recent past is that foreign policy is no longer just about relations between countries. In our current globalized world, foreign policy now includes a country's relationships with a range of actors, including those that exist outside traditional state borders. These might include organizations that are made up of nation-states, such as the United Nations, the European Union, or NATO. It could include multinational corporations (MNCs), such as Wal-Mart, that end up influencing the policies of the country within which they are housed.[11] It might include stateless actors, such as the Palestinians or the Kurds, which act as political entities to influence the policies of other countries. It might include nonstate actors, such as Al Qaeda or ISIS, which exist outside the boundaries of any established country but influence the foreign policy decisions of other countries. Or it might include nongovernmental organizations (NGOs), such as the Sierra Club or Amnesty International, which increasingly play a role in getting policy issues onto the agenda for international discussion.

The presence of actors that exist outside the traditional nation-state has further complicated the foreign policy process. Generally, countries transmit their policy decisions from one to another through recognized diplomatic channels, whether the head of state, an ambassador, a secretary of state or a foreign minister, or through an established bureaucracy. But the actors mentioned above, especially nonstate actors and stateless peoples, typically do not have such channels or representatives, thereby raising questions about how policy decisions will be transmitted or policy requests made. In some cases, heads of state do not want to meet with representatives of some of these actors because they fear that doing so will grant legitimacy—that is, give the nonstate actors the same status that a country has. However, ignoring these actors or uncertainty about how to deal with them does not mean that they do not have a critical role to play in influencing the foreign policy decisions of a state, even a major power like the United States.

National Interest

Foreign policy decisions are made based on *national interest*. But what does that mean? Exactly what is "national interest"? There are a number of theoretical approaches to guide our understanding of this concept.

Different policy-makers are influenced by their own perspectives, which help frame the policy decisions that they make. If foreign policy involves those decisions that are made within a country that are affected by and in turn affect actors and decisions made outside its borders, it is also important to understand some broad theoretical approaches that decision-makers have used to understand those interactions. These broad theoretical areas of focus have influenced the decisions made by different presidents and other policy-makers. So when we talk about Wilson as an "idealist" or Nixon as a "realist," we need to understand what that really means.

The Realist Perspective

In general, relations between countries are the basis of foreign policy. One of the major schools of thought about understanding these relations is the *realist school*, which assumes that nation-states (i.e., countries) are the primary actors in world politics and that each will act in a way that allows it to pursue its key interests or "national interests."

The realist perspective is characterized by the central role that *power* plays, where power is the ability of one actor to influence the behavior of another. Power can be defined in a number of ways, all pertaining to influencing the outcome of a decision.

According to Joseph Nye, a political scientist as well as policy-maker, power can be defined simply as "hard" or "soft." *Hard power* includes both economic and military strength that is used to force others to change their position. In contrast, *soft power* involves persuading others to do what you want through co-option or cooperation, rather than coercion. Soft power relies on values rather than might.[12] On the other hand, Walter Russell Mead divides power into four types: sharp (military), sticky (economic), sweet (culture and ideals), and hegemonic. Sharp, sticky, and sweet together contribute to hegemonic in that they come together and the result is greater than the sum of its parts.[13]

The application of hard or sharp power is at the core of the realist perspective. In general, since its emergence as an imperial power in the nineteenth century, the United States has relied heavily on military power in order to get its way. If the realist perspective assumes that the nation-state is the primary actor in the international system and that it will act in a rational way (to maximize benefits and minimize costs), then states will act to maximize their own power by wielding military or economic might as necessary. At the heart of realist decision-making is the notion that "statesmen think and act in terms of interest defined as power"[14] and that it is in the country's best interest to continue to accrue power using whatever means available.

The United States' decisions to provoke a war with Mexico in 1846 to gain territory and later to respond militarily to the explosion of the battleship USS *Maine* in the harbor in Havana, Cuba, in 1898 are two early examples of realist foreign policy decision-making. Later, in the twentieth century, President Nixon and Henry Kissinger, who served first as national security advisor and then as secretary of state, are both seen as quintessential realist decision-makers, using the threat of military force when necessary, but also knowing how to play one actor (the Soviet Union) against another (China) to the advantage of the United States. Values and moral principles do not play a major role in realist thinking. Rather, the main goal is getting and using power in the belief that power is equated with security.

In the realist perspective, most critical are what are known as *"core interests,"*[15] those that involve the protection and continuation of the state and its people. These tie directly to a country's security and become the central core of any state's national interest. Only when the country's security can be assured can the government make decisions about other aspects of the country. For example, concern about global warming, while important, becomes a far lower priority in the face of a direct military threat.

Liberal/Idealist Perspective

Another major approach to relations between countries is the *liberal* or *idealist school*, which looks at countries as part of a collective body where security is best achieved if countries work together rather than in competition. In contrast to realism, the contemporary idealist or liberal perspective is based on values and on the importance of peoples and nations working together cooperatively. *Liberalism* (not to be confused with the political notions of "liberal" or "conservative") grows from the idealist stress on what unites people and countries and leads directly to the creation and growth of international organizations, such as the United Nations. This perspective, in turn, stresses the importance of countries working together in pursuit of common goals for the betterment of all. Advocacy of free trade policies is an example of the application of this theoretical perspective since the assumption is that all countries will benefit from this form of economic cooperation. The use of soft or sweet power becomes an important element in this tradition, as it is tied to policies rooted in cooperation. The liberal/idealist perspective gained increasing credibility as a framework for foreign policy with the end of the Cold War and the spread of capitalist economics and democracy through the countries that had been part of the so-called Eastern Bloc.

The foreign policies advocated by Woodrow Wilson are perhaps the clearest application of this approach in American foreign policy. (These are discussed in more detail in chapter 2.) From Wilson's decision to enter World War I, justified in part on the need to make the world safe for democracy, to his advocacy for an organization, the League of Nations, that would bring all countries together to thwart expansionist tendencies of other countries, his foreign policy was steeped in idealism. George W. Bush, with his emphasis on the belief of the importance of spreading the values of freedom and democracy, is a more recent example of this way of thinking. (See chapter 6.)

Underlying the goals of the liberal/idealist approach to foreign policy is the idea that the country's security and national interests are better served by working *with* other countries than by trying to compete with or overpower them.

Feminist Perspectives

Another approach to foreign policy and international relations grew out of the *feminist critique*, which advocates the need to look not only at who made policy and why (generally men who followed the realist approach), but also at the impact of those decisions on the people who were most affected and often had the least access to the decision-makers: women and children. And, as feminist writers point out, women have been an important—if unacknowledged—part of U.S. foreign policy.[16]

The *feminist perspective* argues that those who make foreign policy decisions are largely men who have different interests from the groups affected by U.S. policy, especially when the policy decision is to do nothing. (It is important to remember that doing nothing is a policy decision in and of itself.) It focuses more on understanding who has the power and how that power is used rather than on the processes by which decisions are made. The feminist perspective would remind us of the importance of understanding the impact of decisions on all people and of the ways in which gender might influence our understanding of foreign policy decisions.[17]

When we look at the characteristics generally associated with foreign policy they are the traits that we tend to think of as masculine: power, military might, strength, and coercion, to name but a few. In contrast, the notions of cooperation and peace, which are typically associated with women and are seen as feminine, are perceived as less important in ensuring a country's security. However, in order to get a more complete understanding of U.S. foreign policy, we need to look at the world through "gender-sensitive lenses." In doing so, we can see that women are an important part of the foreign policy picture, even though they are often obscured by the prominence of men, and that foreign policy is neither necessarily masculine nor feminine. Rather, it is about making decisions perceived to be in the best interest of the country.

The emergence of women as prominent foreign policy decision-makers both in the United States and in other countries has made it clear that women are as capable of making tough decisions as men. In the United States, former secretary of state Hillary Clinton became the first woman to run for president supported by a major political party and we currently have a female vice president, Kamala Harris; Madeleine Albright and Condoleezza Rice are also examples of women who rose to hold the critical position of secretary of state. Before them, women like Theresa May and Margaret Thatcher in England, Indira Gandhi in India, and Golda Meir in Israel all became prime ministers in their respective countries. However, it is also important to bear in mind that many of the qualities ascribed to these women were masculine in character (ambitious, ruthless, hard-headed, "hawk" versus dove), and not necessarily seen as positive qualities for women to have.[18]

As you will see as you go through this book, most of the decision-makers were men, and women's voices generally did not enter into the process. We have tried to make a point of noting those exceptional cases.

Security and the Concept of Threat

Regardless of which theoretical approach you take—realist, idealist/liberal, feminist—achieving the country's security is paramount. Inherent in the concept of security is also the notion of threat, that is, anything that endangers a country's core interests, people, or territory. Although this generally refers to physical danger, the concept of threat is far broader and can apply to anything that can harm or interfere with the way of life, ideals, philosophy, ideology, or economy of the country. During the Cold War, the primary threat coming from communism was far more than the fear of military attack; communism was also seen as a danger to the democratic ideals and capitalist market economy on which the United States was founded. More recently, the concept of threat has been broadened further to refer to the dangers posed by environmental degradation, the spread of disease, and human rights abuses—all of which run counter to the ideals that are considered fundamental to the United States and to the well-being of its people.

One test of national interest and core values is whether the threat is important enough to go to war about. Would the American public support the decision to deploy U.S. troops against the perceived threat? Clearly, in the face of armed attack on the country, such as the Japanese attack on Pearl Harbor on December 7, 1941, or the terrorist attacks on September 11, 2001, there was little debate about whether a military response was appropriate. But what about the case of human rights abuses abroad, such as those that have taken place in Rwanda or Bosnia or Sudan? More recently, questions have arisen about what, if any, role the United States should play in the bloody civil war in Syria, in which approximately five hundred thousand people, many of whom were civilians, were killed in the first five years of the war and with little indication of a peaceful resolution in sight. Because protecting basic human rights is a central value dear to the United States, should the United States use its military might to help those whose rights are being abused, or who are fighting against an autocratic and repressive dictator? Both Presidents Obama and Trump debated that question with no definitive answer. Clearly, these are much harder questions to answer, and the response can be debated. Some people believe that the United States has a moral responsibility to intervene in those cases. Others believe that fighting against human rights abuses in foreign countries is not in our national interest because it does not affect this country directly. Therefore, they conclude, the United States should not get involved. Because of the need for public support for military intervention, the resulting foreign policy decision as to whether or when to intervene in such cases is an example of the ways in which international and domestic factors coincide.

As the one who sets the foreign policy priorities, it is up to the president to make the case for (military) intervention as being in the national interest, and it is the president who is held accountable by the public. Former assistant secretary of state for democracy, human rights, and labor, John Shattuck, notes that in these cases, "strong public support is unlikely until the president has stimulated it by cogently explaining that the redefinition of U.S. national interests include the prevention of human rights and humanitarian disasters that might destabilize the world."[19] In other words, while it is easy to make the case for war in the event of direct attack on the country or on U.S. citizens, it is far more difficult to explain why it is necessary or in the national interest to get involved in a country on the other side of the world to prevent human rights abuses or humanitarian catastrophe. If the president believes that such intervention is necessary, it will fall on him or her, as the leader of the country, to clearly explain why Americans will be put in harm's way.

A corollary is that once the president makes the decision to intervene militarily, the public must see results, or support for that effort will wane over time. For example, in 2003 President Bush took his case to the Congress and the public and received the support necessary to go to war against Iraq. However, by June 2005, two years after the war was declared "over," with combat troops still fighting and no known exit strategy, public support started to decline.[20] By April 2008, as the presidential campaign was heating up, according to a Pew poll, 52 percent of Americans believed that the war (in Iraq) was going not too well or not at all well, and 57 percent believed that the war was the wrong decision.[21] Regardless of initial support for the war effort, over time and with little end in sight, support started to wane.

Another element of the concept of threat is tied directly to the ways in which the nation perceives its own power and capabilities as well as its perception of the power and capabilities of an adversary. A nation will pursue a foreign policy that it believes will increase its own security and diminish the threat. This suggests that many foreign policy decisions are tied to intangibles, such as perceptions. For example, it is possible to quantify one country's military might, such as the number of fighter aircraft, aircraft carriers, tanks, and troops. But what should also go into this equation (and is much harder to measure) is the nation's willingness to use those capabilities, that is, its *credibility*. This is an intangible but very real factor when one country is trying to determine whether other countries represent a threat or, conversely, how it can protect itself from a threat. Most will agree that a country with no military force or with a military that could easily be overpowered poses little direct threat to the United States. But what about a country such as North Korea or Iran, both of which are believed to be developing nuclear weapons? Each of those countries can be perceived as a threat because not only might it have such weapons, but because of the fear that it might use them. Thus, a country's credibility enters into the foreign policy equation, and perceptions directly affect the making of foreign policy, where credibility is based on the belief that a country has weapons and is willing to use them to achieve its foreign policy goals.

FOREIGN POLICY ORIENTATIONS

How does a country pursue its national interest? Countries have various foreign policy options or orientations available to them. The particular option that the decision-makers choose to pursue assumes a number of things: that they know or have formulated what is in the national interest; that the decision-makers will then make decisions that are tied to or that will further the national interest; and that the first priority will be to ensure the country's security and that of its people.

We will look at a number of foreign policy orientations in this book: *unilateralism, neutrality, isolationism,* and *engagement.* As you will see, one of the ways in which the United States became engaged internationally was by becoming an *imperialist* power, that is, by extending its reach globally. But it did so initially under the umbrella of unilateralism. This apparent contradiction will be explained in more detail in chapter 2. It is important to remember that foreign policy orientations are generalizations or theoretical types and that few countries pursue any one in its purest form. Rather, the application of the particular policy will be a function of the country and its goals *at a given time*.

The United States has predominantly pursued two of these orientations in its history—unilateralism and engagement—although it was isolationist in the period between the two world wars. The United States also declared neutrality to try to avoid involvement in World Wars I and II, unsuccessfully it turns out. Of these orientations, *neutrality* is the only one that has a very specific meaning within the international system. When a nation pursues a policy of neutrality, it chooses *not* to engage in any military, political, or security alliances. In other words, it remains apart from any aspect of the international system that would require it to take sides or get involved militarily. Because of its unique status, a country that is neutral is generally willing to accept specific roles and responsibilities within the international system. Often such a country—Switzerland is a classic example of this—is used as the site for various international negotiations so that no one country in the negotiation has the "home team advantage." Switzerland, moreover, is an international banking center because it is considered "safe." A declaration of neutrality also means that other countries will (or should) respect that position and not invade or attack a neutral nation.

The declaration of neutrality became especially important during the Cold War, when states did not want to be put into a position of having to take sides between the United States and its allies and the Soviet Union and its allies. In fact, a group of countries, primarily smaller developing ones, further assured this special relationship by creating their own bloc called the "neutral nonaligned" (NNA) countries. Led by Egypt under Nasser, Yugoslavia under Tito, and Indonesia under Sukarno, this group of countries met in 1961 to create an organization that would combat colonialism and also assure political and military/security independence for their states at the height of the Cold War. In addition to protecting their countries' national interest by allowing them to remain outside the U.S. and Soviet orbits, these countries also worked together to further a common agenda that would benefit them, including economic cooperation and growth. Many of these countries were very successful at playing the two sides off against each other in order to get economic aid and assistance; both Tito and Nasser were masters at this political maneuvering, for example, for the benefit of their own state.

Unilateralism and Isolationism

In the early years of the United States, the prevailing foreign policy was one of unilateralism,[22] which gave the United States freedom to engage with other countries economically while also protecting it by keeping it out of any formal alliances or agreements. This "policy of aloofness" or political detachment from international affairs was advocated by Thomas Jefferson, George Washington's secretary of state, who saw this as "the best way to preserve and develop the nation as a free people."[23] This approach was consistent with that advocated by other founders of the country. In his often-quoted farewell address as president, George Washington warned the leaders of the new country to "steer clear of permanent alliances with any portion of the foreign world." He asked the country why we should "entangle our peace and prosperity in the toils of European ambition, rivalship, interest, humor, or caprice."[24] And John Adams, the second president, wrote in a letter in 1805 of the principles in foreign affairs that he advocated and followed as president and specifically, that "we should make no treaties of alliance with any European power; that we should consent to none but treaties of commerce; that we should separate ourselves, as far as possible and as long as possible, from all European politics and wars."[25]

What did the policy of unilateralism really mean for the United States? Here, again, it is important to think about national interests *within the context of the United States at that time*. When the United States was founded, the highest priority was to grow from within. As a new country, the greatest need was to pay attention to internal priorities, including political stability and economic independence, and the best way to do that, according to the founders of the country, was to remain outside the framework of European wars. Instead, the emphasis would be on economic strength through trade and commerce. This emphasis was essential to the growth and expansion of the country.

Europe in the eighteenth century was in a constant struggle for power, with France and England especially vying for prominence. America's founders warned the future leaders of the United States that it would not be in the national interest to get involved with those struggles, but rather it would be in the country's interest to stay clear of them. Yet "the evidence suggests that the U.S. economy was at least as dependent on foreign trade in 1790 as it was two hundred years later,"[26] and much of that trade, and in fact the United States economic system, "was inextricably bound up in the British economic system."[27] Hence, while the United States in its early years remained removed from the politics and wars of Europe, it was linked directly to Europe economically.

Pursuing a foreign policy of unilateralism allowed the United States to pick and choose when, where, and how to be involved with other countries, which was what allowed it to grow. Unilateralism provided the framework for geographic expansion through what would become known as America's "manifest destiny," and it allowed the country to strengthen economically through trade and, eventually, industrialization. And as U.S. trade and commerce grew, a military (especially a navy) was needed to protect U.S. interests. In short, unilateralism allowed the United States to become a "great power," or some would say an imperialist power, by the end of the nineteenth century.[28]

Engagement/Internationalism

The other major policy orientation that the United States pursued was one of *engagement*, or *internationalism*, which characterized U.S. foreign policy from 1945 to 2017 and, technically, through the Trump administration.[29] Internationalism deals with the decision to become actively engaged in all aspects of international relations, including the military and political alliances that the United States shunned prior to World War II. Again, the critical question is why the U.S. decision-makers chose to pursue that course of action. How and why was it in the national interest of the United States to become involved militarily and politically as well as economically? And why and how would that change?

An important point is that involvement internationally has both a cooperative and a conflictual component, with a country sometimes pursuing both at the same time. For example, during the Cold War, although the United States and the Soviet Union were major adversaries, they were also trading partners, at least since 1972, because this served the best interests of both countries economically.[30] And while the Bush administration labeled North Korea an "axis of evil" country, under the terms of an agreement signed earlier between the United States and North Korea in 1994, the United States sent fuel to that country.[31] While these might seem to be contradictory policies, they are in the national interest of the United States, as they gave this country an important edge economically, while also ensuring ongoing engagement with an adversary.

THEORY AND CONTEXT

As we have seen above, over the course of its history, the United States has pursued two major foreign policy orientations at different points, first unilateralism and then a policy of internationalism or active engagement in the international system, although at different periods it also was either neutral or isolationist, albeit briefly. Deciding which one to pursue and why, and when and why to break from that particular pattern, was tied to what was perceived to be in the national interest of the United States at various points. It is important to note that each of these approaches represents an ideal type and, as we will see, the actual application of each policy was not nearly as pure.

In order to understand which approach the United States opted for and why, it is necessary to place the particular policy into the context of the period during which it was made. American foreign policy is the result of a number of often-competing priorities and issues, as well as the result of the perspectives of the people who make policy. Therefore, it is important to explore when and why the United States broke from its policy of unilateralism. We must also examine why U.S. policies since the end of the Cold War have been different from those pursued during the Cold War, although all could be termed "internationalist," though for different reasons. In other words, understanding U.S. foreign policy is tied to an understanding of history and the context within which decisions were made—both domestic and international.

Fully understanding and appreciating American foreign policy (or that of any country) requires looking within the nation to see who makes policy and speaks for the nation. Generally, the more developed and democratic the country, the more complex the foreign policy decision-making apparatus. In the United States, policy is generally formulated by the executive branch, specifically, the president, his advisors such as the assistant to the president for national security (the national security advisor), and the secretaries of state and defense, although other components of the executive branch (the bureaucracy) weigh in as well. Other actors, such as Congress, play a role, although a less direct one. The media play both a direct role, through the stories they cover and how they cover them, and an indirect one, as a vehicle through which the public gets its information. But the power of these other groups to influence policy outcomes diminishes the farther they get from the president and the members of the executive branch.[32] Knowing who makes policy and the relationships these various actors have to one another is a critical part of understanding the process of making foreign policy.

IDENTIFYING THEMES

Thus far, we have identified a number of themes that characterize and explain U.S. foreign policy. We can look at the policies based on how involved the United States was with other countries and the extent of that involvement (unilateralism or isolationism versus internationalism or engagement). We can look at who made the policies and the competing role of the president versus the Congress. We can ask who influenced the policies and who are affected by them, both domestic and international actors. And we can ask how U.S. foreign policy at different points in time reflects changes from previous policies and, if there are changes, why these occurred.

One of the points raised in reviewing the history and evolution of U.S. foreign policy is that while the broad shifts might be startling (e.g., unilateralism to engagement), on closer examination hints of those changes actually existed before they were implemented. This, too, is important to note. For example, the ideological battles between democracy and communism following World War II in many ways were extensions of the fight for the spread of democracy advocated by Woodrow Wilson. Hence, as the United States moved into the Cold War, it was possible to hear echoes of earlier ideas about the primacy of democracy and about the need to "make the world safe for democracy." What was different during the Cold War was the fact that military and political engagement in support of those ideals became the norm rather than an exception.

As we explore the evolution of U.S. foreign policy, we will keep returning to these themes in order to place the foreign policy decisions into a broader context for understanding.

WHO MAKES FOREIGN POLICY, AND WHY ARE PARTICULAR DECISIONS MADE?

The Constitution of the United States laid out a framework for making U.S. foreign policy. Like many other decisions made in the early years of this country, the particular approach built into this document was designed to limit the power of any one branch and to ensure that the system of checks and balances would be applied.[33]

The Actors

The executive branch, headed by the president, and the legislative branch, the Congress, are the two parts of the government that have been given most of the responsibility for making—and for implementing—foreign policy. Although the judicial branch (the courts) is usually not considered part of the foreign policy process, it does get involved when a particular law is in dispute, and it has been used to interpret the Constitution in order to clarify the relationship between the other two branches on a range of issues.[34] However, this does not happen very often.

In the early years of the country especially, with a relatively weak and part-time Congress, it is not surprising that the executive branch, primarily the president, set the foreign policy priorities. It was assumed at the time that only the president could look at what was in the national interest and then give the orders necessary for that policy to be implemented. More important, it was also assumed that only the president represented the country as a whole. In an era before cell phones, faxes, and internet, the primary means of communication was through letters and direct conversation. Hence, the president had to rely on information supplied by U.S. diplomats and emissaries who traveled and lived abroad as well as information from other countries' diplomats who served as the representatives of their countries in order to get information relevant to this country's foreign policy. It was the job of these officials to relay information back through the State Department, where the secretary of state could inform and advise the president, who could then make decisions.

Because the means of communication were slow, decisions could be made more deliberately. Crises did not escalate overnight, nor did circumstances change by the minute. Rather, there was an established international order, and the primary shifting that took place was over the relative power that different countries had within that order.

In the late eighteenth century, the United States was a relatively new country compared with the European nations such as Britain or France, or with the Asian nations of Japan and China. Fearing what would happen if the country got involved with those countries, the founders decided that the highest priority for the United States was to establish itself as a nation and to stay removed from those others politically and militarily.

Over time, circumstances changed. Among the most significant in the making of U.S. foreign policy was the growth of the executive branch following World War II, and subsequently the assertion of congressional power into foreign policy decision-making. Later chapters will explore the various changes and the reasons for them; however, a brief overview will help set the stage for what will follow.

Shifting Balance of Power: Executive and Legislative Branches

As the United States grew as a nation, so did U.S. relations with different parts of the world. With more involvement internationally came questions about the wisdom of the decisions that were made and whether the president really did speak in the best interest of the country or whether he represented the interests of a particular group, such as big business. As a result of such questions and the political pressure that came with them, Congress became more assertive in accepting the role it was given in the Constitution to balance the power of the president. Perhaps one of the first assertions of congressional prerogative came after World War I, when the Republican majority in the Senate opposed the creation of the League of Nations advocated by President Wilson. Where Wilson saw this organization as one way to avoid war in the future, the Senate feared the opposite—that being a member of the League would guarantee U.S. involvement in future wars outside the country. This particular issue is discussed in more detail in chapter 2.

The example of the League of Nations illustrates how different interpretations of national interest resulted in a clash between the two branches of government, and it shows the tension that the Constitution created when it assigned foreign policy powers to two branches, albeit different powers, but in the same arena. Specifically, Article II, Section 2 of the Constitution grants to the president the power to make treaties, but "with the Advice and Consent of the Senate . . . provided two thirds of the Senators present concur."[35] In the case of the League of Nations, because the Senate did not concur, the legislative branch prevailed.

There are other areas where the power of the two branches at best overlap or at worst conflict. One of the most dramatic has to do with the decision to go to war. Here, too, the Constitution builds in ambiguities. Article II, Section 2 states, "The President shall be Commander in Chief of the Army and Navy of the United States."[36] But Article I, Section 8 states very clearly, "The Congress shall have Power . . . To declare War."[37]

When Pearl Harbor was bombed, President Franklin D. Roosevelt went to Congress to ask that body to declare war, and Congress complied. Subsequently, the authority of the president to take the United States to war (or even what "war" meant) grew increasingly murky. President Harry Truman did not ask for a declaration of war when the United States went into Korea in 1950. Instead, he issued a statement noting that he had ordered "United States air and sea forces to give the Korean Government troops cover and support," under the auspices of and in response to a request by the United Nations.[38] When President Lyndon Johnson wanted to escalate military operations in Vietnam—which was termed a "limited war" rather than a formal "war"—he did not seek a declaration of war. Instead, he asked that Congress pass a resolution allowing him "to take all necessary measures," thereby giving him a blank check to do whatever *he* deemed necessary to prosecute that war. It can be argued that when Congress did so, it abrogated its responsibilities under the Constitution. Subsequently, Congress sought to return the balance by reversing the Tonkin Gulf Resolution in 1971 and then by passing the War Powers Resolution two years later.

The passage of the War Powers Resolution in 1973 was a clear assertion of congressional authority. Congress also designed this act to ensure that the power of the president to take the country into an undeclared war was balanced by the congressional oversight guaranteed in the Constitution. However, since that resolution was passed, its constitutionality has been questioned, and presidents have found ways to either work outside its strictures or to skirt them. Both Presidents George H. W. Bush and George W. Bush asked Congress to support their decisions to send U.S. troops to fight in the Middle East, in the first case, the Persian Gulf War of 1991, and in the second case, the "war on terror" (against Afghanistan and also Iraq). In both cases, they used the Tonkin Gulf Resolution of 1964 as a model to secure open-ended support for the action rather than requesting a formal declaration of war.[39] Given the brevity of the 1991 Persian Gulf War, the wisdom of congressional approval was not debated subsequently, although it passed initially only by a narrow margin.

That stands in contrast to the case of George W. Bush and the war with Iraq that started in 2003. The longer the conflict continued and as more information became available that made it clear there were no weapons of mass destruction (the original rationale for that war), the more public support dwindled. Waning public support for that war suggests that, in the future, members of Congress undoubtedly will raise questions about the wisdom of voting for open-ended support as they are pressured by their constituents and respond to public opinion.[40] Note that the issue of Iraq came up in the presidential election of 2008, although it was not a factor in the election of 2012. It returned in 2016 because as a senator, Hillary Clinton had supported the decision to go to war, a point that was made repeatedly by Republican candidate Donald Trump as an example of her questionable judgment. The topic came up yet again in the presidential election of 2020 because Joe Biden was one of seventy-seven senators to vote in favor of the war. As noted in the *New York Times*, "He is still trying to explain that choice."[41] The lesson is that especially when a war becomes unpopular, the members of the Senate who voted for it cannot escape their record.

The point here is that tensions do exist between the two branches regarding the conduct of U.S. foreign policy and especially the commitment of troops. Those tensions are exacerbated by domestic political issues, including public (and therefore congressional) support for the mission.

Conflicts between and among the Actors

In addition to the conflicts that exist across the different branches of government because of ambiguities in the Constitution and different interpretations of it, there are often conflicts that take place *within* a branch of government as each vies for power. These can be seen in the legislative branch when a different party controls each of the branches. For example, between 2018 and 2020 the Democratic Party was in control of the House and the Republican Party was in control of the Senate, and each party had its own priorities. This became especially difficult when the two sides were trying to pass an economic stimulus bill in the summer of 2020 to address the economic downturn caused by the coronavirus. In that case, there was a significant difference in the bills passed by each of the two houses, which meant that there was a period when nothing was done while the economy languished. It took until December 2020 for the two houses to reach an agreement, and that was largely because of increasing political pressure.

Another classic case of conflict within a single branch can be seen by looking at the Departments of State and Defense in the Executive Branch. Each of these two is an essential aspect of U.S. foreign and security policy, yet the two are often seen as being competitive rather than complementary. Because each has a different orientation, they can approach the same issue from a very different perspective, leading to interagency competition. In theory, one of the roles of the National Security Council when it was created in 1947 was to serve as a forum within which each of the agencies could present different points of view and argue them out before arriving at an agreed-upon position. However, sometimes it is left up to the president to sort out the priorities.

It has often been the case that there is conflict between the president and his own executive branch. So even though the president makes a policy decision, he depends on the bureaucracy to carry it out, sometimes over the objections of his own cabinet secretary. Because the president has the final word, generally the cabinet secretary will comply. However, in some cases, the disagreements can be extreme. For example, Secretary of State Cyrus Vance strongly objected to President Carter's decision to send in military forces to free the American hostages held in the embassy in Teheran, Iran, in 1979 and ultimately resigned in protest. As it turned out, that mission was a fiasco, which affected perceptions of both President Carter and the United States internationally.

What we have seen during the Trump administration is even more extreme: a virtual war between the president and parts of the executive branch with which he disagrees. This became apparent early in the administration when Trump disagreed with the assessment of the intelligence community that Russia interfered with the 2016 election, preferring instead to take the word of Vladimir Putin.[42] While it is true that senior-level government officials in the executive branch serve "at the pleasure of the president," this president has either fired or forced into retirement government officials who he perceives have not been supportive of him. The result is that, as of August 2020, there was a turnover rate of approximately 88 percent at the level below cabinet secretary, many of whom were replaced by "acting" designees who do not have to be approved by the Senate as required by the "advise and consent" function.[43] The result is lack of continuity among decision-makers but also accountability; these positions are accountable only to the president. This is far from what the founders envisioned when they set up an advise-and-consent function in the constitution to balance the power of the president.

Role of Economics

Despite the claims of pursuing a unilateralist or isolationist foreign policy in the early years of U.S. history, successive presidents made decisions to get involved with various parts of the world. This happened incrementally, first by establishing a "sphere of influence" in the Western Hemisphere (i.e., the Monroe Doctrine and the Roosevelt Corollary), and then by expanding that sphere to encompass more countries, such as Japan and China, in which the United States had economic and business interests.

An important point here, and it is one that can be seen throughout this brief exploration of American foreign policy, is that very often the decision to expand U.S. involvement with different parts of the world was made for economic reasons. In some cases it was to protect business interests, such as the case of U.S. investments in Cuba before the Spanish-American War; in some cases to expand trading opportunities, as was the case with U.S. expansion into Japan in 1853 and China at the end of the nineteenth century. In other cases it was with a desire to increase access to foreign capital and investment, which drove much of America's relations with Britain. The bottom line is that economic motives and the need to protect U.S. businesses often drive foreign policy decisions. These decisions were (and are) made by the president based on his perception of national interest.

Another constant in reviewing the history of U.S. foreign policy is that once the United States started to get involved with a particular part of the world, it did not retreat from that area as it became more involved with other parts. U.S. involvement in different parts of the world can be seen as an inverse pyramid, starting with a narrow base, where involvement was limited to a small number of countries in the early years, growing to a very broad platform at the top by the 1960s, as the United States was involved directly on every continent in some way.

Role of Domestic Politics and Factors

That brings us to the next important generalization about making and understanding American foreign policy—the role that domestic politics and other domestic factors (economic, social, etc.) play. An examination of the history of U.S. foreign policy illustrates clearly the role of domestic politics. For example, support at home for Cold War foreign policy was increased by Senator Joseph McCarthy and his "Red Scare." Conversely, the decision to pull out of Vietnam was accelerated by an American public that was withdrawing its support for the war and was also losing its faith in the government because of the then-breaking Watergate scandal.

Many African Americans in this country are concerned about and question why the United States has not been more involved with Africa, especially given the genocides that took place in Rwanda in the 1990s and in Darfur in Sudan starting in 2004. While Africa has not been a priority, some hoped that would change in an Obama administration, given his family history. Here, too, the easy answer lies, at least in part, with domestic politics. The United States claims that it has (or had) no vital national interest in this region. More important, despite pressure from the Congressional Black Caucus and the commitment of then secretaries of state Colin Powell and Condoleezza Rice to pay more attention to Africa, the reality is that there has not been a critical voting bloc or a powerful domestic political voice for that position, at least when weighed against the voices of those who oppose deploying U.S. forces in distant lands for humanitarian reasons that are not clearly linked to U.S. national interests. President Obama's visit to Africa in June 2013 suggested that perhaps this would change, especially in light of China's growing interest in the continent. However, the reality is that little changed under Obama and certainly not under a Trump administration.

As noted above, economic factors play a major role in influencing the direction of foreign policy decisions. They are often spurred by business interests that are important to the political process as well as the economic well-being of the country. Big business especially tends to have ties to the political system, through lobbies, campaign contributions, and the interrelationship of business and foreign policy/security through what President Dwight Eisenhower called the "military-industrial complex."[44] Hence, U.S. involvement in many parts of the world has often been tied directly to the need to protect economic and U.S. business interests abroad as well as resources such as oil.

WHO IS AFFECTED BY U.S. FOREIGN POLICY DECISIONS?

This brings us to the next logical question: who is affected by U.S. foreign policy decisions? The most obvious answer to this question is those countries with which the United States is involved. But people at home are affected as well. Another category to consider is the least powerful, or the powerless, specifically those who have least access to policy-makers but who are often affected by their decisions. Each of these is explored briefly below.

Impact of U.S. Foreign Policy Decisions on Other Countries

Since foreign policy is a continuous process where a decision made by one country directly affects the decisions made by another, any change in existing policy will have an important and perhaps long-standing impact on other countries. A good example of this is the U.S. relationship to its European allies. Joined together through NATO, the United States and the countries of Europe have remained allies because it was in all their interests to do so. Despite rocky periods, such as French President De Gaulle's decision to remove France from the military structure of NATO in 1966 or many of the European countries' negative responses to the war in Iraq in 2003, the alliance has been able to function as a whole. In fact, after September 11, it was the Europeans, not the United States, who requested invoking Article 5, the collective defense clause, of the NATO treaty in order to allow for a unified NATO response.[45] The Bush administration's decision to go to war against Iraq in March 2003 without UN Security Council approval put it at odds with some of its NATO allies. While some NATO members, such as Great Britain and Poland, supported the United States, others, most notably France and Germany, were outspoken in their objections to this decision.[46] Nonetheless, they all remained allies, bound together by common interests. While the NATO alliance has been stressed further under the Trump administration, there is little reason to believe that it will not survive and become more coherent again under a Biden administration.

Another example is the Cold War, which was premised on competition between the United States and the Soviet Union. The United States based its early Cold War policies on assumptions about Soviet military capabilities and, specifically, the ways in which they lagged behind those of the United States. When the USSR tested an atomic weapon in 1949 and then launched Sputnik in 1957, the United States had to rethink its own policies, including the need to accelerate some of its weapons programs. This led to an arms race that was one of the major factors that contributed to the economic bankruptcy and collapse of the Soviet Union.

This leads to another important conclusion: foreign policy decisions often have unintended consequences. No matter how carefully foreign policy decisions are analyzed and assessed, not all results can be anticipated. It also means that decisions are made based on assumptions and information available at the time. It is only later, as more information becomes available, that the full range of options (and dangers) becomes clear. This often puts the United States, or potentially any country, into a position of making policies that are reactive rather than proactive.

Domestic Constituencies

The American public is directly affected by foreign policy decisions, although different groups are affected in different ways. Foreign policy decisions can affect each of us, whether we are aware of it or not. The *Wall Street Journal* published an article on August 11, 2004, entitled "Sticker Shock at the Lumberyard." The article, which is subheaded "Remodeling Gets Costlier as Price of Wood Surges; Impact of China and Iraq," is a good example of the ways in which foreign policy decisions have an impact on "ordinary" Americans.[47] Although it was written more than a decade ago, the point still holds that in a globalized world, decisions made by one country can have a direct effect on the domestic public here in the United States.

As that article noted, an increase in the price of lumber can be attributed to a number of domestic factors, such as a housing boom in the United States that increased the demand for lumber. Foreign policy comes into this as well: a building boom in China increased demand, a 27 percent tariff on lumber imported from Canada (which supplies 30 percent of all U.S. lumber), and a weak dollar made imports more costly which means that Americans felt the impact on their pocketbooks. Those who are remodeling or renovating a house, doing any home improvement, or buying a new house paid more for lumber than they would have one year earlier.

Almost every group in this country has some representative who is looking out for and advocating for its interests. Virtually every type of business and labor organization has a lobbying group that represents it in Washington, as do special interest groups that have been formed to advocate for policy areas they care about, such as the environment. Even foreign governments have interest groups to represent their point of view. The goal of these various groups is to make sure that policies enacted by the president and Congress will not harm and ideally will help the constituencies they represent.

However, the success of these groups to influence policy decisions will vary, depending on who is in office, how broad their constituency is, and the amount of access that they actually have. For example, under the Clinton administration, environmental groups were extremely successful in advocating for protection of natural wilderness areas and for policies and agreements to protect the environment, such as the Kyoto Protocol. Part of the reason for their success was a president who was sympathetic to their cause and a vice president who was actively committed to improving the environment. In contrast, the administration of George W. Bush, which was tied more closely to business interests, reversed many of the Clinton administration policies to allow logging and road building in national forests, a position the Bush administration justified on the basis of domestic economic priorities. Shortly after taking office, the Obama administration again reversed many of the Bush administration decisions on the environment and shored up his legacy addressing issues pertaining to greenhouse gasses and other environmental issues as a strong advocate for the Paris Climate Change Agreement passed in December 2015. In contrast, one of the first actions taken by Trump when he came into office was to announce that he was withdrawing the United States from the Paris Climate Change Agreement. During his term in office, the Trump administration rolled back many of the Obama-era environmental protections on the grounds that the new policies would help American businesses. All indications are that the Biden administration will reverse Trump-era policies, by executive action if necessary, and return to if not build on the policies of the Obama administration. This can be seen with the number of executive orders signed early in Biden's term, including one for the United States to reenter the Paris Agreement, as he had promised to do during the presidential campaign.

Clearly, each administration responds to a different set of needs, priorities, perception of national interest, and interest groups, and the resultant policies have a direct impact on different groups of Americans. In addition to politicizing the issue domestically, changes in policy send confusing and ambiguous signals to other countries that are trying to make their own policies based, in part, on what the United States is doing. Hence, under a Bush presidency, the countries that worked with the United States to reach agreement in Kyoto had to form a new coalition, recognizing the fact that they likely would have to move forward without U.S. help or support. With the withdrawal of the United States from the Paris Agreement, other countries, especially those in the EU, have emerged as leaders in the fight against global warming and climate change.

The "Powerless": The Feminist Perspective

As noted above, in asking "who is affected by policies," the feminist critique becomes especially important. The feminist critique argues that often those who are most affected by decisions are the ones who are the least powerful and, therefore, with little direct access to those who make the decisions. Who represents the interests of these groups? And is protecting these groups, whose interests fall under the broad category of "human rights" and "humanitarian interests," for example, a valid basis for making foreign policy? Are they tied to U.S. "national interest"?

The case of the Vietnam War is instructive when we look at the groups that are both affected by policy decisions and also most powerless to do anything about them. The "peace movement" grew from a small fringe group of mostly young people in the early days of the war to become all-encompassing. While many in this country still supported the war, the violent actions at Kent State University in May 1970, in response to what was seen as the illegal bombing of Cambodia, which was neutral in the conflict, galvanized members of the "silent majority," some of whom later joined with students to protest the war. Clearly, male students had the greatest stake in the outcome, as they were the ones being drafted to fight and die in Vietnam, but they were also generally removed from the formal political process as they were unable to vote. By 1968 the voices of public opinion were loud enough to keep Lyndon Johnson from running for reelection and were strong enough to persuade Nixon that he needed to find a way out of the war. Furthermore, pressure by the public to give more voice to those who would fight a war resulted in the passage in 1971 of the Twenty-Sixth Amendment to the Constitution, which lowered the voting age to eighteen from twenty-one.[48]

The Black Lives Matter movement that had been slowly growing in the United States for a number of years took on greater urgency in May 2020 following the death of George Floyd, an African American man killed by members of the police in Minneapolis. Not only the American public, but people around the world became galvanized to support social justice. While the issue of police brutality was tied to specific incidents in this country, it became part of a larger movement that touched people in a range of countries and served as a reminder that even the "powerless" can have power when they band together in support of a cause.

SETTING THE STAGE

This chapter introduced some important concepts about American foreign policy that will help frame the approach taken throughout this book. It also laid out some basic questions about the foreign policy process, including asking who makes these decisions and why. However, this introduction to the theories and concepts is just the starting point—now we have to apply them.

The remainder of the book is divided into parts. If part I is the introduction to and framing of the U.S. foreign policy process, the next parts are the applications of that process over time. Part II outlines the formative years when this country was establishing itself as an independent country, eventually becoming an imperialist state as a result of nineteenth-century conquests of Mexico and the indigenous peoples on this continent, and then the territories that were the result of the victory over Spain in the Spanish-American War. It goes through the First World War, the interwar years and then the Second World War. Through these, you can see the process by which the United States moved from unilateralist foreign policy, into neutrality and finally active engagement in the international system. Part III focuses on the Cold War, its origins, and the evolution of the foreign policy framework that would guide the United States until the fall of the Soviet Union in 1991. While this covers a lot of territory, it is really impossible to understand the challenges and angst of the post–Cold War period without having a firm grounding in aspects of the Cold War. Part IV addresses the post–Cold War years, from the presidencies of Clinton through Biden, and how the end of the Cold War upended U.S. foreign policy. Finally, the concluding chapter deals with the Biden administration, new challenges to U.S. foreign policy, and what role the United States can and should play going forward.

The emphasis throughout is to understand why the United States pursued a particular foreign policy orientation at different points in time, when and why the United States deviated from that policy, and the relationship between domestic politics and the foreign policy decisions that ultimately were made. Here, too, we have to look at who made the decision and the role that domestic politics played as well.

The goal of this book is not to pass judgments about the wisdom or "rightness" or "wrongness" of any single foreign policy decision as much as it is to provide the tools for understanding those decisions in the context of the time at which they were made and with the information available then. One of the things that is striking in reviewing the history of U.S. foreign policy is the ways in which history seems to repeat itself, or, put another way, how unwilling American leaders are to learn from the past. For example, during the Spanish-American War and over the objections of the anti-imperialists, McKinley decided to put a military governor in place in the Philippines. While the anti-imperialists warned of the danger of imposing American rule on the Philippines, the imperialists dismissed the concerns, reporting "that there was no 'nationalist sentiment'" and that the Americans "would be welcomed as liberators."[49] Those same words were used by then-Vice President Cheney to describe the U.S. invasion of Iraq in 2003. The anti-imperialists proved to be correct and the United States continued to fight in the Philippines for thirteen years, just as the United States continues to have troops in Iraq. Similarly, as will be discussed in later chapters, the alleged attack on the USS *Maine* stationed in Havana harbor is eerily similar in many ways to the alleged attacks on the *Maddox* and *Turner Joy* in the Gulf of Tonkin in August 1964. The result in both cases was to get the United States more deeply into war with Spain in the case of the *Maine*, and an escalation of the war in Vietnam as a result of the Gulf of Tonkin incident. Despite the fact that the historical record should be clear, the United States repeated the same policies.

As you go through this book, you will see any number of examples where it appears that you had seen them before—the same words, phrases and/or decisions. Probably because you did. Be aware of those instances, for they are instructive about our understanding of the implications of foreign policy decisions, and, as Mead has said, how ahistorical Americans are.

PRIMARY SOURCES

The Constitution of the United States, http://www.archives.gov/exhibits/charters/constitution_transcript.html.

George Washington's Farewell Address to the Nation, https://avalon.law.yale.edu/18th_century/washing.asp.

II

THE FORMATIVE YEARS

2

Unilateralism to Engagement

The Founding to the End of World War I, 1777–1920

In 2016, an unlikely musical, *Hamilton*, based on a biography of Alexander Hamilton, won eleven Tony awards and was breaking box-office records on Broadway and everywhere it played subsequently. According to an interview with *Hamilton*'s creator and star, Lin-Manuel Miranda, "The show, almost entirely sung-through, transforms esoteric Cabinet debates between Jefferson and Hamilton into riveting, delirious rap battles."[1] Why is this such an engaging topic? Surely the music and theatrics are terrific, but ultimately it was the story that captured Miranda's attention. And that battle between Jefferson and Hamilton resulted in a two-hundred-year journey that has taken the United States along a range of different paths, from unilateralism/isolationism to active engagement in the international system. This chapter will explore the foundations of this journey.

The early years of U.S. foreign policy were defined by those men (and they were all men) who believed that the nation's highest priority should be to look inward and build a stable and prosperous country removed from the affairs (and wars) of Europe. This did not mean that the United States would not have overseas involvements. Rather, it meant that foreign policy decisions would involve choosing when, where, and how to get involved with other countries while at the same time building its own.

The first chapter of this book outlined a number of foreign policy orientations, including unilateralism. This policy presumed that the United States would remain removed from the political and military affairs of the rest of the world but would be engaged in limited ways and in areas of its choosing. This chapter will explore the policy of unilateralism (as opposed to isolationism) to describe how the leaders of the United States chose when, where, and how to be involved internationally and how those decisions allowed the country to grow into a great—and imperial—power by the end of the nineteenth century.

We will begin by looking at the perception of national interest at the time that this country was created, and why the founders believed that being removed politically and militarily (i.e., "aloof") from other countries was in the national interest. Nonetheless, as we will see, the country broke from this policy at various points in its early history. Looking at when and why the United States deviated from this policy will give you a better understanding of the foreign policy process as well as the ways in which domestic priorities affected the definition of "national interest" when applied to U.S. foreign policy. It will also give you an understanding of why knowledge of the past can provide insight into the direction that U.S. foreign policy ended up taking at various points in time.

THE BEGINNING

As a newly independent country, the United States had to develop policies and processes for governing domestically and for setting priorities internationally (foreign policy). Much of what the founders of the country did was simply react to (and against) what they had seen in England, especially the tyranny of the monarch. However, they were not in agreement on how to create a new governmental structure that would replace the monarchy they had known and that was the norm at the time.

One of the descriptions of the American experiment, and it was an experiment with a new type of government, was the word *exceptionalism*. Founded on religious principles, the notion of American exceptionalism suggests that this new country had a special role to play that was tied to the unique spirit of this country and the people who founded it. Put another way, "the exceptional calling of the American people was not to *do* anything special in foreign affairs, but *to be* a light to lighten the world" (emphasis in original).[2] This notion of American exceptionalism, the United States as "the city on the hill," would be reprised throughout the history of the country, often used as a justification for U.S. foreign policy decisions as well as for expansion across our own continent.

Creating a Foreign Policy Framework

The Articles of Confederation, drafted in 1777 and ratified in 1781, created a loose union of sovereign states and was the first attempt to frame a new form of government. Given the priorities in the 1770s, the Articles "were designed primarily to facilitate a unified approach to foreign policy and national defense,"[3] with Congress given primary responsibility for speaking on behalf of the whole. In contrast, domestic priorities rested with each of the states. Although the Articles of Confederation failed for a number of reasons, the idea of the country speaking with a single voice on foreign policy remained an important concept that would continue through the evolution of the government to its present form.

A Continental Congress convened in Philadelphia in 1787 specifically to revise the Articles of Confederation. The goal was to create a strong central government that would have responsibility for the domestic affairs of the nation (as opposed to the states) and would speak on behalf of the country on foreign affairs. As embodied in the new Constitution, power in foreign policy would be vested in both a president and Congress, with each given certain tasks to ensure that there would be checks and balances. For example, while the president would be the commander in chief of the armed forces, it would be up to Congress to declare war. While the president, as head of state, could negotiate treaties with foreign governments, two-thirds of the Senate must concur through its "advice and consent" function. In this way the founders believed the national interest of the country would be served because no one person or organization within the government could become too strong, although this can also create conflict, as noted in chapter 1.

The Constitution also specified the powers that would be given to the states as well as to each branch of the federal government, and it reflected many of the divisions that existed within the young country. As is the case today, there were divisions between the rural areas and the cities, between those Americans who were educated and well-traveled and those who were not, between the farmers and the merchants, and between those who lived on the coast and those who were inland. Those divisions also reflected the differences in how each of the groups viewed the world beyond the borders of the United States. Even with these differences, the primary view of the founders at that time was that the president was "the general Guardian of the National interests."[4] Generally, this has not changed; what has ebbed and flowed is the relationship and relative power of the president versus Congress to make foreign policy. This "push-pull" has often led to tensions between the two branches. The sometimes difficult relationship between the branches, as well as the reasons for the tensions, has been ongoing and will be explored in more detail in later chapters.

Beware of Entangling Alliances

The first three presidents of the United States—George Washington, John Adams, and Thomas Jefferson—were wary of foreign involvement that could wreck the young country. Yet each also brought to his position an understanding of the world beyond the United States, as well as the dangers of involvement in foreign wars. Washington was the first commander in chief and, as a general, saw the havoc wrought by war. Adams came to the office with a diplomatic background, as did Jefferson. Each of them feared what would happen if the United States got too involved in the wars of Europe at the expense of "domestic tranquility."[5]

In many ways the primary dispute over U.S. foreign policy and the definition of national interest was between Alexander Hamilton, the first secretary of the treasury, and Thomas Jefferson, the first secretary of state. Hamilton laid out many of his ideas on foreign policy in *The Federalist Papers*, written with James Madison and John Jay between October 1787 and July 1788. Hamilton believed that the United States needed the capability to develop into an important power, with a critical role to be played by an alliance of the government and commerce (business). Because of his emphasis on commerce, he advocated for a navy that could protect America's interests on the high seas, and he wrote of the importance of an army to make sure the United States could withstand the dangers surrounding it, from "British settlements" to "the savage tribes on our Western frontier [who] ought to be regarded as our natural enemies."[6] In *Federalist* Number 41, Madison affirmed what Hamilton had said and also noted the importance of ensuring "security against foreign danger" as one of the most important powers granted to the new American union.[7]

Jefferson saw the world differently. Rather than using limited U.S. resources to create a military, he emphasized trading with other countries and negotiating commercial treaties that would be in U.S. interests. While he allowed that the United States might need a small navy to protect its commercial interests, his priority was in securing the country's place in North America. The Louisiana Purchase of 1803 and the acquisition of the port of New Orleans resulted from Jefferson's desire to promote commerce. The decision to acquire this territory began a pattern of growth and expansion of the United States that would continue for the next fifty years and, ironically, would be aided directly by the decision to build a navy, as advocated by Hamilton.

The primary rivalry for "great power" status in Europe at that time was between France and Britain, each of which was building its empire, sometimes at the expense of the other. Although Spain, the Netherlands, and Portugal had also established themselves as colonial powers in the "new world" by that time, each of the first three U.S. presidents saw France and Britain as the primary threats; however, they did not agree on which was the greater one. What was clear was that the dangers of getting involved in foreign wars or in any rivalry among the major European powers had the possibility of creating a real threat to the homeland.

Despite these dangers, in 1778 the United States entered into an alliance with France, Britain's primary rival. Using realist political thinking, the early founders saw this alliance as a critical balance to the power of Britain, against which the United States was fighting for its independence. Ultimately, relations between the United States and France soured, with some of the early Federalists calling for war against France. From 1796 until 1800 the French claimed the right to seize any ships potentially bound for their enemy (Britain) and seized more than three hundred U.S. vessels. In 1800 the United States and France negotiated a treaty to end this "quasi-war." The United States agreed to drop all claims against France "in exchange for abrogation of the Franco-American Alliance of 1778."[8] This early alliance made clear to the United States the risks of involvement with the major European powers.

On September 17, 1796, George Washington delivered his Farewell Address to the nation upon his retirement after serving two terms as president. This address laid out his perspective on U.S. foreign policy based on his reading of the priorities at the time and the dangers that seemed to threaten the young country. The address contains much detail regarding Washington's understanding of the world at the time and what it meant for the United States going forward. For example, he advised the United States to "observe good faith and justice towards all nations," and that "nothing is more essential than that permanent, inveterate antipathies against particular nations . . . should be excluded; and that, in place of them, just and amicable feelings toward all should be cultivated."[9] He was issuing a warning to the young country about how to deal with all countries, especially those in Europe, in a way that would protect the national interest. And he cautioned that while it is important to trade with other countries, the United States could do so while also remaining politically removed from them, the very definition of "unilateralist" policy. Given the dangers and warnings that Washington laid out, it is logical he would then advocate "our policy to steer clear of permanent alliances," which John Adams, the second president, agreed with.

GEORGE WASHINGTON'S
FAREWELL ADDRESS TO THE NATION
SEPTEMBER 17, 1796

Observe good faith and justice towards all nations; cultivate peace and harmony with all. . . .

In the execution of such a plan, nothing is more essential than that permanent, inveterate antipathies against particular nations, and passionate attachments for others, should be excluded; and that, in place of them, just and amicable feelings towards all should be cultivated. The nation which indulges towards another a habitual hatred or a habitual fondness is in some degree a slave. It is a slave to its animosity or to its affection, either of which is sufficient to lead it astray from its duty and its interest. Antipathy in one nation against another disposes each more readily to offer insult and injury, to lay hold of slight causes of umbrage, and to be haughty and intractable, when accidental or trifling occasions of dispute occur. Hence, frequent collisions, obstinate, envenomed, and bloody contests. The nation, prompted by ill-will and resentment, sometimes impels to war the government, contrary to the best calculations of policy. . . . The peace often, sometimes perhaps the liberty, of nations, has been the victim.

So likewise, a passionate attachment of one nation for another produces a variety of evils. Sympathy for the favorite nation, facilitating the illusion of an imaginary common interest in cases where no real common interest exists, and infusing into one the enmities of the other, betrays the former into a participation in the quarrels and wars of the latter without adequate inducement or justification. It leads also to concessions to the favorite nation of privileges denied to others which is apt doubly to injure the nation making the concessions; by unnecessarily parting with what ought to have been retained, and by exciting jealousy, ill-will, and a disposition to retaliate, in the parties from whom equal privileges are withheld. And it gives to ambitious, corrupted, or deluded citizens (who devote themselves to the favorite nation), facility to betray or sacrifice the interests of their own country, without odium, sometimes even with popularity; gilding, with the appearances of a virtuous sense of obligation, a commendable deference for public opinion, or a laudable zeal for public good, the base or foolish compliances of ambition, corruption, or infatuation.

As avenues to foreign influence in innumerable ways, such attachments are particularly alarming to the truly enlightened and independent patriot. How many opportunities do they afford to tamper with domestic factions, to practice the arts of seduction, to mislead public opinion, to influence or awe the public councils. Such an attachment of a small or weak towards a great and powerful nation dooms the former to be the satellite of the latter. . . .

The great rule of conduct for us in regard to foreign nations is in extending our commercial relations, to have with them as little political connection as possible [emphasis added]. So far as we have already formed engagements, let them be fulfilled with perfect good faith. Here let us stop. Europe has a set of primary interests which to us have none; or a very remote relation. Hence she must be engaged in frequent controversies, the causes of which are essentially foreign to our concerns. Hence, therefore, it must be unwise in us to implicate ourselves by artificial ties in the ordinary vicissitudes of her politics, or the ordinary combinations and collisions of her friendships or enmities. . . .

It is our true policy to steer clear of permanent alliances with any portion of the foreign world; so far, I mean, as we are now at liberty to do it; for let me not be understood as capable of patronizing infidelity to existing engagements. I hold the maxim no less applicable to public than to private affairs, that honesty is always the best policy. I repeat it, therefore, let those engagements be observed in their genuine sense. But, in my opinion, it is unnecessary and would be unwise to extend them.

Available at https://avalon.law.yale.edu/18th_century/washing.asp.

Consistent with the belief that a strong executive should set foreign policy priorities and speak for the country, these men defined the path the United States would take in foreign policy for more than the next century. Initially, at least, the United States remained removed from European politics and did not enter into formal alliances; instead, the goal was to strengthen the country economically by *trading* with those countries. This policy of limited involvement, and the decision to become involved with other countries when and where the United States chose to, became the basis for the U.S. policy of *unilateralism*.

MANIFEST DESTINY, THE
MONROE DOCTRINE, AND WESTWARD EXPANSION

The death of Alexander Hamilton in 1804 meant his voice regarding the direction of U.S. foreign policy was stilled, although his influence and ideas remained important. What guided U.S. foreign policy in the 1800s was the notion of "manifest destiny," or "the belief that it was the destiny of the United States to spread across the continent." Further, "Manifest destiny embodied the conviction that Americans had a higher purpose to serve in the world than others. Theirs was not only a special privilege, but also a special charge:

to protect liberty and to promote freedom" (emphasis added).[10] Examining manifest destiny from that perspective—that higher ideals were central to the founding of the country and it was the role of the United States to serve and promote them—makes it possible to identify a pattern of expansionism, even imperialism, that provided the framework for foreign policy, including the justification for the breaks from the policies of unilateralism and sometimes isolationism that predominated from the founding until World War II.[11]

It is important to remember that most of North America had been colonized by European countries by the end of the eighteenth century. Consequently, if the United States was to expand further, it had two options: it could deal with those countries in a way that could be cooperative (e.g., negotiating treaties) or in a way that could lead to conflict. There seems to be an inherent contradiction between the policies of manifest destiny and expansion versus unilateralism. On the one hand, the United States had no desire to get involved politically with Europe. On the other hand, if it was to grow and enlarge, the United States had to engage in various ways with the same European powers that had already colonized parts of the continent and that could, potentially, threaten the United States. Didn't that mean breaking from a policy that was unilateralist or even isolationist?

What made the desire for expansion compatible with the overall doctrine of unilateralism was the belief that the United States was not engaging in political alliances nor in European politics or wars but was simply protecting itself and fulfilling its mission—its "destiny"—to expand across the continent. Hence, the U.S. conquest of North America did not seem to contradict what Washington had warned of or the course that he and Adams had set.

Domestically, by the early 1800s the young nation became more stable as a democracy with the assurance that the processes and structures of government that had been embodied in the Constitution worked. Events in Europe further helped the United States pursue its manifest destiny. As the United States began its march westward while building an economy based on trade and commerce, Europe was fighting the Napoleonic Wars. The end of those wars in 1815 marked a change in the politics of Europe as alliances and the power balance shifted.

The War of 1812

As the United States was beginning its westward expansion, it took a short detour and ignored Washington's admonitions, getting involved in another war with Europe. In June 1812, the House and Senate both voted for war against England regarding Britain's hostile policies toward U.S. naval ships. In retrospect, the war should never have happened, as Britain had already ordered the navy to avoid clashes with U.S. ships and to avoid the American coasts, which were some of the grounds for the hostilities. However, given the delays in communication at that time, members of the U.S. Congress, who were already angered by what they saw as British interference in North America, were ready to engage in war in the hope of expanding territory on this continent into Canada. The peace treaty signed in December 1814 simply codified what had been the *status quo ante*. The war cost the United States more than two thousand lives and $158 billion.[12] However, "in the minds of most Americans the war achieved its purpose, which was to duke it out with the British and remind the world that while Americans had no intention of meddling in others' affairs, they were fiercely jealous of their own freedom."[13] For those who supported the war, this was a matter of honor for the new country.

The Monroe Doctrine

What had been the Spanish Empire in the new world started to disintegrate as Argentina (in 1816), Chile (1818), and Bolivia (1825) gained their independence from Spain. Meanwhile the United States negotiated with Spain to purchase Florida, which was ceded to the United States in 1819. In 1822 the Monroe administration extended diplomatic recognition to the newly independent Latin American republics of Argentina, Chile, Colombia, Mexico, and Peru.

In 1823 Monroe laid out the policies regarding the U.S. role in the Western Hemisphere. In Europe, the usual intrigues were ongoing, with suggestions that France and Spain were aligning with Russia, Prussia, and Austria to wage war on the new republics in Latin America in order to help Spain regain its territory. In response, Britain proposed that the United States join it to ward off French and Spanish aggression in the New World. What is of note is that the British foreign minister, George Canning, proposed that the United States and Britain issue a joint declaration in opposition to further European intervention in the Americas. This option was considered by Monroe, who sought advice about the wisdom of this union. He contacted former presidents Thomas Jefferson and James Madison, and both affirmed the importance of this joint declaration. However, Secretary of State John Quincy Adams, who was skeptical about British intentions, argued that the interests of the United States would be better served by a unilateral declaration. Monroe ultimately agreed with Adams and on December 2, 1823, he delivered an address to Congress that defined the U.S. position: the United States would continue to stay removed from European affairs but, in turn, the European powers were expected to stay out of the New World, which the United States declared was within its own sphere of influence.

THE MONROE DOCTRINE
DECEMBER 2, 1823

Our policy in regard to Europe, which was adopted at an early stage of the wars which have so long agitated that quarter of the globe, nevertheless remains the same, which is, not to interfere in the internal concerns of any of its powers; to consider the government de facto as the legitimate government for us; to cultivate friendly relations with it, and to preserve those relations by a frank, firm, and manly policy, meeting in all instances the just claims of every power, submitting to injuries from none. But in regard to those continents circumstances are eminently and conspicuously different.

It is impossible that the allied powers should extend their political system to any portion of either continent without endangering our peace and happiness; nor can anyone believe that our southern brethren, if left to themselves, would adopt it of their own accord. It is equally impossible, therefore, that we should behold such interposition in any form with indifference. If we look to the comparative strength and resources of Spain and those new Governments, and their distance from each other, it must be obvious that she can never subdue them. It is still the true policy of the United States to leave the parties to themselves, in hope that other powers will pursue the same course. . . .

Available at https://avalon.law.yale.edu/19th_century/monroe.asp.

With the Monroe Doctrine the United States reiterated its promise not to interfere in European politics. In turn, the Americas were no longer open to European colonization. The only country that now had claim on the continent was the United States.

CONTINUED EXPANSION

The Monroe Doctrine made clear the intentions of the United States to continue to expand on its own continent. Over the subsequent decades, the country did so by annexing Texas (which had won independence from Mexico) in 1845, acquiring the Oregon territories from the United Kingdom in 1846, and expanding into the western part of the country (that is now California, Nevada, Arizona, and parts of Utah and Colorado) in 1848 (see figure 2.1).

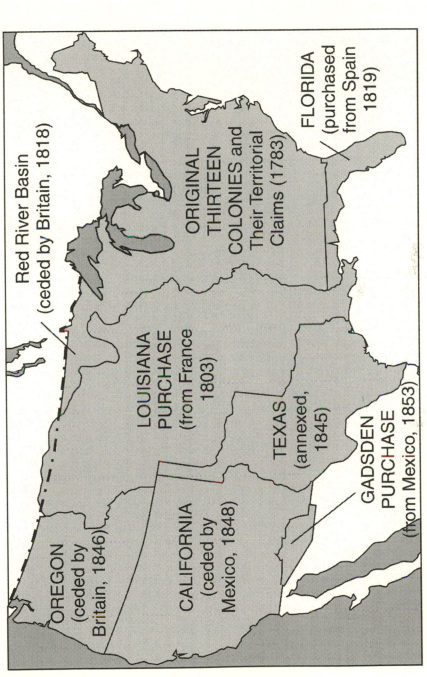

Figure 2.1. U.S. Westward Expansion.

Not all of this was done peacefully. Rather, the United States gained some of that territory as a direct result of war. It is clear that U.S. national interest and priorities at the time were best served by ensuring that the United States was no longer surrounded by foreign powers and by asserting primacy over its own lands, even if that meant war and/or displacing the native peoples. This framework was to guide U.S. foreign policy throughout the nineteenth century and well into the twentieth.

Consistent with the notion that the president defined the national interest especially in the area of foreign policy, when James K. Polk became president in 1844, he made it clear that he would accelerate the policy of territorial expansion toward the west. One of the prizes was the Mexican territory of California, with its port of San Francisco. The other area Polk wanted was the Oregon territory, held by Britain. In the latter case, Polk was willing to negotiate with Britain, building on negotiations started earlier by John Quincy Adams. In June 1846, the British proposed a treaty that Polk accepted and sent to the Senate, which ratified it by a vote of 41 to 14. Despite Polk's claim of "Fifty-four forty or fight," suggesting the territorial lines that would be ideal, he was willing to compromise with a border at the forty-ninth parallel rather than risk the domestic political battles and costs of another war with Britain.

Unlike parts of the Oregon territory, which were described as "wholly unfit for agriculture & incapable of sustaining any considerable population"[14] (and thereby worth giving up), California was seen as worth fighting for. Initially Polk tried negotiating with Mexico to persuade the country to sell California to the United States. When that failed, Polk resorted to the use of hard power and ordered troops to the Rio Grande, the border area, where they quickly engaged with Mexican forces. Congress responded to the clash between U.S. and Mexican forces by endorsing Polk's request for a declaration of war in May 1846.

Mexican-American War

Military historian T. Harry Williams describes the Mexican-American War this way: "The Mexican War has always occupied an ambiguous position in the national historical consciousness. Depending on the prevailing mood of intellectuals and historians, it has been denounced as a wicked war of aggression against a weaker neighbor or justified as an inevitable phase in the expansion [of the United States]." He also describes this war as "significant because of the number of 'firsts' associated with it. It was the first overseas war. . . . It was also America's first successful offensive war, the first in which the strategic objectives were laid out with some clarity before hostilities were joined, and the first to be conducted with a large measure of technical proficiency and with relative efficiency. Finally, it was the first war in which the president really acted as commander in chief."[15]

Although it was controversial, the Mexican-American War (1846–1848) was important to the growth of the United States, a priority at that time, and was seen by the leaders of the country as necessary to secure parts of the hemisphere that the United States claimed as its own. The war added 529,000 square miles to U.S. territory with a loss of thirteen thousand dead and an estimated $97 million in war costs. Plus the United States paid Mexico another $15,000. Nonetheless, the victory over Mexico was celebrated by many as a great success that "confirmed their faith in republicanism and seemed to earn them new respect abroad."[16] However, it also raised the issue of extending slavery into the new territories, setting the country "on the road to civil war."[17]

At the end of the Mexican-American war, U.S. territory extended from the Atlantic Ocean to the Pacific and included the areas now known as Nevada and California, both of which had gold and silver deposits. During the period from December 1845 through the end of the Mexican-American War in 1848, "the United States had grown by about 1.2 million square miles, or about 64 percent."[18] The promise of wealth from gold and silver helped fuel the westward movement of the population that was necessary for the growth of the country. The acquisition of California also meant that the United States had ports on both coasts, which helped further the goals of increasing trade and commerce.

How was this expansion possible? Who paid for the purchase of these new lands or to finance these wars? How could the United States assure the security of this ever-expanding country? In many ways, the answers to these questions can be found in the concept of what we now call *globalization*, which linked the United States to other countries economically, even as it stayed removed politically. In fact, the United States took seriously the need for commerce and trade and depended on foreign investment to provide the funding to sustain much of this growth westward that was seen as critical to the national interest.[19] The only alternative would have been to raise taxes, and that was unpalatable politically. To some Americans this foreign investment was a cause of controversy or resentment, and they were concerned about the influence these investors might have on U.S. policy. But there was little that they could do about it.

The decision to trade with and secure investments from other countries, especially Europe, while positioning itself in the Western Hemisphere is the essence of the early U.S. policy of unilateralism. Pursuing this policy allowed the United States to achieve what it had defined as its national interest, its "manifest destiny," while simultaneously protecting it from the intrigues of Europe.

The American Genocide

One of the points that is often overlooked in talking about manifest destiny and westward expansion was the impact of this policy on the Native American peoples and the Mexicans who had been on the continent and lived on the land way before the Europeans. While manifest destiny is part of the popular lore about the growth of the country, it also "normalizes the successive invasions and occupations of Indigenous nations and Mexico as not being colonialist or imperialist, rather simply ordained progress."[20] Looking at the map in Figure 2.1, it is clear that the "Unorganized" territory that made up much of the Louisiana Purchase becomes "Indian County" as result of the removal of Indians from the southeast United States in the 1830s. And it also shows how much of Mexico was later to be incorporated into the United States in the 1840s; Texas in 1845 and then Mexican American War, 1846–1848.

Early traders and explorers, like Lewis and Clark and Zebulon Pike (who "discovered" and named Pike's Peak in Colorado after himself), were military projects supported by the U.S. government as necessary precursors to westward expansion. Hence, Lewis and Clark were instrumental in gathering information about the many tribes of native peoples who lived in the territory between the Rocky Mountains and the Pacific, while Pike and his group of soldiers were sent to gather information that would later be used for the military invasion that justified the Mexican-American War.[21] Yet, those peoples in the newly annexed territories following the Mexican-American War were Indigenous peoples or Mexican farmers and ranchers who had resisted colonization by the Spanish and Mexican authorities, just as many continued to resist the new regime.

It is important to note that the U.S. government entered into various treaties with different Native American tribes in much the same way as they would enter into a treaty with any sovereign nation during the early to mid-nineteenth century. In doing so, they treated the tribes as if they were sovereign nations, respecting their tribal governing structure and territory. "From 1774 until about 1832, treaties between individual sovereign American Indian nations and the U.S. were negotiated to establish borders and prescribe conditions of behavior between the parties. The form of these agreements was nearly identical to the Treaty of Paris ending the Revolutionary War between the United States and Great Britain. The negotiations ended in a mutually signed pact which had to be approved by the U.S. Congress. Non-tribal citizens were required to have a passport to cross sovereign Indian lands."[22] Later, however, these treaties actually became a way to remove the native peoples from their land. According to the Office of the Historian, "From a legal standpoint, the United States Constitution empowered Congress to 'regulate commerce with foreign nations, and among the several States, and with the Indian tribes.' In early treaties negotiated between the federal government and the Indian tribes, the latter typically acknowledged themselves 'to be under the protection of the United States of America, and of no other sovereign whosoever.'"[23]

Thus, the notion of manifest destiny in a country founded on the ideals of freedom and democracy required the elimination of the Indigenous people and/or appropriating their land. During the administration of Andrew Jackson (1829–1837), a period known as "Jacksonian Democracy," U.S. westward expansion was accompanied by the relocation and even genocide of Indigenous people. Despite signing numerous treaties with various tribes, Jackson "outright rejected their claim of sovereignty. He rationalized removal as a way of saving Indian civilization." During Jackson's term alone, the government acquired more than 100 million acres of Indian land, plus another 30 million acres in the west. "Amidst horrific suffering, more than forty-six thousand Indians were forced from their ancestral lands into the wilderness across the Mississippi."[24]

When Jackson became president, he enacted a systematic approach to Indian removal on the basis of legal precedents. Perhaps most notorious among these was the Indian Removal Act of 1830, which led to the removal of the native peoples from their own ancestral lands to federal lands west of the Mississippi, thereby allowing for white settlements. It should be noted that even at that time, the act was not without controversy, to no avail. In the winter of 1831–1832, the Cherokees, who had resisted the removal, "were herded into prison camps and eventually removed by force, resulting under Jackson's successor, Martin Van Buren, in the infamous "Trail of Tears."[25]

Thus, U.S. westward expansion was accompanied by the relocation and even genocide of the Indigenous people, in part, the result of treaties broken by the U.S. government. Thus, while U.S. expansion across the continent might have been justified as this country's "destiny," it came at a harsh price to its native peoples and the peoples of Mexico. This is also another example of the United States' march toward imperialism that would continue throughout the century.

Expansion into the Pacific

As the United States expanded westward in the mid-nineteenth century, it also was starting to make a mark internationally. With the Atlantic and Caribbean claimed by Europe, and the Atlantic waters nearly exhausted by European whalers, the American whaling trade needed other waters to explore. After 1848, when U.S. territory extended to the Pacific, it was only natural that the United States look in that direction for trade and commerce that would allow it to compete with Europe economically. In 1853, U.S. Commodore Matthew Perry arrived in Japan, a country then untouched by the West. He offered Japan a choice: trade with the United States peacefully or run the risk of war. When he returned early in 1854 with a fleet of ships, Japan granted the United States the right to use the Japanese ports of Shimoda and Hakodate, and by 1856 the United States negotiated a trade treaty with Japan. Japan soon extended similar terms to the European countries of France, Britain, the Netherlands, and Russia, but it was U.S. ambition that opened the country to the West.

The U.S. venture into Japan was an example of the growing power of its navy, initially created to protect U.S. commercial interests but also to be used as an instrument of policy. Here, too, we see one of the apparent contradictions of the policy of unilateralism, that is, the growing U.S. presence globally: "During the period of American innocence and isolation, the United States had forces stationed on or near every major continent in the world; its navy was active in virtually every ocean, its troops saw combat on virtually every continent, and its foreign relations were in a constant state of crisis and turmoil."[26]

Clearly, a unilateralist foreign policy did not mean being removed from the world. Rather, it was interpreted to mean that the United States would chart its own course and become engaged internationally at times and places that it chose when it was perceived to be in the national interest to do so.

THE CIVIL WAR

By the time the American Civil War broke out in 1861, the United States was already on its way to becoming a major economic power. While the countries of Europe had been diverting economic resources toward their militaries, the United States had focused instead on domestic needs. The thriving trade between the United States and England (the United States exported raw materials, especially cotton, to England in exchange for British manufactured goods) tied the two countries closely together and further fueled U.S. economic growth. Pragmatically, one of America's former adversaries became one of its major trading partners.

The Civil War required the U.S. government to divert resources for military purposes necessary to fight that war. According to Paul Kennedy, the Civil War was "the first real industrialized 'total war' on proto-twentieth-century lines."[27] Although the conflict was a brutal and divisive one for the country, it further spurred U.S. industrial growth. As a result, by the end of the war, the industrial output of the United States had increased, and along with that came modernization of military technology. Coupled with the relative stability of the international system in the later part of the nineteenth century, the United States was then able to take its place in the "modern" world.

THE SPANISH-AMERICAN WAR

The Spanish-American War of 1898 represents one of the clearest cases where the United States broke from its unilateralist policy (as defined by political and military aloofness from other parts of the world) to become actively engaged internationally, both militarily and politically, while still remaining clear of "entangling alliances." The United States earlier had acted aggressively against Mexico to acquire contiguous territory seen as essential to the country's manifest destiny. The Spanish-American War represents a different case. The question to ask here is why the United States chose to declare war against Spain, a European country. How did this serve the national interest? Here we see the confluence of international and domestic politics, both of which must be considered in order to answer these questions.

The United States had had a troubled relationship with Spain for decades, as Spain claimed some of the land that the United States wanted for its own. For example, the Florida cession in 1819 was the result of a long diplomatic campaign that was characterized by threats, bribes, and intimidation. At that time, the United States also made it clear to Spain that any attempt by that country to reestablish its control over the colonies in the Western Hemisphere that had gained their independence (e.g., Argentina, Bolivia, and Chile) would result in war between the United States and Spain. This history between the two countries helps frame the issues surrounding the Spanish-American War.

The U.S. decision to go to war against Spain in 1898 resulted from many factors, all of which reflected what was then understood as the "national interest." The result was a more aggressive foreign policy and an expansive, even imperialistic, interpretation of U.S. territory to include the Pacific Ocean. Spain's possession of the Philippines and Guam interfered with the U.S. desire to strengthen its role in the Pacific, especially after the opening of Japan in 1856, which was followed by a treaty with Korea in 1882.[28] And the United States saw Spain's control of the island of Cuba, ninety miles off the coast of the United States, as an infringement on its hemisphere. In addition, American businesses, which had invested millions of dollars in Cuban sugar, were pushing the government to do something about the political instability on the island.

McKinley was elected president in 1896 on the twin promises to protect American business and to free the Cuban people. Because of his experiences in the Civil War, he was reluctant to take the country to war again, but pressure on the president to do something grew. The press exacerbated U.S. claims on Cuba and built pressure to go to war against Spain to "protect" the island. One newspaper, William Randolph Hearst's *New York Journal*, printed a letter written by the Spanish ambassador, Enrique Dupuy de Lôme that had been stolen by Cuban rebels. The de Lôme letter described President McKinley as "weak and a bidder for the admiration of the crowd, besides being a would-be politician who tries to leave a door open behind himself while keeping on good terms with the jingoes of his party."[29] Although the ambassador subsequently resigned, the letter had the desired effect of further inciting "war fever" within the United States when it was published on February 9, 1898.

A few days later, on February 15, 1898, the U.S. battleship *Maine* blew up in Havana harbor, allegedly by an underwater mine, although a later investigation indicated that the explosion was caused internally.[30] Again, the press snapped into action and called for war against Spain, using the slogan "Remember the *Maine*" to rally public support. On April 11, McKinley went to Congress and asked for authority to "intervene" in Cuba, despite the fact that Spain had agreed to give Cuba its independence. Although this was not a formal declaration of war, Spain perceived it as such. In response, Spain declared war on the United States on April 23. By late July, the United States had overwhelmed Spain militarily in the Atlantic (Cuba and Puerto Rico) as well as in the Pacific (the Philippines), and peace negotiations started between the two countries. They signed the Treaty of Paris on December 10, 1898. As a result of the peace negotiations, Cuba was given its independence from Spain, Spain agreed to give Puerto Rico and Guam to the United States, and the United States purchased the Philippines for $20 million. The U.S. position in the Western Hemisphere, from the Atlantic into the Pacific, was secure.

Implications of the Spanish-American War

The United States justified the decision to go to war against Spain in part by the principles put forward in the Monroe Doctrine and the need to solidify its sphere of influence in the Western Hemisphere. Tied to this were humanitarian goals, as some U.S. political leaders believed Cuba needed to be "saved" from Spanish exploitation. An editorial in the *New York Times* of July 30, 1898, titled "Not for Cuba Only," notes that although this was a "war of humanity," to save the Cuban people from the barbarism of its Spanish colonial masters, it also notes that "it is not that alone. Our primary object, the real inspiring cause and chief end sought was the attainment of peace and tranquility at home."[31] Clearly, the decision to go to war was the result of a combination of commercial, political, and growing expansionist sentiments domestically perpetrated in part by political leaders and members of the media.

To be understood fully, this decision must be put into a global context. For the countries of Europe, this was a time of imperialism, as each of the major powers scrambled to claim colonies in Asia and Africa. By confining itself to North America, the United States was being left out of this global power grab that threatened to undermine the place that the country was slowly securing for itself internationally. The Spanish-American War unambiguously made the United States an imperial power, rivaling the major powers of Europe. No longer seen as a new, young country, the United States now had its own colonies, which brought with them responsibilities. The U.S. could no longer be removed from the rest of the world, nor could it only look inward. Rather, its national interest now required that it protect its colonial interests as well as become more involved in world affairs. The foreign policy of the United States was changing.

It also is important to look at the role that domestic politics played in pushing the United States to war against Spain and toward expansionism. First, Americans were united against a common enemy, Spain, for the first time since the Civil War had divided the country. Northerners and southerners fought side by side, thus helping to heal the bitter divisions, at least temporarily. Second, foreign policy, especially the role of the United States in the world, became an important issue in the presidential election of 1900. Theodore Roosevelt, leader of the Rough Riders, who had gained fame during the war, was on the ticket as McKinley's vice president, and he espoused an imperialist/expansionist agenda that he was able to enact once he became president upon McKinley's death in 1901. Finally, we see the power of the press, led by William Randolph Hearst, who used newspapers to foment public sentiment in favor of war. This fact alone marks an important transition in the role of the media in influencing policy.

The Spanish-American War and the defeat of Spain ended more than four hundred years of Spanish power and influence in the Western Hemisphere and Pacific and solidified the role of the United States as the major power in the region. This meant that the United States faced the new century in a different position internationally, and its foreign policy reflected that shift.

THE SCRAMBLE FOR CONCESSIONS

As a result of the Spanish American War, the United States had a firm claim to the Pacific. But by 1899, the "scramble for concessions" in China threatened to leave the United States out of this market which was seen as important for American businesses. While the United States had been distracted by the Spanish-American War, between 1897 and 1899 the European countries had been acquiring territorial rights within parts of China. These "concessions" followed China's defeat in the Opium Wars and a subsequent weakening of the Qing Dynasty. This quickly led to an undermining of the Chinese Empire as European countries and Japan began to carve up China for their own economic gain. To ensure America's place and to protect its own commercial interests in China, Secretary of State John Hay sent his Open Door note to the governments of Germany, Russia, and England; similar notes were subsequently sent to Japan, Italy, and France.[32] These documents called on the other imperialist countries to open their Chinese concessions (areas of interest) to trade and investment equally to all. Hay also requested that countries not interfere with any country's so-called sphere of influence within China. The Open Door notes were another assertion that the United States was a player in the international system and that it could not be taken for granted.

THE ROOSEVELT COROLLARY TO THE MONROE DOCTRINE

In 1902, Venezuela defaulted on debts to many of its European investors. In response, Britain, Germany, and Italy sent gunboats to blockade Venezuela's ports. Within the United States these actions raised old fears that European powers would try to undermine U.S. dominance in the region. In 1904, President Theodore Roosevelt used an address to Congress to state clearly the U.S. position regarding the Western Hemisphere. This came eighty-one years after Monroe delivered his address to the Congress.

EXCERPTS FROM ROOSEVELT COROLLARY TO THE MONROE DOCTRINE PRESIDENT THEODORE ROOSEVELT'S ANNUAL MESSAGE TO THE CONGRESS, DECEMBER 6, 1904

It is not true that the United States feels any land hunger or entertains any projects as regards the other nations of the Western Hemisphere save such as are for their welfare. All that this country desires is to see neighboring countries stable, orderly and prosperous. . . . Our interests and those of our southern neighbors are in reality identical. They have great natural riches, and if within their borders the reign of law and justice obtains, prosperity is sure to come to them. While they thus obey the primary laws of civilized society they may rest assured that they will be treated by us in a spirit of cordial and helpful sympathy. We would interfere with them only in the last resort, and then only if it became evident that their inability or unwillingness to do justice at home and abroad had violated the rights of the United States or had invited foreign aggression to the detriment of the entire body of American nations.

In asserting the Monroe Doctrine, in taking such steps as we have taken in regard to Cuba, Venezuela, and Panama, and in endeavoring to circumscribe the theater of war in the Far East, and to secure the open door in China, we have acted in our own interest as well as in the interest of humanity at large. . . . Nevertheless there are occasional crimes committed on so vast a scale and of such peculiar horror as to make us doubt whether it is not our manifest duty to endeavor at least to show our disapproval of the deed and our sympathy with those who have suffered by it. The cases must be extreme in which such a course is justifiable. There must be no effort made to remove the mote from our brother's eye if we refuse to remove the beam from our own. But in extreme cases action may be justifiable and proper. What form the action shall take must depend upon the circumstances of the case; that is, upon the degree of the atrocity and upon our power to remedy it. The cases in which we could interfere by force of arms as we interfered to put a stop to intolerable conditions in Cuba are necessarily very few. Yet it is not to be expected that a people like ours, which in spite of certain very obvious shortcomings, nevertheless as a whole shows by its consistent practice its belief in the principles of civil and religious liberty and of orderly freedom. . . .

Available at https://www.ourdocuments.gov/print_friendly.php?flash= false&page=transcript&doc=56&title=Transcript+of+Theodore+Roose velts+Corollary+to+the+Monroe+Doctrine+%281905%29.

In this speech, Roosevelt established a policy that built on the principles espoused in the Monroe Doctrine. He gave notice that the Western Hemisphere was the responsibility of the United States and that this country would use military force if necessary to protect its interests. In effect, he laid out the conditions under which the United States would intervene in Latin America, and he also made it clear that the United States would take military action should any country engage in activities that could be seen as detrimental to

U.S. interests. The United States was replacing European imperialist intentions in Latin America with its own, and its own foreign policy was being driven by a realist perspective backed up with its use of hard (military) power.

Roosevelt's term in office was characterized by further U.S. expansion and involvement internationally. By the time Roosevelt became president in 1901, U.S. interests in Asia had been furthered by the Open Door policy that encouraged free and open trade rather than running the risk of having China divided into spheres of influence that might deprive the United States of its opportunity in this new market. In another assertion of U.S. interests in Asia, in 1905 Roosevelt helped negotiate the end to war between Russia and Japan, making sure that Russia would help balance the growing power of Japan. While Roosevelt won a Nobel Peace Prize for these efforts, they were driven in no small measure by Roosevelt's fear that if Japan got too strong, it could threaten U.S. markets and commercial interests in the Far East.

Consistent with Roosevelt's desire to dominate the Caribbean, which was seen as within the U.S. sphere of influence, he supported building a canal across the Isthmus of Panama that would connect the Caribbean with the Pacific Ocean. The canal would also allow the U.S. Navy to move quickly from the Atlantic to the Pacific, making it possible to have one, rather than two, navies to protect U.S. interests.[33] Building the canal was made possible because of Roosevelt's intervention on behalf of Panama's rebellion against existing Colombian rulers. The success of that rebellion allowed the United States to acquire the land through which the canal would be built.

As noted above, the Roosevelt Corollary to the Monroe Doctrine and the building of the Panama Canal are but two examples of growing U.S. involvement internationally. When William Howard Taft, Roosevelt's successor, became president in 1909, he continued the policies started under Roosevelt. Taft pushed U.S. businesses to invest abroad as a way to further solidify U.S. interests. However, the expanding reach of the United States and its businesses meant that greater military involvement was necessary to protect them. Hence, Taft sent U.S. forces into Nicaragua and Honduras in 1910 and 1911, respectively, in order to protect U.S. lives and interests. In 1912, U.S. forces were deployed to Honduras, Panama, Cuba, and China, all in the name of "protecting U.S. interests." A detachment of marines was sent to Nicaragua in 1912 to "protect U.S. interests" and "to promote peace and stability," with a small group remaining until 1925. While some Americans opposed the United States' imperialist adventures, their voices largely went unnoticed. U.S. foreign policy and the place of the United States in the world had changed dramatically.

MARCH TO WORLD WAR I

By 1900 the international economic as well as geopolitical picture had changed. As historian Robert Marks explains, in the eighteenth century (around the time the United States was created), India, China, and Europe each claimed about 23 percent of the world's gross domestic product (GDP). In contrast, by 1900, just after the end of the Spanish-American War, "India accounts for barely 2 percent of world manufacturing output, China about 7 percent, while Europe alone claims 60 percent and the United States 20 percent, or 80 percent of the world total."[34] Industrial growth had allowed the United States to become a major power that would soon overtake Europe (see figure 2.2)

Within the United States, the era of industrialization brought both economic and social changes. The period from 1900 until the outbreak of World War I was a time of reform known as the Progressive Era. Not only did this change the face of labor and business, but it was also a time when the United States continued its international involvement, justified at least in part by the need to support U.S. business interests. The resulting changes in foreign

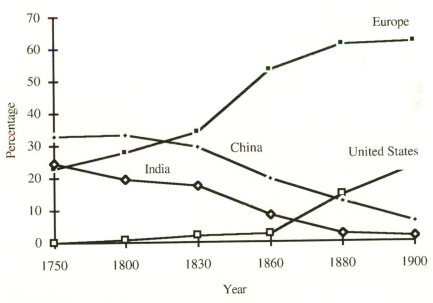

Figure 2.2. World Industrial Output 1750–1900
Source: Originally published in Robert B. Marks, *The Origins of the Modern World: A Global and Environmental Narrative from the Fifteenth to the Twenty-First Century,* 4th ed. (Lanham, MD: Rowman & Littlefield, 2020), 137. Data derived from Paul Kennedy, *The Rise and Fall of the Great Powers* (New York: Vintage, 1987), 149.

policy were characterized broadly as "dollar diplomacy," in recognition of the importance of business and trade.

Woodrow Wilson, a former president of Princeton University, was elected president in 1912 and continued the policies set by his predecessors. The United States was actively engaged in those regions and parts of the world that had been defined as within its sphere of influence and critical to national interest, primarily Latin America and the Pacific. Wilson broadened the rationale for U.S. involvement so that U.S. assistance (and intervention if necessary) was extended to helping other peoples and countries become democratic. Wilson's idealism and commitment to democratic values would characterize his administration and become the basis for active U.S. engagement in the war that would rage in Europe.

Wilsonian Idealism and U.S. Foreign Policy

Wilson outlined the ideals that he valued in and for the United States in his first inaugural address, delivered March 4, 1913. In this speech, we can see the outlines of what was to become known as "Wilsonian idealism."

Initially, U.S. interests in the first years of Wilson's administration centered on Asia, Latin America (primarily Mexico), and the Caribbean. Consistent with his broadened interpretation of national interest, Wilson deployed U.S. military forces to those areas to help protect or maintain order (e.g., in Haiti, China, Dominican Republic) rather than just to protect U.S. interests.

Shortly after Wilson took office, World War I broke out in Europe. Wilson's goal was to keep the United States out of that conflict if possible. On August 4, 1914, he proclaimed the United States *neutral.* On May 7, 1915, the British passenger ship *Lusitania* was sunk by a German torpedo, resulting in the deaths of more than a thousand passengers and crew, including 124 Americans. In response, Wilson had the secretary of state deliver a note to the German ambassador in which the United States reiterated its neutrality but also gave warning that Germany should "not expect the Government of the United States to omit any word or any act necessary to the performance of its sacred duty of maintaining the rights of the United States and its citizens and of safeguarding their free exercise and enjoyment."[35]

In November 1916, Wilson was reelected president, in part because of his campaign slogan that he had kept the United States out of the European war. But ongoing trade with Britain, one of the belligerent nations, was drawing the United States into the conflict. The United States provided Britain and its allies with munitions, food, and raw materials, and it extended loans when the countries could not pay. During the first two years of the war (1914–1916), U.S. trade with Britain and its allies went from $800 million to $3 billion.[36]

EXCERPTS FROM WOODROW WILSON'S
FIRST INAUGURAL ADDRESS
MARCH 4, 1913

We see that in many things that life is very great. It is incomparably great in its material aspects, in its body of wealth, in the diversity and sweep of its energy, in the industries which have been conceived and built up by the genius of individual men and the limitless enterprise of groups of men. It is great, also, very great, in its moral force. Nowhere else in the world have noble men and women exhibited in more striking forms the beauty and the energy of sympathy and helpfulness and counsel in their efforts to rectify wrong, alleviate suffering, and set the weak in the way of strength and hope. We have built up, moreover, a great system of government, which has stood through a long age as in many respects a model for those who seek to set liberty upon foundations that will endure against fortuitous change, against storm and accident. Our life contains every great thing, and contains it in rich abundance. . . .

. . . This is the high enterprise of the new day: To lift everything that concerns our life as a Nation to the light that shines from the hearthfire of every man's conscience and vision of the right. It is inconceivable that we should do this as partisans; it is inconceivable we should do it in ignorance of the facts as they are or in blind haste. We shall restore, not destroy. . . . Justice, and only justice, shall always be our motto.

Available at https://avalon.law.yale.edu/20th_century/wilson1.asp.

Despite Wilson's intentions, he could not keep the United States out of the European war. In August 1915 German forces sank another British passenger ship, the *Arabic*, and then in March 1916 a French steamer, *Sussex*, and more American lives were lost. On January 22, 1917, as he was starting his second term in office, Wilson addressed the U.S. Senate and called for a "peace without victory." Although he did not ask for a declaration of war, he called for an end to the war on terms "which will create a peace that is worth guaranteeing and preserving, a peace that will win the approval of mankind, not merely a peace that will serve the national interests and immediate aims of the nations engaged." And he warned that "victory would mean peace forced upon the loser, a victor's terms imposed upon the vanquished. . . . Only a peace between equals can last."[37] In that prediction he was prescient, for the peace that was ultimately imposed on Germany contributed to the humiliation and economic devastation that fostered the rise of Hitler and Nazism and ultimately another world war. Nonetheless, despite his intentions, Wilson was not successful at keeping the United States out of the war.

The resumption of German unrestricted submarine warfare in February 1917 and attacks on U.S.-flagged merchant ships made U.S. involvement inevitable. U.S. involvement was also spurred with the release of a telegram intercepted by the British sent by German Foreign Minister Arthur Zimmermann to the German Ambassador in Mexico City in January 1917. The so-called Zimmermann Telegram "promised the Mexican Government that Germany would help Mexico recover the territory it had ceded to the United States following the Mexican-American War. In return for this assistance, Germany asked for Mexican support in the war."[38] The Zimmermann Telegram was leaked to the press, and, as was the case with the de Lôme letter and the Spanish-American War, it helped convince the American public of the need to go to war. This implied threat, coupled with the loss of American life by German torpedoes and the recognition that Germany had no interest in seeking a peaceful end to the conflict finally convinced Wilson of the need for the United States to take action. On April 2, 1917, Wilson went before a joint session of Congress and asked for a declaration of war against Germany.

This was the fourth time that a president had asked for a formal declaration of war (the War of 1812, the war with Mexico in 1846, and the Spanish-American War) which was justified by Wilson in the most idealistic terms. "The world must be made safe for democracy. Its peace must be planted upon the tested foundations of political liberty."[39] In other words, the United States was going into this war for high-minded reasons and against an aggressive government that had violated international law. On April 4, the Senate approved the declaration by a vote of 82 to 6, and on April 6, following days of debate, the House approved it by a vote of 373 to 50. Jeanette Rankin from Montana, the first woman to be elected to Congress who had been sworn in four days earlier, voted "no," stating "I want to stand by my country, but I cannot vote for war."[40]

Wilson's understanding of national interest and the ways in which he chose to implement American foreign policy represented a marked departure from the direction that the United States previously had taken. Whatever the actual reasons the United States had for going to war in Europe, Wilson put the decision into idealistic and moralistic terms.[41] Further, his foreign policy in general was tied to a desire to actively extend democracy, thereby changing the U.S. policy posture from one that was unilateralist to one of active engagement internationally.

Wilson's Fourteen Points

On January 8, 1918, about ten months before World War I ended, Wilson again addressed the Congress, giving what has become known as his Fourteen Points speech. Driven in part by his desire to avoid war in the future, the Fourteen Points outlined Wilson's vision to assure justice for all countries and peace in the future by creating an "association of nations . . . for the purpose of affording mutual guarantees of political independence and territorial integrity to great and small states alike."[42] The concept of uniting all states—large and small, powerful and those with less power—into one organization that would allow all of them to work together to thwart the imperialist or expansionist intentions of any one nation was a relatively new idea. Wilson's ideal notion of "collective security" was not to come to fruition, nor could the concept prevent another major war. Nonetheless, it provided the seeds that would eventually grow into the United Nations.

An armistice signed in Paris in November 1918 ended World War I. Wilson, Prime Minister Lloyd George of Britain, Premier Clemenceau of France, and Prime Minister Orlando of Italy negotiated the Treaty of Versailles. In a series of "secret" agreements, each of the allies was granted additional territory that was taken from the defeated countries. The German colonies were parceled out among the allies. New countries—Czechoslovakia and Yugoslavia—were created as the existing European empires were disbanded, and Poland was again recognized as a sovereign state. The treaty imposed reparations on Germany, that is, payments that had to be made to the allies to compensate for the damage caused by the war. The treaty also included provisions for the creation of the League of Nations that would embody many of the principles espoused by Wilson.

Unfortunately, U.S. domestic politics intervened and thwarted Wilson's plans. With an election coming up in 1920, the issue of the League of Nations became highly politicized. The Republican majority in the Senate opposed the creation of the League, as did the Republican candidate for president, Warren G. Harding. This was one of the first times that Congress asserted its will on a foreign policy issue, thereby overriding the president's priorities. An indication of the growing power of the United States was that, without U.S. presence, the League of Nations could not succeed.

Although some of Wilson's goals for American foreign policy were defeated in the face of domestic opposition, many of his ideals and ideas influenced subsequent presidents and resurfaced periodically long after his death.[43]

U.S. INVOLVEMENT IN RUSSIA

In March 1917, while World War I was raging, a revolution in Russia toppled the government of Czar Nicholas II. Some months later, in November 1917, the Bolsheviks, a communist faction led by V. I. Lenin, overthrew the provisional government. Virtually all the European countries sent troops, allegedly to help Russia form a new stable government, although many of the Western leaders wanted to stop the nascent Bolshevik (communist) movement. Hoping to encourage the anti-Bolshevik forces, Wilson sent U.S. troops, which remained in Russia from 1918 through 1920, after World War I ended; nonetheless, the communist forces prevailed.

This involvement by Europe and especially the United States proved to have long-term implications. It planted seeds of mistrust between the communist forces and the Western powers that would continue to fester, finally emerging full blown in the Cold War that followed World War II. The leaders of the Soviet Union did not forget the way in which the Western countries, especially the United States, did not hesitate to intervene in their civil war, including sending troops to their country. In turn, the leaders of the West were already defining the conflict as an ideological one that pitted the forces of democracy against those of communism. While the Soviet Union became an ally of the United States in its fight against Nazi Germany during World War II, the relationship was clouded by this history that continued into and throughout the Cold War.

DOMESTIC ISSUES:
THE EXECUTIVE AND LEGISLATIVE BRANCHES

As we review the foreign policy of the United States from its founding through World War I, one of the patterns that becomes most apparent is the dominance of the president in setting foreign policy priorities. Consistent with the beliefs of the early founders of the country, a strong executive was seen as the critical policy-maker and the one who set the priorities, with Congress playing largely a "balancing" role. As history shows, that generally was the case. Foreign policy was made by the president, working with other members of the executive branch (e.g., the secretary of state). While Congress played a role, it was largely secondary and compliant, with congressional attention more focused on enacting legislation for the growing and industrializing country.

One of the first, and perhaps most dramatic, examples of a departure from this pattern came in the Republican resistance to the League of Nations that was being pushed by Wilson. Article 10 was the heart of the League of Nations treaty; it stipulated that an attack on any member of the League was to be regarded as an attack on all members, and therefore that all should be prepared to go to war in response.[44] Republican opposition to the League was rooted in the concern that Article 10 would bind the United States too closely to other countries in opposition to the country's national interest and policy of unilateralism. The fear was that if the United States were to agree to the terms of the League, then the country could be plunged inevitably into foreign wars, whether or not it would be in its interest to do so.

Given congressional resistance, and knowing that entering into the League would require a two-thirds vote of the Senate, Wilson took his case to the American people, making it part of the presidential campaign of 1920. Harding, the Republican candidate, opposed the League, and his election meant that the United States would not join. Ultimately it was members of the Senate who asserted their feelings in opposition to the League, thereby assuring its defeat, regardless of Wilson's desires.

While an assertion of congressional opposition to presidential priorities was rare at the time, it would become more common later in the twentieth century, setting the stage for ongoing battles between the two branches about the making and implementation of U.S. foreign policy.

THE SHIFTING NATIONAL INTEREST

Although the dominant foreign policy pursued by the United States in the early years of the country was one of unilateralism, it did not take long for that concept to be reinterpreted in light of changing perceptions of national interest. While trade, commerce, and economic relationships were necessary to U.S. growth and prosperity, the founders of the country also saw political and military aloofness from other countries as essential to U.S. well-being. Gradually, however, U.S. prosperity was tied to the country's "manifest destiny" to expand across the continent. In many cases, this meant displacing those who were already on the land, whether European colonial powers or the Native Americans who had been there long before western exploration. Sometimes U.S. expansion was peaceful, as in the case of the Louisiana Purchase. At other times, the desire to grow brought the United States into direct conflict with other countries (e.g., Mexico and Spain) or with the native peoples. In each case, the United States justified that aggression because of national interest.

As the country grew and prospered, U.S. business and investment became more international or global in scope. This also changed the direction of U.S.

foreign policy, as the country had to protect those interests, militarily if necessary, when they were threatened. By 1900, not only had the United States become a major industrial power, but it was emerging as a major political and military force to be reckoned with as well. By that time, U.S. territory had expanded beyond the Western Hemisphere into parts of the Pacific and Asia. Still under the same general foreign policy framework, the United States kept its involvement focused only on those parts of the world defined as being in its national interest. The Spanish-American War of 1898 represented a change in U.S. foreign policy, as the country aggressively declared war on Spain for dubious reasons. Nonetheless, the victory over Spain helped solidify the U.S. position in the world.

Until 1915, the United States remained largely within its own sphere of influence geographically, becoming more actively engaged militarily in the regions it defined as important. As president, Wilson added yet another dimension to the conduct of U.S. foreign policy by injecting ideals and morality as valid and legitimate reasons for intervention; U.S. involvement in World War I was justified in part by high-minded principles espoused by Wilson. These were further articulated in his Fourteen Points and in the creation of a League of Nations that was designed to make war less likely in the future.

By the end of World War I, the United States had established itself as a major power not only in the Western Hemisphere, but in Europe as well. However, if U.S. involvement in World War I is measured against Wilson's "lofty" goals, it proved to be a failure; the war neither ended war forever nor established a universal democratic system. It did change the role of the United States in the international system, but in many ways the leaders of the country did not realize or acknowledge this for some time. In fact, it set the stage for active U.S. engagement during and following World War II.

Walter Russell Mead notes, "With fewer casualties than any other great power, and fewer forces on the ground in Europe, the United States had a disproportionately influential role in shaping the peace." But Mead also notes, "The United States was the only true winner of World War I. . . . World War I made the United States the world's greatest financial power, crushed Germany—economically, America's most dangerous rival—and reduced both Britain and France to a status where neither country could mount an effective opposition to American designs anywhere in the world."[45]

Following World War I, the highest priority of the Harding administration was a "return to normalcy," which meant changing priorities and focusing inward and away from international engagement. This also meant the creation of new laws restricting U.S. immigration and the passage of other laws that limited freedom for anyone thought to be associated with a communist organization. Under existing laws, American women who married foreigners lost their citizenship and could even be deported if they or their husbands were found to be suspect.[46]

By the 1930s, as fascism was growing in Europe, the dominant feeling in the United States was a desire for isolationism in the truest sense. After World War I, although the United States was a stronger and more powerful country internationally, the priorities—the national interest—were again focused inward. While the United States tried to remain outside the politics and problems of Europe and focus again on domestic priorities, it did not take long for the country to engage internationally once again.

As we move forward in our exploration of U.S. foreign policy and get to the Interwar years, we find the United States had to confront a number of challenges, economic as well as military. Further, conflicts brewing in different parts of the world threatened to escalate into yet another world war, which the United States would become involved in despite its best attempts to avoid it. The next chapter will discuss the myriad changes that the United States went through from the period following World War I to the end of World War II. In many ways, this was a period of transition for the United States as it went from isolationism and neutrality to becoming a superpower.

CHRONOLOGY FROM THE FOUNDING TO THE END OF WORLD WAR I

1776	United States declares its independence from Great Britain
1777	Articles of Confederation created
1788	Constitution of the United States ratified
1796	George Washington's Farewell Address to the Nation (September 17, 1796)
1812	War of 1812 between the United States and Britain
1823	Monroe Doctrine (December 2, 1823)
1830	Indian Removal Act leading to the "Trail of Tears"
1846–1848	Mexican-American War
1853	Admiral Perry arrives in Japan; start of U.S. expansion into the Pacific
1861–1865	Civil War
1898	Spanish-American War
1917	U.S. enters World War I
1918	World War I ends

SELECTED PRIMARY SOURCES*

Constitution of the United States, http://www.archives.gov/exhibits/ charters/constitution_transcript.html.

The Federalist Papers, https://www.congress.gov/resources/display/ content/The+Federalist+Papers.

George Washington's Farewell Address, http://avalon.law.yale.edu/18th _century/washing.asp.

Monroe Doctrine (President Monroe's address to Congress, December 2, 1823), https://avalon.law.yale.edu/19th_century/monroe.asp.

de Lôme Letter, https://www.ourdocuments.gov/print_friendly.php?flash= false&page=transcript&doc=53&title=Transcript+of+De+L%26amp% 3Bocirc%3Bme+Letter+%281898%29.

Roosevelt Corollary to the Monroe Doctrine (President Theodore Roosevelt's address to Congress, December 6, 1904), https://www.ourdocu ments.gov/print_friendly.php?flash=false&page=transcript&doc=56& title=Transcript+of+Theodore+Roosevelts+Corollary+to+the+Monroe+ Doctrine+%281905%29.

Woodrow Wilson's Speech to the Congress asking for a Declaration of War against Germany, April 2, 1917, http://millercenter.org/president/ speeches/detail/4722.

Woodrow Wilson's Address to the Congress, January 8, 1918 (Fourteen Points), https://avalon.law.yale.edu/20th_century/wilson14.asp.

* NOTE: These websites were current as of the time we went to press. If they are no longer available, all these documents should be readily accessible online using a search engine. In general, two of the best sources for major primary source documents are the Avalon Project of Yale University, https:// avalon.law.yale.edu/ and the Miller Center of the University of Virginia, https://millercenter.org/. Both are very easy to search online.

From Isolationism to Superpower

The Interwar Years through World War II, 1920–1945

The United States came out of World War I in a strong position internationally although also with a desire to turn inward. Therefore, the United States embraced a policy of *isolationism* during the period between the two world wars (roughly 1920 through 1941). If the foreign policy during the early years of the country was characterized by unilateralism and creeping engagement internationally, the interwar period was a time when the United States preferred to remain removed from the international system as much—and as long—as possible.[1] While isolationism was the stated and overarching foreign policy framework, the reality was that the United States continued to expand and solidify its role internationally.

Policies in the 1920s reflected the domestic political priorities of the time: a commitment to big business and economic growth, as well as the desire to shield the United States from the outside world. This was done by passing laws limiting who could enter the country and through policies that the leaders in Washington hoped would keep the United States out of another European war. As economic depression gripped the country in the 1930s, the highest priority was domestic recovery. Nonetheless, the United States found itself involved internationally, although initially this engagement was limited in scope. While the United States hoped to stay out of the conflict that later escalated into World War II, this proved to be impossible.

This chapter begins with a brief description of the interwar years and the relationship between domestic and foreign policies. The focus will then be on World War II, which brought the United States—and the rest of the world—into the new "atomic age" that changed the conduct of international relations and foreign policy. The chapter concludes with discussion of the ways in which events during World War II ordained the United States' role as a superpower when the war ended, as well as set the stage for the Cold War that followed.

INTERWAR AMERICA

Although U.S. attention was focused inward in the 1920s and 1930s, the reality was that the country was fast becoming one of the most powerful nations in the world. Since the Monroe Doctrine, the United States had established a significant presence in Latin America. The United States also had a dominant place in Asia and the Pacific as early as the turn of the century, and subsequent policies ensured that it would retain that position. Where Europe was devastated by World War I, the industrial strength of the United States grew substantially, fueled in part by the material needs of its European allies who were at war. The combined military and industrial power of the United States meant that it had surpassed even the European countries, which looked to the United States not only for military help (which was limited in World War I) but for economic support.[2]

In addition, building on the precedent set by Wilson, U.S. global dominance was not just military and economic but political and ideological as well. The ideals espoused earlier by Wilson continued to guide U.S. foreign policy. Even subsequent administrations, while more pragmatic than idealistic, pursued a foreign policy that was liberal—even idealist—in nature, tied to the desire to bring countries together and settle their differences through negotiated agreements rather than through armed conflict.

When he was elected president in 1920, Warren Harding inherited a country disillusioned by world war and whose attention was focused inward. Isolationism guided foreign policy, albeit with active involvement externally when it was perceived to be in the national interest. The main priority of the Harding administration was economic growth and commerce, priorities that continued under Calvin Coolidge, who took office on Harding's death in 1923. He was followed by Herbert Hoover, who, before he was elected president in 1928, had served as secretary of commerce. In that role he had declared: "The dominant fact of this last century has been economic development. And it continues today as the force which dominates the whole spiritual, social and political life of our country and the world."[3] This was the attitude that predominated through the 1920s during the administrations of Harding, Coolidge, and Hoover.

For the United States, the 1920s on the whole was a period of economic prosperity and consumerism; the average income rose by over 25 percent between 1920 and 1929.[4] The increase in income coupled with a drop in prices for many luxury items meant that Americans were buying products that they could not have afforded earlier. There were poor and unemployed in the country, but they were largely lost amid the prevailing sense of well-being.

Consistent with the priority to look inward and fearing an influx of foreigners who could disturb the domestic economic balance that existed, Congress passed a series of immigration acts that severely limited the number of people allowed to enter the United States from countries in eastern and southern Europe, especially Russia, Poland, and Italy. These were not the first of the exclusionary acts that were passed by Congress, but they were now directed against a different group of people.[5] In 1921 national quotas for immigrants allowed into the country were imposed; the 1924 Immigration Act further restricted the number of people allowed to enter the country. Not only did the Immigration Act favor those countries with earlier emigration patterns (e.g., northern and western Europe), but it barred all Chinese, Japanese, and people from other Asian countries.[6] In many ways the Act was a reaction to a growing nationalist/nativist sentiment within the United States that sought to "protect" the country from foreigners and to ensure that "undesirables," such as communists, could not enter the country. It was also consistent with isolationism and the desire to be removed from interaction with other countries.

Within the United States, this period also was marked by an increase in tensions between the races, with riots breaking out in many of the major cities. The inequality that was supposed to have ended after the Civil War along with the abolition of slavery clearly remained deep-seated. According to one historian, this was exacerbated by the 1924 Immigration Act, which was "deliberately designed to be both racist and discriminatory."[7] The Ku Klux Klan, which had been dormant, reemerged with its message of hate not limited to blacks but extended to include Jews, Catholics, and anyone else deemed a "foreigner."

This was also the era of prohibition and temperance, as some in the country looked for ways to control the increasing alcohol consumption, greed, gambling, organized crime, and political corruption that many believed were undermining the values of society. However, the imposition of prohibition only exacerbated these vices, as trade in liquor became a new source of wealth and power for organized crime.

Women's suffrage was among the social advances during this period. The passage of the Nineteenth Amendment in 1920 gave American women who were U.S. citizens the right to vote. The international nature of World War I, coupled with recognition of the role that women played to help the war effort, ensured support of the amendment by Wilson and then passage by the Congress in 1919. By 1920, it was ratified by the necessary thirty-six states. However, by no means did this mean real equality for women in this country.

During the 1920s, the primary emphasis of the Republican administrations was on helping and supporting big business, which had foreign policy implications. Congress imposed tariffs to protect American goods, raising duties on farm goods up to 28 percent. However, Europeans retaliated by raising their own tariffs on American goods, thereby making it harder to sell American products abroad. Congress reduced taxes on the wealthiest Americans from 65 to 50 percent and passed the Budget and Accounting Act, thereby giving itself greater oversight over the budget process, consistent with its constitutional responsibilities.

Thus, for most of the 1920s the United States reveled in its prosperity and consumption while at the same time ignoring growing economic, social, and political problems, both domestic and international. By the end of the decade, circumstances changed considerably.

U.S. Foreign Policy, 1920–1930

Although the United States was one of the major powers that emerged after World War I, its policy of limited international engagement evidenced in its foreign policy decisions did not reflect that status. Despite the movement toward isolationism and emphasis on domestic economic growth, the Harding administration did not completely abandon the internationalism or idealism of the previous Wilson administration. Rather, Harding's international focus was largely limited to participation in disarmament conferences in the belief that limiting the growth of weapons would help minimize the chances of war. Clearly, this would be in the best interest of the United States.

In fall 1921, Harding convened a conference in Washington, D.C., to find ways to control the size of countries' navies (especially Japan's) and to limit a possible military buildup that could potentially affect the United States by deflecting its economic growth. The Washington conference resulted in a series of agreements that encouraged all countries involved to respect one another's possessions in the Pacific, and that also limited the size and number of naval vessels they could build.[8] One flaw in these agreements was that they could not be enforced (an important lesson in any arms control agreement). For example, Japan secretly built up to and ultimately exceeded the treaty limits while simultaneously building its air power as it moved toward militarism and aggression. However, the agreements provided at least some sense of stability for the next decade.

Harding died suddenly in 1923 and was replaced by Calvin Coolidge, who completed Harding's term and then won reelection as president in 1924. Like Harding, Coolidge's main priority was domestic economic stability, especially in areas like farming that had not yet recovered from the downturn following the war. And, like Harding, Coolidge was willing to engage internationally in a limited way in order to pursue the desired outcome of keeping the United States out of another war.

In August 1928, representatives of the United States and France co-authored the Kellogg-Briand Pact, idealistically designed to outlaw war. The leaders who signed the pact[9] did so aware of "their solemn duty to promote the welfare of mankind." And they were "persuaded that the time has come when a frank renunciation of war as an instrument of national policy[10] should be made to the end that the peaceful and friendly relations now existing between their peoples should be perpetuated." Most important, the signers of the pact agreed that "the settlement or solution of all disputes or conflicts of whatever nature or of whatever origin they may be, which may arise among them, shall never be sought except by pacific means."[11]

In many ways, the Kellogg-Briand Pact reflected the idealism of the Wilson years and the goals of Wilson's Fourteen Points, which encouraged countries to find ways to avoid war. The pact was signed by sixty-five countries, virtually all that were then in existence, and was ratified by the U.S. Senate.[12] U.S. Secretary of State Frank Kellogg won a Nobel Peace Prize for this effort. Unfortunately, it did not result in ending war as a means of settling disputes between and among nations.

In 1930 another naval conference was convened, this time in London, which brought together the United States, France, Great Britain, Italy, and Japan specifically to extend the limits that they had agreed on at the Washington Conference of 1921. However, the international situation had changed since the earlier conference. Both France and Italy, concerned that the agreement would limit their military power, refused to sign. The London Conference also included an "escalator clause," allowing a country to build more ships if it felt threatened by another country, thereby opening the door to an arms buildup. Despite the optimistic belief that international security could be assured with arms control and arms limitation agreements, war was brewing in Europe.

ESCALATION TO WORLD WAR II: 1930–1941

Despite international idealism and desire to avoid war, World War II was on the horizon. By the early 1930s, fascism was growing in Germany, Italy, and Japan, all of which harbored militaristic and expansionist goals. In 1931, in direct violation of the Nine Power Treaty to respect the integrity of China, Japan conquered the province of Manchuria and created the puppet state of Manchukuo. This was done by a group of Japanese military officials without the backing of the Japanese government. The United States sent a note of protest in response and invoked the Kellogg-Briand Pact in condemning Japan's aggression. In January 1932, Japan bombed the city of Shanghai, another direct violation of China's sovereignty. However, the United States did not intervene; this was outside what was perceived as its national interest at the time and was consistent with the desire to stay removed from international conflicts. Without unanimous action and U.S. participation, the League of Nations was powerless to do anything. In fact, facing censure for its invasion of Manchuria, Japan withdrew from the League, as did Italy following its takeover of Ethiopia in 1935–1936. This sent an important signal that collective defense, as it was constructed at that time, would not succeed in preventing war.

Simultaneously, the world fell into deep economic depression. Although the warning signs were apparent earlier, they were largely ignored until the crash of the New York stock market in October 1929. Economic downturn in Europe and throughout Europe's colonies quickly followed. In 1931, Japan suffered poor harvests, and severe economic dislocations resulted. These economic conditions fueled the fascist movement already growing in Japan, and Germany followed a similar pattern.

The U.S. presidential election of 1932 reflected the disillusionment of the American people and the desire for change. Franklin D. Roosevelt headed the Democratic ticket and defeated incumbent Herbert Hoover by 472 electoral votes to 59. Roosevelt used his first inaugural address on March 4, 1933, to reassure the American people, stating that "the only thing we have to fear is fear itself."[13] At that point, the American people had a lot to fear. As one historian points out, "In 1932, at the height of the Depression, 13 or 14 million Americans, a quarter of the workforce and mainly men, were out of work. Industrial output [which had fueled the U.S. economy] was down by 60 percent."[14] The price of livestock and agriculture (crops) had fallen, which had a devastating effect on the nation's farmers. Given the level of discontent, there was fear that the country might be heading for domestic unrest or even a revolution.[15]

Because of the deteriorating economic situation, Roosevelt's highest priority was domestic needs such as putting people back to work, creating and unifying existing "relief" (social welfare) agencies, and stricter supervision of the banking industry in order to guarantee that the crash of 1929 and the run on the banks that followed would not be duplicated. It was only after he outlined his domestic "program of action" (which was to become the New Deal) that Roosevelt addressed international issues. Even then his attention was not to the war brewing in Europe. Instead he expressed concern about the ways in which a change in "international trade relations" affected the United States.

EXCERPTS FROM FRANKLIN D. ROOSEVELT'S
FIRST INAUGURAL ADDRESS
MARCH 4, 1933

I am certain that my fellow Americans expect that on my induction into the Presidency I will address them with a candor and a decision which the present situation of our Nation impels. This is preeminently the time to speak the truth, the whole truth, frankly and boldly. Nor need we shrink from honestly facing conditions in our country today. This great Nation will endure as it has endured, will revive and will prosper. So, first of all, let me assert my firm belief that *the only thing we have to fear is fear itself*—nameless, unreasoning, unjustified terror which paralyzes needed efforts to convert retreat into advance [emphasis added]. In every dark hour of our national life a leadership of frankness and vigor has met with that understanding and support of the people themselves which is essential to victory. I am convinced that you will again give that support to leadership in these critical days. In such a spirit on my part and on yours we face our common difficulties. . . .

Our greatest primary task is to put people to work. This is no unsolvable problem if we face it wisely and courageously. It can be accomplished in part by direct recruiting by the Government itself, treating the task as we would treat the emergency of a war, but at the same time, through this employment, accomplishing greatly needed projects to stimulate and reorganize the use of our natural resources. . . .

Finally, in our progress toward a resumption of work we require two safeguards against a return of the evils of the old order; there must be a strict supervision of all banking and credits and investments; there must be an end to speculation with other people's money, and there must be provision for an adequate but sound currency.

There are the lines of attack. I shall presently urge upon a new Congress in special session detailed measures for their fulfillment, and I shall seek the immediate assistance of the several States.

Through this program of action we address ourselves to putting our own national house in order and making income balance outgo. Our international trade relations, though vastly important, are in point of time and necessity secondary to the establishment of a sound national economy. I favor as a practical policy the putting of first things first. I shall spare no effort to restore world trade by international economic readjustment, but the emergency at home cannot wait on that accomplishment. . . .

I am prepared under my constitutional duty to recommend the measures that a stricken nation in the midst of a stricken world may require. These measures, or such other measures as the Congress may build out of its experience and wisdom, I shall seek, within my constitutional authority, to bring to speedy adoption.

But in the event that the Congress shall fail to take one of these two courses, and in the event that the national emergency is still critical, I shall not evade the clear course of duty that will then confront me. I shall ask the Congress for the one remaining instrument to meet the crisis—*broad Executive power to wage a war against the emergency, as great as the power that would be given to me if we were in fact invaded by a foreign foe* [emphasis added].

Available at https://avalon.law.yale.edu/20th_century/froos1.asp.

Roosevelt alluded to the situations in Europe and the Pacific, both of which were moving toward war, and to the need for the United States to face the crisis if national interests were threatened. To meet these joint crises, domestic and international, Roosevelt also informed the American public that he was "prepared under my constitutional duty to recommend the measures that a stricken nation in the midst of a stricken world might require." And while he asked for the help of the Congress to take whatever actions were necessary (as specified in the Constitution), he also made it clear that he would invoke his executive power should that become necessary if Congress did not act.[16]

In this inaugural address, Roosevelt foreshadowed a number of themes that became more prominent in his administration, and as the United States headed toward war. First was the priority to focus inward and address the devastating economic situation facing the country. In his speech, when Roosevelt addressed the international situation, he did so in a way that made it clear that U.S. national interest was affected negatively because of the decline in international trade. By asking for the help of Congress, Roosevelt showed that he understood the relationship between the president and the Congress. However, he also raised the possibility of acting outside the bounds of Congress should that become necessary. This was the statement of a strong executive, which made it possible for Roosevelt to do what he outlined as being in the best interest of the country.

Given domestic priorities, it is not surprising that during Roosevelt's early years the United States tried to continue a policy of isolationism not only with respect to Europe and the Pacific but toward Latin America as well. Many of the countries in that region were also suffering from economic disruption and inflation along with political instability as economic conditions worsened. Rather than get involved in Latin America, traditionally an area of U.S. interest, Roosevelt's approach was to assure the countries to the south that they would be treated as equals and with respect. Roosevelt pledged that the United States would be a "good neighbor," but he retreated from involvement in Cuba and Mexico, two countries that had been defined earlier as within the U.S. sphere of influence.[17]

Neutrality Acts

The outbreak of war between Italy and Ethiopia in May 1935 prompted Congress to pass a series of laws (1935, 1936, 1937 and 1939), that prohibited the United States from providing arms or money to the belligerents or from sending U.S. ships into harm's way. Congress hoped that these "neutrality acts" would keep the United States out of the European war.

In 1937 war broke out between Japan and China, which threatened U.S. interests in China. The United States sent a note of condemnation to Japan claiming that this was in violation of existing agreements, including the Open Door policy and the terms of the Washington Conference. Japan responded that because of changing circumstances, the Open Door was no longer applicable, in effect putting the United States on notice that Japan would not comply with any existing agreement.

In September 1938, in an attempt to stop German aggression without going to war, the leaders of Britain and France met with Hitler in Munich and agreed that Germany could annex part of Czechoslovakia in exchange for the promise of peace. One year later, despite his pledge, Hitler attacked Poland. Britain and France, both of which had promised to support Poland, declared war on Germany. War in Europe was inevitable; the lesson learned was that appeasement would not work.

During this period Roosevelt continued to appeal for peace internationally. He sent letters to Hitler and to Mussolini in Italy in September 1938 and in 1939, trying to persuade them to seek peace and affirming U.S. neutrality in the situation in Europe. In November 1939, Congress passed another neutrality act, but this time amended it to allow the belligerents to purchase war munitions and materials from the United States as long as they paid cash and carried the purchases in their own ships. "That was as far as American public opinion would go at that point; it was a step away from complete isolation, but a long way from intervention in Europe's quarrels."[18] Nonetheless, the United States was creeping toward involvement in the European war.

Even before the United States got involved in World War II at all there was discussion about whether doing so would be in the national interest of the country. In fact, there was a group within the United States who wanted the country to remain isolationist and removed from the wars in Europe, as evidenced by the passage of the neutrality acts. Isolationist senator Arthur Vandenberg, a Republican from Michigan and the unofficial spokesman of Senate Republicans on foreign policy matters, prior to the bombing of Pearl Harbor advocated strict neutrality and a rigid arms embargo to prevent American involvement in the war. He proved to be prescient when he wrote that "'We have thrown ourselves squarely into the power politics and power wars of Europe, Asia, and Africa. We have taken the first step upon a course from which we can never hereafter retreat.'"[19]

From Neutrality to Nonbelligerency

On June 10, 1940, Roosevelt spoke at the University of Virginia in Charlottesville and outlined a subtle shift in U.S. foreign policy from "neutrality" to "nonbelligerency." He said that the United States subsequently would pursue "two obvious and simultaneous courses: we will extend to the opponents of force the material resources of this nation; and, at the same time, we will harness and speed up the use of those resources in order that we ourselves in the Americas may have equipment and training equal to the task of any emergency and every defense." While he made it clear that "we still insist on the need for vast improvements in our own social and economic life," he also warned that the United States would gear up for a war footing should it become necessary.[20] One year later, it would.

The presidential election of 1940 was hard fought. Roosevelt's opponent, Wendell Wilkie, accused Roosevelt of trying to drag the country into the war. Nonetheless, the two candidates were not as far apart on foreign policy as it first appeared. Wilkie supported Roosevelt's policy to get the country on a war footing and to aid ally Great Britain. Both men favored instituting a draft, which Congress passed in September. But as the election got closer, Wilkie's campaign rhetoric appeared to become more extreme. He warned about the dangers of sending American men into a foreign war. He implied that the United States had no direct interest in the war and, therefore, that Americans should not fight and die in Europe. Ultimately, Roosevelt defeated

Wilkie and won an unprecedented third term as president. According to one historian, Roosevelt believed that "in the interests of the United States, Great Britain had to be supported both up to the limits his own public support and the law of neutrality would permit."[21] Roosevelt began to prepare the country for the possibility of war.

In his message to Congress on the "state of the union" in January 1941, Roosevelt spoke of the "four freedoms," which became a call to the American public to go to war if necessary. Roosevelt reminded the American public why the country went to war in the past, "for the maintenance of American rights and for the principles of peaceful commerce," and that the war then raging on four continents was for the "armed defense of democratic existence." He reminded the country that "thinking of our children and their children, we oppose enforced isolation for ourselves or for any part of the Americas." And he presaged the U.S. reaction to the Japanese attack on Pearl Harbor when he warned, "As long as the aggressor nations maintain the offensive, they—not we—will choose the time and the place and the method of their attack."[22]

Roosevelt ended this speech with a call for personal sacrifice so that all Americans could respond to the call of "a world founded on four essential freedoms." These were freedom of speech and expression, freedom to worship God in one's own way, freedom from want, "which will secure to every nation a healthy peacetime life for its inhabitants," and freedom from fear—all to be guaranteed "everywhere in the world." Then, drawing on the idealism and appeal to moral virtue that had permeated much of American foreign policy since Wilson, Roosevelt called for a moral world order characterized by "cooperation of free countries, working together in a friendly, civilized society."[23] Hence, almost one year before the United States formally became involved in World War II, Roosevelt set the stage for U.S. involvement by asking the American public to sacrifice and by reminding them that the United States had a unique role to play in the world.[24]

Two months later, in March 1941, Congress passed the Lend-Lease Act, allowing the United States to assist countries whose defense was seen as vital to the United States by lending or leasing them war supplies, equipment, or material. In August 1941, Roosevelt met with British prime minister Winston Churchill off the coast of Newfoundland, Canada, and issued the Atlantic Charter, affirming common principles "for a better future for the world." In this document, the two leaders reiterated many of the principles that Roosevelt had already laid out in his Four Freedoms speech, but they also echoed many of the ideas and ideals originally articulated by Wilson.[25] This statement moved the United States even closer to war.

WAR

U.S. entry into the war became inevitable when the Japanese attacked Pearl Harbor on December 7, 1941. On December 8, Roosevelt went to Congress and asked for a declaration of war against Japan. Three days later, Germany and Italy declared war on the United States. The United States was at war in both Europe and the Pacific.

FRANKLIN D. ROOSEVELT'S ADDRESS TO CONGRESS REQUESTING A DECLARATION OF WAR DECEMBER 8, 1941

Yesterday, December 7, 1941—*a date which will live in infamy*—the United States of America was suddenly and deliberately attacked by naval and air forces of the Empire of Japan [emphasis added].

The United States was at peace with that Nation and, at the solicitation of Japan, was still in conversation with its Government and its Emperor looking toward the maintenance of peace in the Pacific. Indeed, one hour after Japanese air squadrons had commenced bombing in the American Island of Oahu, the Japanese Ambassador to the United States and his colleague delivered to our Secretary of State a formal reply to a recent American message. And while this reply stated that it seemed useless to continue the existing diplomatic negotiations, it contained no threat or hint of war or of armed attack.

It will be recorded that the distance of Hawaii from Japan makes it obvious that the attack was deliberately planned many days or even weeks ago. During the intervening time the Japanese Government has deliberately sought to deceive the United States by false statements and expressions of hope for continued peace.

The attack yesterday on the Hawaiian Islands has caused severe damage to American naval and military forces. I regret to tell you that very many American lives have been lost. In addition American ships have been reported torpedoed on the high seas between San Francisco and Honolulu.

Yesterday the Japanese Government also launched an attack against Malaya.

Last night Japanese forces attacked Hong Kong.

Last night Japanese forces attacked Guam.

Last night Japanese forces attacked the Philippine Islands.

Last night the Japanese attacked Wake Island. And this morning the Japanese attacked Midway Island.

Japan has, therefore, undertaken a surprise offensive extending throughout the Pacific area. The facts of yesterday and today speak for themselves. The people of the United States have already formed their opinions and well understand the implications to the very life and safety of our Nation.

As Commander in Chief of the Army and Navy I have directed that all measures be taken for our defense. But always will our whole Nation remember the character of the onslaught against us. No matter how long it may take us to overcome this premeditated invasion, the American people in their righteous might will win through to absolute victory. I believe that I interpret the will of the Congress and of the people when I assert that we will not only defend ourselves to the uttermost but will make it very certain that this form of treachery shall never again endanger us.

Hostilities exist. There is no blinking at the fact that our people, our territory, and our interests are in grave danger. With confidence in our armed forces—with the unbounding determination of our people—we will gain the inevitable triumph, so help us God.

I ask that the Congress declare that since the unprovoked and dastardly attack by Japan on Sunday, December 7, 1941, a state of war has existed between the United States and the Japanese Empire.

Available at http://docs.fdrlibrary.marist.edu/tmirhdee.html.

Although it took the bombing of Pearl Harbor for the United States to enter the war officially, it is clear that the country had been moving toward involvement for some time. Roosevelt's speeches for at least one year prior to the attack were preparing the country for what appeared to be inevitable. In addition, U.S. policies—gearing up industrially to help the war effort, assuring that the United States was prepared should it become necessary to go to war, moving from neutrality to nonbelligerency—were all designed to get the United States ready to enter the war. In many ways, the United States had no choice. It was one of the major powers in the world; by 1938, it had overtaken Britain and Germany as the greatest manufacturing producer.[26] The United States had been inching past isolationism, and Roosevelt was building public support for war, including warning the American people of the sacrifices they would have to endure for important reasons: fighting against forces of tyranny and oppression.

Once the United States was involved with World War II, it played a unique role as a military leader, fighting both in the European and Pacific theaters. Clearly, this was also a period in which the United States was solidifying its place as a world power. Both Roosevelt and then Truman, who followed as president, were aware of the fact that whatever the United States did would set the stage for the period that would follow the end of the war and the reconfigured postwar political and military order. Therefore the decisions that they made during the war would have longer-term implications.

Executive Order 9066

One of the great ironies is that while the United States was waging a war to fight the forces opposing democracy and freedom, it also passed one of the most inhumane policies seen in the United States since slavery. On February 19, 1942, President Roosevelt signed Executive Order 9066 authorizing the evacuation of Japanese living on the West Coast to "relocation centers," where they spent the remainder of the war. Roosevelt had come under increasing pressure from military and political advisors to address the growing fear in this country of the possibility of another attack by the Japanese or sabotage from Japanese in this country. Inherent in this was also racism against Asians in general, and the Japanese in particular, that had been part of the culture of this country for decades.

Executive Order 9066 states that "the successful prosecution of the war requires every possible protection against espionage and against sabotage to national-defense material, national-defense premises and national-defense utilities." As such, it authorizes the secretary of war and the military commanders to designate areas from which "persons" may be excluded and, similarly, areas to which those people can be relocated. It is important to note that this order does not specifically name Japanese, but it was applied against that group of people, as well as some of German and Italian descent.[27]

Many of these people were American citizens, and some had family members serving in the U.S. military. Over the six months after this Executive Order was signed, over a hundred thousand men, women, and children of Japanese descent were moved to the relocation centers, generally located in remote areas in the west.[28] This policy was indicative of the fear that pervaded the country following the attack on Pearl Harbor.

Preparing for Peace

The war also created strange, if fleeting, international alliances. It was not surprising that the United States joined with Britain and France, two traditional allies, to fight Nazi Germany. However, a new alliance was created when the Allied forces joined with the Soviet Union's communist leader, Joseph Stalin, to fight against Germany. Although the alliance with the Soviet Union was a necessary part of the war effort, Roosevelt and especially Churchill were suspicious of Stalin's motives as well as his ideology. This alliance lasted until the war ended and Germany was defeated. Shortly thereafter, the Soviet Union, led by Stalin, became the major threat to the United States and the countries of Western Europe.

By 1944, when it was clear that the Allied forces would win the war, one of Roosevelt's priorities was to start to prepare the country for peace. In January 1944, he again faced the Congress and the American public to describe "the state of the union." In this speech, Roosevelt not only predicted the end of war but prepared the country for a return to postwar normalcy, with an emphasis on domestic issues once again, as this speech dealt with both winning the war and the need "to maintain a fair and stable economy at home." To address both of these priorities, Roosevelt made a number of recommendations that he claimed would amount to a new bill of rights appropriate for the time. Although Roosevelt would not live to see World War II end, he set the stage for what would follow.

FRANKLIN ROOSEVELT'S STATE OF THE UNION SPEECH JANUARY 11, 1944

This Nation in the past two years has become an active partner in the world's greatest war against human slavery. We have joined with like-minded people in order to defend ourselves in a world that has been gravely threatened with gangster rule. But I do not think that any of us Americans can be content with mere survival. Sacrifices that we and our allies are making impose upon us all a sacred obligation to see to it that out of this war we and our children will gain something better than mere survival. We are united in determination that this war shall not be followed by another interim which leads to new disaster—that we shall not repeat the tragic errors of ostrich isolationism—that we shall not repeat the excesses of the wild twenties when this Nation went for a joy ride on a roller coaster which ended in a tragic crash. . . .

In the last war such discussions, such meetings, did not even begin until the shooting had stopped and the delegates began to assemble at the peace table. There had been no previous opportunities for man-to-man discussions which lead to meetings of minds. The result was a peace which was not a peace. That was a mistake which we are not repeating in this war. . . .

The one supreme objective for the future, which we discussed for each Nation individually, and for all the United Nations, can be summed up in one word: Security. And that means not only physical security which provides safety from attacks by aggressors. It means also economic security, social security, moral security—in a family of Nations. . . .

The best interests of each Nation, large and small, demand that all freedom-loving Nations shall join together in a just and durable system of peace. In the present world situation, evidenced by the actions of Germany, Italy, and Japan, unquestioned military control over disturbers of the peace is as necessary among Nations as it is among citizens in a community. And an equally basic essential to peace is a decent standard of living for all individual men and women and children in all Nations. Freedom from fear is eternally linked with freedom from want. . . .

It is our duty now to begin to lay the plans and determine the strategy for the winning of a lasting peace and the establishment of an American standard of living higher than ever before known. We cannot be content, no matter how high that general standard of living may be, if some fraction of our people—whether it be one-third or one-fifth or one-tenth is ill-fed, ill-clothed, ill housed, and insecure. This Republic had its beginning, and grew to its present strength, under the protection of certain inalienable political rights—among them the right of free speech, free press, free worship, trial by jury, freedom from unreasonable searches and seizures. They were our rights to life and liberty. As our Nation has grown in size and stature, however—as our industrial economy expanded—these political rights proved inadequate to assure us equality in the pursuit of happiness. We have come to a clear realization of the fact that true individual freedom cannot exist without economic security and independence. . . .

. . . We have accepted, so to speak, a second Bill of Rights under which a new basis of security and prosperity can be established for all regardless of station, race, or creed. Among these are: The right to a useful and remunerative job in the industries or shops or farms or mines of the Nation; The right to earn enough to provide adequate food and clothing and recreation; The right of every farmer to raise and sell his products at a return which will give him and his family a decent living;

The right of every businessman, large and small, to trade in an atmosphere of freedom from unfair competition and domination by monopolies at home or abroad; The right of every family to a decent home; The right to adequate medical care and the opportunity to achieve and enjoy good health; The right to adequate protection from the economic fears of old age, sickness, accident, and unemployment; The right to a good education. All of these rights spell security. And after this war is won we must be prepared to move forward, in the implementation of these rights, to new goals of human happiness and well-being. America's own rightful place in the world depends in large part upon how fully these and similar rights have been carried into practice for our citizens. For unless there is security here at home there cannot be lasting peace in the world. . . .

I have often said that there are no two fronts for America in this war. There is only one front. There is one line of unity which extends from the hearts of the people at home to the men of our attacking forces in our farthest outposts. When we speak of our total effort, we speak of the factory and the field, and the mine as well as of the battleground—we speak of the soldier and the civilian, the citizen and his Government. Each and every one of us has a solemn obligation under God to serve this Nation in its most critical hour—to keep this Nation great—to make this Nation greater in a better world.

Available at http://www.fdrlibrary.marist.edu/archives/pdfs/state_union.pdf.

THE IMPACT OF WORLD WAR II

We are not going to describe the course of World War II, as that information is readily available elsewhere. However, what is important is assessing the legacy and impact of the war on the United States and the evolution of the international system that followed. In many ways, World War II was a product of the twentieth century because of the role technology played; the attack by Japanese aircraft on the naval base at Pearl Harbor was a reminder that all countries were suddenly vulnerable to such surprise attacks. Further, the war ended with the decision to use the newest technology, the atomic bomb. The emergence of these new technologies not only changed the way war was fought but also set the stage for the Cold War that would follow.

The United States became fully mobilized for the war effort, which led to some important changes domestically. Because men were drafted, women had to take on new roles domestically, including going to work to keep industry running. As women accepted these new roles, they were given more responsibility and proved themselves as professionals and corporate leaders, which had repercussions in the decades following the war. African Americans lobbied for greater integration, especially in light of a controversy that emerged during the election of 1940 about the segregation of the army. This push for integration also had important—and long-term—social implications for civil rights.[29]

Technology and World War II

Pearl Harbor was a wake-up call about the role of technology in redefining a country's security. At a time when oceans could only be breached by ship, surprise attack was difficult because of the time involved. Pearl Harbor made clear what air power could do and mean. Suddenly, the United States and other countries were vulnerable, as this new technology could be used to attack in a way that had not been seen before. The role of air power changed the nature of warfare as well. Unlike World War I, where much of the war was fought on the ground and in the trenches, during World War II all countries depended on aerial bombing. This did not totally erase the need for ground or sea battles, as the history of World War II shows. Instead, it offered the belligerents more and different opportunities and ways to fight the enemy.

For example, the Battle of Britain in 1940 was an ongoing attack by German bombers sent to bring destruction on Britain. This part of Hitler's strategy of attrition against Britain was made possible by air power. British bombers attacked Germany as early as 1941, joined by U.S. air forces in 1942. The Germans responded with V-1 and V-2 flying bombs and rockets against Britain. While the Allies tried to confine their attacks to industry and "high-value" targets such as railroads, it was inevitable that civilians were killed and cities destroyed. Similarly, the German bombing of London and other parts of England did not differentiate between military and civilian targets. This showed both the strengths and weaknesses of the new technology: while it allowed countries to attack one another on their homeland, where they were most vulnerable, the risk to civilians increased and, with that, the number of noncombatant casualties. The allied bombing of Dresden, Germany, and the firebombing of Tokyo, Japan, are also examples of the destructive power of air attacks, which virtually leveled both cities and resulted in the deaths of hundreds of thousands of civilians.[30]

In June 1944, with the Germans apparently on the run, the Allies crossed the English Channel, landed on the beach at Normandy, France, and began the ground attack that would bring the war in Europe to a close. The fighting intensified in fall 1944, making the war the primary campaign issue in the U.S. presidential election in November. President Roosevelt and his running mate, Harry Truman, were elected overwhelmingly. In December, one month after the election, the final defeat of Germany began with the Battle of the Bulge. On May 8, 1945, not quite one month after the death of President Roosevelt, Germany signed the terms of unconditional surrender. However, fighting continued in the Pacific, leaving it up to President Truman to end that war.

The Decision to Bomb Hiroshima and Nagasaki

As president, Roosevelt was aware of the role of technology and the importance of dominating technologically. In 1939, before the United States was even involved in World War II, Albert Einstein wrote a letter to Roosevelt specifically to inform him about recent research "on chain reactions utilizing uranium [that] made it probable that large amounts of power could be produced by a chain reaction and that, by harnessing this power, the construction of 'extremely powerful bombs . . . ' was conceivable."[31] Einstein believed, and wrote in his letter, that research was already underway on this idea supported by the German government, and that the United States should be prepared to move ahead as well. Einstein was working with Leo Szilard, a physicist who had emigrated from Hungary to flee the Nazis, and was among the most vocal of those advocating for the creation of this type of weapons program. Along with a number of other scientists, such as Edward Teller, they saw it as their responsibility "to alert Americans to the possibility that German scientists might win the race to build an atomic bomb and to warn that Hitler would be more than willing to resort to such a weapon."[32] Roosevelt responded to Einstein that he had ordered a committee to study this possibility, and then formally approved of this uranium research in October 1939.

In May 1942, to make sure that the United States retained an edge, Roosevelt authorized the creation of the Manhattan Project, which brought together some of the greatest scientists of the time. The team's goal was to determine whether it was possible to split the atom and create a chain reaction that would result in the release of energy. If this energy could be harnessed and controlled, as some physicists thought, then the United States would be able to create a new and very powerful weapon.

On July 16, 1945, the new weapon was tested successfully in the desert near Alamogordo, New Mexico. The project was so secret that even Vice

President Truman was unaware of its existence. Yet, when he became president, Truman was the one who had to make the decision to use the weapon. With the war in Europe over, U.S. forces were concentrated in the Pacific, and the Americans stepped up their bombing of Japanese cities, resulting in hundreds of thousands of civilian deaths.

On both military and moral grounds, scholars have thoroughly debated the decision to drop the atomic bombs, especially since Japanese defeat appeared inevitable.[33] Nonetheless, Truman ultimately made the decision to use the atomic bomb to force a quick end to the war, thereby minimizing further American casualties. On August 6, 1945, the *Enola Gay* dropped an atomic bomb, dubbed "Little Boy," on the city of Hiroshima, Japan, killing more than 70,000 people. Three days later, on August 9, a second bomb, called "Fat Man," was dropped on the city of Nagasaki. The atomic age had begun.

On August 6, the White House issued a press release: "With this bomb we have now added a new and revolutionary increase in destruction to supplement the growing power of our armed forces. In their present form these bombs are now in production and even more powerful forms are in development." The release continued: "It is an atomic bomb. It is a harnessing of the basic power of the universe. The force from which the sun draws its power has been loosed against those who brought war to the Far East."[34]

In this release, the White House noted the role of technology and how it had changed the face of warfare. "Before 1939, it was the accepted belief of scientists that it was theoretically possible to release atomic energy. But no one knew any practical method of doing it. By 1942, however, we knew that the Germans were working feverishly to add atomic energy to the other engines of war with which they hoped to enslave the world. But they failed."[35]

On September 2, 1945, Japan surrendered. In retrospect, it is clear that more than simply military reasons affected the decision to drop the atomic bombs. Influencing that decision was the desire to send a signal to the Soviet Union about U.S. military supremacy.[36] Once the war—and the need for the alliance—ended, the suspicion that characterized the relationship between the United States and the Soviet Union returned. The seeds of the Cold War that would follow World War II were already planted.

Implications of the Decisions to Drop the Atomic Bombs

As we have seen in this chapter, some of the foreign policy decisions that emerged during this period proved to be very controversial; the decisions to drop an atomic bomb on Japan twice in a period of three days remains contested to this day. In retrospect it is clear that the use of the atomic bombs was designed not only to end the war with Japan but also to send a signal to the

Soviet Union and any other potential adversary about U.S. capabilities as well as its credibility—that is, not only did the United States have these weapons of mass destruction, but it was willing to use them.

Historian and student of Japanese culture Bill Gordon wrote an essay in 2000, "Reflections on Hiroshima," in which he draws on a range of sources to support his conclusion that "no justification exists for the dropping of the atomic bomb on Hiroshima."[37] His argument reflects what other critics of the decision say: there was little military justification at that point, as Japan was already on the verge of collapse and surrender, and even if Hiroshima had been warranted, there is little to support the decision to drop a second weapon on Nagasaki. According to historian Brian McNulty, "President Harry S. Truman's decision to use the atomic bomb on two Japanese cities remains one of the most passionately debated historical events of the twentieth century. . . . Some respected historians say the bombing was avoidable at best, and analogous to Nazi war crimes at worst." McNulty also notes, "While . . . historians agree on the bomb's necessity [because of the conduct of the war to that point], some question the necessity of dropping the Nagasaki bomb only three days after Hiroshima."[38] Hence, not only is the decision to drop one bomb contested, but the question of whether the second one was needed is cause for ongoing discussion and debate. Nonetheless, what is important to remember is that the decision was made in the heat of the war, based on the information available, and bearing in mind the national interest at that time.

THE UNITED NATIONS: DEFINING THE POSTWAR WORLD

The horrors of World War II reinforced the importance of preventing such catastrophes in the future. Planning for the creation of an organization that could bring countries together with that goal had begun before World War II even ended. President Roosevelt and Prime Minister Churchill worked together to bring this idea to fruition.

As a vice presidential candidate in 1920, Franklin Roosevelt supported the need to approve a "general plan" of the League of Nations.[39] Over time, however, it was perceived that "the organization's inherent structure and its rules of procedure were grossly inadequate to the basic task of safeguarding peace and preventing war."[40] Roosevelt supported the basic idealistic philosophy on which the League was structured, but he believed that an organization such as the League could not succeed if it required unanimous action by all member states. In other words, while he agreed with the values of cooperation and collective security in principle, he also understood the importance of power and the need to inject realist thinking if such an organization were to succeed.

The principles embodied in the short document called the Atlantic Charter, which Roosevelt and Churchill negotiated in August 1941, ultimately led to the creation of the United Nations.[41] Note that they worked on this document before the United States had even formally entered World War II, but clearly, Roosevelt was anticipating that step and the need to start planning for the postwar world. The two leaders sent the text of the charter to Stalin for his endorsement, but Stalin saw it as an attempt at Anglo-American domination. Stalin told British foreign secretary Anthony Eden that the charter seemed directed against the Soviet Union.[42] The idealistic visions of a world that could avoid war were counterbalanced by the schism growing between East and West.

Creation of the United Nations

Despite Stalin's reservations, on January 1, 1942, representatives of the Soviet Union and China joined President Roosevelt and Prime Minister Churchill in signing the Declaration of the United Nations. The following day, twenty-two other countries signed as well, all of which were countries then at war with the Axis powers. They also agreed to remain united and not to sign any peace agreement individually with the Axis countries. Although the idea of a "united nations" then referred to the Allied countries, it quickly grew into the skeleton for an international peacekeeping and collective security organization.[43] Planning for the nascent organization continued with an eye toward learning the lessons of the League of Nations so that its weaknesses would not be repeated. Planners recognized the need for countries to work together in opposition to any aggressor nations (i.e., liberalism) balanced against the use of power and military might if and/or when necessary (i.e., realism).

One of the highest priorities was finding funding for the new organization. The framers (primarily the British and Americans) also had to address the problem of assuaging Soviet suspicions as well as the fears of smaller countries that they would be overwhelmed by the power of the larger ones. During these early years (1942 through 1943) in the midst of war, the mood within the United States was changing and becoming more international in outlook. This aided Roosevelt in his task to build domestic support for the new United Nations while also planning for the postwar order, although he still had to overcome the objections of isolationists, such as Senator Arthur Vandenberg of Michigan, if the treaty were to be ratified by the Senate.

Roosevelt and Churchill met first with Chiang Kai-shek of China[44] in Cairo, Egypt, and then the two men met Stalin in Tehran, Iran, to discuss the war effort and what would follow the end of the war. In his Christmas Eve message to the American public on December 24, 1943, Roosevelt reflected on these meetings and noted that "those four powers must be united with and cooperate with all the freedom-loving peoples of Europe, and Asia, and Africa, and the Americas. The rights of every Nation, large or small, must be respected and guarded as jealously as are the rights of every individual within our own republic." He also noted that "the overwhelming majority of all the people in the world want peace. Most of them are fighting for the attainment of . . . peace that is as strongly enforced and durable as mortal man can make it. If we are willing to fight for peace now, is it not good logic that we should use force if necessary, in the future, to keep the peace?"[45] In this message, he was reinforcing the idea that force might be necessary in order to continue to assure peace not only at the present, but in the future. And he reminded the American public that the end of the war was not yet in sight, although these world leaders were in the process of thinking about, and preparing for the peace to follow. The creation of a United Nations was part of that thinking.

By the summer of 1944, formal talks on the new organization were well under way. The organization would consist of a Security Council, a General Assembly, an International Court of Justice, and a Secretariat, with other agencies to address specific issues (especially economic and social) to be brought in as needed. The primary purposes of the organization were to maintain peace (using force if necessary) and to foster cooperation among all nations, leading to the common good. The leaders agreed that all countries should be bound by the decisions of the new organization, but they had questions about how best to achieve this. The structure of the Security Council would include permanent members, each of which would have a veto in recognition of the power that each held, both politically and militarily. This structure also acknowledged the reality that any action would require them to act in unanimity, and therefore ideally would foster cooperation among them. The General Assembly would be composed of all member nations and would be vested with broad authority, in contrast with the Security Council, which was primarily charged with peacekeeping.

Negotiations on the details continued through 1944. The four major powers issued a statement following a conference at Dumbarton Oaks in Washington, D.C., titled "Proposals for the Establishment of a General International Organization."[46] The proposals included expanding the Security Council to five permanent members (the big four countries plus France) and six rotating members elected by the General Assembly. In addition to the International Court of Justice, the new structure would include an Economic and Social Council and a Military Staff Committee to direct the forces that would be employed in the event of a UN military action.

It is important to remember that Roosevelt had to present this idea at a time when the United States was in the midst of war that was costly in terms of lives and money. Yet it was also a period in which the United States was clearly solidifying its place as a world leader. The challenge facing Roosevelt was how to put forward, during the war, a framework for this international organization that would help avoid such conflicts in the future, bearing in mind that this would not succeed without getting the support of Congress, including the isolationists who saw the world very differently than he did. On April 25, 1945, less than one month after Roosevelt's death, delegates from forty-six nations gathered in San Francisco for a conference on the UN. The basic structure of the organization agreed to at that time was the one negotiated at Dumbarton Oaks. Despite ongoing political issues, the goals of the organization were paramount, and the delegates approved the charter of the UN. President Truman submitted it to the Senate, which voted to ratify the charter on July 28, 1945. Then on December 4, 1945, the Senate voted 65 to 7 to approve full participation in the United Nations.

The UN was to embody the lessons of the League of Nations, and in many ways, it was successful. But, as history has shown, no organization could successfully ensure that war would be avoided. Although optimistically and idealistically the new organization would force the United States and the Soviet Union to work together, the tensions of the Cold War were already in place.

On the whole, the American public supported the notion of an organization that would help deter or avoid war. By the end of World War II, the American people had also come to the realization that the United States could no longer resort to isolationism or even unilateralism in its foreign policy. Rather, the United States would have to become actively engaged in the international system.

FROM ISOLATIONISM TO ENGAGEMENT

The period following World War I was a time when the United States turned inward once again, reverting to an isolationist foreign policy. Yet the decade following the war was one in which the United States was engaged diplomatically, for example, initiating the Kellogg-Briand Pact and convening the Washington Conference, in the idealistic belief that negotiations and agreements could avoid conflict and war in the future. It did not take long for this premise to be questioned. Once Japan invaded China and Hitler began his relentless drive for power, no international agreement would stop them. Furthermore, even the League of Nations, which had specifically been created as an instrument of collective security, proved to be powerless unless all countries agreed to work together to stop the aggression of any one.

Under a succession of presidents, the highest priority of the United States was to remain removed from the conflicts escalating in the Pacific and Europe. Yet, as Roosevelt saw, that would be impossible. The best he could do was to justify the reasons for U.S. involvement in these foreign wars and prepare the American public for the sacrifices they would have to make once the country went to war. The bombing of Pearl Harbor made U.S. involvement inevitable. The surprise attack also gave notice to all nations of the dangers inherent in new technology.

The way that World War II was conducted was important for a number of reasons. The advent and use of new technology made it clear that whatever country had the best and most advanced technology would be in a position of power internationally. This meant that even before World War II ended, the rush to technological dominance that characterized much of the Cold War had begun. During the war, the United States feared that Germany would be the first country to get new technology and then use it against the Allies. This drove the development of new weapons by the United States. The fact that the United States was able not only to build but also to use atomic weapons made an important point both during and after the war.

By the end of World War II, the international order had changed. The United States emerged from that war as the major power and was well positioned internationally. War had not been fought on its mainland, thus, unlike the European countries and Japan, it had an intact industrial base. The U.S. economy was thriving. The country was the dominant military power as well, with a close relationship that had developed between the economy and the military sector, or what Eisenhower would later call "the military-industrial complex." Further, the United States was instrumental in creating a structure that would define the postwar world, embodied internationally in the United Nations.

The Domestic Context for the Postwar Period

Domestically, the country faced a number of challenges with the end of the war. The return of men in uniform displaced women who had been in the workforce and who had taken on greater roles both in their homes and in society. Following the war there was a return to a more "traditional" family that was fostered by the growth of the new suburbs. Nonetheless, within twenty years, women were fighting for access to jobs, status, and pay equal to that of their male counterparts. African Americans, who had fought in the war, returned home only to face discrimination, and they, too, felt that a promise had been broken. This led directly to the civil rights movement that started in the 1950s and really took hold early in the 1960s.

The period following World War II was difficult as the United States adjusted to a changing international order as well as these domestic issues. It would be up to Harry Truman to lead the country through these many domestic and international issues. The post–World War II period, known as the Cold War, provided a framework that would guide U.S. foreign policy for the next 45 years.

CHRONOLOGY, 1920–1945

1928	Kellogg-Briand Pact, outlawing war as an instrument of foreign policy
1929	Global economic depression starts
1931	Japan captures Manchuria
1932	Franklin D. Roosevelt elected president
1935	First Neutrality Act passed
1937	War breaks out between China and Japan
1938	Munich Agreement as an attempt to "appease" Hitler and avoid war
1941	Lend-Lease Act passed (March)
	Bombing of Pearl Harbor by Japan (December)
1942	Roosevelt signs Executive Order 9066
1945	Germany surrenders (May 7)
	U.S. drops atomic bomb on Hiroshima (August 6) and Nagasaki (August 9)
	Japan surrenders (September 2)

SELECTED PRIMARY SOURCES

Kellogg-Briand Pact (1928) https://avalon.law.yale.edu/20th_century/kbpact.asp.

Franklin Roosevelt's First Inaugural Address, March 4, 1933, http://avalon.law.yale.edu/20th_century/froos1.asp.

Roosevelt's Charlottesville Address, "From neutrality to nonbelligerency," June 10, 1940, https://millercenter.org/the-presidency/presidential-speeches/june-10-1940-stab-back-speech.

Roosevelt's "Four Freedoms" speech, January 6, 1941, https://www.americanrhetoric.com/speeches/fdrthefourfreedoms.htm. (Note that there is an audio version of this speech at the same site.)

Roosevelt's speech to Congress asking for a declaration of war, December 8, 1941, http://docs.fdrlibrary.marist.edu/tmirhdee.html.

Executive Order 9066, signed February 19, 1942, https://www.archives.gov/files/historical-docs/doc-content/images/japanese-relocation-order.pdf.

Roosevelt's State of the Union speech, January 11, 1944, http://www.fdrlibrary.marist.edu/archives/pdfs/state_union.pdf.

White House Press Release, August 6, 1945, https://www.trumanlibrary.gov/library/research-files/press-release-white-house.

III

THE COLD WAR

4

The Making of a Superpower

The Evolution of U.S. Cold War Policy, 1945–1968

The Cold War that emerged following the end of the Second World War provided the framework for United States foreign policy from 1946 until the end of the Soviet Union in 1991. During that forty-five-year period, the United States was engaged internationally in virtually every part of the world, drawn to various areas in part as a way to offset Soviet/communist influence. In many ways, that made the making of foreign policy during that time relatively easy.

In order to understand why the post–Cold War period was so difficult for the United States it is necessary to have a firm grounding in the Cold War and how it pervaded all aspects of U.S. policy, both domestic and international. Hence, this chapter will provide a rather detailed exploration of the genesis of U.S. Cold War policy and how that policy was implemented. The structure and framework of the Cold War stand in stark contrast to the lack of both after the Cold War ended.

This chapter will explore the period from the end of the Cold War through the administration of Lyndon Johnson. It was during this period that U.S. Cold War policy was defined, and also was the period of greatest tension between the United States and the Soviet Union. The next chapter will cover the period from the Nixon through the Reagan administrations (1969–1989), which captures the period leading up to the end of the Cold War. As you go through these chapters, it will be important to note the themes that have emerged and the ways in which the United States solidified its position as a major power.

BACKGROUND OF THE COLD WAR

Two countries emerged in positions of global power at the end of World War II: the United States, which came out of the war with its homeland intact, its economy strengthened by the war effort, and its military unsurpassed technologically, and the Soviet Union, which had joined with the United States and the Western allies against Germany, but which was also charting its own course. One of the unintended consequences of the end of World War II was that it set the stage for the Cold War that followed by pitting these two "superpowers," as they came to be called, against each other. Neither of these two countries specifically wanted or sought this power; in fact, in the 1920s and 1930s, each had pursued an isolationist foreign policy, preferring to focus on domestic priorities rather than trying to secure a place of power internationally. Yet World War II thrust both countries into positions of international leadership that became even more important after the war ended. The Soviet Union emerged from the war as one of the most powerful countries in Europe, while the United States was the only country strong enough to "balance" that power, and it was in the United States' interest to do so.[1]

In contrast, the relative power of those countries that had been dominant before World War II (e.g., the countries of western Europe—France, the United Kingdom, and Germany—and Japan) waned as they were forced to look inward, rather than outward, in order to recover from the devastation of the war. The result was a restructuring of the international system into a bipolar world in which the forces of democracy and free-market capitalism, embodied by the United States and its allies, faced the Soviet Union and its allies, the forces of communism.

Rather than the traditional "hot war," where countries fought one another directly on the battlefield, this was a "cold war," or a period of ongoing tensions played out in a number of arenas. First, the Cold War was a war of *ideology*, which assumed that the two divergent approaches (democracy and communism) could not coexist peacefully. Therefore, one side would have to emerge as dominant.

One of the misconceptions that guided U.S. foreign policy during the Cold War was the belief that communism was a single monolithic force. This suggested that *all* communist countries, whether China or Vietnam or even some of the left-leaning movements in Africa and South America, were loyal to and supported (and were, in turn, supported by) the Soviet Union. This belief gave rise to the domino theory that ultimately led to U.S. involvement in Southeast Asia. According to the domino theory, if one country in Southeast Asia became communist, then the other neighboring countries would fall like a row of dominoes and similarly become communist. Hence, any incursion of communism had to be stopped before it spread.

The Cold War was also a *political* war in which the two approaches, democracy and communism, were seen as antithetical to each other, leading inevitably to conflict. The belief in the expansive political nature of communism not only had foreign policy implications for the United States but important domestic ones as well. The growth of McCarthyism and the Red Scare in the 1950s created a domestic atmosphere that supported U.S. foreign policy priorities.

The Cold War involved *military* confrontation, albeit indirect. While no war was fought directly between the United States and the Soviet Union, the two sides fought each other through "proxy wars." The battleground on which Cold War conflicts were fought expanded dramatically to include countries in Latin America and Africa as well as Asia. Often the Soviet Union and sometimes the People's Republic of China backed communist-led insurgencies and communist-leaning leaders, and the United States backed virtually any government or force that was not communist. These proxy wars made it possible for the two superpowers to avoid a direct military confrontation that could, potentially, lead to nuclear holocaust. The outcome was the same—victory for the forces of democracy or communism—but the danger to the rest of the world from nuclear weapons was diminished. What neither side seemed to consider (especially in the early years) was the desire of other countries, such as India and Pakistan, to acquire nuclear weapons so that they could better deter—or if necessary—fight their own enemies. As more countries entered the "nuclear club," it potentially upset the balance of power between the United States and the Soviet Union.

Finally, the Cold War was a war of *economics*. The United States and its allies were steeped in capitalist free-market economics. In contrast, the Soviet Union followed a communist economic system, where the state planned the economy and owned the means of production. Although the conflict between these two systems appeared to be secondary to political, military, and ideological competition, in reality, economics pervaded many of the foreign policy decisions that the United States made, especially in the early years of the Cold War. For example, the Marshall Plan to aid European recovery had its roots in the U.S. desire to expand markets for its own goods and the need for stable trading partners that would not be tempted to turn to communism. This made economic tools important elements of the U.S. foreign policy of containment and set the precedent of using foreign aid (i.e., money) as an instrument of foreign policy.[2]

The Cold War period was an especially important time in the evolution of U.S. foreign policy. As we shall see in this chapter, domestic and international policies and priorities came together as the United States revised and strengthened not only its military but its decision-making apparatus to support the goals and needs of this new "cold" war. It was a time when domestic and international politics merged through movements like the Red Scare, which helped build domestic support for policies that were seen as necessary for success in the Cold War. We see the role of a strong executive as a series of presidents—starting with Harry Truman—provided the guidance and direction for a new course of action. Then, in the belief that presidents had overstepped their powers, we see Congress asserting its constitutional authority and oversight role. And, most important, we see the creation of a framework for American foreign policy that is rooted in unapologetic internationalism and engagement. Not only did the United States move beyond unilateralism or isolationism, but it did so in a way that left no doubt about the country's belief in itself and its dominance in the new world order. The concept of national interest changed dramatically after World War II, and all aspects of U.S. policy during the Cold War were designed to promote the "new" national interest.

This chapter will also illustrate the ways in which perceptions affect the making of foreign policy. Stalin's speech in February 1946 reinforced the perception that George Kennan already had of the Soviet Union and its intentions, and Kennan's perceptions were quickly translated into policy recommendations. In turn, the U.S. policy of containment affirmed Soviet concerns of being encircled by hostile countries and the need for them to build their own military to deter and defend against any possible attack. In short, we see the making of a classic "security dilemma" or a situation where the actions of one state to ensure its security are seen as a direct threat to another state which responds with its own military buildup. While each state was enacting policies perceived to be ensuring its own security, in effect it was creating a situation of insecurity, something that becomes especially apparent in retrospect.

THE EARLY YEARS OF THE COLD WAR

In many ways, the origins of the Cold War can be traced to 1917 and the Russian Revolution. As noted in chapter 2, U.S. troops remained in Russia from 1918 through 1920 to fight against the Bolsheviks (communists). This action was not forgotten by subsequent Soviet leaders and was part of the reason for their suspicion and mistrust that they had of the United States. On the other hand, the United States and its allies (primarily Great Britain) harbored their own suspicions of Stalin and his intentions. Although it was in all sides' interest to fight together against the Germans during World War II, it was not long after the war ended that a chasm emerged between the former allies.

Germany surrendered in May 1945. In July, the leaders of the three major victorious wartime powers (Truman, Churchill, and Stalin) met in Potsdam,

Germany, to address the postwar order in Europe. Since Germany had been instrumental in instigating two world wars, the allies wanted to make sure that what they perceived as German militarism was held in check. Thus, they divided Germany among the four powers (the three plus France), which together ultimately decided the future of that country. Berlin, the capital of Germany, was similarly divided among the four. Physically it was located in the heart of what was to become the Soviet sector of East Germany, so Berlin, more than any other place, became a barometer of the level of Cold War tensions.

As noted in chapter 3, the war against Japan ended with the dropping of two atomic bombs. This, too, was important as the United States entered the Cold War, for it sent a signal that the world was entering a new era in military warfare. The United States was aware of the fact that if U.S. scientists could create this type of weapon, so could Soviet scientists, and the nuclear era was born.

Just as Roosevelt had prepared the American people for participating in World War II before the United States officially entered the war and then started preparing them for the peace before World War II ended, so Truman began setting the stage for the Cold War before it started. In October 1945, he gave a major foreign policy address in New York City that became known as the "Fundamentals of American Foreign Policy." In this statement he outlined twelve points that he said would now guide U.S. foreign policy. Some of the points are reminiscent of Franklin Roosevelt's Four Freedoms speech, in which he pledged to support the basic freedoms to which all people are entitled.[3] For example, Truman stated his belief that all peoples "should be permitted to choose their own form of government by their freely expressed choice," and he spoke of the need for the establishment of "freedom from fear and freedom from want."[4]

Truman also used this statement to send a signal, especially to Stalin, about U.S. intentions in the emerging world order. For example, he made it clear that the United States had "no plans for aggression against any other state, large or small. We have no objectives which need clash with the peaceful aims of any other nation." And he warned Stalin and any other potential aggressor, "We shall approve no territorial changes in any friendly part of the world unless they accord with the freely expressed wishes of the people concerned." He also foreshadowed some of the major postwar programs: "By the combined and cooperative action of our war Allies, we shall help the defeated enemy states establish peaceful democratic governments of their own free choice."[5] But he also made it clear that "We seek to use our military strength solely to preserve the peace of the world. For we now know that this is the only sure way to make our own freedom secure. That is the basis of the foreign policy of the people of the United States."[6] In stating this, Truman also outlined what would become an important aspect of U.S. Cold War policy: That the military would become an instrument of American foreign policy.

Suspicions about Soviet intentions were confirmed in February 1946 when Joseph Stalin gave a speech in which he noted that in the wake of the victory of World War II, "the Soviet social system is a fully viable and stable form of organization and society," despite the Western assertions that "the Soviet social system was a 'dangerous experiment' that was doomed to failure." He also noted the strength of the Soviet armed forces, and that the Red Army is "a first-class modern army, equipped with the most up-to-date armaments, led by most experienced commanders."[7] Achieving this would require planning and economic development, as well as mobilization of the Soviet people behind the war effort, so Stalin concluded by reminding the people that "all are engaged in one common cause" that unites the Soviet people. Although World War II was behind them, Stalin was telling the people of the Soviet Union that they won because of their planning, their military strength, and their will, all of which they would need as they look to the future. Clearly, this speech sent an important message to the West as evidenced by the telegram that U.S. diplomat George Kennan sent back to Washington approximately two weeks later.

George Kennan and Early Cold War Policy

The foreign policy that the United States pursued during the Cold War had its origins in 1946 and 1947. In order to understand the evolution of U.S. Cold War foreign policy, it is important to examine in some detail the critical events and ideas that framed the policy decisions that the United States made during these early years.

The assessment of George Kennan, a U.S. diplomat stationed in Moscow, reinforced the beliefs about a fundamental clash between the two countries and ideologies. In February 1946, Kennan sent a document to Washington that became known as "the Long Telegram." This document and Kennan's subsequent article "The Sources of Soviet Conduct" (the X Article), published in 1947, helped crystallize the thinking of U.S. policy-makers and changed the course of U.S. foreign policy.[8] Both documents warned about an aggressive Soviet Union and the need for the United States to be prepared to counter that aggression anywhere in the world. For the analyses he put forward and the impact that he had, Kennan has become known as one of the critical architects of U.S. Cold War foreign policy, especially the policy of containment.

The Long Telegram

Kennan sent the Long Telegram from Moscow on February 22, 1946, describing the Soviet threat as he saw it. The document, intended as information for the president and secretary of state, was in five parts and began with the statement that the "USSR still lives in antagonistic 'capitalist encirclement' with which in the long run there can be no permanent peaceful coexistence."[9]

EXCERPTS FROM GEORGE KENNAN'S "THE LONG TELEGRAM" FEBRUARY 22, 1946

Answer to Dept's 284, Feb 3 [13] involves questions so intricate, so delicate, so strange to our form of thought, and so important to analysis of our international environment that I cannot compress answers into single brief message without yielding to what I feel would be dangerous degree of over-simplification. I hope, therefore, Dept will bear with me if I submit in answer to this question five parts, subjects of which will be roughly as follows:

(One) Basic features of post-war Soviet outlook.

(Two) Background of this outlook

(Three) Its projection in practical policy on official level.

(Four) Its projection on unofficial level.

(Five) Practical deductions from standpoint of US policy.

I apologize in advance for this burdening of telegraphic channel; but questions involved are of such urgent importance, particularly in view of recent events, that our answers to them, if they deserve attention at all, seem to me to deserve it at once. There follows

Part One: Basic Features of Post War Soviet Outlook, as Put Forward by Official Propaganda Machine Are as Follows:

(a) USSR still lives in antagonistic "capitalist encirclement" with which in the long run there can be no permanent peaceful coexistence. . . .

In course of further development of international revolution *there will emerge two centers of world significance: a socialist center, drawing to itself the countries which tend toward socialism, and a capitalist center, drawing to itself the countries that incline toward capitalism. Battle between these two centers for command of world economy will decide fate of capitalism and of communism in entire world* [emphasis added]. . . .

Part Two: Background of Outlook Before examining ramifications of this party line in practice there are certain aspects of it to which I wish to draw attention.

First, it does not represent natural outlook of Russian people. Latter are, by and large, friendly to outside world, eager for experience of it, eager to measure against it talents they are conscious of possessing, eager above all to live in peace and enjoy fruits of their own labor. Party line only represents thesis which official propaganda machine puts forward with great skill and persistence to a public often remarkably resistant in the stronghold of its innermost thoughts. But party line is binding for outlook and conduct of people who make up apparatus of power—party, secret police and Government—and it is exclusively with these that we have to deal. . . .

Part Three: Projection of Soviet Outlook in Practical Policy on Official Level

We have now seen nature and background of Soviet program. What may we expect by way of its practical implementation? Soviet policy, as Department implies in its query under reference, is conducted on two planes: (1) official plane represented by actions undertaken officially in name of Soviet Government; and (2) subterranean plane of actions undertaken by agencies for which Soviet Government does not admit responsibility. . . .

On official plane we must look for following: (a) Internal policy devoted to increasing in every way strength and prestige of Soviet state: intensive military-industrialization; maximum development of armed forces; great displays to impress outsiders; continued secretiveness about internal matters, designed to conceal weaknesses and to keep opponents in dark. . . .

(b) Wherever it is considered timely and promising, efforts will be made to advance official limits of Soviet power. For the moment, these efforts are restricted to certain neighboring points conceived of here as being of immediate strategic necessity, such as Northern Iran, Turkey, possibly Bornholm. However, other points may at any time come into question, if and as concealed Soviet political power is extended to new areas. . . .

(e) Russians will strive energetically to develop Soviet representation in, and official ties with, countries in which they sense Strong possibilities of opposition to Western centers of power. This applies to such widely separated points as Germany, Argentina, Middle Eastern countries, etc.

Part Four: Following May Be Said as to What We May Expect by Way of Implementation of Basic Soviet Policies on Unofficial, or Subterranean Plane, i.e., on Plane for Which Soviet Government Accepts no Responsibility.

Part 5: [Practical Deductions from Standpoint of US Policy] *In summary, we have here a political force committed fanatically to the belief that with US there can be no permanent modus vivendi that it is desirable and necessary that the internal harmony of our society be disrupted, our traditional way of life be destroyed, the international authority of our state be broken, if Soviet power is to be secure* [emphasis added]. . . .

For those reasons I think we may approach calmly and with good heart problem of how to deal with Russia. As to how this approach should be made, I only wish to advance, by way of conclusion, following comments: (One) Our first step must be to apprehend, and recognize for what it is, the nature of the movement with which we are dealing.

(Two) We must see that our public is educated to realities of Russian situation.

(Three) Much depends on health and vigor of our own society. World communism is like malignant parasite which feeds only on diseased tissue.

(Four) We must formulate and put forward for other nations a much more positive and constructive picture of sort of world we would like to see than we have put forward in past.

(Five) Finally we must have courage and self-confidence to cling to our own methods and conceptions of human society. After Al, the greatest danger that can befall us in coping with this problem of Soviet communism, is that we shall allow ourselves to become like those with whom we are coping.

KENNAN

Available at: https://digitalarchive.wilsoncenter.org/document/116178. pdf.

Kennan saw the Soviet leadership as defining a world in conflict that are "insoluble by means of peaceful compromise." And based on the premises that he put forth, he concluded that "relentless battle must be waged against socialist and social-democratic leaders abroad." Hence, Kennan made clear that the United States would face an ongoing battle that would pit this country against the Soviet Union.

In the remainder of the telegram, Kennan documented how he arrived at his conclusions and drew a distinction between the outlook of the Russian people and the attitudes of the Soviet leadership. This is an important distinction between the "official" policy of the government, and the people with whom the United States has no quarrel. However, it is important to note that in his analysis, it is the Communist Party line that made peaceful coexistence between the two countries impossible. He also reiterated the Soviet Union's drive for power, which, of course, put it in conflict with the United States. In Part Five, Kennan prescribed what U.S. policy should be to counter the Soviet intentions, beginning with the need to recognize the nature of the enemy and to prepare the United States to fight against it.

It is instructive to note that about six months later, the Soviet ambassador to the United States, Nikolai Novikov, sent a cable from Washington to Moscow in which he painted a similar portrait of the United States.[10]

The X Article

One year later, in 1947, Kennan published an article titled "The Sources of Soviet Conduct" in the journal *Foreign Affairs* under the pseudonym "X." This article went further than the Long Telegram in outlining ideas for the future U.S. foreign policy of containment. By publishing in *Foreign Affairs*, a respected journal read by policy-makers among others, Kennan made his points publicly. In fact, one of the most important aspects of the article was that it was directed at the American public, or at least those members of the public who studied and cared about foreign policy (i.e., "the attentive public") as well as decision-makers. In doing so, Kennan built support for the policies he believed would be most important for the United States to win the emerging Cold War, a point he made explicitly in The Long Telegram.

In the X article, he reprised themes outlined in the Long Telegram, such as "the innate antagonism between capitalism and socialism." And he warned that out of the antagonism "flow many of the phenomena that we find disturbing in the Kremlin's conduct of foreign policy: the secretiveness, the lack of frankness, the duplicity, the wary suspiciousness, and the basic unfriendliness of purpose." From that he concluded, "This means that we are going to continue for a long time to find the Russians difficult to deal with." As he outlined the characteristics that influence Soviet behavior, he also noted that the "cumulative effect of these factors is to give to the whole subordinate apparatus of Soviet power an unshakable stubbornness and steadfastness in its orientation. This orientation can be changed at will by the Kremlin but by no other power."

Kennan then put forward his recommendations for the United States: "In these circumstances it is clear that the main element of any United States policy toward the Soviet Union must be that of a long-term, patient but firm and vigilant *containment* of Russian expansive tendencies" (emphasis added). With that, Kennan articulated the basic tenets that would guide U.S. foreign policy through the Cold War, premised on an expansionist and aggressive Soviet Union and the need for the United States to contain those tendencies. He also described some of the ways that the United States could contain the USSR: "The Soviet pressure against the free institutions of the western world is something that can be contained by the adroit and vigilant application of counterforce at a series of constantly shifting geographical and political points."[11]

While Kennan made it clear in this article that he thought the Soviet Union was far weaker than the United States and the West, he also warned that the Russian leaders were dedicated to the success of their cause and that they had the patience to wait and continue their fight. He was prescient when he noted that "Russia, as opposed to the Western world in general, is still by far the weaker party, that Soviet policy is highly flexible, and that Soviet society may well contain deficiencies which will eventually weaken its own total potential." (This would not happen until approximately forty-four years later, when the Soviet Union imploded in August 1991.) But, for the short term, Kennan argued it was up to the United States to do whatever it had to do to contain the Soviet Union.[12]

The X article not only outlined the containment policy that was the framework of American foreign policy during the Cold War, but it also sowed the seeds for the U.S. alliance system that followed by encouraging the United States to align with countries surrounding the Soviet Union in support of the common goal of containing the USSR. While this strategy helped limit Soviet expansion by making it clear that if the USSR went into any of those countries it would have to deal with the United States, it also sent a signal to the Soviet Union, which perceived that it was being surrounded by hostile countries. The result was to exacerbate the cycle of mistrust and suspicion that characterized much of the Cold War.

1947: OUTLINING U.S. COLD WAR POLICY

The Truman Doctrine

A series of communist takeovers in countries of Eastern Europe followed World War II. Bulgaria and Yugoslavia elected communist majority governments in 1945, and communist governments were created in Hungary, Poland, and Romania in 1946. In addition, the Soviet Union retained its control of the Baltic republics of Latvia, Lithuania, and Estonia after World War II. Not only did these lead to the creation of a "Soviet bloc" in Eastern Europe, but they validated Kennan's warnings of an expansionist Soviet Union (see figure 4.1).

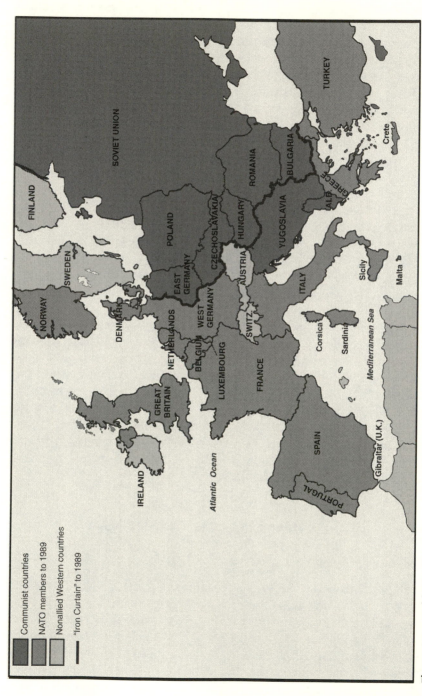

Figure 4.1. Cold War Europe.

Communist countries

NATO members to 1989

Nonallied Western countries

"Iron Curtain" to 1989

SOVIET UNION

FINLAND

NORWAY

SWEDEN

DENMARK

GREAT BRITAIN

IRELAND

NETHERLANDS

BELGIUM

LUXEMBOURG

WEST GERMANY

EAST GERMANY

POLAND

CZECHOSLAVAKIA

AUSTRIA

SWITZ.

HUNGARY

ROMANIA

YUGOSLAVIA

BULGARIA

ALB.

GREECE

TURKEY

FRANCE

ITALY

SPAIN

PORTUGAL

Gibraltar (U.K.)

Corsica

Sardinia

Sicily

Malta

Crete

Atlantic Ocean

Mediterranean Sea

The situation in Greece, engaged in civil war since 1945, grew very serious from the perspective of the United States. Britain had been sending money and troops to Greece in support of the forces defending the monarchy against communist insurgents. However, by 1947 it could no longer afford to do so. Instead, it would be up to the United States to pick up the slack. Similarly, unrest in Turkey and Soviet pressure on that country furthered U.S. concerns about Soviet intentions regarding Europe.

Thus, by 1947 the world was divided into two camps centered on the United States and the Soviet Union: West versus East. Drawing on the warnings put forward in the Long Telegram and the X article, Truman delivered a speech to the U.S. Congress in March 1947 outlining what became known as the "Truman Doctrine." In this speech, Truman formalized the policies that the United States would pursue, as well as the reasons behind them. It was a clear articulation of U.S. policies and intentions at the start of the Cold War.

EXCERPTS FROM THE "TRUMAN DOCTRINE" PRESIDENT HARRY S TRUMAN'S ADDRESS BEFORE A JOINT SESSION OF CONGRESS ON GREECE AND TURKEY MARCH 12, 1947

The gravity of the situation which confronts the world today necessitates my appearance before a joint session of the Congress. The foreign policy and the national security of this country are involved. One aspect of the present situation, which I wish to present to you at this time for your consideration and decision, concerns Greece and Turkey.

The United States has received from the Greek Government an urgent appeal for financial and economic assistance. Preliminary reports from the American Economic Mission now in Greece and reports from the American Ambassador in Greece corroborate the statement of the Greek Government that assistance is imperative if Greece is to survive as a free nation. I do not believe that the American people and the Congress wish to turn a deaf ear to the appeal of the Greek Government.

Greece is not a rich country. Lack of sufficient natural resources has always forced the Greek people to work hard to make both ends meet. Since 1940, this industrious and peace loving country has suffered invasion, four years of cruel enemy occupation, and bitter internal strife. . . . As a result of these tragic conditions, a militant minority, exploiting human want and misery, was able to create political chaos which, until now, has made economic recovery impossible. . . .

The very existence of the Greek state is today threatened by the terrorist activities of several thousand armed men, led by Communists, who defy the government's authority at a number of points, particularly along the northern boundaries. A Commission appointed by the United Nations Security Council is at present investigating disturbed conditions in northern Greece and alleged border violations along the frontier between Greece on the one hand and Albania, Bulgaria, and Yugoslavia on the other. Meanwhile, the Greek Government is unable to cope with the situation. The Greek army is small and poorly equipped. It needs supplies and equipment if it is to restore the authority of the government throughout Greek territory. Greece must have assistance if it is to become a self-supporting and self-respecting democracy.

The United States must supply that assistance. . . . There is no other country to which democratic Greece can turn [emphasis added]. No other nation is willing and able to provide the necessary support for a democratic Greek government.

The British Government, which has been helping Greece, can give no further financial or economic aid after March 31. Great Britain finds itself under the necessity of reducing or liquidating its commitments in several parts of the world, including Greece. . . .

Greece's neighbor, Turkey, also deserves our attention. The future of Turkey as an independent and economically sound state is clearly no less important to the freedom-loving peoples of the world than the future of Greece. The circumstances in which Turkey finds itself today are considerably different from those of Greece. Turkey has been spared the disasters that have beset Greece. And during the war, the United States and Great Britain furnished Turkey with material aid. Nevertheless, Turkey now needs our support.

Since the war Turkey has sought financial assistance from Great Britain and the United States for the purpose of effecting that modernization necessary for the maintenance of its national integrity. That integrity is essential to the preservation of order in the Middle East.

The British government has informed us that, owing to its own difficulties can no longer extend financial or economic aid to Turkey. *As in the case of Greece, if Turkey is to have the assistance it needs, the United States must supply it. We are the only country able to provide that help* [emphasis added]. . . .

One of the primary objectives of the foreign policy of the United States is the creation of conditions in which we and other nations will be able to work out a way of life free from coercion. This was a fundamental issue in the war with Germany and Japan. Our victory was won over countries which sought to impose their will, and their way of life, upon other nations.

To ensure the peaceful development of nations, free from coercion, the United States has taken a leading part in establishing the United Nations. The United Nations is designed to make possible lasting freedom and independence for all its members. We shall not realize our objectives, however, unless we are willing to help free peoples to maintain their free institutions and their national integrity against aggressive movements that seek to impose upon them totalitarian regimes. This is no more than a frank recognition that totalitarian regimes imposed on free peoples, by direct or indirect aggression, undermine the foundations of international peace and hence the security of the United States. . . .

I believe that it must be the policy of the United States to support free peoples who are resisting attempted subjugation by armed minorities or by outside pressures [emphasis added]. I believe that we must assist free peoples to work out their own destinies in their own way. I believe that our help should be primarily through economic and financial aid which is essential to economic stability and orderly political processes.
. . .

Available at https://avalon.law.yale.edu/20th_century/trudoc.asp.

In his speech, Truman specifically identified Greece and Turkey as two major areas of concern to the United States. He also noted that the United States is now the only country which could supply the assistance needed, especially in light of the fact that Great Britain could no longer afford to do so. With this statement, Truman made it clear that the United States would take on the global role that the British had played earlier; thus, the power balance shifted from Europe in general and Britain in particular to the United States. It also set the United States on a particular course of action not only in Greece and Turkey but in other parts of the world as both Britain and France withdrew from their colonial commitments and the United States replaced them as the major power. With that relative change in status, the United States became the major imperial power in the West.

Leading to the call for the Congress to act, Truman uttered the words that have often been quoted: "I believe that it must be the policy of the United States to support free peoples who are resisting attempted subjugation by armed minorities or by outside pressures."[13] To support these beliefs, Truman asked Congress to authorize $400 million in assistance to Greece and Turkey. Congress authorized the funds, and the role of the United States as the defender of countries fighting communist aggression was established. The United States was now firmly committed to using its hard power, economic and military, as well as its soft power (i.e., its influence) to support its allies and in opposition to communism.

The Truman Doctrine had a number of other important foreign policy implications. It established the precedent of using foreign aid and economic assistance as an instrument of foreign policy, something that continued through the duration of the Cold War and continues to the present (post–Cold War) period. It also made clear to the Soviet Union and to all other countries that the United States would use military force not only within its own hemisphere (Monroe Doctrine) or when democratic ideals were threatened (Wilsonian perspective) but in support of any country fighting communism anywhere in the world.

The National Security Act of 1947

When Truman outlined a new and more muscular direction in U.S. foreign policy, he also needed to create a governmental structure that would ensure its implementation. The bureaucratic structure for the conduct of U.S. foreign policy had been in place virtually since the creation of the country, when the foreign policy orientation was very different. That structure no longer was appropriate for a world in which the United States was going to be playing a dominant role. With the advent of the Cold War, the military became an important and overt instrument of U.S. foreign policy; the success of U.S. foreign policy was tied directly to military might. For the United States to play a major role globally, not only did it have to have a robust military force (capability), but it had to be perceived as willing to use that force in support of its foreign policy goals (credibility). Therefore, the country needed a structure that more firmly linked the military to the civilian sides of policy-making.

President Truman designed the National Security Act to create a structure that would accomplish these various goals, all of which were seen as necessary for success in the Cold War. Until the events of 9/11 precipitated rethinking the national security and intelligence sectors, the National Security Act of 1947 was the most sweeping change made to the military and foreign policy apparatus since the country was founded.[14]

The National Security Act of 1947[15] did a number of things. The War and Navy departments were merged into a single Department of Defense (DoD), which was more appropriate for the new direction in U.S. foreign policy. The DoD was to be headed by a civilian, and each military service would be headed by a civilian secretary who reported to the secretary of defense.[16] It authorized the establishment of a Central Intelligence Agency (CIA) headed by a director of central intelligence; the ability to keep track of the Soviet Union and other adversaries was seen as essential to preparing for and winning the Cold War. The act provided for the creation of a National Security Council (NSC) charged with coordinating domestic, military, and foreign policies relating to national security. The membership of the NSC would consist of the secretaries of state and defense with other officials (such as the director of the CIA and the chair of the Joint Chiefs of Staff) serving as advisors as needed. Starting in 1953, under President Eisenhower, the NSC staff was headed by an assistant for national security. Initially, this job involved little more than serving as secretary to the NSC; however, over time, and as U.S. foreign policy became more complex, the role of national security advisor grew so that now that position serves as one of the most important advisors to the president.

With the passage of the National Security Act, the United States was better equipped militarily as well as from a policy-process perspective to wage the Cold War.

The Marshall Plan

As Congress debated the Truman Doctrine, in June 1947 Secretary of State George C. Marshall delivered a commencement address at Harvard University outlining the basic principles for the postwar recovery of Europe. Marshall proposed a specific plan for European economic recovery to be implemented over the next several years in the belief that only if Europe were strong economically could it withstand any attempt at communist insurgency. But it also put the burden on the Europeans to determine their own needs: "Before the United States Government can proceed much further in its efforts to alleviate the situation and help start the European world on its way to recovery, there must be some agreement among the countries of Europe as to the requirements of the situation and the part those countries themselves will take in order to give proper effect to whatever action might be undertaken by this Government. It would be neither fitting nor efficacious for this government to undertake to draw up unilaterally a program designed to place Europe on its feet economically. This is the business of the Europeans."[17]

In response, Britain and France took the lead and invited twenty-two European countries, including the Soviet Union and its Eastern European allies, to a conference to draw up an outline for European reconstruction that could be presented to the United States. Although the USSR and members of the Eastern bloc refused to participate, virtually all the countries of Western Europe did, and on September 23, 1947, they submitted a report to the United States on general European needs.

On April 3, 1948, President Truman signed into law the European Recovery Act, widely known as the Marshall Plan. It provided for $5.3 billion specifically for European economic recovery for the following year. During the period from 1948 through 1950, the United States spent $12 billion in economic aid for Europe, more than half of which went to Britain, France, and West Germany. This infusion of money gave those countries the impetus they needed to begin to recover from the war. And, as planned, they became major trading partners of the United States (and, through the European Union, remain so today).

The Marshall Plan not only strengthened the economic systems of the partner countries, but by doing so, it helped stabilize their political systems as well. By forcing the countries of Europe to work together, it created the early framework for what would later grow into the European Union. It tied the United States more firmly to Western Europe, and it solidified the role of the United States as global leader. But it also exacerbated the divide between Western Europe and the countries of Eastern Europe, which were pulled more firmly into the Soviet orbit.

By 1947, just two years after World War II ended, the United States had secured its place as a "superpower" politically, militarily, and economically. Further, it had transformed its foreign policy into one that was actively engaged internationally, and its foreign policy–making process was restructured to support that perspective. And Congress and the American public supported this direction for the country.

THE ESCALATION OF THE COLD WAR: BERLIN TO KOREA

A coup in Czechoslovakia in February 1948 brought a communist government to power and furthered U.S. concerns about an expansionist Soviet Union. Those fears were made even more real in June 1948, when the Soviet Union closed all roads through East Germany into Berlin, blocking land access to the city. The United States saw this as an act of Soviet aggression against an ally and felt that it had to respond. The United States led a massive airlift that lasted one year. During that period, all necessary supplies, including food, clothing, and medicines, were brought into West Berlin by air (see figure 4.2). This served as a reminder that the United States would not forget its allies, and would support them using the U.S. military as necessary. It was an important signal to send to the allies, as well as the Soviet Union. Stalin lifted the blockade in June 1949, but this would not be the last time that Cold War tensions were played out in this divided city.

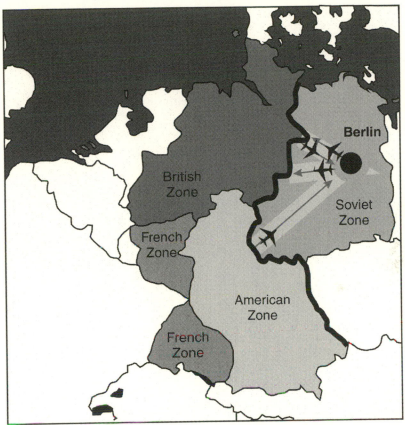

Figure 4.2. Germany after World War II Showing Allied Airlift to Berlin.

The Creation of NATO

The Berlin blockade reinforced the importance of U.S. military involvement
in Europe as well as the critical role of the United States in deterring the
Soviet Union. The desire by the United States and Europe to formalize their
relationship as well as to build on the need to contain communism contributed
directly to the creation of the North Atlantic Treaty Organization (NATO)
in April 1949. At the heart of the North Atlantic Treaty is Article 5, which
unequivocally links the United States and Europe with its statement of collective security and mutual support.

> The Parties agree that an armed attack against one or more of them in Europe or
> North America shall be considered an attack against them all and consequently
> they agree that, if such an armed attack occurs, each of them, in exercise of the

right of individual or collective self-defense recognized by Article 51 of the Charter of the United Nations, will assist the Party or Parties so attacked by taking forthwith, individually and in concert with the other Parties, such action as it deems necessary, *including the use of armed force, to restore and maintain the security of the North Atlantic area* (emphasis added).[18]

Note that Article 5 does not *require* a military response to an attack, but leaves that option open. In many ways, this statement of collective security/ defense is similar to the one outlined in Article 10 of the League of Nations charter, that the collective power of nations working together would be sufficient to deter any aggressive nation.[19] In contrast to the earlier League of Nations, what made the NATO alliance credible was the link between the United States and its allies in Western Europe and, as evidenced by the Berlin blockade, the willingness of the United States to use its military power to support its allies when necessary. Further, while the members of the Senate feared that Article 10 of the League of Nations charter could embroil the United States in a war that they did not want, the political and military realities of the Cold War period required U.S. commitment.

The NATO treaty contains other components that were—and remain— important politically, if not necessarily militarily. For example, Article 2 specifically references the "further development of peaceful and friendly international relations by strengthening their free institutions. . . . They will seek to eliminate conflict in their international economic policies and will encourage economic collaboration between any or all of them."[20] While this made it clear that these like-minded countries (democratic and capitalist) would work together and cooperate, it further divided East and West.[21] In general, NATO represents one of the clearest, and also most enduring, examples of the U.S. postwar alliance system designed to contain communism.

The End of the Decade

As the 1940s drew to a close, the United States had not only asserted itself as a major power, but it was expanding its reach internationally, including into areas such as the Middle East. This can be seen clearly with U.S. support of the creation of Israel in 1948. The state of Israel was the result of longstanding controversy and dispute in the region going back to 1917 and the Balfour Declaration, which called for the creation of a Jewish homeland in the area then called Palestine. The British Peel Commission report, released in 1937, recommended that Palestine be partitioned into a separate Arab and Jewish state. This plan was adopted by the UN in 1947, and the British withdrew from the area, leading to increasing violence. In 1948, the UN agreed to the creation of the state of Israel as a Jewish homeland. The United States was the first country to officially recognize the new country, and has remained a staunch supporter ever since. It should be noted that the creation of a second Arab state has not yet happened, and is the root of much of the conflict over a "two-state solution" today.[22]

Two events occurred in 1949 that served as harsh reminders to the United States about the dangers of the Cold War. In September 1949 the Soviet Union tested an atomic bomb, making it the second country to acquire this new weapon of mass destruction. This happened years before the United States anticipated that the Soviets had the technology to do so. With that test, the world really was bipolar, and the United States could no longer count on technological domination to assure the defeat of the USSR.

Then, in October 1949, after years of civil war, Mao Tse-tung (Mao Ze-dong) proclaimed the creation of the People's Republic of China (PRC), a communist state. Despite the fact that Chinese and Soviet communism were different and that each country was pursuing separate goals,[23] to U.S. policy-makers the creation of the PRC was another indication of the spread of communism, which they believed was monolithic and out for world domination. This perception colored many of the foreign policies that they made during the Cold War.

By 1950 the United States was established as a major power in European affairs. Further, it had started to play an active role in the Middle East with its support of the state of Israel. In 1953 the United States cemented its place in that region when it supported the overthrow of Prime Minister Mohammad Mosaddegh in Iran. Eisenhower wanted a pro-U.S. leader in Iran because of its strategic location bordering the Soviet Union as well as its supply of oil (which Mosaddegh had nationalized). Thus, Eisenhower ordered the CIA to work with the Iranian military to overthrow Mosaddegh. With the help of the United States, Shah Mohammad Reza Pahlavi was restored as leader of Iran following a coup in August 1953, regaining the role he had had before Mosaddegh took power two years earlier. Iranian resentment toward the United States grew because, as one scholar noted, the shah was seen as "holding the American proxy in the Persian Gulf—as the protector of America's interests."[24] Those feelings would come to a head during the Iranian revolution of 1979 and the seizure of the U.S. embassy in Tehran.

NSC 68

In the 1950s, the United States was flexing its muscles internationally. The National Security Act established the bureaucratic structure necessary for the United States to act as a global superpower. The Truman Doctrine and Marshall Plan clearly outlined the active role that the United States would take in Europe, and the creation of NATO reinforced the ties between the United States and its European allies. And the United States was willing to play an active role in parts of the world, such as the Middle East, in which it had not been involved before. However, all of these actions were guided by the strong belief in the need to contain communism led by the Soviet Union.

In April 1950, two months before the outbreak of war in Korea, the NSC issued a report to President Truman known as "NSC 68: United States Objectives and Programs for National Security." This document laid out the bipolar nature of the Cold War world and, like the Long Telegram, reinforced the belief that the goal of "those who control the Soviet Union and the international communist movement is to retain and solidify their absolute power, first in the Soviet Union and second in the areas not under their control." And because the United States is the "principal center of power in the non-Soviet world and the bulwark of opposition to Soviet expansion [it] is the principal enemy whose integrity and vitality must be subverted or destroyed . . . if the Kremlin is to achieve its fundamental design."[25] It was this document that became "the seminal Cold War blueprint that portrayed the Soviet Union as an implacable foe bent on world domination, requiring a massive U.S. military buildup."[26] The analysis put forth in NSC 68 (which was classified until 1975) led to the conclusion that the United States had to build up its military forces (conventional and nuclear) in order to meet its commitments and confront—and deter—the Soviet threat. Any questions about Soviet intentions were laid to rest in June, when war broke out on the Korean peninsula.

War in Korea

By the time that war in Korea started in June 1950, the United States had been involved in Asia for about a century. However, it was the U.S. occupation of Japan following the end of World War II that made the United States a major presence in that region. When civil war broke out on the Korean peninsula, precipitating invasion by the Soviet-backed North into the U.S.-backed South, Truman felt that the United States had to act on behalf of its ally, South Korea.

Truman asked Secretary of State Dean Acheson to bring the issue before the United Nations Security Council, which condemned the invasion as a breach of the peace agreed to at the end of World War II. Voting when the Soviet ambassador was absent (and therefore could not veto the action),[27] the Security Council agreed to call for an end to fighting and required the invading armies of the North to withdraw to the thirty-eighth parallel, an arbitrary dividing line that had been established earlier. When this did not happen, on

June 27 the UN Security Council called on member states to aid South Korea, created a special military command, and invited the United States to lead it.

Truman never asked Congress for a formal declaration of war. Since this was not an act of war but merely a "police action" in support of the United Nations, he used his power as commander in chief and issued a statement consistent with the Security Council request: "I have ordered United States air and sea forces to give the Korean Government troops cover and support." He concluded the statement by asserting, "I know that all members of the United Nations will consider carefully the consequences of this latest act of aggression in Korea in defiance of the Charter of the United Nations. A return to the role of force in international affairs would have far-reaching effects. The United States will continue to uphold the rule of law."[28]

Initially under the leadership of U.S. General Douglas MacArthur,[29] the Korean War continued until an armistice was signed between North Korea and the United Nations on July 27, 1953. The armistice drew the dividing line between North and South Korea at the thirty-eighth parallel (where it had been before the war broke out) and established a demilitarized zone, patrolled by UN forces, to separate the two sides.

Approximately thirty-five thousand Americans lost their lives in this Korean War which was the first example of active U.S. military engagement under the new Cold War framework. The military was an important instrument of U.S. foreign policy and was used directly to support the foreign policy and ideological goals of confronting communism, a clear commitment to realist political thinking backed up by the use of hard power. The war was fought on the basis of President Truman's power to commit forces, and without a congressional declaration of war. It was a clear assertion of U.S. global superiority. But given the tenuous relationship between the United States and the Soviet Union, both of which had nuclear weapons, it was also a reminder of how fragile the peace could be as well as the dangers of war between the superpowers.

The Cold War at Home

To be successful, foreign policy needs the support of the American public, which is often unsophisticated about the details. Hence, the U.S. leadership simplified the policy into a depiction of democracy versus communism or "good" versus "evil." Truman helped draw the lines in some of his speeches, but actual events coupled with the media coverage of those events reinforced the notion of a divided world. It was the rise of Senator Joseph McCarthy and the subsequent Red Scare that brought the Cold War home.

In February 1950, McCarthy gave a speech in which he charged that there were more than two hundred communists in the State Department.[30] He followed this with speeches on the floor of the U.S. Senate, where he talked about "loyalty risks." Although many viewed him as an extremist and a demagogue, his attacks got the attention of the press and the public. McCarthy spoke in terms that the "average" American could understand, and his charges resonated. The Senate held investigations and hearings to look into McCarthy's allegations. Ultimately, the Senate censured him, and both McCarthy and the charges he made were discredited, but not before the damage was done and many innocent people suffered. Nonetheless, McCarthy and the Red Scare created the atmosphere at home that contributed directly to building support for U.S. military and foreign policy during the Cold War.

The Domino Theory

North Korea's invasion of South Korea exacerbated America's fears of communism and gave ammunition to those in Washington who felt that the United States was not doing enough to contain communism. Journalist Stewart Alsop wrote, "We are losing Asia fast" (referring not only to Korea but to China as well). He went further when he warned that after China, "the two pins in the second row are Burma and Indochina. If they go, the three pins in the next row, Siam, Malaya, and Indonesia, are pretty sure to topple in their turn. And if all of Asia goes . . . magnetism will almost certainly drag down the four pins of the fourth row, India, Pakistan, Japan and Philippines."[31] This belief, that if one country were to fall to communism others would follow, became the rationale for increasing support to South Korea, and it was the basis for the domino theory that contributed directly to the U.S. decision to get involved in Vietnam in the 1960s.

EISENHOWER

The decade of the 1950s was characterized by brinkmanship and ongoing tensions between East and West. Both the United States and Soviet Union arrived at policies that each felt would solidify its own power as well as send signals to the other country. This suggests that foreign policy and military decisions made by the United States during this period not only were designed to further those policies deemed to be in the national interest but also were based on a perception of the ways in which each country viewed the other. We will examine the policies and decisions made during this period from those multiple perspectives.

In 1952 the United States elected Dwight Eisenhower president based in part on his pledge to "bring the boys home from Korea." In June 1953, about six months after Eisenhower took office, the Korean War ended with the signing of an armistice. The United States deployed troops to help patrol the border between North and South Korea and reaffirmed its commitment to protect its allies against communism. With the war in Korea, the United States expanded its reach and demonstrated that it would use military force when necessary to contain communist aggression.

The United States made some of its foreign policy decisions during this period in reaction to external events over which it had no control. For example, Stalin's death in 1953 just before the Korean War ended had a direct impact on U.S. policies. So much of U.S. foreign policy was tied to *perceptions* about the Soviet Union that Stalin's death led to uncertainty about who would succeed him and what that would mean for Soviet decision-making. In 1956, after three years of unclear leadership, Nikita Khrushchev came to power. He used a "secret" speech at a session of the twentieth congress of the Communist Party of the Soviet Union to denounce Stalin and declare that "coexistence" would become the goal of Soviet foreign policy.[32] The speech was widely covered and, taken together with announcements of Soviet reductions in armaments, might have signaled a significant change in international relations. This was not to be; the Soviet army quickly quashed the Hungarian revolution of 1956, which served as a reminder not only of Soviet military power but of its willingness to use it.

Doctrine of Massive Retaliation

Committed to the policy of containment, Eisenhower's foreign policy built on the recommendations of NSC 68 as well as the advice of "cold warriors" such as Secretary of State John Foster Dulles. Eisenhower shifted U.S. foreign policy to rely more heavily on weapons of mass destruction as the primary deterrent against Soviet aggression. One of the critical factors to Eisenhower was how to protect the nation without wrecking the economy. The answer was nuclear weapons, which were cheaper to produce than conventional weapons. In March 1954, the National Security Council (NSC) and the Joint Chiefs of Staff (JCS) signed off on documents declaring that "atomic weapons would be used at the outset of general war."[33]

Eisenhower asked Secretary of State John Foster Dulles to deliver a speech on the topic to the Council on Foreign Relations, which he did on January 12, 1954. Titled "The Strategy of Massive Retaliation," the speech outlined the Eisenhower strategy and reasons for it, and depicted the Soviet Union as planning to "divide and weaken the free nations by overextending them . . .

so that they come to practical bankruptcy." If this were to come true, it would assure victory for the Soviet Union. To meet this threat, Dulles announced the new policy that would assure "a maximum deterrent at a bearable cost." According to Dulles, "The way to deter aggression is for the free community to be willing and able to respond vigorously at places and with means of our choosing." The assumption was that in the event of attack, the United States would respond quickly and forcefully, using nuclear weapons. This decision meant that the United States would now "depend primarily upon a great capacity to retaliate, instantly, by means and at places of our choosing." This would enable the Department of Defense and the JCS to "shape our military establishment to fit what is our policy, instead of having to try to be ready to meet the enemy's many choices."[34] Massive retaliation was to remain the primary military policy of the United States into the 1960s. With the advent of the hydrogen bomb and nuclear weapons, and apparent technological superiority, the United States had a credible threat that if this country or its allies were attacked by the Soviet Union (or China), the response would be overwhelming, and hence, would serve as a deterrent to any attack against the United States or its allies. However, the success of this strategy was premised on U.S. military superiority.

That assumption was put to rest in October 1957 when the Soviet Union launched a satellite, known as *Sputnik*, using a rocket that had a range of five thousand miles (capable of hitting the United States). The fact that the Soviets had this capability came as a surprise to the United States, which had not yet tested its own long-range rocket (ICBM) successfully. As a result of *Sputnik*, there was a fundamental shift in the perceived balance of power between the United States and the Soviet Union; the Soviet Union had apparently surpassed the United States.[35] This came at a time when U.S. foreign policy was premised on the idea of military balance or even U.S. superiority, and it contributed to the acceleration of the arms race that had already started.

The Suez Crisis

In general, the Eisenhower years were characterized by international tension and a tenuous balance of power. The Suez Canal crisis of 1956 disrupted the delicate balance that existed in the Middle East. It also caused strains between the United States and France and Britain, its closest European allies. Precipitated by Egyptian president Nasser's nationalization of the Suez Canal, Britain and France conspired with Israel to overthrow the Egyptian leader. Israel invaded Egypt in October 1956, allegedly to destroy bases that had been used against Israeli settlers. As agreed, the British and French governments immediately claimed that the war would put passage through the

Suez Canal in danger and called for a cease-fire. When Nasser rejected this, the countries launched an attack against Egypt. Britain, France, and Israel all denied that they had colluded, and with U.S. pressure, the UN negotiated a cease-fire. All sides suffered as a result of this adventure. The British prime minister resigned, and the British government lost prestige within the British Commonwealth. The attack by Israel fueled the hatred between Israel and the Arab peoples. The United States was angered that it had not been told of this plan by three of its allies. To many in the United States and Western Europe, Suez was an unnecessary distraction during a time of Cold War tension.

The U-2 Incident

In May 1960, Eisenhower was looking forward to a summit meeting with Khrushchev in Paris that was to be his final major diplomatic act before his term ended. However, just before that meeting, the Soviet Union shot down a U.S. U-2 spy plane that had been flying over the USSR.[36] Even more embarrassing to Eisenhower, the pilot, Francis Gary Powers, was captured alive by the Soviet Union.[37] A series of events followed, starting with Eisenhower's claims that a "weather plane" had been lost. When the Kremlin published a photograph of the plane along with the claims that the pilot was alive, Eisenhower faced a dilemma: admit that he lied about the plane, or say that he was unaware of its mission. Either way, the outcome would not be good for Eisenhower and perceptions of the United States, and it virtually guaranteed that the summit would fail. As reporter James Reston wrote in the *New York Times*, "This was a sad and perplexed capital tonight, caught in a swirl of charges of clumsy administration, bad judgment and bad faith."[38]

In many ways, this event set the tone for the election of 1960. The Cold War to date had been a delicate balancing act that included not only military might, as defined by actual numbers of weapons, but also perceptions. The U-2 incident and the subsequent failure of the Paris summit held in August 1960 were further indicators that the perception of balance had shifted in favor of the Soviet Union. It is little wonder that one of John F. Kennedy's major election themes was a "missile gap" and that the United States was losing the arms race to the USSR.[39]

THE KENNEDY YEARS

John F. Kennedy defeated Eisenhower's vice president, Richard Nixon, in the election of 1960 and became president. While the American public saw Kennedy as youthful, handsome, and energetic, the Soviet Union perceived him as young and inexperienced. Here, too, perceptions became reality as that image of Kennedy played into the decisions that the Soviet Union made during Kennedy's brief tenure in office whereas the foreign policy decisions made by Kennedy defined the direction of U.S. foreign policy for the next decade.

One of the defining themes of the election was the alleged missile gap that favored the Soviet Union at the expense of the United States. But, more important, this equation was part of the perceptions that each of the two sides had of its role internationally, and of one another. In October 1961, Kennedy asked Roswell Gilpatric, deputy secretary of defense, to use a speech he was scheduled to give at a convention of the Business Council "to implode the myth of the missile gap more fully than anyone had done in public."[40] As was true of so many things during this time, this public speech was meant to send a very clear signal to Khrushchev. In this speech, Gilpatric enumerated the number of nuclear weapons that the United States had, stressing that the U.S. nuclear arsenal was second to none, and that the United States would not be cowed by Soviet threats. In the speech he said that "The Soviet's bluster and threats of rocket attacks against the free world—aimed particularly at the European members of the NATO alliance—must be evaluated against the hard facts of United States nuclear superiority." He also foreshadowed the doctrine of flexible response when he noted that "We are determined to have flexibility in our choice and mobility of weapons, and in our capacity to respond to repeated crises in the long run without the dislocation of our entire economy."[41] According to at least one analysis, this speech also conveyed to Khrushchev the need for a response, which Khrushchev did by placing Soviet medium-range ballistic missiles in Cuba, ninety miles off the U.S. coast.[42] We will return to what became known as the Cuban Missile Crisis below.

Berlin

In August 1961, after he had been in office about seven months, Kennedy faced a crisis over Berlin. The crisis was foreshadowed in a speech that Khrushchev made in January 1961, just before Kennedy's inauguration, when he threatened to annex West Berlin. Although Khrushchev had threatened this before, any crisis had been averted. However, this time, at a summit meeting in June 1961 between Khrushchev and Kennedy, Khrushchev warned the American president that the Soviet Union would be willing to go to war over Berlin. Kennedy had his national security team look at options. The Soviets demanded that the Western powers evacuate West Berlin, and Khrushchev threatened to sign a peace treaty with East Germany, a move that would have further isolated the western sectors of the city. When Kennedy refused to comply with Khrushchev's demands, the Soviets sealed East Berlin from the

West by erecting a wall. That wall became a symbol of the Cold War divisions between East and West; when the wall came down in November 1989, it was a tangible sign that the Cold War was over.

Berlin was an early crisis for the Kennedy administration. But Kennedy faced other areas of crisis and even conflict that further defined U.S. foreign policy under Kennedy and beyond. Two specific areas that had long-term implications for U.S. foreign policy were Cuba and Southeast Asia—specifically Vietnam.

Cuba

With the Monroe Doctrine, the Spanish-American War, and the Roosevelt Corollary, the United States had defined Cuba as being within its sphere of influence. Therefore, the United States initially welcomed Fidel Castro when he overthrew Cuban dictator Fulgencio Batista in 1959, believing that Castro would create a democracy on the island. However, in 1960, when Castro turned to the Kremlin for aid and support, the United States became concerned about the danger of creeping communism in its own hemisphere.

When Kennedy became president, he inherited and accepted a plan drawn up by the Eisenhower administration for a CIA-backed invasion of Cuba, executed with the help of Cuban exiles in the United States. The plan assumed that once the Cuban exiles landed in Cuba and the Cuban people learned about the invasion, they would rise up and overthrow Castro. But the Bay of Pigs invasion in April 1961 was a disaster. Not only did the people of Cuba not rise up, but virtually every member of the invading force was either killed or captured.

Kennedy gained respect domestically when he spoke to the American public and took responsibility for what happened. "There's an old saying that victory has a hundred fathers and defeat is an orphan. I am the responsible officer of the government," he said.[43] In contrast, the failed invasion undermined his credibility internationally by reinforcing the perception that he was inexperienced and not up to the task of managing U.S. foreign policy. At a time when perceptions mattered, this sent an important signal to the Soviet Union that, no doubt, helped prompt the other big crisis in Cuba during Kennedy's term.

The Cuban Missile Crisis

The Cuban Missile Crisis of October 1962 was a critical turning point in the course of the Cold War. There are many reasons why the Soviet Union chose to put missiles in Cuba: the United States had invaded the island the year before, and the Soviet Union wanted to protect its client state; it was an assertion of Soviet superiority designed to send a signal to China;[44] Khrushchev wanted to demonstrate leadership domestically by taking a bold step internationally; it sent a signal in response to the Gilpatric speech suggesting that the Soviet Union lagged behind the United States. But there is little doubt that the Soviet Union did so at least in part in the belief that, as a result of what happened at the Bay of Pigs, Kennedy simply was not strong enough to stop it.

The Cuban Missile Crisis undoubtedly was the most dangerous confrontation of the Cold War, a time when the two superpowers were indeed "eyeball to eyeball."[45] President Kennedy and his closest advisors reviewed a range of options and, as tensions grew, opted for a naval blockade of the island of Cuba coupled with "back-channel" diplomacy. In retrospect, it was the decision to pursue both courses of action simultaneously that made a peaceful resolution of the crisis possible.

Countless volumes have been written about the Cuban Missile Crisis.[46] Suffice it to say, the successful—and peaceful—resolution of the conflict led to an increase in stature internationally for both Kennedy and the United States and a concomitant diminishment of both Khrushchev's and the Soviet Union's prestige. At a time when perception of balance was relative (in that a relative increase in one side came at the expense of the other), this was an important shift. In part as a result of this gamble in Cuba, Khrushchev was removed from power shortly thereafter.

In 1992, thirty years after the missile crisis, former U.S., Soviet, and Cuban officials met in Havana to discuss and explore the circumstances of the event. Following that conference Robert McNamara, who had been Kennedy's secretary of defense, revealed that "the two nations were much closer to nuclear conflict than was previously realized."[47] McNamara also disclosed that he had learned at the conference that Soviet officials "had sent Havana short-range nuclear weapons and that Soviet commanders there were authorized to use them in the event of American invasion. . . . The short-range nuclear weapons were in addition to medium-range nuclear weapons that would have required authorization from Moscow to use." Given the new information, McNamara concluded, "The actions of all three parties were shaped by *misjudgments, miscalculations* and *misinformation,*" and that "in a nuclear age, such mistakes could be disastrous" (emphasis added).[48]

Nonetheless, the outcome of the Cuban Missile Crisis changed the momentum of the Cold War by shifting the balance back in favor of the United States.[49]

Vietnam

The other area of tension growing at this time that affected U.S. foreign policy far beyond the Kennedy administration was Vietnam. During the presidential transition, Eisenhower warned the newly elected president about the dangers in Southeast Asia including communist-backed insurgencies in Vietnam and Laos. The French colony of Indochina gained its independence after defeating France at Dien Bien Phu in 1954. This victory was followed by an agreement signed in Geneva to divide Vietnam at the seventeenth parallel until elections could be held two years later. The United States did not sign the agreement but promised to abide by its terms, pledging support to the government of Ngo Dinh Diem in the south. The northern part of the country was controlled by communists under Ho Chi Minh, who had led the fight for independence against the French. The elections were not held in 1956 as agreed to, and unrest continued to fester.

The seeds for protracted U.S. involvement in Southeast Asia were sown under Eisenhower when he sought congressional approval for limited U.S. involvement in the region. Congress then made clear its opposition to unilateral U.S. involvement to replace France, which had withdrawn after its defeat in 1954. Referring to the popularity of Ho Chi Minh, then senator John F. Kennedy, according to one historian, "warned that no amount of military aid could conquer 'an enemy which has the support and covert appeal of the people.'"[50]

At the time, Laos was in the midst of an uprising led by communist Pathet Lao forces allied with the Vietnamese communists (Vietminh). Eisenhower felt that Laos, rather than Vietnam, would be the trouble spot, and he warned Kennedy that the conflict in Laos was potentially destabilizing to the region. Eisenhower said of the communist insurgency that it was "the cork in the bottle . . . whose removal could threaten all of Southeast Asia." And in late 1960, as he was leaving office, Eisenhower warned, "We cannot let Laos fall to the Communists, even if we have to fight—with our allies or without them."[51]

Shortly after he took office, in March 1961, Kennedy made a statement on Laos echoing Eisenhower's concerns: "The security of all of Southeast Asia will be endangered if Laos loses its neutral independence. Its own safety runs with the safety of us all. . . . I want to make it clear to the American people, and to all the world, that all we want in Laos is peace, not war."[52]

However, it was Vietnam, not Laos that proved to be the real dilemma. International negotiations settled the conflict in Laos in 1962 with an agreement that guaranteed neutrality for the country.[53] At the same time, the unrest in Vietnam grew, led by popular leader Ho Chi Minh, who continued to gain strength against the despised (and U.S.-backed) Diem. The Kennedy administration was very concerned about "losing" Vietnam, one of the "dominos," to communism, as noted earlier in this chapter. Kennedy was also concerned about what such a loss (or even continued conflict) might mean for the rest of Southeast Asia, including Laos and Cambodia, both of which were neutral nations. To assuage this concern, in 1961 Kennedy authorized sending about four hundred U.S. Special Forces (Green Berets) to Vietnam and one hundred military advisors to aid Diem in the South. Nonetheless, Diem was overthrown and assassinated on November 2, 1963, and the civil war in Vietnam escalated. By the time of Kennedy's death three weeks later on November 22, 1963, there were twenty-three thousand Americans in the country.[54] The United States clearly was committed to Vietnam, and the president had yet to seek authorization from Congress. It was this "quagmire" that Lyndon Johnson had to deal with, and that would affect not only U.S. foreign policy, but domestic policy and politics as well.

JOHNSON: VIETNAM, AND THE GREAT SOCIETY

After Kennedy's assassination, Vice President Lyndon Johnson became president and inherited the problem of Vietnam. Johnson had had a long career in Congress, first in the House of Representatives and then in the Senate, where he served as majority leader from 1955 until he became vice president in 1961. That experience influenced the ways in which Johnson made decisions and especially his understanding of the need for congressional support for those policies that he thought were important.

Johnson came into office committed to making change domestically by enacting a series of laws to promote what became known as "the Great Society." However, Johnson also was aware that an unpopular and costly war in Vietnam could put his domestic policies at risk. A Congress that was pressured by constituents because of the war would be far less likely to compromise or support presidential initiatives in other (domestic) areas.[55] The policies of the Johnson administration clearly illustrate the confluence of domestic and international politics and how one can easily affect—and derail—the other.

The Tonkin Gulf Resolution

By 1964 domestic turmoil within the United States was increasing. The civil rights movement was growing in strength, as was the women's movement. Leaders like Martin Luther King Jr. energized the Black community, and the Vietnam War became a rallying cry as minorities were disproportionately being asked to fight—and die—there. Johnson knew that there was a direct relationship between what would happen in Vietnam and domestic politics.

In 1970, after he was out of office, Johnson reflected on the dilemma that he had faced as president, trying to balance the escalating war effort and domestic reforms. At that time Johnson told historian Doris Kearns Goodwin, "If I left the woman I really loved—the Great Society—in order to get involved with that bitch of a war on the other side of the world, then I would lose everything at home. All my programs. All my hopes to feed the hungry and shelter the homeless. All my dreams to provide education and medical care to the browns and blacks and the lame and the poor. But if I left that war and let the Communists take over South Vietnam, then I would have been seen as a coward and my nation would be seen as an appeaser and we would find it impossible to accomplish anything for anybody anywhere on the entire globe."[56] Hence, Johnson believed that the United States would have to continue to fight in Vietnam, regardless of the costs.

The war in Vietnam escalated slowly, and still Johnson did not have official congressional authorization to send troops into combat. From his experience in Congress, Johnson knew that he needed to have congressional backing and domestic support for the war effort. His opportunity to get these came in August 1964 when two U.S. destroyers, the *Maddox* and the *Turner Joy*, were allegedly fired on in the Gulf of Tonkin. The first attack against the *Maddox* came on August 2; however, a second one, two days later, was questionable. The commander of the *Maddox* later admitted that he did not think they were fired on at all. Rather, he indicated that "weather effects" and "overeager" sonar operators were probably to blame rather than an attack by the North Vietnamese. Nonetheless, the incident gave Johnson the excuse to seek congressional support for the war.[57]

On August 5, 1964, Johnson sent a message to Congress. The thrust of his public statement was the need for the United States to honor its commitments to meet communist aggression in Southeast Asia under the terms of the Southeast Asia Collective Defense Treaty (SEATO), approved in 1955 as part of the Cold War alliance system.[58] Johnson asked Congress "to join in affirming the national determination that all such attacks will be met, and that the United States will continue in its basic policy of assisting the free nations of the area to defend their freedom."[59]

On August 7, 1964, Congress passed a joint resolution as Johnson requested. (The text of the resolution had been drawn up months earlier.) The resolution was sent with Johnson's message to the Congress in which he outlined the events that precipitated the resolution. It is important to note that the message to the Congress is far longer than the actual resolution. The heart of the resolution, and the power that Johnson sought, is found in Section 1: "The Congress approves and supports the determination of the President, as Commander in Chief, *to take all necessary measures* to repel any armed

attack against the forces of the United States and to prevent further aggression" (emphasis added). Section 3 keeps the resolution active until "the
President shall determine that the peace and security of the area is reasonably
assured . . . *except that it may be terminated earlier by concurrent resolution
of the Congress*" (emphasis added).[60]

Congress debated the resolution for two days before the House passed it
on a 416 to 0 vote, and the Senate by a vote of 88 to 2. One of the two members of the Senate who voted against the resolution was Oregon Republican
Wayne Morse, "who objected to the resolution on the basis of his belief that
the resolution was indirectly a declaration of war and that it violated Article
1, Section 8, of the U.S. Constitution."[61] The other was Democratic Senator
Ernest Gruening of Alaska, who called the resolution "a predated declaration
of war."[62]

The Tonkin Gulf Resolution is significant for a number of reasons. First,
it gave Johnson virtually open-ended permission to take whatever actions he
deemed necessary in Vietnam. Second, it left the timing open ended so that
the resolution (and the powers that went with it) would remain in force until
either the president determined that the circumstances had changed or Congress terminated it, which it did in January 1971. And third, it clearly shifted
the policy-making balance of power. Despite questions of constitutionality,
when Congress passed the Tonkin Gulf Resolution, it gave the power to initiate military action to the president. (Congress would reassert itself and take
some of that power back under President Nixon.) In remarks made when he
signed the resolution into law on August 10, 1964, Johnson said that it stood
"squarely on the corners of the Constitution," and "confirms and reinforces
powers of the Presidency."[63]

After the resolution passed, Johnson escalated the war in Vietnam. By
1966, 450,000 American troops were in Vietnam, and General William Westmoreland, commander of U.S. forces in Vietnam from 1965 through 1968, requested an increase to 542,000 by the end of 1967.[64] By mid-1967, according
to one historian, "Westmoreland conceded that if his request for an additional
200,000 men was granted, the war might go on for as long as two years. If
not, he warned, it could last five years or even longer."[65] In other words, the
United States was in the midst of what came to be known as a quagmire.
Fighting intensified during this period, and so did battle deaths; the number
of Americans killed in action rose to 13,500 by late 1967.[66] In order to keep
the war effort going, draft calls increased as well. The increase in number of
men drafted coupled with growing American casualties and no end in sight
to the conflict contributed to opposition to the war at home.

The Great Society

While Johnson was dealing with the Vietnam War, domestically he continued to push his Great Society policies. In 1964 in response to the civil rights movement, Congress passed the Civil Rights Act, outlawing discrimination in public accommodations and in the use of federal funds, and giving more protection in voting rights. With pressure coming from the Civil Rights movement, passage of this bill carried a powerful message that change is possible when the voice of the people is heard in Washington, a message that would be applied a few years later by anti-war protesters. In 1965, under Johnson's direction, Congress also passed the Medicare Bill, a housing bill, the Voting Rights Act, an Economic Opportunity Act to fight the "war on poverty," a Clean Air Act, and measures to create a new Department of Housing and Urban Development and National Foundations for the Arts and Humanities. Between 1965 and 1968, Congress passed five hundred reform laws, made possible in part by Johnson's understanding of and ability to work with the legislative branch.

While these represented a great success for Johnson's domestic priorities, the war in Vietnam continued to escalate and was taking a toll economically. In order to continue to pay for the war effort, ultimately Johnson had to cut back on spending for the domestic programs that he had fought so hard to enact. The size of the federal deficit rose, as did taxes. And public discontent over the course and conduct of the war was growing.

In January 1968, the situation in Vietnam worsened. During the cease-fire in place for the lunar new year—the Tet holiday—the forces of the North launched a major surprise offensive. The Tet offensive lasted about one month, and even though the South "won," defined by a greater number of North Vietnamese troops lost than South Vietnamese or U.S. forces, it was a propaganda victory for the North. The media played and replayed images of North Vietnamese and Viet Cong troops attacking the South, including the U.S. embassy in Saigon, which raised questions in the minds of the public about who really was winning the war. Walter Cronkite, the anchor of CBS nightly news and known as "the most trusted man in America," having recently returned from Vietnam, concluded his broadcast on February 27, 1968, with a commentary in which he said, "To say that we are closer to victory today is to believe, in the face of the evidence, the optimists who have been wrong in the past. To suggest we are on the edge of defeat is to yield to unreasonable pessimism. To say that we are mired in stalemate seems the only realistic, yet unsatisfactory, conclusion."[67] This was at a time when news anchors did not inject their own editorial comments into the broadcasts. Thus, this commentary further fueled the antiwar movement at home.

In March 1968, at the time of the first Democratic primary contest for the presidency, Johnson's approval rating had dropped to 26 percent. When peace candidate Eugene McCarthy (Democratic senator from Minnesota) won 42 percent of the vote in the New Hampshire primary, it sent a strong signal to Johnson about how the public felt about his performance.[68] On March 31, Johnson, in a televised address to the American people, announced "a unilateral halt of all United States air and naval bombardment of most of the populated areas of the north." He called on the North Vietnamese government to join peace negotiations that would bring an end to the war.[69] And then he announced: "I shall not seek, and I will not accept, the nomination of my party for another term as your President."[70] He later said that he had had enough: "I felt that I was being chased on all sides by a giant stampede coming at me from all directions. On one side, the American people were stampeding me to do something about Vietnam. On another side, the inflationary economy was booming out of control. Up ahead were dozens of danger signs pointing to another summer of riots in the cities. I was being forced over the edge by rioting blacks, demonstrating students, marching welfare mothers, squawking professors, and hysterical reporters."[71]

Johnson learned an important lesson in American foreign policy: it doesn't matter how successful a president is domestically, because an unpopular war will make a difference at the polls. While Americans generally vote economics and "pocketbook" issues, when the country is fighting a war that involves the deaths of Americans in a country far away and with a dubious relationship to national interest, foreign policy will become a more important issue.

THE END OF THE DECADE: CHANGES IN U.S. POLICY

If one of the major characteristics of the Eisenhower years was an arms buildup in order to ensure the ability for massive retaliation to deter an attack and to meet it should one occur, under Kennedy and Johnson the policy officially shifted. The idea of "flexible response" was developed during Eisenhower's second term in office and was tied to the idea that nuclear war did not have to be the only option, but that there had to be ways to fight a limited nuclear war should conflict arise. In short, this approach would allow the United States to apply its technological superiority against "the manpower advantage of the communist world, so that the certainty of a credible military response would exist at whatever level adversaries chose to fight—without the risk of committing suicide." [72] Hence, this strategy would give the United States more military options. However, Eisenhower rejected this concept of limited nuclear war, believing that if there were to be a war, the United States must be able to fight it using every weapon in its arsenal on the assumption that the Soviet Union would do so as well.

Flexible response became official U.S. policy during the Johnson administration; it was adopted as NATO policy as well in 1967. This strategy would allow the United States and its allies to respond to an attack by a hostile nation using whatever military force might be most appropriate, ranging from conventional to the use of nuclear weapons. At a time when the Cold War was still driving U.S. foreign policy, this offered a greater deterrent against Soviet aggression as well as a possible response in the event of attack on the United States or its allies.

U.S. Cold War foreign policy still relied on having a strong military to deter an attack and/or to respond in the event of an attack. However, flexible response shifted U.S. military policy from one that relied primarily on nuclear weapons to deter attack and to respond if necessary to include conventional weapons as part of the deterrent and response as well. It is important to note that this policy was developed while the United States was mired in a conventional war in Vietnam.

The 1960s into the 1970s

The United States entered the 1960s as the alleged underdog in the missile gap with the Soviet Union, which was the basis for a major arms buildup that continued even after the revelation that the missile gap was a myth. The Berlin crisis of 1961 reinforced the vulnerability of the United States and its allies as well as serving as a reminder of the potential costs of a nuclear confrontation between the United States and the Soviet Union. That danger was reinforced in 1962 with the Cuban Missile Crisis, and the threat that came from the Soviet deployment of nuclear missiles to Cuba; it was not until thirty years later that the full extent of the dangers posed by that event became known. Under Kennedy, the United States became embroiled in a war in Vietnam, which would eventually lead to Johnson's decision not to run for reelection, and to the presidency of Richard Nixon.

By the end of the decade, "the arsenals [of the United States and Soviet Union] swelled beyond numbers ever previously imagined, and plans for fighting—and possibly winning—a nuclear war emerged as too tempting to pass up.[73] Hence, the United States shifted its military thinking to rely on a strategy of flexible response, which combined conventional and nuclear weapons capabilities. While this was directed at the Soviet Union, the United States was losing a conventional war in Vietnam. At a time when perceptions mattered, this conveyed a weakness on the part of the United States.

Nixon came into office in 1972 as the quintessential realist politician. He was determined not to have the United States lose a war on his watch. But, more important, both he and Henry Kissinger, his national security advisor and then secretary of state, saw that the United States could play an important—and new—role internationally. Thus, even with another nuclear buildup, and amid the Vietnam War, the 1970s also introduced the U.S.-Soviet arms control process and the policy of détente that was to further alter the relations that the United States had with the Soviet Union and also China. These themes will be explored in more detail in chapter 5.

CHRONOLOGY, 1946–1968

1945	World War II ends
1946	Kennan sends "The Long Telegram"
1947	Kennan published "The X Article"
	Truman Doctrine
	National Security Act passed
1948	European Recovery Act (Marshall Plan) passed
	Berlin Blockade (1948–1949)
	State of Israel created
1949	Creation of NATO
	Creation of the PRC
	Soviet Union tests an atomic bomb
1950	NSC 68
	War breaks out in Korea
1953	Death of Stalin
1954	U.S. adopts doctrine of Massive Retaliation
1956	Khrushchev comes to power in Soviet Union
	Suez crisis
1957	Soviet Union launches Sputnik
1960	U.S. U-2 plane shot down over Soviet Union
1961	Berlin Wall erected
	Bay of Pigs
1962	Cuban Missile Crisis
1964	Gulf of Tonkin incident/Resolution passed
1965	Tet offensive
1968	Johnson announces he will not seek reelection
	Antiwar movement grows

SELECTED PRIMARY SOURCES

Truman's Navy Day address, https://millercenter.org/the-presidency/presidential-speeches/october-27-1945-navy-day-address.

Kennan, "The Long Telegram," https://digitalarchive.wilsoncenter.org/document/116178.pdf.

Kennan, "The X Article" ("The Sources of Soviet Conduct"), https://www.digitalhistory.uh.edu/disp_textbook.cfm?smtID=3&psid=3629.

Truman, "Special Message to the Congress" (Truman Doctrine), http://avalon.law.yale.edu/20th_century/trudoc.asp.

National Security Act of 1947, http://global.oup.com/us/companion.websites/9780195385168/resources/chapter10/nsa/nsa.pdf.

George Marshall speech at Harvard, https://www.marshallfoundation.org/marshall/the-marshall-plan/marshall-plan-speech/.

Treaty of the North Atlantic Treaty Organization, http://www.nato.int/cps/en/natolive/official_texts_17120.htm.

NSC 68, https://fas.org/irp/offdocs/nsc-hst/nsc-68.htm.

Gulf of Tonkin Resolution, https://avalon.law.yale.edu/20th_century/tonkin-g.asp.

Walter Cronkite "We are mired in stalemate," https://www.digitalhistory.uh.edu/active_learning/explorations/vietnam/cronkite.cfm.

Johnson's address to the nation, March 31, 1968, https://millercenter.org/the-presidency/presidential-speeches/march-31-1968-remarks-decision-not-seek-re-election.

The Cold War Continued

Nixon through Reagan, 1969–1989

This chapter continues the progression of U.S. foreign policy through the Cold War period leading up to 1989 and the presidency of George H. W. Bush. Most people would say that the beginning of the end of the Cold War came in 1989, when East Germany opened its borders to the West, and the Berlin Wall came down in November. That contributed to the democratic revolutions that swept many of the Eastern European countries formerly under the sway of the Soviet Union. In many ways, though, the Cold War actually ended in 1991, with the breakup of the Soviet Union. At that point, the United States emerged as the last (and only) superpower.

As you go through this period, you will note that although the basic framework has remained the same, that is, the United States/democracy versus the Soviet Union and communism, there are also some significant changes. Some of those start under the administration of Richard Nixon, who, despite being a virulent anti-communist, instituted the policy of "détente," or reconciliation, with the Soviet Union, while also changing U.S. relations with what was then-known as "Red China." So although it would be another twenty-plus years before the Cold War actually ended, the possibility of a changing world order was already starting to be seen.

NIXON

Richard Nixon defeated Johnson's vice president Hubert Humphrey in the 1968 election and became president in January 1969. He inherited the war in Vietnam as one of his major foreign policy issues. The Vietnam War was fought against the backdrop of the Cold War; one of the most important foreign policy legacies of the Nixon administration was the way he handled two of the major communist adversaries of the United States, the Soviet Union and China, while also trying to extricate the country from Vietnam. Guided in part by Henry Kissinger, who served first as national security advisor and then as secretary of state, Nixon pursued a policy of détente, or reconciliation, with the Soviet Union and began the process that resulted in opening diplomatic relations with China. These two competing trends, fighting communism in Southeast Asia on the one hand and reconciliation with major communist powers on the other, are among the most interesting facets of the evolution of U.S. foreign policy in the period.

Nixon and Vietnam

Both Nixon and Kissinger had come into office defending the U.S. commitment in Vietnam. "Nixon had insisted that the presence of U.S. troops in Southeast Asia had helped contain an expansionist China and given the 'free' Asian nations time to develop stable institutions." In fact, Nixon was quoted as saying, "Whatever one may think of the 'domino theory,' it is beyond question that without the American commitment in Vietnam, Asia would be a far different place today."[1] However, it also did not take long for them to realize that the war had to end, and to end "honorably." Furthermore, both men also realized that the future international order and role of the United States within it would depend on ending the war in Vietnam. "Their grand design included at least a limited accommodation with the Soviet Union and China, and they felt that they must extricate the United States from the war in a manner that would demonstrate to these old adversaries resoluteness of purpose and certainty of action, a manner that would uphold U.S. credibility with friends and foes alike."[2] Thus, Nixon saw the future international role of the United States, as well as his legacy, tied to Vietnam, and he also saw the interrelationship between U.S. policy in Vietnam and future policy with both the Soviet Union and China.

Nonetheless, the Vietnam War escalated during the Nixon years while he attempted to negotiate a peace. As opposition to the war grew domestically, and with no response to U.S. overtures for peace, Nixon changed the strategy for fighting the war by reducing the number of troops on the ground and relying more heavily on attacks from the air. These included bombing North Vietnamese sanctuaries in neutral Cambodia, a policy that Nixon tried to keep secret. In 1969, in response to growing public dissatisfaction with the war, Congress passed a nonbinding "Sense of the Senate" resolution that told the president he could not commit additional troops or encumber funds for the war without the express permission of that body. Although this did not have the force of law, it sent the important message that Congress was not pleased with the conduct of the war and that its members were "hearing" their constituents. It was also a clear assertion of congressional will regarding its constitutional powers, in many ways foreshadowing the revocation of the Tonkin Gulf Resolution and the open-ended powers it granted to the president. The messages from Congress as well as the public were among the items that caused Nixon to rethink the strategy.

In July 1969, while on a major international trip that included his only visit to Vietnam, Nixon unveiled what became known as "the Nixon Doctrine." While the United States would still support countries struggling against communism by providing economic and military assistance, there would be a shift away from the deployment of U.S. combat units that would result in a large number of U.S. casualties. A month earlier, in June 1969, after a meeting with Vietnamese president Nguyen Van Thieu, Nixon announced that twenty-five thousand U.S. forces would be withdrawn from Vietnam to be replaced by South Vietnamese forces. Reports at the time speculated that the new guidelines were prompted by the growing anti-war movement in the United States and by the belief that the withdrawal would help quiet the movement. The administration feared that the anti-war movement was helping to fuel North Vietnam's reluctance to negotiate. The concern was that public pressure at home, with a growing anti-war movement, would force Nixon into a weaker bargaining position just so that he could end the war.[3]

Nixon presented his doctrine to the American public in a speech that he gave on November 3, 1969, in which he returned to the major shift in U.S. foreign policy that he had outlined in July. He began by reminding the American public why we were in Vietnam at all, and then asked, rhetorically, what is the best way forward? He said that the United States would keep all its treaty commitments, would continue to provide a "shield" if "a nuclear power threatens the freedom of a nation allied with us" or threatens a nation that the United States considers "vital to our security," and that the United States would furnish military and economic assistance." But he also made it clear that it would be up to the nation directly threatened "to assume the primary responsibility of providing manpower for its defense." In other words, the United States would no longer be expected to provide combat troops. And he concluded by appealing to "the great silent majority" to support him and his plan to bring the war to an end.[4] In a poll taken shortly after that speech, Nixon hit a 67 percent approval rating, among the highest of his presidency.[5]

Implementing this new policy, in April 1970, Nixon informed the country that over the next year he had authorized the withdrawal of more than one hundred fifty thousand ground troops from Vietnam. However, by the end of the month, the public was shocked to learn that U.S. forces had entered

Cambodia, which was neutral in the conflict. This led to outrage and protests across the country. Public anger grew when on May 4, 1970, National Guard troops shot and killed four students who were protesting at Kent State University in Ohio. Many college and university campuses across the country suspended classes so that students and faculty could protest the war and the policies of the Nixon administration. Protestors went to Washington to demand that Congress take action to bring the war to an end. Public opinion against the war was growing.

To help assuage some of the outpouring of opposition to the war, and especially to the inequality of the draft as more men of color were being drafted while white men were finding ways to avoid military service or even flee to Canada, Nixon worked with Congress to change the process by which men were brought into the military. As of December 1969, after Nixon signed an Executive Order, men were selected randomly and assigned a draft number based on a lottery tied to birth days. This process of "random selection" was seen to be more fair, as who could be drafted was decided arbitrarily. In addition to the first draft lottery held in December 1969, subsequent ones were held from 1970 to 1975. This was part of a process to transition military service from a draft to an all-volunteer force that was phased in starting in 1973. This represented a major change in the way in which people were recruited into the military, with the All-Volunteer Force (AVF) the military structure that exists today.

Nonetheless, domestic opposition to the war continued to grow, especially as it became clear that there was no peace treaty forthcoming. Opposition was exacerbated by the secret incursion into Cambodia, thereby violating the sanctity of a neutral nation. Congress debated the wisdom of the Tonkin Gulf Resolution and the power it had given to the president, and opposition to the "blank check" in the resolution grew. In response to the growing concerns about the conduct of the war, as well as the president's virtually unchecked ability to escalate it, on January 12, 1971, Congress repealed the Gulf of Tonkin Resolution. Along with this, two Senators, John Cooper (R-KY) and Frank Church (D-ID) proposed an amendment "to cut off all funds for American military operations in Cambodia after June 30."[6] This was passed by the Senate but not the House, so it was never enacted. This was followed by another amendment that, had it been passed, would have required the administration to withdraw all American forces from Vietnam by the end of 1971. While these never became law, they further fueled opposition to the war, as well as made clear the growing battles between the president and Congress over the conduct of the war. The last of the American forces in Cambodia left on June 30, 1970. However, the "strategic bombing" of the country continued.[7]

By 1970, eager to find a way to end the war, Kissinger began "secret" peace negotiations with North Vietnam. Meanwhile, Nixon continued to authorize bombing Vietnam and Cambodia while also drawing down the number of U.S. combat troops in Vietnam. In 1972, even with the troop withdrawals, there were more than forty thousand Americans stationed in Vietnam.[8] While much of the public already wanted the conflict to end, details continued to emerge that further fueled opposition to it. In the summer of 1971, a military court found Lieutenant William Calley guilty of war crimes for the massacre in the town of My Lai in 1968 and sentenced him to life imprisonment (for which he served three years of house arrest). But this also brought to the public's attention once again the brutality of this war. At the same time, the *New York Times* began publishing a top-secret internal history of the war leaked by Daniel Ellsberg, a former Defense Department official. The so-called *Pentagon Papers* "appeared to confirm what antiwar critics had been saying—that the government had repeatedly misled the public about what it was doing in Vietnam and the success attained."[9] By 1971, public opposition was growing even more, with 71 percent of the public agreeing that the United States had erred in sending troops to Vietnam, and 58 percent seeing the war as "immoral."[10] This put even more pressure on Nixon and Kissinger to end the war.

Once again, there was a confluence of domestic and international politics here. Going into the presidential election of 1972, as violence continued in Vietnam, the Democrats nominated George McGovern, a senator from South Dakota and an outspoken dove who had been vocal in his opposition to the war. While Nixon was sure that he would defeat McGovern in the election, he had many reasons to want to end the war. Kissinger continued to negotiate with the North Vietnamese, trying to work out a political settlement. On October 31, just before the election, Kissinger stated publicly that "peace is at hand," although negotiations continued. When an agreement was not reached, and with Nixon reelected in a landslide, in December the United States "unleashed the most intensive and devastating attacks of the war" in what became known as "the Christmas bombing."[11] The intensity of this attack gave the North Vietnamese reason to return to the negotiating table. The negotiations resumed in Paris and on January 27, 1973, a cease-fire agreement was signed. In 1975, after Nixon had resigned as president, Vietnam was unified as a communist country. Approximately fifty-nine thousand Americans had died in Vietnam.

In May 1975, approximately one month after the fall of Vietnam, then secretary of state Henry Kissinger drafted a memo to President Gerald Ford outlining what he saw as the major lessons of the war. Although the memo was never sent or signed, it is now available publicly and has some important insights. Among the lessons Kissinger notes are "the importance of absolute honesty and objectivity in all reporting, within and from the Government as well as from the press." Another lesson is "a dedication to consistency," in terms of the reasons given for going to war, and then for seeing that war through." And he speaks in this memo of the need to "ask ourselves whether it was all worth it, or at least what benefits we did gain."[12]

If they had been applied by Johnson in 1964, those lessons and others that Kissinger articulated in this memo might have changed the decisions that Johnson made and altered the course of the war. They also might have altered decisions made by subsequent presidents, such as George W. Bush's decision to invade Iraq in 2003 (see chapter 6).

War Powers

Congress's repeal of the Gulf of Tonkin Resolution in 1971 was the first step in the assertion of congressional authority to regain some control of the foreign policy process and to begin, once again, to enforce the checks and balances between the two branches outlined in the Constitution. As the war went on with no end in sight, and as protests grew, Congress came under increasing pressure to limit what was seen as the abuse of presidential power regarding the ability to commit the United States to war. The impetus to do something was pushed further by the Watergate scandal and by questions about the integrity of the president. In response to these growing concerns, on November 7, 1973, Congress passed Public Law 93-148, known as the War Powers Resolution.[13]

The War Powers Resolution's stated purpose is "to fulfill the intent of the framers of the Constitution of the United States and insure that the collective judgment of *both* the Congress and the President will apply to the introduction of United States Armed Forces into hostilities, or into situations where imminent involvement in hostilities is clearly indicated" (emphasis added).[14] The law clearly asserts that anytime U.S. forces will be sent into hostile or even potentially hostile situations, the president must consult with and report to Congress. It also specifies the need for consultation between the president and Congress before introducing troops into hostility, and it contains the provisions under which the president must report to Congress "in the absence of a declaration of war." The resolution was designed to limit the possibility of giving any subsequent presidents the blank check that Johnson and Nixon had to commit the United States to conflict and to escalate that conflict without a formal declaration of war. It also was designed to make it very difficult for Congress to once again cede all its war-powers authority to the president.[15] As we will see in later chapters, however, that was not to happen.

Nixon vetoed the bill and questioned its constitutionality, as have subsequent presidents (who have generally complied with it), but Congress overrode the veto. Specifically, presidents have questioned the provisions in Section 5, "Congressional Action," under which the president must end the use of force within sixty days unless Congress authorizes otherwise (5 b) and which require that forces be removed "if the Congress so directs by concurrent resolution" (5 c). Critics argue that these provisions usurp the president's constitutional power as commander in chief. And there are always questions of enforcement.[16] Nonetheless, the War Powers Resolution had the desired effect of putting the president on notice that he should report to Congress before deploying U.S. troops. That then puts the burden on Congress to determine how to respond. In that sense, the law helped reaffirm the balance in roles and responsibility between the executive and legislative branches.

The Soviet Union, Détente, and Arms Control

As the war in Vietnam was growing, so were the number of nuclear weapons worldwide and various countries' expenditures for defense.[17] The vast number of nuclear weapons formed the basis of "mutually assured destruction"—or MAD—the deterrent allegedly keeping the United States and Soviet Union from attacking each other or their allies. By early 1972, the military was rethinking its nuclear targeting options to allow the president to choose from a range of response scenarios in case of attack. Underlying these changes were questions raised by Nixon but especially Kissinger who noted that "given the parity in the nuclear balance, the president could no longer assume that the Soviets would back down before a crisis turned violent." This led Kissinger to ask, among other things, "How . . . do you most effectively deter nuclear war? Failing that, how do you limit nuclear war once it broke out—what sorts of targets would you need to hit, and what sorts of weapons would you need to fire?"[18] It is important to note here that the various scenarios outlined, and the options available to the president to respond, dealt with China as well as the Soviet Union, as both were seen as major U.S. adversaries.

As the military and political planners were looking at targeting options, Kissinger and Nixon were coming to the conclusion that "there was no scenario in which using nuclear weapons would give the United States—or any country—an advantage."[19] Hence, there had to be another approach. To help get spending and weapons proliferation under control, the Soviet Union and United States entered into a process of discussion and negotiation designed to control the spread of nuclear weapons.

The arms control process started in 1969 and was part of détente, defined by Henry Kissinger as "an environment in which competitors can regulate and restrain their differences and ultimately move from competition to cooperation."[20] One of the things that makes this policy and the arms control process in general so intriguing from the perspective of American foreign policy is that it is a liberal/idealistic approach (the notion of cooperation) employed by a decision-maker (Kissinger) who, in many ways, was the ultimate realist. The process resulted in a successful agreement, the Strategic Arms Limitation Treaty (SALT I), signed in 1972, and set the stage for subsequent agreements. More important, it made relations between the United States and the Soviet Union more *predictable* by establishing an ongoing forum for discussion and conversation that continued through the duration of the Cold War and beyond. Regardless of the level of tension between the two countries, the discussion and negotiation process continued in the belief that it was in the national interest of both.

SALT I satisfied the immediate needs of both countries. "The Soviet Union gained recognition of its status as the United States' equal; the United States gained a commitment from the Soviet Union to moderate its quest for permanent power in the world."[21] SALT I did not stop the arms race; rather, it set limits for specific nuclear weapons, providing a ceiling up to which both sides could build, and then allowed both sides to channel additional resources into other weapon systems. The main value of this Anti-Ballistic Missile (ABM) Treaty was that it banned defenses against long-range missiles. At a time when both countries had enough nuclear delivery systems to obliterate each other, this was seen as an important step and was an acknowledgment that "the vulnerability that came with the prospect of instant annihilations could become the basis for a stable, long-term, Soviet-American relationship."[22]

According to the Office of the Historian, U.S. Department of State, "SALT I is considered the crowning achievement of the Nixon-Kissinger strategy of détente." It was the first time that the two countries had agreed to *limit* the number of nuclear weapons in their arsenals.[23] And it set a precedent for ongoing talks between the United States and the Soviet Union that would continue, extending to talks between the United States and Russia after the Cold War ended.[24]

Nixon and Europe

Nixon's strategic vision, which included a reordering of U.S. foreign and military policy as defined by détente with the Soviet Union and a changing relationship with China (below), depended to a large extent on having a strong and stable relationship with the countries of Western Europe. Thus, Nixon went to Western Europe on his first trip outside the United States as president in February 1969, including a trip to NATO headquarters. In a statement at the start of the trip Nixon said, "The purpose of this trip is to underline my commitment to the closest relationship between our friends in Western Europe and the United States. I would like to lift these relationships from a concern for tactical problems of the day to a definition of common purpose." And regarding NATO in particular, he asserted that "the Alliance, held together in its first two decades by a common fear, now needs the sense of cohesiveness supplied by common purpose."[25] The importance of the U.S. relationship with the countries of Western Europe was further affirmed in an address given by Henry Kissinger who said that "they [countries of Western Europe] are the oldest and closest allies and also because a stable world is inconceivable without a European contribution."[26]

At a time when perceptions of the United States globally was being undermined by the war in Vietnam, Nixon and Kissinger both felt that the relationship with Europe needed to be reaffirmed and strengthened and that one of the best ways they could do that was a formal visit by the president. It also reinforced the idea that the United States would consult with its allies prior to, or in addition to, engaging in negotiations with adversaries, and that the United States had foreign policy priorities beyond just Vietnam. At that time, these were all important messages to send to the European allies.

As it turns out, many of the policies that the Nixon administration pursued, such as a radical change in U.S. monetary policy in 1971 that effectively ended the Bretton Woods system that had been in place since the end of World War II, enraged the allies as they were made without any consultation.[27] Despite the positive start, the U.S. relationship with Europe was eclipsed by other priorities. Europe's attention was also elsewhere, as the countries of the European Economic Community (EEC) became focused on enlargement of that organization. In effect, "the United States pursued policies deemed to be in its own national interest, often at the expense of Europe, while at the same time the European countries were developing their own policies, both individually and collectively that minimized or excluded the United States."[28]

China and Normalization

As was the case with arms control and détente with the Soviet Union, in many ways only an administration known for its virulent anticommunist position could begin the process of normalizing relations with China.[29] The United States did not recognize the PRC, referring to the Nationalist government of Taiwan as "China." But in 1971, Nixon sent Kissinger to Beijing to begin the process of "normalization." The desire for rapprochement between the two countries was born of *pragmatism*, not idealism. For China, closer relations with the United States would serve as an important balance to China's growing antagonism with the Soviet Union. For the United States and for Nixon in particular, stronger relations with China would allow him to play China against the USSR, appear to weaken China's ties to Hanoi at a time when the course of the Vietnam War was not going well, and help Nixon politically by allowing him to run for reelection in 1972 by stressing what he had done to help achieve a more peaceful world, rather than by having the Vietnam War as the main foreign policy focus.

In February 1972, President Nixon visited mainland China, the first American president to do so. At the end of the trip, Nixon issued a statement known as the Shanghai Communiqué that has defined U.S. policy toward China and Taiwan since that time. Using language that had been negotiated earlier, the document states, "The United States acknowledges that all Chinese on either side of the Taiwan Strait maintain there is but one China and that Taiwan is part of China. The United States does not challenge that position. It reaffirms its interest in a peaceful settlement of the Taiwan question by the Chinese themselves." This phrase articulates the "one China" policy that remains in place today. In the document the United States also declared, "With this in mind, it [the United States] affirms the ultimate objective of the withdrawal of all U.S. forces and military installations from Taiwan. In the meantime, it will progressively reduce its forces and military installations on Taiwan *as the tension in the area diminishes*" (emphasis added).[30] Thus the United States will maintain forces and serve as a protector to Taiwan as long as it perceives there is danger of armed attack by China and forceful attempt to take over the island, that is, until the status quo changes. Because of this initiative, seven years later, in 1979 under President Carter, the United States established full diplomatic relations with China.

Nixon, the quintessential realist politician, had successfully orchestrated rapprochement with the Soviet Union and China, thereby easing Cold War tensions and shifting the balance of global international relations. By putting a process into place for ongoing negotiations between the United States and the Soviet Union, he ensured that the two sides would continue to communicate, which would also help minimize tensions. And he negotiated an end to the war in Vietnam, although belatedly. Nonetheless, by the time of his resignation his foreign policy successes were lost in the face of deep domestic divisions and political scandal.

Gerald Ford

When Nixon resigned in August 1974, Gerald Ford succeeded him. Ford had been appointed vice president by Nixon when the sitting vice president, Spiro Agnew, resigned in October 1973. Prior to becoming vice president, Ford had been a popular member of Congress, serving as minority leader of the House during Johnson's tenure as president. As a member of the Congress and critic of many of Johnsons' policies, Ford understood Washington and the political process and felt the impact of the Watergate scandal as well as Nixon's resignation. When he took office, Ford's primary goal was to restore the faith of the American people in government in general and in the presidency in particular. One of his most controversial decisions was to grant Nixon an unconditional pardon, which he did on September 8, 1974, believing that this was an important step in healing the country after the scandal of Watergate.[31]

In foreign policy, he had to face the unification of Vietnam as a communist country, which was seen as a major blow to the United States, but he also helped broker an interim peace agreement between Egypt and Israel, thereby paving the way for the Camp David Accords that was concluded by his successor, Jimmy Carter. Perhaps the most difficult part of Ford's presidency, though, was inheriting an economy with rampant inflation (up to 12 percent in 1974) and a growing recession. In many ways, the situation that he faced as president was an impossible one.

CARTER

Jimmy Carter defeated Gerald Ford in the election of 1976. A Washington outsider—a peanut farmer and then governor of the state of Georgia—Carter believed in the need to restore the perception of integrity to the government and he ran as someone who could bring a new tone to Washington. He also wanted to help the country recover from the "Vietnam hangover" that followed the U.S. defeat in Vietnam and that made the United States hesitant to get involved in any international conflict.

In his campaign and early in his presidency, Carter brought back to foreign policy the idealist perspective advocated by Woodrow Wilson, and he vowed to make the fight for human rights the centerpiece of his foreign policy agenda. In March 1977, eight weeks after he became president, Carter addressed the UN General Assembly and reiterated that commitment to global human rights. In this speech, Carter addressed a range of topics, but made clear the U.S. commitment to human rights around the world:

> The search for peace and justice also means respect for human dignity. All the signatories of the U.N. Charter have pledged themselves to observe and to respect basic human rights. Thus, no member of the United Nations can claim that mistreatment of its citizens is solely its own business. Equally, no member can avoid its responsibilities to review and to speak when torture or unwarranted deprivation occurs in any part of the world.

The basic thrust of human affairs points toward a more universal demand for fundamental human rights. The United States has a historical birthright to be associated with this process.[32]

In this speech, he also affirmed the importance of the arms control process, which he committed to continue. And foreshadowing other important foreign policy efforts, he stated that "We are also working to resolve in amicable negotiations the future of the Panama Canal," which succeeded. And in the Middle East, another important foreign policy priority, he stated that "we are doing our best to clarify areas of disagreement, to surface underlying consensus, and to help to develop mutually acceptable principles that can form a flexible framework for a just and a permanent settlement."[33] This, too, was to come to fruition with the Camp David Accords.

Nonetheless, while the Carter administration pursued the foreign policy perceived as consistent with the basic tenets on which the United States was founded (freedom and liberty for all), it also angered many of the international leaders who saw this as a direct attack on their domestic policies. For example, Carter angered the Soviet Union by praising Soviet dissidents who had dared to speak up against the government. Despite Carter's stated desire to work for peace, his remarks and many of his policies only exacerbated international tensions.

The Carter Administration: Successes and Failures

The Carter years were marked by a series of both dramatic successes and notable failures in foreign policy. The successes included the Camp David Accords signed in March 1979, the first major agreement between Israel and an Arab nation (Egypt), which resulted in Israel's withdrawal from the Sinai. (President Carter subsequently won a Nobel Peace Prize for this accomplishment.) He also successfully negotiated the treaties returning the Panama Canal to the control of Panama and making the canal a neutral waterway open to all shipping traffic after 1999. The United States was given the permanent right to defend the waterway and its neutrality. Carter outlined his desire to pursue both of these initiatives in his initial address to the General Assembly. However, the Panama Canal treaties resulted in a fight between the president and Congress. Given an increasingly assertive Congress that did not see why the treaties were to the advantage of the United States, Carter had to fight for their passage at great political cost.

One high-profile failure was the Carter administration's response to the Soviet deployment of a new missile, the SS-20, which had the range to hit targets in Western Europe from launch pads in the Soviet Union. At that point, none of the U.S. and NATO missiles in Western Europe had the capability to strike targets in the Soviet Union. But what was of greater concern to the European allies were questions about the extent of U.S. commitment in the event of an attack. Their fear was articulated by German Chancellor Helmut Schmidt in a speech he gave to the International Institute for Strategic Studies in London on October 28, 1977. In this speech, Schmidt questioned the reliability of the United States as an ally, and "urged the United States to deploy a new generation of theater nuclear weapons having the range to hit Soviet targets from inside Western Europe—in short, missiles that matched the capabilities of the Soviet SS-20s."[34]

The implications of this speech were tremendous. It raised questions about the reliability of the United States, but also about the United States and NATO's ability to deter and respond to a Soviet attack. The U.S. response to the Schmidt speech led to another of the major foreign policy fiascos in the Carter administration and further questioning of U.S. leadership. The United States initially responded to Schmidt's call by developing a plan to deploy new medium-range missiles to Europe (Pershing II and Ground Launched Cruise Missiles) and in December 1979, NATO agreed to the plan, although the weapons were never deployed. At the same time, another new weapon, the enhanced radiation warhead (ERW), popularly known as the neutron bomb, was being developed by the United States. Amid popular outcry against this weapon that was said to kill people while leaving buildings intact, Carter still was willing to go ahead with it, although he required that the NATO allies would have to ask for it. This proved to be a great political dilemma for Germany, but Schmidt asked for the weapons nonetheless, as long as at least one other country similarly requested it. Then in April 1978, Carter decided to cancel the project. Not only did this anger Schmidt, but it further raised questions about U.S. reliability. By the time that Carter left office, the U.S. relationship with its European allies was undermined significantly and the perception was of a United States that had been weakened significantly.

While the issue of nuclear weapons in Europe was playing out, Carter and Soviet President Brezhnev were engaged in another set of arms-control negotiations. This one continued the arms control process that started with SALT I and then the 1974 Vladivostok Accord signed by President Ford and Brezhnev, which built on the ABM agreement and further limited nuclear arms buildup. Despite Brezhnev's suspicions of Nixon, Kissinger and the process of détente, negotiations continued,[35] and talks were resumed with the Carter administration. On June 18, 1979, the two sides signed what became known as the SALT II agreement.

Unfortunately, this agreement was doomed for a number of reasons, including its opposition by a number of prominent security analysts in Washington. While "the treaty advocates portrayed it as a modest but significant achievement," to the opposition it "was a disaster because it left the Soviet missiles with superior megatonnage and throw-weight, creating an imbalance."[36] As that political debate continued with Washington, what ultimately doomed the approval of the treaty by the Senate was the Soviet invasion of Afghanistan in December 1979. As a result, "détente was declared dead."[37] Carter canceled proposed wheat sales to Russia; prohibited U.S. athletes from participating in the Olympics, which were scheduled to begin in Moscow in July 1980; and withdrew SALT II from Senate consideration for ratification. This contributed to a resurgence of Cold War attitudes and tensions.

Perhaps the most spectacular foreign policy failure of the Carter years was the Iranian revolution and the way in which Carter handled the taking of American hostages at the embassy in Tehran in November 1979.[38] Day after day nothing happened, as network news anchors, such as Walter Cronkite, began each broadcast with an announcement about how many days the hostages had been held captive inside the U.S. embassy in Tehran. This contributed to an undermining of public confidence in Carter, and when he finally did authorize a rescue attempt, it was over the objections of members of his cabinet, such as Secretary of State Cyrus Vance, who resigned in protest. The rescue attempt on April 24, 1980, was a dismal failure, and the entire experience on top of four years of economic recession, high gas prices, unparalleled inflation, and other domestic economic woes contributed directly to Carter's defeat at the polls in November 1980 by Ronald Reagan.

Carter's administration is instructive for understanding the course of American foreign policy. In part, Carter inherited the economic problems that were the result of years of war as well as domestic ills and bad decisions by the previous administrations. He chose to pursue a foreign policy based on values and idealism at a time when pragmatism and realism probably would have been more successful. He saw issues in black-and-white terms and presented them to the American public and to the world in that way. While this encouraged and empowered some, it also inflamed and alienated others, both at home and abroad. Implementing foreign policy successfully requires domestic support as well as international cooperation, and Carter was not able to get either. It was only after the Cold War ended, and years after he stepped down as president and took on the role of "elder statesman," that Carter came to play an important role internationally in pursuit of peace and human rights, winning a Nobel Prize for his efforts.

By the end of the Carter administration, the United States was still suffering from "Vietnam hangover" and national self-doubt. Its global leadership was under question, and relationships with the European allies were frayed. It was these negative forces that Ronald Reagan came into office determined to fight. For Reagan, the United States was still a superpower, and it had to start acting like one again.

SELECT MAJOR U.S.-SOVIET ARMS CONTROL AGREEMENTS DURING THE COLD WAR AND BEYOND

Signed	Treaty and Signatories
1963	Limited Test Ban Treaty (signed by U.S [Kennedy].-Soviet Union-Great Britain).
1968	Nuclear Non-Proliferation Treaty (NPT) (signed by 191 countries).
1972	Anti-Ballistic Missile Treaty (SALT I) (signed by U.S. [Nixon] and Soviet Union). On December 13, 2001, President Bush announced that the United States was withdrawing from this treaty.
1974	Vladivostok Agreement (signed by U.S. [Ford] and Soviet Union).
1979	Strategic Arms Limitation Treaty (Salt II) (signed by U.S.[Carter] and Soviet Union.
1987	Intermediate-Range Nuclear Forces (INF) Treaty (signed by U.S. [Reagan] and Soviet Union). On August 2, 2019, the Trump administration announced its intention to withdraw from this agreement.
1991	Strategic Arms Reduction Treaty (START) (signed by U.S. [George H.W. Bush] and Soviet Union).
1992	Open Skies Treaty (signed by 35 countries). On May 21, 2020, President Trump announced that the United States would be withdrawing from this treaty.
1993	START II (signed by U.S. [George H. W. Bush] and Russia).
1996	Comprehensive Test Ban Treaty (CTBT) (signed by 184 countries). Although the United States signed the CTBT, it has not ratified it.
2010	New START (signed by U.S. [Obama] and Russia).

REAGAN

The 1980s started with the election of Ronald Reagan, who early in his administration referred to the Soviet Union as "the evil empire." He promoted building a weapons shield to protect the United States from incoming Soviet missiles, and he increased spending for defense and the military. In other words, he did everything that a Cold War president needed to do. And just as President Kennedy stood next to the Berlin Wall in 1963 to proclaim, "Ich bin ein Berliner,"[39] in 1987 President Reagan, at a speech in Berlin, told Mikhail Gorbachev, then leader of the Soviet Union, to "tear down this wall."[40] Two years later, in 1989, that would happen. If Cold War tensions could be measured by policies regarding Berlin, then the fall of the Berlin Wall was the best indicator that the old order literally was crumbling. It would take two more years for the Soviet Union to fall. After years of waiting for this to happen, was the United States ready for it when it did?

From Cold War to Democratic Revolutions

"On the day of Mr. Reagan's inauguration as president in 1981," writes one historian, "the Iranians released their American hostages. That closed a humiliating and frustrating episode."[41] One can speculate as to why Iran chose to release them on that day; suffice it to say, it provided a powerful start to the Reagan administration. Whereas Jimmy Carter's administration ended in apparent failure, Ronald Reagan came into office the image of American strength. No longer would U.S. foreign policy be based on "soft" ideas, such as human rights, but it would once again be tied to strength and power.[42] While the American public might have yearned for such a change, it came at a price.

Reagan's election signaled a return to a strong executive whose administration defined the policies and the priorities of the nation at that time. And, for the most part, despite its earlier assertions of oversight, Congress complied with and approved Reagan's domestic policies and priorities, even though they resulted in budget deficits. In what became known as "the Reagan Revolution," Reagan focused his attention on domestic issues, especially the economy. He cut taxes across the board and, concomitantly, slashed social programs, many of which had been in place since the New Deal. He focused on "supply-side economics" that promised prosperity by putting more money into the hands of people who would spend it, thereby stimulating the economy. He blamed the recession that hit the country in 1981 and 1982 on residual effects of Carter's policies (as opposed to the long-term impact of Vietnam), and when the economy started to recover before the congressional elections of 1984, he took the credit. And Reagan authorized an increase in spending for defense in order to counter what he had called "America's weakened defense" during the election campaign.

Reagan successfully energized the American public and instilled a sense of pride in the country once again. The United States returned to the policies of "us versus them," good versus evil, democracy versus communism, that had been part of the Cold War rhetoric but were tempered under Carter. Reagan's hardline rhetoric, such as his "evil empire" speeches in June 1982 and March 1983,[43] reawakened Cold War fears in the Soviet Union as well as within many in the United States.

The hostile rhetoric put the Soviet Union on warning that the Cold War was not over. In response, the Soviet leadership once again denounced the United States. In the words of one historian, "Matters were not helped when, within a few months of Mr. Reagan's inauguration, America's nuclear force was twice in one week activated following erroneous computer warnings that Soviet missile attacks were on the way."[44] Hence, U.S. foreign policy during at least the first years (1981–1985) of Reagan's eight years in office was characterized by increasingly hostile rhetoric, an arms buildup, and a sense that the United States was reliving the policies of decades earlier, before détente and arms control.[45] In contrast, his second term (1985–1989) was characterized by a period of détente with the Soviet Union and a resurgent United States that was becoming a global leader once again. Another way to describe these eight years was that they "marked a time when the superpowers came closest to both a catastrophic war and a grand peace."[46]

When the Berlin Wall fell in 1989, then president George H. W. Bush as well as Reagan took the credit. Yet the end of the Cold War was the result of the confluence of many factors; Reagan just happened to be president when a series of critical events started to unfold. Shortly before he left office, when asked about the role he had played in facilitating the end of the Cold War, Reagan referred to himself as "a supporting actor." When asked at a press conference who deserved the credit for the changes in the Soviet Union that ultimately led to the end of the Cold War, Reagan replied that "Mr. Gorbachev deserves most of the credit, as the leader of this country."[47]

There is little doubt that Reagan's policies of increasing spending for defense and ratcheting up the hostile rhetoric pushed an already significantly diminished Soviet Union to the brink. The priority of Mikhail Gorbachev, who became general secretary of the Communist Party of the Soviet Union in 1985 following the deaths of first Yuri Andropov and then Konstantin Chernenko just as Reagan was beginning his second term in office was to demilitarize the Soviet Union so that much-needed resources could be diverted to the depleted economy. Further, since he came of age in the post-Stalin era,

Gorbachev had a different perspective on the West than previous leaders, and he saw Europe and Russia as sharing a "common home."[48]

By that time, Reagan was receptive to Gorbachev's ideas and was willing to work with him on implementing new policies. Reagan believed that a change in the direction of the Soviet Union would be in the best interests of the United States and therefore modified his own approach over time, becoming less "cold warrior" and more the diplomat whose primary goal was to encourage Gorbachev to continue down the new path that he had chosen. Doing this required personal contact, and the two leaders met periodically to outline areas of common interest. By the end of the Reagan administration, the Cold War was on a course to its inevitable end.[49]

Continuing the Arms Control Process

Reagan's administration can be divided into two parts, each coinciding with four years, or one term. Reagan's first term in office was characterized by hostile rhetoric and an arms buildup that Reagan saw as necessary to offset the general perception of U.S. weakness after Carter. But early in his administration the allied (NATO) leaders told Reagan that the Pershing II missiles developed under Carter could not be deployed in Europe unless the United States also put forward an arms-control proposal. One suggestion was that Reagan propose a ban on all nuclear weapons in Europe. "This would require the Russians to dismantle hundreds of their SS-4, SS-5, and SS-20 missiles—in exchange for which the United States would cancel the Pershing II and Ground Launched Cruise Missiles, which had not yet been deployed."[50] If successful, this approach would require the Soviet Union to get rid of their existing weapons while the United States only had to pledge not to deploy weapons that were not yet in the field. This came to be known as the "zero option" and became the basis for future discussions between Reagan and Gorbachev.

Before the two sides were to get to the zero option, tensions would continue to grow once again. On March 23, 1983, in a televised speech, Reagan announced the creation of a new weapons system that could detect and stop Soviet missiles before they could attack the United States. Formally named the "Strategic Defense Initiative," the system quickly became known as "Star Wars." Despite the skepticism of the military, Reagan believed that this system could work and "envisioned it as a shield that could protect the United States—and, as we shared the technology, the entire world—thus rendering nuclear weapons obsolete."[51] However, as Fred Kaplan also notes, "He [Reagan] could not have known it at the time, but his Star Wars speech kicked off the most intense year of the Cold War since the Cuban Missile Crisis two decades earlier."[52]

EXCERPTS FROM RONALD REAGAN'S "STAR WARS" SPEECH
MARCH 23, 1983

My fellow Americans, thank you for sharing your time with me tonight.

The subject I want to discuss with you, peace and national security, is both timely and important. Timely, because I've reached a decision which offers a new hope for our children in the 21st century, a decision I'll tell you about in a few minutes. And important because there's a very big decision that you must make for yourselves. This subject involves the most basic duty that any President and any people share, the duty to protect and strengthen the peace.

At the beginning of this year, I submitted to the Congress a defense budget which reflects my best judgment of the best understanding of the experts and specialists who advise me about what we and our allies must do to protect our people in the years ahead. That budget is much more than a long list of numbers, for behind all the numbers lies America's ability to prevent the greatest of human tragedies and preserve our free way of life in a sometimes dangerous world. It is part of a careful, long-term plan to make America strong again after too many years of neglect and mistakes.

Our efforts to rebuild America's defenses and strengthen the peace began 2 years ago when we requested a major increase in the defense program. . . .

The defense policy of the United States is based on a simple premise: The United States does not start fights. We will never be an aggressor. We maintain our strength in order to deter and defend against aggression—to preserve freedom and peace.

Since the dawn of the atomic age, we've sought to reduce the risk of war by maintaining a strong deterrent and by seeking genuine arms control. "Deterrence" means simply this: making sure any adversary who thinks about attacking the United States, or our allies, or our vital interests, concludes that the risks to him outweigh any potential gains. Once he understands that, he won't attack. We maintain the peace through our strength; weakness only invites aggression. . . .

After careful consultation with my advisers, including the Joint Chiefs of Staff, I believe there is a way. Let me share with you a vision of the future which offers hope. It is that we embark on a program to counter the awesome Soviet missile threat with measures that are defensive. Let us turn to the very strengths in technology that spawned our great industrial base and that have given us the quality of life we enjoy today.

What if free people could live secure in the knowledge that their security did not rest upon the threat of instant U.S. retaliation to deter a Soviet attack, that we could intercept and destroy strategic ballistic missiles before they reached our own soil or that of our allies?

I know this is a formidable, technical task, one that may not be accomplished before the end of this century. Yet, current technology has attained a level of sophistication where it's reasonable for us to begin this effort. It will take years, probably decades of effort on many fronts. There will be failures and setbacks, just as there will be successes and breakthroughs. And as we proceed, we must remain constant in preserving the nuclear deterrent and maintaining a solid capability for flexible response. But isn't it worth every investment necessary to free the world from the threat of nuclear war? We know it is.

In the meantime, we will continue to pursue real reductions in nuclear arms, negotiating from a position of strength that can be ensured only by modernizing our strategic forces. At the same time, we must take steps to reduce the risk of a conventional military conflict escalating to nuclear war by improving our nonnuclear capabilities. . . .

America does possess—now—the technologies to attain very significant improvements in the effectiveness of our conventional, nonnuclear forces. Proceeding boldly with these new technologies, we can significantly reduce any incentive that the Soviet Union may have to threaten attack against the United States or its allies. . . .

I clearly recognize that defensive systems have limitations and raise certain problems and ambiguities. If paired with offensive systems, they can be viewed as fostering an aggressive policy, and no one wants that. But with these considerations firmly in mind, I call upon the scientific community in our country, those who gave us nuclear weapons, to turn their great talents now to the cause of mankind and world peace, to give us the means of rendering these nuclear weapons impotent and obsolete.

Tonight, consistent with our obligations of the ABM treaty and recognizing the need for closer consultation with our allies, I'm taking an important first step. I am directing a comprehensive and intensive effort to define a long-term research and development program to begin to achieve our ultimate goal of eliminating the threat posed by strategic nuclear missiles. This could pave the way for arms control measures to eliminate the weapons themselves. We seek neither military superiority nor political advantage. Our only purpose—one all people share—is to search for ways to reduce the danger of nuclear war.

My fellow Americans, tonight we're launching an effort which holds the promise of changing the course of human history. There will be risks, and results take time. But I believe we can do it. As we cross this threshold, I ask for your prayers and your support.

Available at http://www-personal.umich.edu/~mlassite/internetdocuments467/reaganstarwars.html.

What brings challenges also brings opportunities; by 1985 and the start of Reagan's second term in office, the situation changed relatively quickly from a period of tensions that had characterized the earlier years, to one conducive to cooperation. Soviet leader Konstantin Chernenko died on March 10, 1985, and was succeeded by Mikhail Gorbachev, resulting in a significant change in the relationship of the two countries. This is an example of the ways in which individual leaders can make a huge different in shaping national and even international policies.

Gorbachev came into office recognizing the many problems that the Soviet Union was facing, made worse by a resurgent arms race. Reagan remained suspicious of this new leader and his intentions; nonetheless, the two agreed to a meeting in November 1985 near Lake Geneva. By the time that the summit ended, the two leaders "released a joint statement declaring that nuclear war 'cannot be won and must never be fought.'"[53] Following that summit, the two leaders kept in touch, meeting again for a summit in October 1986 in Reykjavik, Iceland. And that started a significant change in the policies of the two nations toward one another, and, while they might not have known it at the time, this was the start of the end of the Cold War.

Reagan and Gorbachev actively pursued arms control talks as part of their mutually beneficial policy agenda. The meeting between the two men in Reykjavik, Iceland, in 1986 initially appeared to be a failure, yet it led directly to the treaty limiting intermediate-range nuclear weapons (INF) signed in December 1987. This INF treaty specified the destruction of all land-based missiles with a range of between 500 and 5,500 kilometers (which could strike from Europe into Soviet territory and vice versa), with specific provisions for onsite inspection. Not only was this treaty seen as important because it eliminated a certain type of weapon system, but it laid the groundwork for further arms control agreements, leading to the destruction of other types of weapons. As was the case with Richard Nixon, whose anticommunist stance made it possible for him to negotiate with both the Soviet Union and China without charges that he was "selling out" the country, Ronald Reagan, another "cold warrior," was able to negotiate successfully with Gorbachev.

Iran-Contra

In the West, Reagan was celebrated for helping to bring about the fall of communism. But the Iran-Contra affair was a different type of foreign policy situation that also defined this administration. "Iran-Contra" refers to a complex set of policies and actions that led to congressional hearings and a federal commission to explore what really happened. One outcome of Iran-Contra was a clear statement of presidential responsibility. It is also another example of the assertion of congressional oversight regarding the executive branch. And it raised—and then clarified—some important points about who holds ultimate responsibility for making and implementing U.S. foreign policy, something that had become fuzzy over time.

A revolution in Nicaragua in 1980 resulted in the overthrow of the Somoza regime, which had been supported by the United States. It was replaced by the left-leaning Sandinista government, which the Reagan administration saw not only as communist but also as a potential threat to U.S. influence in Latin America. Hence, overthrowing the new Sandinista government by supporting a group of rebels, known as the Contras, became a U.S. policy priority. However, within the United States, public opinion polls indicated that the American people did not support military involvement in Nicaragua, which led the government to try to conceal any possible involvement in the conflict. In 1984, in response to CIA actions to mine the harbors of Nicaragua, Congress passed the Boland Amendment, making it illegal to support "directly or indirectly, military or paramilitary operations in Nicaragua." This was one of three amendments limiting U.S. action in Nicaragua. Ignoring this prohibition, members of the National Security Council (NSC) staff devised an undercover operation to aid the Contras secretly, through third-party support.[54]

In 1986, stories surfaced that the United States had secretly sold weapons to Iran, an enemy of this country since the revolution of 1979, with the profits from the sale funneled to the Contras. Further, in exchange for getting the weapons, Iran promised to ensure the release of hostages being held in Lebanon. When asked about the reports of this linkage, Reagan denied the basic facts. But critical questions remained unanswered, and the president convened a special commission to investigate. As a result of the commission's investigations and findings, most of the blame fell on Robert (Bud) McFarlane,

Reagan's former national security advisor, and NSC staff member Colonel Oliver North, who was found guilty of lying to Congress in hearings about the incident. It was clear that the whole scheme was set up in a way that sheltered the president and vice president by keeping the details from them. (During the Watergate hearings, this approach was known as "plausible deniability.")

Although neither President Reagan nor Vice President George H. W. Bush was charged with or indicted on any specific crime related to Iran-Contra, the uncertainty about whether they were—or were not—involved raised important questions about who is responsible for making and implementing U.S. foreign policy, and what responsibility the president does or should have when illegal actions are committed by members of the administration in the name of foreign policy or "national interest."

The Tower Commission and Report

The special review board convened to look into Iran-Contra was headed by former Republican senator John Tower. The other two members were former Democratic senator and secretary of state Edmund Muskie and Brent Scowcroft, a retired air force general who had been national security advisor to President Ford (and who would become George H. W. Bush's national security advisor). The goal of the Tower Commission was to look into the allegations and then issue a report on what happened. It was this report, published in 1987, that provided the clearest picture of Iran-Contra. But the report did something else; it clarified, once again, the relationships among the various actors who make foreign/national security policy (for in this case they were interchangeable) for the country, and it made it clear that ultimate responsibility rests with the president.

EXCERPTS FROM THE *TOWER COMMISSION REPORT*

Ours is a government of checks and balances, of shared power and responsibility. The Constitution places the President and the Congress in dynamic tension. They both cooperate and compete in the making of national policy. . . .

The Constitution gives both the President and the Congress an important role. The Congress is critical in formulating national policies and in marshalling the resources to carry them out. But those resources . . . are lodged in the Executive Branch. As Chief Executive and Commander-in-Chief, and with broad authority in the area of foreign affairs, it is the President who is empowered to act for the nation and protect its interests. . . .(6)

The primary responsibility for the formulation and implementation of national security policy falls on the President [emphasis added]. . . . [T]he departments and agencies—the Defense Department, State Department, and CIA bureaucracies—tend to resist policy change. [This makes it incumbent upon the president to] bring his perspectives to bear on these bureaucracies for they are his instruments for executing national security policy. . . . His task is to provide them leadership and direction. (87)

The Tower Commission Report: The Full Text of the President's Special Review Board (New York: Random House, 1997).

After years in which it appeared that a strong president was leading the country at the expense of congressional oversight, the Tower Commission report served as a reminder about the difficulties and complexities of making foreign policy. It also provided a warning of how easily the system can go awry when the president is not really in control of nor taking responsibility for those who work under him. It also reaffirmed the important oversight role of Congress.

THE COLD WAR AND BEYOND

By the time Reagan left office in 1989 to be replaced by his Vice President George H. W. Bush, it was clear that the world was changing. The framework that had defined U.S. foreign policy since the end of the Cold War was in the process of disintegrating. When Bush took office, it was not clear exactly when this would happen or what would precipitate the changes. But it would come to Bush and his successors to try to define a new direction for U.S. foreign policy, absent the Cold War framework. As we will see in the next few chapters, that proved to be a very challenging task.

CHRONOLOGY, 1969–1988

1970   Kent State leading to growing opposition to the war in Vietnam
1971   Congress repeals the Gulf of Tonkin Resolution
1972   SALT I/ABM Treaty signed by U.S. and Soviet Union
        Nixon's trip to China; release of Shanghai Communique
1973   Congress passes the War Powers Resolution over Nixon's veto
        Vietnam Peace Accord signed
1974   Richard Nixon resigns as president
        Vladivostok Accord signed by the U.S. and Soviet Union
1975   Vietnam unified as a communist country
1979   Camp David Accords signed by Israel and Egypt
        SALT II signed by U.S. and Soviet Union
        Soviet invasion of Afghanistan
        American hostages taken at embassy in Tehran, Iran
1981   American hostages released
1983   Reagan's "Star Wars" speech
1986   Mikhail Gorbachev comes to power in Soviet Union
        Iran-Contra breaks
1987   INF Agreement signed by the U.S. and Soviet Union

SELECTED PRIMARY SOURCES

Richard Nixon's Address to the Nation on the War in Vietnam, November 3, 1969, https://millercenter.org/the-presidency/presidential-speeches/november-3-1969-address-nation-war-vietnam.

War Powers Resolution, Public Law 93-148, 93rd Congress, H.J. RES. 542, November 7, 1973, "Joint Resolution Concerning the War Powers of Congress and the President," https://avalon.law.yale.edu/20th_century/warpower.asp.

Text of SALT I/ABM Treaty https://history.state.gov/milestones/1969-1976/salt.

Pentagon Papers https://www.archives.gov/research/pentagon-papers.

Text of the Shanghai Communique, "Joint Statement Following Discussions with Leaders of the People's Republic of China," February 27, 1972, https://history.state.gov/historicaldocuments/frus1969-76v17/d203.

Address by President Jimmy Carter to the UN General Assembly," March 17, 1977, https://2009-2017.state.gov/p/io/potusunga/207272.htm.

Ronald Reagan Speech to the British Parliament, June 8, 1982, https://millercenter.org/the-presidency/presidential-speeches/june-8-1982-address-british-parliament.

Ronald Reagan speech to the National Association of Evangelicals in Florid, March 8, 1983, https://www.reaganfoundation.org/library-museum/permanent-exhibitions/berlin-wall/from-the-archives/remarks-at-the-annual-convention-of-the-national-association-of-evangelicals-in-orlando-florida/.

Ronald Reagan "Star Wars Speech," March 23, 1983, http://www-personal.umich.edu/~mlassite/internetdocuments467/reaganstarwars.html.

IV

THE POST–COLD WAR PERIOD

6

The Period of American Hegemony

Bush-Clinton-Bush, 1989–2009

"**W**ithout the Cold War, what's the point of being an American?"[1] As author and political analyst Andrew Bacevich tries to answer that question, he notes that "As the Soviet Union passed out of existence, Americans were left not just without an enemy but even a framework for understanding the world and their place in it. . . . Where there had been purposefulness and predictability, now there was neither."[2] What would replace this framework now that the United States finally had "won" the Cold War?

Thus far, we have identified a number of broad themes that help explain the direction of U.S. foreign policy from the nation's founding through the Cold War, as well as some of the decisions that were made and why. Under the leadership of a series of strong presidents, with domestic and congressional support, and as a result of changing international conditions, the United States became a major power militarily, politically, and economically. President Truman altered the foreign policy decision-making apparatus (i.e., the bureaucracy) to allow the government to implement more effectively the policies of a "superpower" during the Cold War, which lasted about forty-five years. However, the structure, framework, and approach that were then in place made it more difficult for the country to make the adjustments required for a post–Cold War world.

The 1980s started with the election of Ronald Reagan, who early in his administration referred to the Soviet Union as "the evil empire." He promoted building a weapons shield ("Star Wars") to protect the United States from incoming Soviet missiles, and he increased spending for defense and the military. In other words, he did everything that a Cold War president needed to do. And while it was not yet known at that time, the increase in spending was matched by a Soviet increase that helped contribute to the economic is-

169

sues that ultimately led to the end of that country and the demise of the Cold War. The question then became: what will replace it?

When Reagan's vice president, George H. W. Bush, took office as president in 1989 it was already apparent that the Cold War international order was disintegrating. Democratic revolutions would sweep through Eastern Europe in 1989 and into the early 1990s. One after another, the communist governments fell and were replaced by democratically elected leaders who believed in capitalist market economies. President Bush proclaimed the creation of a "new world order," as distinguished from the "old" Cold War order.

After decades of proclaiming that the West would inevitably win the Cold War, it did. Yet it happened so suddenly that all the United States could do was react to international events: wars in the Middle East, ethnic strife and genocide in Yugoslavia and countries in Africa, and an apparent increase in terrorism. Although the United States was the only superpower, the global hegemon, that did not mean that the path forward was obvious or easy. Divisions arose within the U.S. government as well as between the United States and its closest allies about what policies to follow to meet these new challenges. While hints of many of these challenges were present during the Cold War, they were either ignored or dealt with as "sideshows" to the more important issue of U.S.-Soviet relations. The Cold War goal of containing communism (broadly defined) provided the focus for all aspects of U.S. policy since 1945. After 1989,[3] the United States had new and different challenges to face. And without the Cold War framework as its guide, U.S. foreign policy often appeared rudderless.

Brent Scowcroft, national security advisor to President George H. W. Bush, describes the changes this way: "The cold war was an intense concentration on a single problem. . . . And suddenly, historically in the blink of an eye, that world came to an end, and it was replaced by a world without the existential threat of the Cold War. If we made a mistake, we might blow up the planet—that was gone. Instead there were one hundred pinprick problems."[4] Or, put another way, "Only in the post–Cold War period did the internal affairs of other countries become the primary focus of American foreign policy."[5]

Only the United States was now in a position "to transform domestic and economic practices in selected places around the world. . . . America's enormous power, the vast superiority in disposable resources over all other countries that the 1991 Gulf War demonstrated, is the pervasive underlying cause of the direction that post–Cold War foreign policy took."[6] As Mandelbaum describes it, "Americans . . . have always believed that they have a vocation to improve the world, and have always wished to carry it out by *helping others become more like themselves*" (emphasis added).[7] This harkens back to the start of the country, and the idea of "American exceptionalism" and the "City on the Hill," of the United States with a special role to play in the world. As the global hegemon, the United States had the power but also the will to affect change. But, as we will see in this chapter, the United States was not always successful in achieving its goals.

This chapter focuses on the period from 1989 and the start of the administration of George H. W. Bush, through the administrations of Bill Clinton and then George W. Bush. The emphasis will be on what the changing international order meant for U.S. foreign policy without the Cold War framework as its guide. We begin with the prelude to the end of the Cold War, including the fall of the Berlin Wall, the implosion of the Soviet Union, and the democratic revolutions that swept the countries of the former Eastern Bloc. We will then review the Clinton administration and conclude with George W. Bush, whose administration can really be divided into two parts: before and after 9/11.

GEORGE H. W. BUSH AND THE "NEW WORLD ORDER"

Despite Iran-Contra, Reagan left office a popular president. He was succeeded by his vice president, George H. W. Bush. But the world in which Bush took office in January 1989 was changing quickly. The country of Yugoslavia was disintegrating and on the path to ethnic conflict. The government of Somalia was collapsing, leaving the country in a state of chaos and clan warfare. In May 1989, Hungary began the process of opening its border with Austria, one of the first signs of the cracks between the East (Hungary) and West (Austria) and on November 9, 1989, the Berlin Wall came down. The Solidarity Party, led by Lech Walesa, gained power in Poland, and by Christmas 1990 the (communist) Polish People's Republic was replaced by the democratic Republic of Poland. Other countries in the Soviet Eastern European bloc started the process of removing their communist leaders and replacing them with democratically elected governments. And the Soviet economy was declining steadily, leading to the assumption that change in that country was inevitable.

In contrast to the optimistic response to the transitions taking place throughout Eastern Europe, in June 1989 the government of China brutally and violently cracked down on students calling for reform who were protesting in Tiananmen Square in Beijing. As many as two thousand were believed killed in that incident. At a time when democracy appeared to be sweeping most of the communist countries of Eastern Europe, government hold was tightened in China.

Amid uncertainty about the direction of the Soviet Union or Eastern Europe, the Bush administration pursued a tentative and status quo foreign policy, preferring to limit U.S. involvement internationally. Nonetheless, Bush also recognized the significance of the changes taking place. As international events were unfolding rapidly, President Bush spoke of the creation of "a new world order" that would emerge in the wake of communism. He coined the phrase in a speech on September 11, 1990, in which he used Iraq's invasion of Kuwait the month before to outline his vision for the future. At that time, he said, "At this very moment, they [American soldiers] serve together with Arabs, Europeans, Asians, and Africans in defense of principle and the dream of a *new world order*" (emphasis added).[8] In other words, in a rapidly changing world, old adversaries, such as the United States and the Soviet Union, could work together and share responsibilities that would make for a better future.

Unfortunately, while the Cold War was ending, other "hot wars" were emerging that would require the attention of the United States. The most immediate of these was Iraq's invasion of Kuwait.

The Persian Gulf War

On August 2, 1990, Iraq invaded Kuwait, an ally of the United States, which provided the impetus for the Bush administration to get involved internationally. Shortly after the invasion, the Security Council passed Resolution 660 condemning the action, demanding immediate withdrawal of Iraqi troops from Kuwait, calling upon Iraq and Kuwait to enter into negotiations to settle their differences, and reserving the right to meet again as necessary.[9] Over the next few months, President Bush and members of the administration used the United Nations to build support for a military response to this act of aggression. When Iraq did not comply with Resolution 660, on November 29, 1990, the Security Council passed Resolution 678 authorizing "member states . . . to use all necessary means to uphold and implement Resolution 660 . . . and to restore international peace and security to the area."[10] The Security Council also set a deadline of six weeks for Iraq to withdraw from Kuwait. Otherwise, the UN would authorize military force.

As early as September 1990, shortly after the invasion, when it became apparent that the United States might get involved in an armed conflict, Bush knew that he would need approval from Congress under the terms of the War Powers Resolution. According to his memoirs, Bush used the Gulf of Tonkin Resolution as a model so that he, too, could get the same kind of open-ended support from Congress that President Johnson had been given in 1964.[11] In addition, Bush met with congressional leaders from both parties to build support for his position. In the meantime, UN Secretary-General Javier Perez de

Cuellar tried to resolve the situation peacefully to avoid armed conflict. On January 9, 1991, Secretary of State James Baker met with the Iraqi deputy prime minister, Tariq Aziz, in Geneva and warned him that the only way to avert war was for Iraq to comply with Resolution 678 and withdraw completely from Kuwait.

On January 10, Aziz made it clear that Iraq would not comply with the terms stated. At that time, joint resolutions were introduced into both houses of Congress authorizing the deployment of U.S. forces to Iraq under the terms of the UN resolution.[12] This gave the president the authorization to use U.S. military forces consistent with the terms of the War Powers Resolution. On January 12, both houses of Congress voted to support the joint resolution; the House vote was 250 to 183, and the Senate vote was 52 to 47, "the smallest margin ever to vote for war."[13] The attack started early in the morning (Iraq time) on January 17, 1991.

The war lasted forty-three days and resulted in the defeat of Iraq and its withdrawal from Kuwait. Most notable about this effort is that "the coalition," as it was known, of military forces working with the United States was not tied to traditional alliances but rather was made up of forces drawn from a range of countries that came together in pursuit of a common outcome. For the first time since World War II, the United States and the Soviet Union cooperated and worked together on the same side—a remarkable event.

In addition, the Persian Gulf War was a true product of new technology both within the military and the media. While coverage of the Vietnam War earned it the moniker of "the first television war" for the nightly news coverage of battles and body bags, the Persian Gulf War was the first war carried live on cable news, leading to what has become known as "the CNN effect." For the first time, the American people as well as the rest of the world got "live" coverage of what was happening in Baghdad and throughout Iraq and Kuwait. This changed expectations of what war coverage should be, something that would be taken even further during the presidency of George W. Bush, when reporters were "embedded" with troops to cover the 2003 war against Iraq.

Since the first Persian Gulf War, and given the subsequent decision to invade Iraq by then President George W. Bush, much has been written and analysis done about the decision made by the first President Bush *not* to invade Iraq at that time but to stay with the mission of getting Iraqi forces out of Kuwait, and not go after Saddam Hussein. Brent Scowcroft, then National Security Advisor to George H. W. Bush, when asked about that decision said, "That was not unfinished business. We early on decided it was not up to us to drive him from power. And, as you know, in much of foreign policy you never have a complete success." When pushed further about this decision,

Scowcroft offered the administration's rationale, which is telling given the events that subsequently transpired. Scowcroft said that they could have gone on to Baghdad, but "it would've changed the whole character of the conflict into one where we were occupiers in a hostile land. Our troops would've been subjected to guerilla activity. And we had no strategy for getting out. And that was a situation which I thought would be a disaster to get into."[14] As you will see below, that assessment describes the situation following the decision to send U.S. troops into Iraq in 2003 with no clear exit strategy.

The End of the Soviet Union

In August 1991, shortly after the Persian Gulf War ended, there was an attempted coup in the Soviet Union. With Mikhail Gorbachev under house arrest at his vacation home in the Crimea by hard-liners who had initiated the coup, it was Boris Yeltsin, then leader of the Soviet republic of Russia, who faced the rebels. Standing on a tank in front of the "Russian White House," Yeltsin declared that he would be in charge of all security forces on Russian territory until order was restored. With that statement, as well as the forceful image of him facing down the troops, Yeltsin emerged as the de facto leader of the country. The end of the Soviet Union was near. On December 8, 1991, the leaders of the Soviet republics of Russia, Ukraine, and Belarus announced the end of the Soviet Union, leading to the creation of a new Commonwealth of Independent States (CIS). This was confirmed on December 21 at a meeting of representatives of eleven of the former Soviet republics. The end of the old Soviet Union was finalized on December 25, 1991, when Mikhail Gorbachev resigned as president of the USSR and Boris Yeltsin became president of Russia, the largest and most powerful of the former Soviet republics.

The dissolution of the Soviet Union, and with it the end of the Cold War, came as a surprise to the United States. While leaders of the United States and other Western countries had long called for this as well as for the victory of democracy over communism, the reality is that few actually thought it would happen. Since 1991, one of the questions that political scientists, historians, and policy makers have asked is whether the United States was responsible for the end of the Soviet Union. But the death of the Soviet Union was the result of the confluence of a number of factors. These ranged from the perceived need to continue an arms buildup, which had a detrimental effect on the Soviet economy, to the democratic revolutions sweeping Eastern Europe, which clearly undermined the power of the Soviet government, to the liberalizing policies of Mikhail Gorbachev, which suggested that change was possible. As one historian noted, "Collapse, when it finally came, had come from within."[15]

The Balkans and Ethnic Conflict

Even with the euphoria surrounding the end of the Cold War, U.S. foreign policy remained unsettled. The existence of ethnic warfare and genocide in countries around the world became more prominent when not overshadowed by the Cold War. According to noted foreign policy analyst Leslie Gelb, the Bush administration "did not understand that these nasty civil wars could become breeding grounds for terrorists. . . . Bush's team performed better in putting the old world's problems to bed than in getting ahead of the new ones."[16] Somalia and especially the wars in the former Yugoslavia illustrate that point, which went beyond the Bush administration to bedevil the Clinton administration that followed.

The country of Yugoslavia had been artificially created after World War I, and its diverse ethnic groups (Serb, Croat, and Bosnian Muslim primarily) had been held together in part by the strength of the country's leader, Josip Tito. After his death in 1980, and with no designated successor, nationalist leaders emerged and called for independent states for each of the ethnic groups (e.g., "Serbia for the Serbs"). This meant that it was simply a question of time until the country dissolved into civil and ethnic warfare as each group vied for territory and power.[17]

On June 25, 1991, Croatia and Slovenia, two of the six republics that made up Yugoslavia, declared their independence.[18] Two days later, on June 27, the first of the wars that would wrack the Balkans for the next eight years began. The Yugoslav-Slovene War lasted ten days, until the UN negotiated a settlement. This falsely conveyed the idea that these "little" ethnic wars in the Balkans could be resolved quickly by negotiation. However, the crisis grew and the conflict spread, leaving the United States to decide whether or how to deal with this situation. The dilemma facing the Bush administration was defining what was in the national interest. On the one hand, this was a war being fought in Europe, close to U.S. allies. This raised concerns that if the United States did not take action, the situation would escalate and the United States would no longer have a choice as to whether or not to get involved. On the other hand, the war was outside the formal NATO guidelines area, it was in a country with which the United States had little involvement, and therefore it would be a stretch to see it as directly relevant to U.S. national interest.

President Bush chose to deal with the situation using a combination of diplomacy (soft power) and threats (hard power). He sent Secretary of State James Baker to meet with Serbian leader Slobodan Milosevic to warn him not to take military action that would make the situation worse. On the whole, though, it fell to the Europeans to address the deteriorating situation in what remained of Yugoslavia, and the Bush administration was content to leave this "European problem" to the Europeans. But the problem would not go away; rather, it would be left to the Clinton administration to decide how to deal with it.

The administration of George H. W. Bush was a period of transition in U.S. foreign policy. Initially the victory in the Gulf War suggested that the post–Cold War period would be a time of shifting alliances created as necessary to meet specific threats. This suggested a flexibility in U.S. foreign policy that the Cold War had not allowed. Further, it indicated that Congress would be willing to grant to a president "permission" to use force against a specific enemy even when the United States was not directly threatened, as long as the case could be made that "national interest" was at stake. It also showed that the American public could and would support such a war, even in a distant country.

This new era in U.S. foreign policy also carried dangers that were not yet fully formed or understood. Ethnic conflict and genocide in other countries were threats to human rights but were difficult to articulate to the American public in a way that tied them to U.S. national interest. It was far more difficult to justify military involvement in a distant country on humanitarian grounds than on economic ones. In short, the concepts of "threat" and "national interest" were starting to have different meanings outside the context of the Cold War.

Going into the presidential election of 1992, war was underway in the Yugoslav republic of Bosnia, the Bush administration was debating what to do about the conflict in Somalia, and unrest was building in Haiti, a country within the traditional U.S. sphere of influence. But overshadowing these foreign policy issues was a faltering economy. President Bush's popularity had gone from a high of 89 percent in February 1991, at the start of the ground war in Kuwait, to a low of 29 percent in July 1992, about four months before the election.[19] With the foreign policy victory in the Persian Gulf behind them, the American public wanted to know what President Bush would do to address the domestic economic situation. It was Bush's challenger Bill Clinton who seemed to have the answers.

THE CLINTON YEARS

To meet domestic concerns raised during the campaign, candidate Clinton focused on the economy and the recession that was sweeping the country. In fact, the admonition "It's the economy, stupid" was coined by James Carville, Clinton's chief election strategist, who posted it on the campaign's office walls as a reminder of the importance of the economy in the upcoming election. The words have since become part of election lore![20] The budget deficits that had started under President Reagan were taking their toll domestically, and Clinton, accusing President Bush of being out of touch with America, promised to "focus like a laser beam on the economy." Clinton's priority was going to be domestic politics and economics, but like other presidents before him, once in office Clinton discovered that international events have a way of interfering. Thus, Clinton had to balance domestic priorities with responses to foreign policy crises.

Clinton suffered two foreign policy disasters early in his administration, in Haiti and Somalia, both of which affected his views on foreign policy and the role of the president. Those situations directly influenced his subsequent decisions about Bosnia and later Kosovo, and his decision not to intervene in the genocide in Rwanda. And, in a clear example of the interaction between domestic and international politics, a Republican-controlled Congress and questions about the president's personal conduct further limited his foreign policy options.

With the end of the Cold War, the United States was the last remaining superpower. This gave the United States a unique and important role in the international arena. Without the Cold War, foreign policy priorities shifted once again; no longer would the focus be on using the military to deter a single (communist) threat. Instead, Clinton's acknowledgment of a globalized world meant recognition of the interdependence of countries and a return to trade and economic relations as a central component of U.S. foreign policy. "Economic engagement—increasing cross-border trade and investment—became the keystone . . . of its [Clinton administration's] foreign policy in general." In this approach, "the administration found a basis for engagement with the world that seemed suited to the new, post–Cold War circumstances."[21] This focus on economics and trade was a marked departure from previous policies, especially for a Democratic president, and it set the stage for the some of the changes that continued into the twenty-first century. Clinton's approach was pragmatic rather than ideological, and that seemed appropriate for the order that seemed to be emerging to replace the Cold War. This is not to suggest that the military was unimportant. In fact, while the military would still have to be prepared to fight two wars simultaneously (which was the established military posture), ideally it could also be used as a force for good in support of human rights and humanitarian missions that were the result of emerging ethnic and civil conflicts. But many of these idealistic (i.e., Wilsonian) goals were derailed by domestic politics, specifically the conflict between President Clinton and Congress, as well as by international political realities. Looking at a number of issues that Clinton had to address, and how he chose to do so, is instructive for understanding the problems associated with American foreign policy after the Cold War and in a globalized world. What is also

important to note, is how all these crises—Somalia, Haiti, Bosnia, Rwanda—
were unfolding simultaneously as Clinton was also trying to deal with the
economic downturn at home which was his priority.

The Clinton administration holds important lessons about the impact of
domestic politics and the ways in which domestic and foreign policy are
intertwined. It also serves as a reminder that international events cannot be
controlled by a president who is often forced to react to them and how, without the Cold War framework, international relations became unpredictable.

Somalia

U.S. involvement in Somalia predated President Clinton; it originated in a
decision made by President George H. W. Bush in December 1992 (after
he was defeated by Clinton in November) to send troops into Somalia on a
humanitarian mission. This case serves as an example of how ill-prepared
the United States was to meet the challenges that it would face after the Cold
War. It also shows the ways in which foreign policy decisions often are made
in reaction to events.

The ouster of dictator Mohamed Siad Barre in 1991 resulted in instability
and clan warfare in Somalia that, coupled with years of drought, led to widespread famine and internal chaos. Although in August 1992 Bush had ordered
an airlift of food as a short-term solution, it became clear that more help was
needed. The NSC held a series of meetings throughout November, *after the
U.S. presidential election*, to determine what to do to address the situation,
which was seen as a humanitarian crisis. In one meeting on November 25,
Bush was given three possible options: "increased support for existing UN
efforts, a U.S.-organized coalition effort but without the participation of
American ground troops, or a major U.S. effort to lead a multinational force
in which U.S. ground troops took the leading role." Then chair of the Joint
Chiefs of Staff, Colin Powell, "expressed concern about the use of ground
troops." After "a broad discussion," President Bush decided that if other
countries would join the effort, "U.S. combat troops would lead an international force to Somalia."[22]

The United States deployed troops to Somalia in December 1992 on a humanitarian mission to ensure that food was distributed to those who needed
it. The deployment was authorized with the promise that U.S. forces would be
out by Inauguration Day in January 1993. U.S. diplomat Robert Oakley was
sent to Somalia to try to negotiate among the various clan leaders in order to
restore some stability to the country. Despite earlier promises, when Clinton
came into office, U.S. ground troops were in Somalia with no end to their
deployment in sight.

By the end of summer 1993, about six months after Clinton took office, the administration faced a series of issues regarding Somalia. First, there did not seem to be an easy diplomatic solution to the problem. Second, in what was becoming a pattern, Congress was asking questions and raising issues about the role of the U.S. forces in Somalia. Finally, Clinton was facing the possibility of U.S. intervention in the growing war in Bosnia, and he saw the two as related. Clinton told his advisors, "Unless we can get the Somalia mission under control . . . it's going to be very hard to convince Congress to provide the forces to implement an agreement on Bosnia."[23] Nevertheless, U.S. troops had already been deployed to Somalia by the previous administration.

On October 3, 1993, U.S. forces staged a raid in the city of Mogadishu to capture the warlord Mohamed Farrah Aidid and his top lieutenants, but the United States paid a high price for that military action. The battle fought on the streets of Mogadishu resulted in hundreds (perhaps thousands) of Somali casualties and the death of eighteen Americans. U.S. public opinion was directly affected by pictures of a dead American soldier being dragged through the streets of Mogadishu.[24] This battle, "the largest firefight Americans had been involved in since Vietnam,"[25] evoked strong reactions from Congress as well as the public. Clinton addressed the American public to remind them of why U.S. troops were in Somalia, but he faced a dilemma. To leave would send a message about U.S. impotence in the face of nonstate actors, such as the warlords in Somalia. But staying would only put more U.S. soldiers in harm's way with an unclear objective. Clinton set a deadline of March 31, 1994, for a political settlement to be finalized so that U.S. troops could be withdrawn. The reaction to this solution among Republican members of Congress was especially hostile. For example, Senator Nancy Kassebaum (R-KS) stated, "I can think of no further compounding of the tragedy that has occurred there for our forces than to have them withdraw and see what started out to be a very successful, noble mission end in chaos."[26] Clinton also was criticized for sending troops into a mission that they were not prepared for and then for wanting them to withdraw in order to save more lives.

Clinton learned a lesson from this about sending U.S. troops to distant lands that were seen as removed from American national interests. As a result of Somalia, the Clinton administration chose not to intervene in the genocide that took place in Rwanda in 1994.[27] But perhaps more important, it helped frame the Clinton administration's perceptions regarding whether—and when—to intervene for humanitarian reasons.

Haiti

As Clinton was dealing with the situation in Somalia, another potential crisis was growing in Haiti. Half of the Caribbean island of Hispaniola, Haiti was well within the U.S. sphere of influence going back to the days of the Roosevelt Corollary. Consequently, instability in Haiti put Clinton into a position where he felt that he had to act. This military action also proved to be disastrous and further reinforced the president's as well as congressional and public perceptions about the limits to U.S. military involvement.

President Clinton came into office a strong supporter of Jean-Bertrand Aristide. Aristide was Haiti's first democratically elected president, but he was overthrown in a military coup in 1991, eight months after his election. The United States brokered an accord between Aristide and Haiti's military rulers stipulating that Aristide would return to power on October 30, 1993. U.S. forces were then to be sent to Haiti as part of a UN contingent to train Haitians in engineering (such as building roads and other infrastructure) and to help serve as an internal police force.

In September 1993, the CIA reported that the Haitian leaders did not intend to keep the agreement. Nonetheless, some in the Clinton administration felt that the United States had to live up to its side of the agreement. Clinton authorized the deployment of a naval ship to Haiti carrying engineers and other forces to fulfill the U.S. commitment. When the ship arrived on October 11, 1993, it was met by a mob, many armed with guns and other weapons, while the police simply stood by. The Haitian leaders refused to guarantee the safety of the U.S. forces, and the ship anchored in the harbor, awaiting orders. On October 12, Washington ordered the ship to leave without allowing the forces to set foot in the country, and this became another foreign policy embarrassment for Clinton.

Clinton felt pressed to intervene in Haiti at least in part for domestic political reasons—to avert the possibility of an influx of Haitian refugees into the United States. Further, a significant African American constituency wanted to see the United States do something to help end the military dictatorship in Haiti. Despite his desire to respond to domestic concerns, Clinton learned quickly the limits of U.S. force in the face of civil unrest and without the support of the people and government that it was allegedly trying to help.

In addition, Clinton provoked Congress by not seeking congressional approval to send troops to Haiti, arguing that he possessed "executive authority" to do so. In response, Congress passed a resolution stating that "the President should have sought and welcomed congressional approval before deploying U.S. forces to Haiti."[28]

In 1994, with the situation in Haiti still unresolved, Clinton ordered a larger invasion force to the island. However, prior to their landing, former president Carter was able to negotiate a deal with rebel Haitian leader Cedras, allowing him to leave the island and authorizing American troops to come in to restore order.

Clinton learned harsh lessons from Haiti, another foreign policy debacle that undermined his credibility. To the members of Congress, it was an abuse of the power of the president, which further exacerbated the strains that already existed between the two branches.

The Balkans

When candidate Clinton was campaigning for the presidency against George H. W. Bush, he condemned Bush for not acting more forcefully to address the situation in the Balkans. By the time Clinton took office as president in January 1993, the siege of Sarajevo, which became the longest siege in modern history to that time, was well under way, and stories of the genocide taking place throughout Bosnia were already hitting the American media. The issues were far from clear-cut, and explaining to the American public why involvement in this area would be in U.S. national interest would be difficult. As a result, Clinton called this "the most frustrating and complex foreign policy issue in the world today."[29]

Under Clinton, the United States pursued a bifurcated policy toward the Balkans. Policy was characterized either by an overwhelming desire not to get involved, which was the attitude of the administration toward the war in Bosnia in 1993 and into early 1994, or by the impulse to jump in and take a leadership role, which the United States did later in 1994. The former was the result of a number of factors: the harsh lessons of Somalia and Haiti of the difficulties of a humanitarian mission; the desire to let the Europeans take the lead under UN auspices (through the United Nations Protection Forces, or UNPROFOR); and concern about getting support of Congress and the public at a time when Clinton's popularity was low.[30] The decision to take a leadership role in the Balkans was the result of a change in the political landscape so that once the administration decided it was time to act, it did so decisively, resulting in a negotiated end to the war.

One of the events that prompted the Clinton administration to act was the "Sarajevo Market Massacre" on August 28, 1995, which resulted in the deaths of thirty-seven civilians, with eighty-eight wounded. It prompted a public outcry that provided the political support Clinton needed. Pushed by the United States, NATO accelerated its air strikes against Serb targets. This helped provide the military cover necessary for the Bosnian and Croat forces to launch a major ground offensive in preparation for the start of negotiations that would bring an end to the war. Negotiations were held at Wright-Patterson Air Force Base outside Dayton, Ohio, under the leadership of Assistant Secretary of State Richard Holbrooke. The major political leaders of Serbia (Milosevic), Croatia (Tudjman), and Bosnia (Izetbegovic) participated in the discussion, and in November 1995, President Clinton announced that an agreement had been reached. The peace agreement was signed in Paris on December 14, 1995, and the war in Bosnia ended.[31] Unfortunately, that was neither the end of war in the Balkans nor of U.S. military involvement there.

Kosovo and the Clinton Doctrine

The 1997 report "National Security Strategy for a New Century" suggests that U.S. military intervention may be appropriate "to respond to, relieve, and/or restrict the consequences of human catastrophe."[32] The willingness to use military force in this way defines what has been called the "new interventionism," one of the foundations of the Clinton Doctrine that was central to justifying the operation in Kosovo in 1999. This doctrine has at its core many of the ideals that Jimmy Carter espoused when he spoke of the need to make human rights central to U.S. foreign policy, and it echoes the earlier ideas of Woodrow Wilson.

Kosovo was another foreign policy issue that Clinton faced. The Dayton Peace Accords that ended the war in Bosnia did nothing to address the ethnic violence growing in the Serb province of Kosovo. Kosovo had been declared an "autonomous province" in 1963. But it had few rights until the Yugoslav constitution of 1974 allowed the province to write its own constitution, thereby giving it the same status as the six republics of then-Yugoslavia. After Serbian leader Milosevic came to power in 1987, the Serb minority in Kosovo increasingly repressed the Albanian majority, imposing more and more restrictions on what they could and could not do. In 1997, violence erupted when a group calling itself the Kosovo Liberation Army (KLA) began a series of terrorist-type attacks against the Serbs. Under the auspices of the European Union, a negotiation was called to take place at Rambouillet, outside Paris, in the hope of averting armed conflict. The negotiators gave Milosevic an ultimatum: withdraw from Kosovo or risk NATO military action. When the talks failed, the United States and Europe had little choice but to follow through on their threat, and in March 1999, NATO began bombing Serbia.

Kosovo was a difficult situation for the United States in many ways. While there was little doubt that human rights abuses were taking place, there were also divisions among the NATO allies as to what form an intervention should take. Clinton made it clear that he would not authorize sending U.S. ground forces into Kosovo, which put him at odds with the allies, especially Britain, and it publicly sent a signal as to military limits; one official in the Clinton administration later claimed that to state this so publicly had been a mistake.[33] Clinton did agree to support air strikes.

Clinton understandably was cautious about the deployment of U.S. military forces at this time. He had easily won reelection in 1996 because of domestic reasons. The economy was doing well, and despite a hostile Republican Congress, Clinton's public approval rating hit a high of 73 percent in December 1998.[34] In 1999, at the same time that he was facing decisions about Kosovo, he was under investigation for his affair with White House intern Monica Lewinsky. He was under additional scrutiny by Congress because he did not seek congressional approval for the earlier U.S. involvement in Bosnia and Kosovo, which he claimed had not been needed because these were NATO (as opposed to U.S.) missions. However, to the Republican-controlled Congress, this was part of a pattern of presidential disregard for congressional oversight.

With U.S. support, NATO made a decision to begin bombing Serbia; the attacks started in March 1999 and continued as a NATO operation tied to the need to assure international intervention when human rights abuses call for it or when it is in support of humanitarian goals. However, Clinton came under scrutiny regarding the U.S. policy on Kosovo. On the one hand, there were those who felt that the United States should have become involved sooner because of the clear human rights abuses. On the other hand, there were questions about whether Clinton had overstepped his responsibilities by agreeing to deploy U.S. troops and aircraft without broad support by Congress.

NATO Enlargement

Clearly Clinton saw the important role that NATO had played during the Cold War, and the role that it could play in a post–Cold War world by ensuring a unified response to so-called out of area conflicts, such as the war in Bosnia. The notion of expanding NATO eastward, to include the former countries of Eastern and Central Europe, was identified by the Clinton administration as a priority that would also be an assertion of U.S. leadership within the alliance. In March 1993, shortly after Clinton came into office, a number of political leaders were in Washington for the dedication of the U.S. Holocaust Memorial Museum. Czech president Vaclav Havel had the opportunity to meet with the new president and urged him to move NATO eastward to include the new democracies as an assertion of shared values and common defense. Although this was articulated in Article 2 of the NATO Treaty,[35] it was always secondary to Article 5 and collective security. Through 1993, as war was escalating in Bosnia, support was growing within the United States for the concept of NATO enlargement. "In January 1994, in the first European trip of his presidency, Clinton met with other NATO leaders in Brussels and reaffirmed the notion that Alliance membership should be open to new members."[36] A new

Partnership for Peace program was created within the alliance as the first step toward formal enlargement of NATO.

The notion of enlargement was not without controversy both domestically and within NATO. On both sides of the Atlantic there were questions about costs associated with a larger alliance. For example, countries in the former Eastern Bloc had military equipment that was obsolete, and there was a question of who would pay to upgrade it. Enlargement raised questions about Article 5 commitment, and whether an alliance that included more countries that were within the sphere of the former Soviet Union would be obliged to defend them in case of attack. And, of course, Russia saw NATO enlargement as a direct threat. Nonetheless, the plan to enlarge the alliance moved forward.

Hungary, Poland, and the Czech Republic were the first three countries to join the enlarged alliance, which became official in April 1999, as part of the celebration of the fiftieth anniversary of NATO. This was to be the first round of enlargement, with later rounds to include more countries. While, as Clinton anticipated, the movement toward NATO enlargement put the United States in a position of leading the alliance once again, it also opened fissures within the alliance over who should be invited to join and when, what the costs would be, who would pay, and a host of other such questions. The decision also alienated Russia, which "never came to regard expansion as fair, legitimate, or indeed anything other than a betrayal of Western promises and an assault on Russian prerogatives and interests. By alienating Russia, NATO expansion undercut Western and American goals in Europe. It turned Russia against the remarkably favorable post–Cold War settlements."[37] Ultimately, this brought a period of relative peace between Russia and the West to an end, leading to a growth in tensions once again.

Economics: Trade and Globalization

In his book *Mission Failure*, Michael Mandelbaum wrote "During the Cold War years . . . in the hierarchy of the American government's concerns, issues involving the international economy took second place to matters of national security." And he notes that "international economics had been a branch of foreign policy." The Clinton administration, coming after the end of the Cold War, reversed that order; "much of its foreign policy became a subset of its economic policy."[38] In many ways, then, Clinton was the first Cold War president to try to construct a different approach to foreign policy, one that was more consistent with the post–Cold War world in which the United States faced no major military threat but where interactions were tied to trade and economics.

Thus, in approaching foreign policy from a different perspective, Clinton understood that the world was changing and becoming more interconnected economically, a phenomenon referred to as "globalization." The economic failure of one country could have repercussions for other countries, and therefore it was in the United States' national interest to be sure that the global economy was strong. Clinton also understood that technology altered the way international business was conducted. Just as détente with the communist countries was best achieved by conservative Republicans, so was free trade pursued more successfully by a president from the Democratic Party, which was traditionally aligned with labor and was seen as protectionist.

With bipartisan support and despite objections from the largely Democratic unions, which claimed that it would result in the loss of jobs, Clinton successfully enacted the North American Free Trade Agreement (NAFTA) in 1994, uniting the United States, Canada, and Mexico. NAFTA strengthened both economic and political ties among the three countries, and years after the agreement went into effect, there is little evidence that it resulted in a loss of jobs in the United States, which was the main fear.[39] In 1995, when Mexico was in financial crisis, the Clinton administration provided that country with a $12.5 billion loan. While this was seen as a significant risk at the time, it not only stabilized the country, but Mexico repaid the loan within two years. This further strengthened the ties between the two countries.[40]

It is now clear that Clinton had an understanding of some of the changes taking place in the international system and was able to use them to strengthen the United States economically. While he had his foreign policy failures, notably Haiti and Somalia, his understanding of economics, both domestic and international, can be seen as one area of success.

The Environment: The Kyoto Protocol

Protecting the environment is one of the areas that falls under the heading of "common good" in that it is something that affects all countries and peoples; environmental degradation knows no national boundaries.[41] Countries can assume that it is not only in their national interest but in the interest of all nations to ensure that the quality of the environment is protected, and that it is incumbent upon them to work together to achieve this goal; this is a position that the liberal theorists would take. Or countries can take the "free rider" position and assume that other countries will take the lead and that they do not have to spend the money or invest resources in this policy area since others will do it for them—and they will benefit anyway. Thus, it is up to each nation-state to ask whether and how it is in their best interest to work on improving the environment and what will happen if they don't.

When Clinton became president, his vice president, Al Gore, had a strong commitment to the environment that went back to his days studying at Harvard.[42] First in Congress and then as part of the Clinton administration, Gore made the environment a priority; as a result, the United States took the lead in working toward a climate change agreement.

Under U.S. leadership, the Kyoto Protocol to the United Nations Framework Convention on Climate Change (known as the Kyoto Protocol) was adopted in 1997. The Kyoto Protocol is linked to the UN Framework Convention on Climate Change (UNFCC). The Protocol sets binding targets for thirty-seven industrialized countries and the European community which have committed "to reducing their emissions by an average of 5 percent against 1990 levels over the five-year period 2008–2012." The Protocol places a higher burden on the developed countries and was designed to assist all countries to adapt to "the inevitable effects of climate change" and to help facilitate the development of techniques that can help increase resilience to climate change impacts. Of special importance, however, is that "The major distinction between the Protocol and the Convention is that while the convention *encouraged* industrialized countries to stabilize GHG emissions, the Protocol commits them to do so."[43]

To ensure that the goals associated with protecting the environment that grew from the Kyoto Protocol were met, subsequent meetings were scheduled annually to bring the international community together for further discussion and negotiation. In general, the goal of these various international meetings was to frame follow-up agreements to move forward issues surrounding climate change.

Despite some of its flaws, the Kyoto Protocol was seen as an important first step toward reducing global greenhouse gas emissions. In addition, it provided a framework for the next steps that the international community needed to take in controlling those emissions. And, perhaps more important, it made the United States one of the global leaders in confronting environmental issues.

After a number of subsequent international meetings that built on this beginning point, and again with U.S. leadership (this time under President Obama), in December 2015, the international community agreed to the United Nations Framework Convention on Climate Change, commonly known as the Paris Agreement for the city in which it was signed.[44]

Terrorism

One of the hallmarks of the post–Cold War world was the emergence of non-state actors playing a major role in the international system. At a time when politicians are debating how to ensure the safety and security of the United States, a brief look at the pattern of terrorism during the Clinton years leading to the attacks of September 11 is instructive.[45] Perhaps the most important point is that "state-sponsored terrorism"—such as the acts perpetrated or supported by Libya, Syria, and Lebanon—has declined overall and is being replaced by a growth of independent organizations, many of which are seen as extremist and radical.[46] This pattern created a foreign policy dilemma for Presidents Clinton and then George W. Bush of how to respond to attacks that are not tied to a nation-state (country). Since international relations and international law are based on and assume a nation-state as the primary actor, there are few guidelines about how a country should interact with, or respond to, a nonstate actor.

According to Gelb, "When terrorists tried to blow up the World Trade Center in 1993, and later struck U.S. embassies in Africa, he [Clinton] did nothing at all for five years, until 1998 when he ordered small cruise missile attacks against Afghanistan and Sudan. These erratic, fragmentary, and feeble acts showed that Clinton [and his administration] had no comprehension of the nature and magnitude of the growing global terrorist threat, let alone what to do about it."[47] In a world in which perceptions become reality, the administration's inability to respond sent a signal that one could argue contributed to the attacks of 9/11.

In September 1998, Clinton addressed the UN General Assembly, and global terrorism was one of the central points of his talk. At that time, he admonished the international community that "all nations must put the fight against terrorism at the top of our agenda." He warned that terrorism is not only an American problem, but "a clear and present danger to tolerant and open societies and innocent people everywhere." And he also said, "If terrorism is at the top of the American agenda—[it] should be at the top of the world's agenda." He then offered common solutions to the problem, especially the need for countries to work together to counter this threat. He concluded that "together we can meet it and overcome its threats, its injuries, and its fears with confidence."[48] Despite this optimistic call for international unity against a common threat, terrorist acts against Americans (and also U.S. allies) increased.

In the aftermath of September 11, 2001, significant questions have been raised about what was then known about the terrorist cells acting in or against the United States, and whether the Clinton administration should have done more to stop Al Qaeda. Those questions might never be answered.

RETHINKING U.S. FOREIGN POLICY UNDER CLINTON

Domestically, ensuring a thriving economy takes precedence over foreign policy situations, even those perceived as failures. As outgoing president in January 2001, Clinton had an approval rating of 67 percent, "the highest of any outgoing president since modern polling began—even surpassing Dwight Eisenhower and Ronald Reagan."[49]

By the end of the Clinton administration it was clear that U.S. foreign policy had no overarching framework as it did during the Cold War. Rather, each of the two immediate post–Cold War presidents, George H. W. Bush and Bill Clinton, had a different emphasis and both seemed unsure as to how to address the emergence of ethnic conflicts and civil wars and the humanitarian and human rights crises that accompany them. The result was the emergence of policies that were inconsistent and often opaque. While the Bush administration showed little doubt about the need to send U.S. troops to the Persian Gulf in the wake of Saddam Hussein's invasion of Kuwait or to deploy troops to Somalia to aid the humanitarian crisis unfolding there, he was unwilling to send troops to the former Yugoslavia, preferring instead to leave that to the Europeans to deal with. Similarly, Clinton appeared to be aggressive in his deployment of U.S. troops to Haiti for a mission that became a foreign policy fiasco and that raised questions about both his and the United States' intentions regarding the use of force.

The administration of George W. Bush, who followed Clinton, started in controversy when the contested presidential election of 2000 was decided by the Supreme Court, and it ended in controversy as well because of the results of decisions that were made in the wake of 9/11. While few would dispute the trauma of September 11, 2001, many have debated and continue to debate the wisdom of the administration's decisions to go into Afghanistan and especially Iraq for the disruption that those attacks caused in each of the two countries, the resulting regional instability that contributed to the growth of terrorist groups such as ISIS,[50] and the economic impact these wars had on the United States. The decision to attack Iraq in 2003 was especially suspect in light of the uncertain evidence provided about alleged weapons of mass destruction.

GEORGE W. BUSH: FROM ELECTION TO 9/11

While the Bush administration initially came into office with a call for a neo-unilateralist, almost isolationist foreign policy, it took the attacks of September 11, 2001, to forge a new direction for U.S. foreign policy. Suddenly, the United States was actively involved internationally, following an "either you are with us or against us" brand of foreign policy. Relatively quickly the United States went from trying to remain disengaged to an almost Wilsonian brand of interventionism tied to the imposition of democracy around the world.

The foreign policy of George W. Bush can be divided into two parts: before and after 9/11. The implications of the shift in foreign policy were far-reaching, as the United States, in seeking to establish itself as a global leader following the attacks, ended up pursuing policies that alienated many of its traditional allies. The post 9/11 period was also characterized by the growing threat from terrorism, which, as we will see, was a difficult one for the United States to counter as it was not tied to any nation-state but to a group that was harder to define—and to fight. Some argue that the decisions made in the wake of 9/11 contributed to the growth of terrorist groups, such as ISIS, that bedeviled the Obama administration that followed Bush.

During the presidential campaign of 2000, then-candidate George W. Bush made it clear that the United States would chart its own course in foreign policy. Bush indicated that under his administration, the United States would return to a more unilateralist policy characterized by actions consistent with what the president perceived to be in the national interest. He stressed his desire to strengthen ties south of the border (especially to Mexico), rather than look primarily to the traditional allies in Europe. And he made it clear that the United States should not be in the business of "nation building," stating his intention to pull U.S. troops out of places like the Balkans. In short, candidate Bush outlined a marked shift in the direction of U.S. foreign policy, especially compared with that of his predecessor, Bill Clinton, and even his father, George H. W. Bush.

The events of 9/11 significantly altered the priorities of the Bush administration, creating the "global war on terror" and making this the highest foreign policy priority. From that time forward, all aspects of Bush administration foreign and security policy stemmed from, and were justified by, the need to support the war on terror. It was the desire to spread freedom and democracy that ultimately was used to justify the United States decision for war in Iraq, eclipsing the initial rationale for the attack, which was "regime change" and the desire to eliminate the spread of weapons of mass destruction allegedly found in Iraq. And despite his willingness to use military force, a realist characteristic, Bush's emphasis on spreading freedom and democracy is inherently idealist in perspective.[51]

Contested Election and Implications for U.S. Foreign Policy

In order to put the Bush administration's decisions into broader perspective, it is necessary to go back to the election of 2000, which was fraught with controversy. Marked by questions about election fraud in Ohio, a critical swing state, and the "hanging chads" and "butterfly ballots" in Florida, the election was characterized by accusations of irregularities in voting procedures as well as the ways in which ballots were counted. The Florida issue was especially contentious, and ultimately the issue of a recount went to the U.S. Supreme Court for a decision. On December 12, 2000, by a vote of 5 to 4, the members of the Court ordered a halt to a recount, thereby overruling the verdict of the Florida Supreme Court and effectively ensuring the election of George W. Bush as president.

Despite—or because of—his disputed victory in the presidential election, Bush moved quickly to fulfill the campaign promises he made, many of which involved a reversal in the patterns of foreign policy set by the Clinton administration. In June 2001, over the objections of the European allies as well as many environmentalists in the United States, Bush declared that the 1997 Kyoto Protocol to the UN Framework Convention on Climate Change "was fatally flawed in fundamental ways," and that the United States would not participate in that agreement but would offer an alternative, which it never did. The United States, Bush said, was committed to "work within the United Nations framework and elsewhere to develop with our friends and allies and nations throughout the world an effective and science-based response to the issue of global warming."[52] These statements left other countries wondering how the United States was going to live up to this commitment or to others that had been made by previous administrations, as the Bush reaction seemed to be especially negative toward anything done by the Clinton administration.

Bush also withdrew the United States from the 1972 Anti-Ballistic Missile Treaty (SALT I) so that the United States would not be constrained by its terms in developing new weapon systems, especially a ballistic missile defense system. In addition, he said that the United States would limit continued engagement in the Middle East peace process, which had been a hallmark of U.S. foreign policy since the Carter years. In effect, Bush halted the Oslo process that had been pursued by Clinton. In another repudiation of his predecessor's policies, Bush also suspended talks with North Korea and criticized the agreement signed in 1994 by the United States and North Korea under the Clinton administration.[53] He said that the United States would not send additional troops to the Balkans as part of the peacekeeping force deployed there in 1995 following the end of the war, and implied that he would withdraw those that were there. And he made it clear that the United States should not be in the business of "nation building," a direct slap at previous administrations' foreign policy decisions, including his father's.

These early policy decisions led to criticism domestically and internationally about the direction of U.S. foreign policy. The European allies charged that this policy of unilateralism was undermining the basis of U.S. (and European) national security. They also raised concerns not only about the apparent destruction of the existing foreign policy framework, but about what (if anything) Bush was putting in its place. To many opponents both within and outside the United States, the perception was that the Bush administration's policies were tied to the desire to please special interests and were made for domestic political reasons rather than in the greater national interest. These criticisms stopped abruptly on September 11, 2001.

September 11 and the Responses

Using the military actively as an instrument of foreign policy was the hallmark of Bush administration foreign policy after September 11. On that day hijackers captured four aircraft, crashing two into the World Trade Center in New York and one into the Pentagon in Washington. The fourth, which by all accounts was also headed to Washington, crashed in Pennsylvania after passengers wrested control of the aircraft from the hijackers and diverted it from its target. The responses to these events are instructive as they pertain to U.S. foreign policy.

One of the most immediate effects of September 11 was that NATO invoked Article 5 for the first time in its history. The North Atlantic Council issued a press release on September 12, 2001, affirming that Article 5 "stipulates that in the event of attacks falling within its purview, each Ally will assist the Party that has been attacked by taking such action as it deems necessary. Accordingly, the United States' NATO Allies stand ready to provide the assistance that may be required as a consequence of these acts of barbarism."[54] By early October, under the framework of Article 5, NATO had started to deploy Airborne Early Warning Aircraft (AWACS) to the United States. However, it should be noted that this was the *only* act that NATO took in support of the United States at that time, not because NATO did not want to do more—in its role as a collective security alliance, NATO was prepared to work with the United States to formulate a response to the attack—but because the United States, under the Bush administration, preferred to work outside the NATO framework, or any other formal alliance, in determining next steps.

Acting unilaterally, the Bush administration thereby determined how to respond to the attacks.[55] The administration quickly began exploring military options, including "a strike against al Qaeda forces in Afghanistan, where Osama bin Laden had been given sanctuary by the country's Taliban government, led by Muslim fundamentalists who had imposed a rigid Islamic regime."[56] The decision to attack Afghanistan was to be part of a larger "global war on terror" that would not end "until every terrorist group that had attacked Americans in the past, up to and including the 9/11 assaults, or might launch attacks in the future, had been destroyed."[57] As political scientist Peter Irons described it, perhaps the more important point about the decisions that Bush made was that "the 9/11 attacks created abrupt, far-reaching changes in the nation's political and military situation—changes that would, in turn, *raise significant constitutional issues*" (emphasis added).[58] These issues pertained to the decision to prosecute the war not only with Afghanistan but also with Iraq, and especially in the expansion of the role of the executive branch to make decisions not only about military and foreign policy, but also about domestic issues—all justified under the broad umbrella of the war on terror.

War with Afghanistan

After gathering intelligence information that linked the hijackers to the terrorist group Al Qaeda, based in Afghanistan, the Bush administration made the decision to send military forces to attack that country and oust the Taliban government, which supported and harbored terrorists. Consistent with the terms of the War Powers Act,[59] the president consulted with Congress and got its support for this venture. According to the president, this was a clear-cut case of an attack on the United States and a military response to that attack. The draft joint resolution was sent to the leaders of the House and Senate on September 12, 2001. It was passed by the Senate on September 14 by a vote of 98 to 0, and in the House later that same day by a vote of 420 to 1.[60]

The critical part is Section 2, "Authorization for Use of United States Armed Forces," which states that "the President is authorized to use all necessary and appropriate force against those nations, organizations, or persons he determines planned, authorized, committed, or aided the terrorist attacks that occurred on September 11, 2001, or harbored such organizations or persons, in order to prevent any future acts of international terrorism against the United States by such nations, organizations or persons." The document also makes it clear that "nothing in this resolution supersedes any requirement of the War Powers resolution."[61] (See chapter 5 for a description of the War Powers Resolution.)

In the signing statement that accompanied his signature, Bush asserted that S.J. Res. 23 "recognized the authority of the *President* under the Constitution to take action to deter and prevent acts of terrorism against the United States."

He also stated that "in signing this resolution, *I maintain the longstanding position of the executive branch regarding the President's constitutional authority to use force*, including the Armed Forces of the United States" (emphasis added).[62] Although the president made it clear that he was complying with the terms of the War Powers Resolution and that the military action requested was necessary to protect the American people and homeland, he was also asserting what he saw as the authority of the president to make these decisions.

However, some in Congress were already concerned about the broad scope of the war on terror envisioned by Bush. After some compromises, Bush signed the resolution into law on September 18, 2001, and less than three weeks later, on October 7, 2001, the United States launched ground and air strikes against Afghanistan.[63]

Despite the reservations expressed by some in Congress, few argued with the president's decision to respond to the attacks of September 11 by attacking Afghanistan. In fact, Bush's public approval rating hit a high of 90 percent following September 11, the highest popularity rating ever recorded.[64] The swift military victory over the Taliban in Afghanistan proved that the Bush administration was willing to take a decisive stand militarily when it mattered, reinforcing the confidence of both the allies and the American public in the president and his policies. What Bush did not take into account at that time was the fact that removing the Taliban from office was not going to end the war in Afghanistan.

The initial decision to attack Afghanistan, one of the known homes for Al Qaeda bases, was seen as justified and, on the whole, was received positively both at home and abroad. British Prime Minister Tony Blair stated that "even if no British citizens had died [in the attacks of September 11], it would be right to act. This atrocity was an attack on us all."[65] Within a few months the war expanded and ultimately became a NATO mission. The International Security Assistance Force (ISAF) was created as a UN-mandated, NATO-led international force in December 2001 after the United States had ousted the Taliban regime. It was created initially to assist the Afghan Transitional Authority to reconstruct the country. Although other countries joined in this NATO mission, the United States had the largest number of troops deployed.

Despite the lofty goals of ousting the Taliban, confronting Al Qaeda, mounting a serious NATO mission, and rebuilding the country, the war in Afghanistan did not go as planned. In fact, between 2001, when the war with Afghanistan started, and January 2009, when the Obama administration came into office, attention given to Afghanistan by the United States became secondary to what became the major foreign policy issue of the Bush years: the war with Iraq.[66]

The Bush Doctrine and the War with Iraq

By early 2002, Bush made it clear that the United States would not stop with the attack on Afghanistan but would expand the war on terror. In his State of the Union speech in January 2002, Bush identified Iraq, Iran, and North Korea as an "axis of evil," and he stated that "some governments will be timid in the face of terror. . . . If they do not act, America will."⁶⁷ He followed that up with a speech on March 11, 2002, the six-month anniversary of September 11. At that time, he said, "Our coalition must act deliberately, but *inaction is not an option*" (emphasis added).⁶⁸ In other words, President Bush was sending notice to the American public and the world that the war on terror was going to expand beyond Afghanistan.

The Bush Doctrine, as it was popularly known, became the basis for the decision to go to war against Iraq in March 2003 and to do so without the formal backing of the international community. Formally titled the "National Security Strategy of the United States," the document, which was issued in September 2002, puts forward a new direction for American foreign policy: "While the United States will constantly strive to enlist the support of the international community, *we will not hesitate to act alone, if necessary, to exercise our right of self-defense by acting preemptively*" (emphasis added).⁶⁹

This doctrine states clearly and unequivocally that the United States is justified in going to war *preemptively* against any group that potentially threatens the country or its allies, and that it will do so alone if necessary. This is a departure from the policies that the United States followed since the end of World War II, when much of its foreign policy was tied to formal alliances and the belief that security is best achieved if countries work together against a common enemy, rather than trying to defeat the enemy alone. The United States had never before threatened to go to war preemptively, previously relying on its military might to act as a deterrent against attack. Furthermore, it is a marked departure from the stated idealistic goals of the Bush administration that now made clear it would be relying on U.S. hard power to do whatever it thought was necessary. For the first time since the Cold War, the United States was relying on its military might to pursue its foreign policy goals. And, once again, foreign and security policy became inextricably linked.

The Path to War with Iraq

The path to war in Iraq can clearly be traced back to the first Persian Gulf War and allowing Saddam Hussein to continue in power, according to a number of members of the George W. Bush administration. Further, it became "the first test case in the Bush administration's new foreign policy doctrine of America's right not only to preeminence in world affairs, but to preemption, by military might if necessary, of whatever threats it perceives to its security at home and abroad."[70] The decision to go into Iraq was not without dissenters even within the administration. Secretary of State Colin Powell, who had been the military director of the first Persian Gulf War, warned of the possible dangers of such a mission and at a meeting with the president in August 2002 was quoted as saying "'We'd own a country.'" And he also made the case that building international support would be essential "not only to legitimize any war in the eyes of the world, but also to lay the groundwork for the postwar reconstruction of Iraq."[71]

Despite the suspicion that Bush and the Neocons[72] had of international organizations like the UN, Bush saw the necessity of going to that organization. In a speech before the General Assembly in September 2002, Bush made it clear that unless Iraq complied with the UN Security Council Resolutions to allow weapons inspectors back into the country, actions would be taken, and he also left no doubt that the United States would go it alone if that should become necessary.[73] But Germany was already voicing opposition to any war in Iraq, as was France, which were pushing for the need to focus on the inspectors and only later on the threatened consequences. In other words, it is clear that six months before the war with Iraq there were already disagreements brewing between the United States and some of its closest European allies as to next steps. Only Great Britain was showing complete support.

While Bush was pressing the international community through the UN, he was already building support in Congress for a military action. On September 19, he sent a draft of a resolution to Congress asking for authority "to use 'all means he determines to be appropriate, including force' to disarm and dislodge Saddam Hussein."[74] Aware of the 2002 congressional election campaign and the need to build support for its position both domestically and internationally, the administration continued to use the same story line about weapons of mass destruction through the fall. On October 2, 2002, Bush submitted to Congress a resolution authorizing the use of force against Iraq. The resolution itself includes a litany of all of Saddam Hussein's wrongdoings for more than a decade, going back to the first Persian Gulf War and even earlier. It describes an Iraq that was building weapons of mass destruction and demonstrated willingness to use such weapons in the past; the clear implication is that it will do so again, this time against the United States. And it *suggests* that Iraq was somehow involved in the attacks of 9/11—"Whereas the attacks on the United States of September 11, 2001, underscored the gravity of the threat posed by the acquisition of weapons of mass destruction by international terrorist organizations"—although it does not mention Iraq by name in that particular clause.[75]

The resolution then concludes with these important clauses: "Whereas the President and Congress are determined to continue to take all appropriate actions against terrorists and terrorist organizations, including those nations, organizations, or persons who planned, authorized, committed, or aided the terrorist attacks that occurred on September 11, 2001, or harbored such persons or organizations"; and then, "Whereas the President has authority under the Constitution to take action in order to deter and prevent acts of international terrorism against the United States" the "President *is authorized to use the Armed Forces of the United States as he determines to be necessary and appropriate*" (emphasis added).[76] It is also interesting to note that this resolution refers explicitly to Public Law 107-40, which authorized the use of force "against those responsible for the recent attacks launched against the United States"[77] and was used to authorize the war with Afghanistan.

On October 11, 2002, the resolution was passed by both houses—in the Senate by a vote of 77 to 23 and in the House by a vote of 296 to 133—and it was signed into law by President Bush on October 16, 2002. All the dissenters were Democrats with the exception of Republican Senator Lincoln Chaffee of Rhode Island, who subsequently was voted out of office. The U.S. attack against Iraq began on March 19, 2003.

The administration also started a concerted public campaign to make the case for military action against Iraq. Directed at both the American public and U.S. allies, the administration put forward two interrelated arguments: "One was that Iraq had ominous, if still largely unspecified and unproven ties, to Al Qaeda. The other was that Saddam remained determined to build a nuclear weapon that could directly threaten the United States and the world."[78] It should be noted that both of these allegations had been debated within the government.

The political pressure by the United States and some of its allies was enough for Iraq to authorize the return of the weapons inspectors, but under pressure from the United States in November, the Security Council also passed Resolution 1441, which gave Iraq "a final opportunity to comply with its disarmament obligations under relevant resolutions of the Council" or "it will face serious consequences as a result of its continued violations of its obligations."[79] Although Iraq allowed inspectors back into the country and released thousands of pages of files on its weapons program, the Bush administration was quick to announce that Iraq was not fully in compliance. Early in 2003, the governments of France and Germany noted that Iraq was complying and should be given additional time. What seemed to be happening was that the United States was pushing for war while many of the allies were willing to wait.

Bush took the opportunity of the State of the Union message in January 2003 to make the implicit case for war against Iraq.

EXCERPTS FROM GEORGE W. BUSH STATE OF THE UNION ADDRESS JANUARY 28, 2003

Mr. Speaker, Vice President Cheney, members of Congress, distinguished citizens and fellow citizens, every year, by law and by custom, we meet here to consider the state of the union. This year, we gather in this chamber deeply aware of decisive days that lie ahead.

You and I serve our country in a time of great consequence. . . .

To protect our country, we reorganized our government and created the Department of Homeland Security, which is mobilizing against the threats of a new era. . . .

We must work together to fund only our most important priorities. I will send you a budget that increases discretionary spending by 4 percent next year, about as much as the average family's income is expected to grow. And that is a good benchmark for us: Federal spending should not rise any faster than the paychecks of American families. . . .

Our second goal is high quality, affordable health for all Americans. . . .

Our third goal is to promote energy independence for our country, while dramatically improving the environment. I have sent you a comprehensive energy plan to promote energy efficiency and conservation, to develop cleaner technology, and to produce more energy at home. . . .

Our fourth goal is to apply the compassion of America to the deepest problems of America. For so many in our country—the homeless, and the fatherless, the addicted—the need is great. Yet there is power—wonder-working power—in the goodness and idealism and faith of the American people. . . .

The qualities of courage and compassion that we strive for in America also determine our conduct abroad. The American flag stands for more than our power and our interests. Our founders dedicated this country to the cause of human dignity, the rights of every person and the possibilities of every life. This conviction leads us into the world to help the afflicted, and defend the peace, and confound the designs of evil men.

In Afghanistan, we helped to liberate an oppressed people, and we will continue helping them secure their country, rebuild their society and educate all their children, boys and girls.

In the Middle East, we will continue to seek peace between a secure Israel and a democratic Palestine.

Across the Earth, America is feeding the hungry. More than 60 percent of international food aid comes as a gift from the people of the United States.

As our nation moves troops and builds alliances to make our world safer, we must also remember *our calling, as a blessed country, is to make the world better* [emphasis added]. . . .

To date we have arrested or otherwise dealt with many key commanders of Al Qaeda. They include a man who directed logistics and funding for the September the 11th attacks, the chief of Al Qaeda operations in the Persian Gulf who planned the bombings of our embassies in East Africa and the USS Cole, an Al Qaeda operations chief from Southeast Asia, a former director of Al Qaeda's training camps in Afghanistan, a key Al Qaeda operative in Europe, a major Al Qaeda leader in Yemen.

All told, more than 3,000 suspected terrorists have been arrested in many countries. And many others have met a different fate. Let's put it this way: They are no longer a problem to the United States and our friends and allies.

We are working closely with other nations to prevent further attacks. America and coalition countries have uncovered and stopped terrorist conspiracies targeting the embassy in Yemen, the American embassy in Singapore, a Saudi military base, ships in the Straits of Hormuz and the Straits of Gibraltar. We've broken Al Qaeda cells in Hamburg and Milan and Madrid and London and Paris—as well as Buffalo, New York.

We've got the terrorists on the run. We're keeping them on the run. One by one the terrorists are learning the meaning of American justice.

As we fight this war, we will remember where it began: here, in our own country. This government is taking unprecedented measures to protect our people and defend our homeland. . . .

Now, in this century, the ideology of power and domination has appeared again and seeks to gain the ultimate weapons of terror. Once again, this nation and our friends are all that stand between a world at peace, and a world of chaos and constant alarm. Once again, we are called to defend the safety of our people and the hopes of all mankind. And we accept this responsibility.

America is making a broad and determined effort to confront these dangers. We have called on the United Nations to fulfill its charter and stand by its demand that Iraq disarm. We are strongly supporting the International Atomic Energy Agency in its mission to track and control nuclear materials around the world. We are working with other governments to secure nuclear materials in the former Soviet Union and to strengthen global treaties banning the production and shipment of missile technologies and weapons of mass destruction.

In all of these efforts, however, America's purpose is more than to follow a process. It is to achieve a result: the end of terrible threats to the civilized world. All free nations have a stake in preventing sudden and catastrophic attacks, and we're asking them to join us, and many are doing so. Yet the course of this nation does not depend on the decisions of others.

Whatever action is required, whenever action is necessary, I will defend the freedom and security of the American people. . . .

Twelve years ago, Saddam Hussein faced the prospect of being the last casualty in a war he had started and lost. To spare himself, he agreed to disarm of all weapons of mass destruction.

For the next 12 years, he systematically violated that agreement. He pursued chemical, biological and nuclear weapons even while inspectors were in his country.

Nothing to date has restrained him from his pursuit of these weapons: not economic sanctions, not isolation from the civilized world, not even cruise missile strikes on his military facilities.

Almost three months ago, the United Nations Security Council gave Saddam Hussein his final chance to disarm. He has shown instead utter contempt for the United Nations and for the opinion of the world. . . .

It is up to Iraq to show exactly where it is hiding its banned weapons, lay those weapons out for the world to see and destroy them as directed. Nothing like this has happened. The United Nations concluded in 1999 that Saddam Hussein had biological weapons materials sufficient to produce over 25,000 liters of anthrax; enough doses to kill several million people. He hasn't accounted for that material. He has given no evidence that he has destroyed it. . . .

Our intelligence sources tell us that he has attempted to purchase high-strength aluminum tubes suitable for nuclear weapons production. Saddam Hussein has not credibly explained these activities. He clearly has much to hide.

The dictator of Iraq is not disarming. To the contrary, he is deceiving. . . .

The United States will ask the U.N. Security Council to convene on February the 5th to consider the facts of Iraq's ongoing defiance of the world. Secretary of State Powell will present information and intelligence about Iraqi's—Iraq's illegal weapons programs, its attempts to hide those weapons from inspectors and its links to terrorist groups.

We will consult, but let there be no misunderstanding: *If Saddam Hussein does not fully disarm for the safety of our people, and for the peace of the world, we will lead a coalition to disarm him* [emphasis added]. . . .

We seek peace. We strive for peace. And sometimes peace must be defended. A future lived at the mercy of terrible threats is no peace at all.

If war is forced upon us, we will fight in a just cause and by just means, sparing, in every way we can, the innocent.

And if war is forced upon us, we will fight with the full force and might of the United States military, and we will prevail. . . .

Available at https://www.washingtonpost.com/wp-srv/onpolitics/tran scripts/bushtext_012803.html.

As noted in the State of the Union speech, in February, Secretary Powell went to the United Nations to make the case against Saddam Hussein and to persuade other countries of the need to go to war. France, Russia, and China all defied the United States, arguing that the inspectors needed more time, while Bush ordered troops and combat helicopters to the Persian Gulf in anticipation of a conflict. As the various sides tried to reach a diplomatic solution to this impasse, the United States continued to deploy troops to the region. A UN Resolution that had been pending was withdrawn in the face of mounting opposition, and UN Secretary General Kofi Annan warned that without the support of the Security Council, the legitimacy of any military action would be questioned. Nonetheless, the decision was made and on March 19, 2003, President Bush announced to the American public that "at this hour American and coalition forces are in the early stages of military operations to disarm Iraq, to free its people, and to defend the world from grave danger."[80]

In authorizing that attack without United Nations approval, Bush charted another new course for U.S. foreign policy. The war against Iraq became the defining moment for the Bush administration. Unlike his father, who was able to build a strong international coalition before mounting the 1991 Persian Gulf War, George W. Bush had the support of only a few nations and, perhaps more important, that action was directly opposed by many of the United States' traditionally strongest allies, especially France and Germany.[81]

This resulted in a significant schism between the United States and its allies, which proved to be especially damaging at a time when the United States was building support for, and needed to sustain allied commitment to, the ongoing war in Afghanistan.

War with Iraq and Its Aftermath

Where the first Persian Gulf War in 1991 was covered widely in the media (the "CNN effect"), the 2003 invasion was characterized by reporters "embedded" with troops, thereby enabling the U.S. public to watch the progress of the war in virtually real time and with first-person commentary. The course of the first phase of the war, "shock and awe," was swift and apparently successful. The initial military attack was sufficient to bring about the end of the regime of Saddam Hussein. In a show of victory aboard the USS *Abraham Lincoln* on May 2, 2003, Bush spoke under a banner that declared, "Mission Accomplished." However, that declaration of victory proved to be premature. What Bush did not count on was the difficulty of both ending the war and building the peace.[82]

Much has been written about the issues and problems associated with the war in Iraq,[83] and we are not going to review or critique the decision here. Suffice it to say, the decision to invade Iraq without UN or allied support had a devastating impact on perceptions of the United States internationally.[84] It also divided the country domestically. Further, the longer the war continued, the more skeptical the American public and especially the allies became. But this did not stop George W. Bush from winning a second term in the election of 2004. When it comes right down to it, the American public does not like to change leaders during a war. And, as Bush kept reminding the American public, he was a wartime president. It was not until later in Bush's second term and then after Obama took office as president in January 2009 that the full impact of many of Bush's decisions started to be felt.

The Iraq War and the Economy

In his State of the Union speech on January 29, 2002, Bush made it clear that "it costs a lot to fight this war [in Afghanistan]. We have spent more than a billion dollars a month—over $30 million a day—and we must be prepared for future operations." And, he continued, "My budget includes the largest increase in defense spending in two decades—because while the price of freedom and security is high, it is never too high. Whatever it costs to defend our country, we will pay."[85] What was not, and could not, have been anticipated at the time of that speech was the additional costs of fighting two wars simultaneously, one in Afghanistan and the other in Iraq, or the longer-term costs to deal with the veterans of the two wars. According to a nonpartisan Congressional Budget Office (CBO) report released in 2011, the estimated costs for Iraq from fiscal year 2003, when the war started, through fiscal year 2011, when the report was compiled, was $805.5 *billion*.[86] According to an analysis in *Bloomberg News*, "Direct federal spending on the war through 2012 will reach $823 billion" and that does not include the resulting payment on the debt accumulated for the war or ongoing costs for veterans of that war.[87]

The economic drain from the "war on terror" was significant, especially the decision to pay for the war by borrowing and increasing budget deficits rather than by raising taxes. This had a longer-term impact on the economy and was among the challenges that Obama faced as president. The major point here is that the decision to expand the war on terror, while initially popular with many Americans, also had longer-term economic consequences as the country had to pay the price for the "guns versus butter" decisions that had been made.

Freedom and Democracy for All

Despite candidate Bush's claim that the United States should not engage in nation building, as President Bush began his second term, not only was the United States engaged in doing so in Iraq, but Bush's inaugural address suggested that the United States would continue its involvement globally, pursuing the Wilsonian ideals of freedom and democracy for all. The war on terror in general and the war in Iraq in particular were part of President Bush's broader policy agenda to spread freedom and democracy. He articulated this concept in his second inaugural address when he said, "There is only one force of history that can break the reign of hatred and resentment, and expose the pretensions of tyrants, and reward the hopes of the decent and tolerant, and that is the force of human freedom." And in language reminiscent of an earlier era, he continued, "So it is the policy of the United States to seek and support the growth of democratic movements and institutions in every nation and culture, with the ultimate goal of ending tyranny in our world."[88]

In his foreign policy decisions following September 11, and especially going into his second term, Bush appeared to be drawing on Wilsonian idealism using America's military might to accomplish his goal.[89] The term coined by the administration to describe this foreign policy direction was "practical idealism," which refers to "the policy's underlying premise that in a post-Sept. 11 world, America's national security is tied directly to the spread of free and open societies everywhere, including the Middle East."[90]

In his book *Winning the Right War*, foreign policy analyst Philip Gordon notes that the Bush administration, early in its second term, started to recognize the reality that an America "that is popular, respected, reliable, and admired has a far better chance of winning needed cooperation than an America that is not." Gordon also contends that the administration was aware of the high price it paid "for gratuitously alienating allies and that diplomatic efforts to repair relations were worthwhile."[91] This awareness resulted in an effort by then secretary of state Condoleezza Rice to attempt to mend relations with the allies by traveling to Europe. President Bush made similar trips, including one to European capitals in June 2008, dubbed his "farewell tour." According to one account of that visit, "the question of his legacy hangs over his eight-day visit to Europe." But this account also notes the fact that the war in Iraq "did more to strain relations with Europe—not to mention with the Muslim world—than any issue since Ronald Reagan deployed intermediate missiles in Europe in 1984 at the height of the cold war. As a result, he [Bush] remains deeply unpopular in Europe, as he does at home."[92]

What is clear is that during most of its tenure, the Bush administration was trying to define a new direction for U.S. foreign policy in the post–Cold War world and that despite the administration's protestations to the contrary, this policy was formulated in response to external events. In many ways, these events and the Bush administration's reactions to them defined the direction of U.S. foreign policy for the early part of the twenty-first century. They are also further proof that regardless of how much a president might try to initiate a particular course of action, ultimately he or she will be forced to react to the most immediate and pressing issues that arise.

Shortly before he left office, December 2008 polls show that Bush's approval rating had dropped to 24 percent and his disapproval rating had gone up to 68 percent. The only group that overwhelmingly remained supportive was conservative Republicans.[93]

It is important to note that it was not just his decisions about Iraq that undermined Bush's popularity at home. Domestic events, such as his handling of Hurricane Katrina and the failure to enact some of his signature policies such as Social Security and immigration reform, combined with skepticism about what was going on in the prison at Guantanamo in the wake of Abu Ghraib and the deteriorating situation in Iraq and Afghanistan contributed to rising doubts among the American people about Bush's leadership. The lack of consultation with the Congress and the perception of the ill treatment of prisoners as well as apparent abuses of the rights of U.S. citizens through legislation such as the Patriot Act also undermined America's moral leadership both at home and abroad.

PRESIDENT BUSH AND WILSONIAN IDEALISM

In writing about Bush and the influence of the neocons, one political scientist writes that "the problem with the Bush reaction to 9/11 was not merely in its unilateral and comprehensive nature. It was also in the administration's insistence on discussing the challenges in *moralistic, religious, and even missionary terms* (rather than in political ones)" (emphasis in original). In so doing, Bush defined the terrorist challenge as a "biblical struggle of good versus evil" that resulted in the loss of support both at home and abroad, despite the overwhelming sympathy that the United States got immediately following the attacks.[94]

In that regard, Bush is often equated with Wilson in the zeal with which he pursued the ideals of promoting democracy and pursuing a foreign policy based on values. However, Bush did not learn all the lessons of history, specifically, that values such as "democracy" and "freedom" cannot be imposed, nor will the rest of the world see the fight in quite the same way.

As noted in chapter 2, Wilson had changed the underlying framework of American foreign policy to inject values, such as democracy, which he saw as a universal given. Bush tempered that set of values with his own beliefs of the United States as an imperial power with a preordained role to play in the world. These values guided his decisions to go to war with Iraq. However, "As the Iraq war turned into a protracted and costly struggle, both the rationale for the American presence in Iraq and the aim of the war shifted substantially. The Iraq war was less about relinquishing Iraq of its weapons of mass destruction than about bringing freedom and democracy to the Middle East."[95]

Clearly, Bush's foreign policy embodies some of the idealism of Wilson with the imperialism of McKinley and Theodore Roosevelt. In understanding the impact of this blend of foreign policy orientations, Judis summarizes it well when he states that "America's true power has always rested not only in its economic and military strength, but in its determination to use that strength *in cooperation with others* on behalf of the equality of individuals and nations" (emphasis added).[96]

The Iraq War: A Postscript

On November 17, 2008, just after the election that would bring Barack Obama to the White House, the governments of the United States and Iraq signed a Status of Forces Agreement (SOFA) that would govern the withdrawal of American troops from Iraq. Under the terms of this agreement, all U.S. forces "shall withdraw from all Iraqi territory no later than December

31, 2011." The agreement also specifies clearly that "all United States *combat* forces shall withdraw from all Iraqi cities, villages and localities no later than the time at which Iraqi Security Forces assume full responsibility for security in an Iraqi province, *provided that such withdrawal is completed no later than June 30, 2009*" (emphasis added).[97] In other words, according to the terms of the agreement, while the government of Iraq acknowledges the need to look to the United States to "support" Iraq "in its efforts to maintain security and stability in Iraq," the primary responsibility would fall to the government of Iraq.

As the time got closer for the withdrawal of U.S. forces from Iraq, concerns mounted in both countries. An article in the *New York Times* on June 25, 2009, summarized the ambivalence surrounding this withdrawal. On the one hand, to Iraqi Prime Minister Nuri al-Maliki, the event was seen as a "great victory" and one that "he compares to the rebellion against British troops in 1920." The Americans, for their part, have been willing "to suspend virtually all American operations—even in support roles—for the first few days in July to reinforce the perception that Mr. Maliki desires: that Iraq's security forces are now fully in control of Iraq's cities." However, according to this news report, "the deadline has provoked uncertainty and even dread among average Iraqis, underscoring the potential problems that Mr. Maliki could face if bloodshed intensifies."[98] The concern, clearly, is a return to the sectarian violence that characterized much of the war prior to the increase in the number of American troops, known as "the surge," early in 2007. In light of the violence that has been occurring in Iraq since this agreement, that concern was prescient.

Under the terms of the Status of Forces Agreement, there would not be a total withdrawal of U.S. troops; thousands would remain in Iraq but with their role shifted from combat to support—primarily training and advising. They would also conduct operations "that the Iraqis could not yet do on their own, like emergency medical evacuation."[99] A paramount goal for both Iraq and the United States was to stress the importance of Iraq as a sovereign nation headed by a democratically elected leader (Mr. Maliki), and to ensure that, eventually, a sense of "normalcy" would return to that country. The SOFA allows for continued U.S. assistance "to strengthen the political and military capabilities of the Republic of Iraq to deter threats against its sovereignty, political independence, territorial integrity, and its constitutional federal democratic system."[100]

The last U.S. combat forces left Iraq prior to the December 2011 date negotiated in the SOFA; although an American military presence remains in that country, sectarian violence continues and the government remains shaky. Despite the goal of replacing Saddam Hussein with a democratic form of government, that has not yet happened. "By the time the American military left, Iraq had still not passed a major milestone in the life of any successful new democracy: the peaceful handover of power to an opposition party."[101]

In July 2016 the issue of the veracity of the claims of weapons of mass destruction that were the alleged justification for the war in Iraq came to the forefront again when a British independent Iraq Inquiry Committee released a report that concluded that "Britain, like the United States, used flawed intelligence to justify the invasion, that Iraq posed no immediate national security threat, that the allies acted militarily before all diplomatic options had been exhausted and that there was a lack of planning for what would happen once Mr. Hussein was removed."[102] Despite the fact that Prime Minister Blair was advised by diplomats and ministers of their concern about the U.S. plan, Blair chose to override their objections and support Bush's decision to invade Iraq. The results of the decision to invade Iraq continue to haunt both Britain and the United States and have affected both countries' foreign policy decisions subsequently. "The legacy of Iraq kept Britain from joining the United States in bombing Syria over its use of chemical weapons. It was also a factor in President Obama's decision to back away from a military strike on Syria's chemical weapons facilities, and to delay military activity there against the Islamic State."[103]

When he came into office in January 2009, President Obama inherited the situation created by Bush: disarray in Iraq, instability in Afghanistan, and the growth of terrorist groups, especially ISIS. How to handle these became part of the discussion and debate in the presidential election of 2008. How to actually address them became part of the foreign policy decisions that the new administration had to make.

If foreign policy is a continuous process, as we indicated in chapter 1, then how could an Obama administration turn aside or reverse the course of Bush administration policy? Or how could the new administration enact policies that would better reflect the changing political and security realities?

In the next chapter, we will explore the policies of the Obama and then Trump administrations in order to draw some lessons for the future of American foreign policy. While Obama continued the basic framework of U.S. foreign policy outlined by Bush, Trump completely upended virtually all aspects of then-existing foreign policy, calling into question some basic assumptions about and understanding of the way foreign policy is, or should be, made.

CHRONOLOGY 1989–2009

1989   Berlin Wall comes down
             Democratic revolutions in Eastern and Central Europe
             Tiananmen Square crackdown in China

1990	Iraq invades Kuwait
1991	Persian Gulf War
	Start of breakup of Yugoslavia; first Balkan war
1992	War in Bosnia-Herzegovina
	Somalia
1993	Haiti
1994	Genocide in Rwanda
1995	Dayton Agreement ends war in Bosnia
1997	First round of NATO enlargement
	Kyoto Protocol signed
1999	War in Kosovo
2001	Attacks of 9/11
	U.S. invades Afghanistan
2003	U.S. invades Iraq
2005	Hurricane Katrina hits the U.S.
2008	Status of Forces Agreement (SOFA) with Iraq

SELECTED PRIMARY SOURCES

George H. W. Bush "New World Order" speech, September 11, 1990, https://millercenter.org/the-presidency/presidential-speeches/september-11-1990-address-joint-session-congress.

"Authorization for use of military force against Iraq," Public Law 102-1, Joint Resolution, January 14, 1991, https://www.govinfo.gov/content/pkg/STATUTE-105/pdf/STATUTE-105-Pg3.pdf#page=1.

UN Security Council Resolution 660, http://unscr.com/en/resolutions/660.

Text of the North Atlantic (NATO) Treaty, https://www.nato.int/cps/en/natolive/official_texts_17120.htm.

Authorization to use military force against Afghanistan, January 3, 2001, https://www.govtrack.us/congress/bills/107/sjres23/text.

George W. Bush, "State of the Union Address," "Axis of Evil," January 29, 2002, http://georgewbush-whitehouse.archives.gov/news/releases/2002/01/20020129-11.html. A video of the address is available at the same site.

Text of Kyoto Protocol, https://unfccc.int/resource/docs/convkp/kpeng pdf.

"Authorization for Use of Military Force Against Iraq Resolution of 2002," https://www.congress.gov/bill/107th-congress/house-joint-resolution/114/text

George W. Bush, "President Thanks World Coalition for Anti-Terrorism Effort: Remarks on the Six-Month Anniversary of the September 11 Attacks," https://georgewbushwhitehouse.archives.gov/news/releases/2002/03/20020311-1.html.

"The National Security Strategy of the United States of America," September 2002, https://georgewbush-whitehouse.archives.gov/nsc/nss/2002/.

George W. Bush State of the Union Address January 28, 2003 https://www.washingtonpost.com/wp-srv/onpolitics/transcripts/bushtext_012803.htm.

George W. Bush, second inaugural address, January 20, 2005, http://www.npr.org/templates/story/story.php?storyId=4460172.

Obama and Trump

2009–2021

When Barack Obama came into office in January 2009, he inherited instability in the Middle East as a result of the wars started by his predecessor in Afghanistan and Iraq with the attendant economic downturn that accompanied them. By the time he left office, the U.S. economy was humming and the unemployment rate was at a near record low of 4.7 percent, less than half of the high of about 10 percent reached in October 2009, Obama's first year in office.[1] During his first term, the Middle East went through political changes because of the "Arab spring" in 2010–2011 with the civil war in Syria as one of the results; that war continues even as we go to press. The civil war in Syria resulted in a humanitarian crisis, something that Obama seemed unwilling or unable to address, while leaving Bashar al-Assad in power.

Obama's successor, Donald Trump, when accepting the Republican nomination for president in 2016 went through a litany of all that was wrong domestically and internationally, claiming that "I alone can fix it." As he left office in January 2021, he leaves behind for his successor: an economy in disarray and barely recovering from the impact of the coronavirus pandemic; the aftermath of that virus, which was peaking in the second or even third wave going into 2021; the United States isolated from its allies as well as estranged from most major international organizations; and a trail of broken agreements, all of which were consistent with Trump's perception that it was in the United States' best interest to go it alone. What happens next, whether the United States can—or should—regain its place as a global leader will be up to Joe Biden, the new president.

As we go through this period in the history of U.S. foreign policy, it will be important to note the direction that Obama wanted to take the country and why, and then to contrast that with decisions made by his successor, Donald

Trump, and why he made the decisions that he did. Doing so will lead to some important lessons about U.S. foreign policy, and what happens when a new president dramatically shifts direction.

PRESIDENT OBAMA AND HIS FOREIGN POLICY DIRECTION

As we consider President Obama and his foreign policy legacy, an article in the *New York Times* published in May 2016 is especially telling: "President Obama came into office seven years ago pledging to end the wars of his predecessor, George W. Bush. On May 6 [2016], with eight months left before he vacates the White House, Mr. Obama passed a somber, little-noticed milestone: he now has been at war longer than Mr. Bush, or any other American president."[2] As a candidate, Obama campaigned on the need to end the war in Iraq and he was awarded the Nobel Peace Prize in 2009 for his desire to rid the world of nuclear weapons. When he left office, neither of those things had come to fruition.

The start of Obama's second term in 2012 was characterized by increasing partisan gridlock domestically but also by chaos internationally, which seemed to continue throughout that term. Among the international issues that Obama faced at the start of his second term were civil war in Syria, unstable situations in Iraq, Afghanistan, and Libya, Russia flexing its muscles, eventually resulting in the invasion and takeover of Crimea in 2014, and China becoming more blatant about its intentions to equal if not overtake the United States as a global power. These issues remained when Obama left office in 2017 with U.S. troops still in Iraq and Afghanistan. Some of these events are the result of situations beyond the control of the president and the United States for, as we have seen, no matter how much a president wants to be proactive, often there is no choice except to react or respond to external events. As president, ultimately it was up to Obama to determine what was in the U.S. national interest and changing U.S. priorities during his administration. The full extent of Obama's legacy will not be known for a while, but even in the short term, some assessment is possible.

THE OBAMA ADMINISTRATION IN RETROSPECT

The 2008 election brought Barack Obama to office as the first African American president. Candidate Obama distinguished himself by his lofty rhetoric, which the country wanted to hear in the midst of two foreign wars and economic recession. By the election of 2012, the optimism that characterized the 2008 election was replaced by a sense of reality. Those who had supported Obama were disappointed that he did not seem to live up to all his promises, a task made more difficult by a divided government after the election of 2010. That said, Obama did manage to put into place the Affordable Care Act ("Obamacare"), which was the first major change in U.S. health policy since the introduction of Medicare in 1965. But it came at the price of political capital.

While focusing on domestic issues, especially the economy and passage of the Affordable Care Act, the international situation remained a challenge. What was especially disconcerting about the ongoing instability in the Middle East was the belief (or fear) that it contributed to the growth of terrorism and the assumption that the United States was actually less safe, a concern about their own countries felt by many of the U.S. allies as well. What seems to have become a proliferation of terrorist attacks alleged to have been perpetrated by individuals associated with ISIS led to an increasing sense of fear on both sides of the Atlantic. In June 2016, three suicide bombers who had allegedly entered Turkey from the ISIS stronghold of Raqqa, Syria, exploded bombs in the major airport in Istanbul, killing forty-two and wounding scores of others. While no group immediately came forward to take credit, experts believe that ISIS was behind it. This followed other major coordinated attacks in Paris in November 2015 that left 130 dead and many more wounded, and a similar attack in Brussels in March 2016 that resulted in thirty-two dead and hundreds wounded. It was believed that at least one person, who was subsequently captured, was involved with both these attacks. Another attack in Nice in July 2016 occurred during Bastille Day celebrations resulting in the death of eighty-four and hundreds wounded. Although the latter attack was believed to have been perpetrated by a "lone wolf" who allegedly had sympathy for ISIS, it contributed to an atmosphere of fear, which is what terrorists hope to achieve.

The United States was reminded of the dangers faced at home when, in June 2016, forty-nine people were shot to death and scores hospitalized, some in critical condition, following a shooting at a gay nightclub in Orlando, Florida. Although the shooter allegedly pledged allegiance to ISIS, it remains unclear whether ISIS was involved in any way, or whether the shooter was simply stating his political convictions. This followed an attack in San Bernardino, California, in December 2015 when a husband-and-wife team attacked a holiday party, resulting in the deaths of fourteen people. The husband was born in the United States to a Pakistani family while his wife was from Pakistan. They initially connected online and then met in person in Saudi Arabia where they married. As posted online, the pair allegedly had been radicalized and pledged allegiance to the Islamic State.

During a volatile presidential election season in 2016, these attacks sparked a major debate within the United States about immigration, access to guns, and what can be done to identify and stop terrorist attacks. The ease with which people can cross borders has been blamed for these attacks and raised fears that other attacks will follow. One result has been a backlash against immigrants and refugees, especially Muslims who are trying to escape the ongoing conflicts in the Middle East and parts of Africa. This anti-Muslim sentiment has been fueled by the growth of right-wing anti-immigrant parties throughout Europe as well as the rhetoric of the 2016 U.S. presidential campaign. That sentiment is threatening to obscure the aid and assistance needed not only by the refugees but by the countries that are facing extreme humanitarian crises because of conflict.

As we explore Obama's foreign policy and the legacy that he left, there are a number of positives that could not have been anticipated when he first came into office. Perhaps one of the most important changes was the Obama administration's decision to establish full diplomatic relations with Cuba. Initially announced by the two countries in December 2014, the move toward "normalization" and full diplomatic recognition culminated in the reopening of the U.S. embassy in Havana in July 2015. The last time there was an embassy in Cuba was January 1961; the embassy was closed and ties between the two countries severed at the height of the Cold War. While there were many within the United States who opposed the decision to change the relationship, especially Cuban ex-pats who fled to the United States, many also applauded it as a sign that we were truly moving into a new era.

Similarly, not without controversy was the decision to negotiate a treaty with Iran to limit its development of nuclear weapons in exchange for lifting of economic sanctions. The agreement was negotiated in spring 2015 between Iran, the United States, and the other four permanent members of the Security Council (United Kingdom, France, Russia, China) plus Germany and the European Union, known as the P5 + 1. Democrats passed a procedural vote of support for the agreement, successfully blocking a Republican resolution to reject the agreement. This allowed it to go into effect as an "executive order," rather than a formally ratified treaty. As of January 2016, the White House issued a statement that touted the successes of the agreement,[3] although this became an issue in the presidential campaign later that year and was quickly rejected by the incoming Trump administration.

In Paris, in December 2015, the successful conclusion of a climate change agreement to limit the growth of greenhouse gas emissions was seen by his supporters as another of Obama's successes as well as a credit to his ability to bring different nations together in pursuit of common goals. His opponents, however, disparaged the agreement, claiming it was another way in which

Obama was undercutting U.S. economic growth. The lesson here is that politics can put a negative political spin on something that can be seen as being important for the greater good.

The lesson for American foreign policy during the Obama administration is that despite the greatest and most proactive plans, events can intervene that take priority and disrupt proposed foreign and domestic policy agendas.

CHALLENGES FACING THE OBAMA ADMINISTRATION

It appeared that the major issue of the presidential election campaign of 2008 would be the United States' place in the world following the Bush administration. Writing in *Foreign Affairs* in 2007, then candidate Obama confronted what he saw as the failures of American leadership, and he issued a call for the United States to "rebuild the alliances, partnerships, and institutions necessary to confront common threats and enhance common security."[4] Candidate Obama echoed many of those themes in a speech in Berlin in July 2008, when he said that "we know that sometimes, on both sides of the Atlantic, we have drifted apart, and forgotten our shared destiny." He continued, "Just as American bases built in the last century still help to defend the security of this continent, so does our country still sacrifice greatly for freedom around the globe."[5] Once again, the emphasis appeared to be on the ideals of freedom and sacrifice that had been themes in U.S. foreign policy since Woodrow Wilson. But, unlike his predecessor George W. Bush, if elected president, Obama indicated that he was going to do this in a way that was consultative, with an emphasis on building and/or rebuilding the partnerships and alliances that were a mainstay of U.S. foreign policy in the past and that would allow the United States to regain its place as a global leader.

As a candidate in 2008, Obama was criticized during the primaries by his Democratic rivals and then by John McCain, his Republican opponent, for his naivety in stating that he wanted to reach out to, and negotiate with, hostile countries such as Iran. But Obama remained adamant that the most effective foreign policy would not be based solely on reliance on military might, but must be balanced with cooperation, negotiation, and diplomacy. Generally, he remained true to these values during his tenure in office.

Just a few months prior to the 2008 election, the global economic crisis hit and eclipsed all other issues in the campaign. Rightly or not, the United States was being blamed for the economic downturn that affected not only it, but also most of the rest of the world. A 2008 Pew poll found that "the U.S. image is suffering almost everywhere," due, at least in part, to the fact that "in the most economically developed countries, *people blame America for the financial crisis*" (emphasis added).[6] Thus, the emphasis of the campaign quickly shifted to economics, although Obama also made it clear that, if elected president, among his first priorities would be ending the war in Iraq, giving renewed attention to the war in Afghanistan, closing the prison camp at Guantanamo Bay, and, in general, working to restore the United States' position and prestige in the world. Although foreign policy is generally not a major concern to the American electorate, especially during a time of economic crisis, Obama's proposed package of economic reforms coupled with foreign policy priorities helped sway the public; Obama was elected along with a significant Democratic majority in the House and Senate.

Obama and Iraq and Afghanistan

After eight years in which U.S. influence internationally waned and its power—especially soft power—was undermined, many around the world as well as at home were eager to see in what direction Obama would take the United States. As he made clear in his first inaugural address, Barack Obama came into office facing critical challenges to United States foreign and security policy. In that address on January 20, 2009, Obama identified what his U.S. foreign policy priorities would be as president. To all who were watching and listening, both at home and abroad, he sent these words: "Know that America is a friend of each nation and every man, woman, and child who seeks a future of peace and dignity, and that *we are ready to lead once more*" (emphasis added).[7]

Philip Gordon notes that simply "having a new face in the White House will itself do much to restore many allies' disinclination to work closely with the United States."[8] While that was true initially, the burden was on the Obama administration to show that it could follow through on its campaign promises and that the United States could and would lead once again. As the results of the Pew Global Attitudes Project noted, "When Barack Obama is sworn in as America's new president in January [2009], he will inherit two wars in distant lands, one highly unpopular and the other going badly, along with a worldwide financial crisis that is being measured against the Great Depression. He will confront the prospect of destructive global climate change and the spread of nuclear weapons to rogue states."[9] In short, President Obama began his presidency facing a number of challenges, both domestic and international.

As promised during the campaign, once he became president, Obama turned his attention to Afghanistan. In remarks he made on March 27, 2009, shortly after taking office, Obama made it clear that there would be a new direction: "So I want the American people to understand that we have a clear and focused goal: to disrupt, dismantle, and defeat al Qaeda in Pakistan and

Afghanistan, and to prevent their return to either country in the future." He framed the changes in policy by noting that "our troops [in Afghanistan] have fought bravely against a ruthless enemy. . . . Afghans have suffered and sacrificed for their future. But for six years, Afghanistan has been denied the resources that it demands because of the war in Iraq. Now, we must make a commitment that can accomplish our goals." And in words that harkened back to the idealism of the past, he continued, *"That is a cause that could not be more just"* (emphasis added).[10]

With that, he announced the deployment of additional U.S. troops to Afghanistan to engage in direct combat with the Taliban and to help secure the borders, but also to train the Afghan forces specifically for the purpose of building an Afghan army. Clearly the goal was to strengthen the Afghan military so that the United States could be involved for a limited amount of time and with specific goals in mind, and then leave. This initial deployment was to be followed up by a "surge" of troops announced in December 2009 to assist the Afghan military. At the end of May 2016, toward the close of Obama's time in office, the United States had more than 4,000 troops in Iraq and about 9,800 in Afghanistan, far fewer than the 200,000 American troops in the two countries at the start of the Obama administration, but also a far cry from ending U.S. involvement.[11]

In his speech in March 2009, Obama made a few important points: not only was leaving Iraq and Afghanistan an important goal, but the United States simply could no longer afford to stay. Iraq and Afghanistan had already cost $1 trillion, and he also suggested "that some conflicts, no matter how morally worthy, are simply not worth the cost."[12]

In contrast to Afghanistan, in some ways, the course for the U.S. withdrawal from Iraq was set by the outgoing Bush administration. When he was running for president, "Barack Obama proposed a fixed deadline for withdrawing U.S. combat troops from Iraq, though few experts considered this a realistic proposal." Bush claimed that such a plan would lead to certain defeat in Iraq while the Democrats continued to press for a withdrawal. However, in November 2008, before leaving office Bush agreed to "a three-year deadline for the withdrawal of all U.S. troops after having insisted during the campaign that such a deadline would be totally irresponsible." It was that Status of Forces Agreement (SOFA) that became the starting point for the new Obama administration. What is especially important to note about the agreement was that neither this, nor any of the other proposals suggested, "linked withdrawals to an Iraqi political settlement, even though every counterinsurgency expert argued that this linkage was absolutely essential."[13]

Clearly, Iraq was not a war of Obama's making, and his administration consistently made it clear that it was not a war that he would have chosen to fight. That decision was made by his predecessor, leaving the United States committed for a number of years but with an apparent end point because of the terms of the SOFA. However, as Obama learned, withdrawing combat troops from Iraq did not equate with the end of conflict. Despite Obama's desire to negotiate a way to maintain a small U.S. military presence in order to ensure some stability in the country, talks between the United States and Iraq collapsed, and, consistent with the SOFA, U.S. combat forces withdrew as of December 2011. According to one news report, "Without American forces to train and assist Iraqi commandos, the insurgent group Al Qaeda in Iraq is still active in Iraq and is increasingly involved with Syria."[14]

Obama had also made it clear that his focus would be on the war in Afghanistan, which he felt suffered under the Bush administration's attention to Iraq. In one of many speeches that he gave on the subject as a candidate for office, Obama claimed that by focusing on Iraq, "we did not finish the job against al Qaeda in Afghanistan. We did not develop new capabilities to defeat a new enemy, or launch a comprehensive strategy to dry up the terrorists' base of support. We did not reaffirm our basic values, or secure our homeland." And he outlined the direction that his administration would take, emphasizing his main points: "The first step must be getting off the *wrong battlefield* in Iraq, and taking the fight to the terrorists in Afghanistan and Pakistan" (emphasis added).[15]

While dealing with these two wars, Obama was able to accomplish something that the Bush administration could not do: locate and kill Osama bin Laden. On Sunday, May 2, 2011, President Obama made the following announcement: "Tonight, I can report to the American people and to the world, the United States has conducted an operation that killed Osama bin Laden, the leader of al Qaeda, and a terrorist who's responsible for the murder of thousands of innocent men, women, and children." In his brief statement Obama also made it clear that "we must also reaffirm that the United States is not— and never will be—at war with Islam."[16] However, he also noted that the raid took place in Abbottabad, Pakistan, and in so doing, the United States was engaged in a military action in Pakistan, an erstwhile ally. The result was strained relations with that country at a time when the United States was still engaged in conflict in neighboring Afghanistan.

RELATIONS WITH THE MIDDLE EAST

Ties to the Islamic World

From the time that he came into office Barak Obama understood that diminished relations with the Islamic world was one of the major results of the

Bush administration policies and that he was in a unique position to try to heal that. Although he is a Christian, he had spent some of his childhood in Indonesia, the world's most populous Islamic country. He saw outreach to the Islamic world as important to mend fences as well as to establish U.S. credibility among the Islamic nations. He began the process by making a speech about U.S. relations with the Islamic world in June 2009, about five months after taking office, and did so in a Muslim country, Egypt. The speech had far-reaching consequences, despite the fact that "the Islamic world" is far greater than any one country or way of thinking.

The decision to give the speech at Cairo University in Egypt was, in itself, fraught with symbolism. While some were puzzled by his choice of Egypt, which had been less than democratic in presidential elections as well as having a relatively poor human rights record, the White House stressed the importance of Cairo as the "heart of the Muslim world." Furthermore, the speech in Cairo would virtually guarantee a Palestinian audience— important if negotiations between Israel and the Palestinians were to succeed, another of Obama's goals—as well as send an important symbolic message by choosing the first country to sign a peace agreement with Israel as the venue.

The speech itself was closely watched and was parsed not only for what it did say but also for what it did not. Obama began by recognizing the tensions that emerged between the United States and the Muslim world in general as well as acknowledging the need for a "new beginning," and outlined specific issues that the United States and the Islamic world could confront together. And he echoed a point that he had made during a speech in Ankara, Turkey, a few months prior and that he would reprise in his statement following the death of bin Laden: *"America is not—and never will be—at war with Islam"* (emphasis added). However, he also made it clear that the United States will "relentlessly confront violent extremists who pose a grave threat to our security—because we reject the same thing that people of all faiths reject: the killing of innocent men, women, and children."[17]

In saying this, President Obama drew an important distinction between the Islamic people and the terrorists or extremists who attacked and threatened the United States and its allies. In contrast to his predecessor, Obama made it clear that he understood the difference between a war of necessity (Afghanistan) and war of choice (Iraq), and that he would engage in the latter only when it becomes necessary. He also stressed that his emphasis would be on the use of diplomacy and soft power.

EXCERPTS FROM REMARKS BY
PRESIDENT OBAMA ON A NEW BEGINNING
JUNE 4, 2009
CAIRO UNIVERSITY, EGYPT

Thank you very much. Good afternoon. I am honored to be in the timeless city of Cairo, and to be hosted by two remarkable institutions. For over a thousand years, Al-Azhar has stood as a beacon of Islamic learning; and for over a century, Cairo University has been a source of Egypt's advancement. And together, you represent the harmony between tradition and progress. I'm grateful for your hospitality, and the hospitality of the people of Egypt. And I'm also proud to carry with me the goodwill of the American people, and a greeting of peace from Muslim communities in my country: Assalaamu alaykum. . . .

I've come here to Cairo to seek a new beginning between the United States and Muslims around the world, one based on mutual interest and mutual respect, and one based upon the truth that America and Islam are not exclusive and need not be in competition [emphasis added] Instead, they overlap, and share common principles—principles of justice and progress; tolerance and the dignity of all human beings. . . . There must be a sustained effort to listen to each other; to learn from each other; to respect one another; and to seek common ground. . . .

. . . I have known Islam on three continents before coming to the region where it was first revealed. That experience guides my conviction that partnership between America and Islam must be based on what Islam is, not what it isn't. And I consider it part of my responsibility as President of the United States to fight against negative stereotypes of Islam wherever they appear. . . .

And so in that spirit, let me speak as clearly and as plainly as I can about some specific issues that I believe we must finally confront together. . . .

In Ankara, I made clear that *America is not—and never will be— at war with Islam* [emphasis added]. We will, however, relentlessly confront violent extremists who pose a grave threat to our security— because we reject the same thing that people of all faiths reject: the killing of innocent men, women, and children. And it is my first duty as President to protect the American people. . . .

So America will defend itself, respectful of the sovereignty of nations and the rule of law. And we will do so in partnership with Muslim communities which are also threatened. The sooner the extremists are isolated and unwelcome in Muslim communities, the sooner we will all be safer. . . .

Too many tears have been shed. Too much blood has been shed. All of us have a responsibility to work for the day when the mothers of Israelis and Palestinians can see their children grow up without fear; when the Holy Land of the three great faiths is the place of peace that God intended it to be; when Jerusalem is a secure and lasting home for Jews and Christians and Muslims, and a place for all of the children of Abraham to mingle peacefully together as in the story of Isra when Moses, Jesus, and Mohammed, peace be upon them, joined in prayer. . . .

This last point is important because there are some who advocate for democracy only when they're out of power; once in power, they are ruthless in suppressing the rights of others. So no matter where it takes hold, government of the people and by the people sets a single standard for all who would hold power: You must maintain your power through consent, not coercion; you must respect the rights of minorities, and participate with a spirit of tolerance and compromise; you must place the interests of your people and the legitimate workings of the political process above your party. Without these ingredients, elections alone do not make true democracy. . . .

The issues that I have described will not be easy to address. But we have a responsibility to join together on behalf of the world that we seek—a world where extremists no longer threaten our people, and American troops have come home; a world where Israelis and Palestinians are each secure in a state of their own, and nuclear energy is used for peaceful purposes; a world where governments serve their citizens, and the rights of all God's children are respected. Those are mutual interests. That is the world we seek. But we can only achieve it together.

I know there are many—Muslim and non-Muslim—who question whether we can forge this new beginning. Some are eager to stoke the flames of division, and to stand in the way of progress. Some suggest that it isn't worth the effort—that we are fated to disagree, and civilizations are doomed to clash. Many more are simply skeptical that real change can occur. There's so much fear, so much mistrust that has built up over the years. But if we choose to be bound by the past, we will never move forward. And I want to particularly say this to young people of every faith, in every country—you, more than anyone, have the ability to reimagine the world, to remake this world.

We have the power to make the world we seek, but only if we have the courage to make a new beginning, keeping in mind what has been written. . . .

Available at https://obamawhitehouse.archives.gov/the-press-office/remarks-president-cairo-university-6-04-09.

In identifying the issues that countries need to address together, Obama focused on many that were of special interest to his audience in the Middle East and Islamic world, including the countries of Iraq and Israel and the Palestinian people. And in a point directed especially to Iran, he spoke of the need to stop the spread of nuclear weapons. In a clear criticism of Egyptian President Mubarak as well as other autocratic leaders, Obama also spoke of those who "once in power . . . are ruthless in suppressing the rights of others."[18] Implied in his words was not the rhetoric of "regime change" or "axis of evil," but rather, the recognition that ultimately it must be up to the people of the state to make decisions about their form of government. Clearly, the United States would help promote the ideals that are important by providing economic aid and assistance, expanding access to education, technological development, and so on. But to be effective, it would have to be a partnership, and the goals that he outlined could be achieved only if countries work together.

In retrospect, it is possible to ponder whether those words helped foment the nascent rebellion that led to the Arab Spring and the Egyptian uprising and overthrow of Mubarak in February 2011. What Obama could not have anticipated was the subsequent election of Mohamed Morsi from the Muslim Brotherhood and his ouster by the military in July 2013, leading to political chaos and violence in Egypt.

Iran and the Nuclear Arms Deal

In January 2002, then president George W. Bush referred to Iran as one of the three "axis of evil" countries, with Iraq and North Korea as the other two. As is often the case, external events helped to create an atmosphere that was conducive to talks with Iran during the Obama administration. Hassan Rouhani was elected president of Iran in June 2013 on a platform of political and economic reform. Soon after, Secretary of State John Kerry met with Iran's Western-leaning foreign minister Mohammad Javad Zarif in what was described as "the first high-level talks between the two countries since the Islamic Revolution thirty-four years earlier," talks that Kerry described as "productive and cordial,"[19] thus setting the stage for further discussions. Working with the other members of the Security Council plus Germany, Iran, and the so-called P5+1 group made progress on negotiations leading ultimately to the signing of the Joint Comprehensive Plan of Action (JCPOA) more commonly known as the Iran nuclear deal in July 2015.

It is clear that Iran was willing to engage in an agreement at that point, as the economic sanctions that had been imposed by the international community were having an impact on the country. In fact, these sanctions "had a political impact . . . because the country [Iran] had only one significant source of income, the sale of energy. By limiting energy imports the sanctions put considerable economic and therefore political pressure on the regime."[20] Those sanctions helped contribute to the election of Rouhani and the apparent desire to change the relationship with the rest of the world in a way that would benefit Iran. Hence, the stage was set for reaching an agreement that would limit progress on the Iranian nuclear program while also ensuring that the economic sanctions would be lifted contingent on Iran's compliance with the terms.

This 159-page agreement included "the most intrusive inspection procedures of any nuclear arms control pact in history, blocking all of Iran's possible paths to a nuclear weapon. In exchange for dismantling its nuclear programs, the P5+1 nations would lift economic sanctions that they'd imposed on Iran after discovering its covert uranium enrichment plants, which were illegal under the Non-Proliferation Treaty."[21] This agreement was consistent with Obama's stated goal of ridding the world of nuclear weapons (for which he won a Nobel Peace Prize in 2009), and he saw this as an important step toward ensuring world peace. The treaty drew opposition from many of the Republicans in Congress and also from Israel, who were opposed to any agreement with the government of Iran. Other countries in the region that were putative allies of the United States, such as Saudi Arabia, Turkey, and Egypt, were also wary of the agreement and of U.S. motives. But it was the Congress that provided the greatest hurdle to the success of the agreement. Facing opposition in Congress, Obama did not submit it for ratification by the Senate, instead claiming that the United States had entered into an "executive agreement," which was within the purview of the president. Because it was not a formal treaty that had been ratified by the Senate, the Trump administration could easily withdraw from it as noted below, despite the fact that there was ongoing evidence that Iran was complying with the terms.

The United States and Israel

In going to Cairo and also in a separate meeting with Israeli Prime Minister Netanyahu, Obama also made it clear that the United States would again be an active participant in peace talks between Israel and the Palestinians. Working toward Middle East peace had been a priority of the United States in the past but had languished under the Bush administration. In contrast, Obama signaled early on that the United States would be actively engaged in the peace process once again. The decision to appoint George Mitchell as special envoy to the Middle East was a sign of the seriousness with which this administration took the Middle East negotiations. Mitchell, the former Senate majority leader, had been appointed by President Clinton to help negotiate a settlement in Northern Ireland, which resulted in the signing of the Good Friday Agreement in 1998. Appointing Mitchell was proof positive of this administration's commitment to the peace process.

In 2008, Mitchell began negotiating with Israel and the Palestinians following meetings that were held between Obama and Secretary of State Hillary Clinton and the major actors in the region. Mitchell's goal was to build trust that would ensure an atmosphere conducive to an agreement.[22] However, Obama and his team quickly learned that wanting something to happen in the world of foreign policy is not the same as making it happen. In May 2011, after years of meeting with the Israelis and Palestinians, the White House announced that Mitchell was resigning his position "as the chief United States envoy to the Israelis and Palestinians amid growing frustration over the impasse in peace talks."[23] Not only did this end the negotiations, but years of tense relations between the United States and Israel followed. In part, this was due to the difficult personal relationship between Obama and Israel's Prime Minister Netanyahu. With the appointment of John Kerry as Secretary of State at the start of the second term of the Obama administration, resuming negotiations between Israel and the Palestinians became a high priority once again, as did "resetting" the relationship between the United States and Israel. However, these good intentions did not come to fruition.

In January 2015, in violation of established protocol, then Speaker of the House John Boehner issued an invitation to Israel's prime minister Benjamin Netanyahu to address a joint session of Congress specifically about the negotiations between the United States and Iran. The speech was scheduled for March 3, two weeks before Israel's elections, thus making it a highly charged political event in both the United States and Israel. Obama refused to schedule a formal meeting with Netanyahu, and a number of members of Congress, primarily Democrats, refused to attend the congressional session. A successful negotiation to the Israeli-Palestinian issue will not be part of Obama's legacy, although the Trump administration took this on as part of its foreign policy agenda. This is discussed in more detail below.

The "Arab Spring" and Civil War in Syria

Ensuring stability in the Middle East became even more important in the wake of the revolutions and unrest that swept the region at the end of Obama's first term. A rebellion that began in Tunisia in December 2010 led to the ouster of that country's president, Zine El Abidine Ben Ali, in January 2011. Thanks to technology and the ease with which information could be transmitted, the popular uprising against autocratic leaders quickly spread to other countries in the region, including Libya, where fighting continued through the summer, ending in October 2011 when Gaddafi was captured and then killed.

Egypt, an important ally of the United States, was another country affected by the revolutions of the Arab Spring. In the midst of the political unrest, on February 11, 2011, Hosni Mubarak stepped down after more than thirty years as president, to be replaced initially by the military and then by Muslim Brotherhood candidate Mohammed Morsi following elections in June 2012. In July 2013 Morsi was deposed in a coup and was replaced as president by Abdul Fattah al-Sisi, the former head of Egypt's armed forces. Al-Sisi resigned from the military in March 2014 and ran successfully for president of Egypt; he was sworn in on June 8, 2014. Having al-Sisi elected president was important to the relationship between the United States and Egypt, which is a major recipient of U.S. foreign aid. The more than $1 billion a year in military aid that the United States gave to Egypt would be cut off if Morsi's overthrow was deemed a military coup.

Al-Sisi was elected to a second four-year term as president in 2014, and on the surface, it appeared that Egypt finally had a democratic government. That was not to last, however. Al-Sisi's allies in the parliament worked to change the constitution to eliminate term limits, meaning that al-Sisi could serve beyond the time his term in office was officially scheduled to end in 2022. The changes also strengthened the military and extended the powers of the president over the courts and judges. Many of these changes were passed in April 2019 during a time when al-Sisi was on a visit to Washington to meet with President Trump. After Trump proclaimed him to be a "great president," al-Sisi was further empowered and has continued to consolidate his powers.[24]

Civil War in Syria

The civil war in Syria exacerbated an already unstable situation in the Middle East. Unlike the uprisings in Tunisia, Libya, and Egypt that collectively formed what has become known as "The Arab Spring," the outbreak of violence in Syria in 2011 did not result in the overthrow of ruler Bashar al-Assad but rather led to an all-encompassing civil war. By 2012, fighting had reached the capital city of Damascus and the major commerce center of Aleppo, as the rebel forces battled the military arm of the government. How to respond to this created a dilemma for the Obama administration.[25]

In August 2014, the imminent genocide of thousands of Yazidis who had fled their villages for the Sinjar mountains near the Iraq-Syria border to escape ISIS finally prompted U.S. action. Obama authorized air strikes against ISIS with assistance by Kurdish forces, Britain, and a number of other countries, which saved thousands of lives. Obama also made it clear, however, that he would not deploy American ground forces to fight in Syria.

Despite the success of this intervention as a humanitarian mission, what remains controversial is that Obama mounted these attacks without congressional authorization. As air attacks continued against ISIS forces in Syria as well as Iraq, justified on humanitarian grounds as well as the need to send a signal to the terrorist group, questions remained as to whether the president needed congressional authorization, a delicate political issue domestically. This issue surfaced again in the run-up to the presidential election of 2016.

As we go to press in 2021, the civil war in Syria continues to bedevil the United States and its allies. What began in March 2011 as a popular uprising against the Assad regime has grown into a bloody civil war that had claimed the lives of more than 380,000 people as of April 2020, with the death toll continuing to rise.[26] In addition, the UN High Commissioner for Refugees has estimated that more than 5.5 million people have fled Syria, with almost seven million displaced within the country.[27] Since the summer of 2012 the ancient city of Aleppo has become a major battleground, divided between government and rebel forces. Seen as a major prize, it has been the focus of attacks that have resulted in the deaths of thousands of civilians, with hundreds of thousands more at risk.

On July 22, 2013, the House and Senate both voted to approve the Obama administration's plans to initiate a CIA operation to send weapons shipments to opposition fighters in Syria. But this decision was not without controversy, and it reflected the partisan politics already playing out in Washington, as well as clearly illustrating the complexity of the situation. On the one hand, Democratic members of Congress as well as those in the administration claimed that "it will allow the administration to exert leadership and coordinate the many streams of aid flowing to the rebels from other countries, including sophisticated surface-to-air missiles coming from Saudi Arabia and other countries in the Persian Gulf."[28] They also claimed that this involvement would ensure that the arms would go to members of the Free Syrian Army rather than extremists fighting on behalf of President Bashar al-Assad and that it would help establish U.S. ties with the opposition movement. On the other hand, Republican members of Congress argued that this proposal did not do enough and that the United States should be taking a stronger stand. However, at a time when the United States finally seemed to be extricating itself from the wars in Iraq and Afghanistan, few members of Congress seemed willing to risk U.S. involvement in another war in the Middle East without any clearly defined national interest. As the bloodshed and humanitarian crisis caused by the war continues, questions remain about whether the United States and/or its European allies should have been more actively involved.[29]

Writing in the *Wall Street Journal* in July 2012 columnist Gerald F. Seib posed two important questions that are worth thinking about not only for the Obama administration but also for the Trump administration that followed: "Does the U.S., with a shrunken checkbook and a weary military, have the power to steer events [in the Middle East]? And does the U.S., tired after a decade of war in Iraq and happy to be growing less dependent on Middle East oil, even care enough to try?"[30] What is clear is that the region cannot be ignored and that there are no easy answers that can be tied to U.S. national interest. Nonetheless, the Middle East became grist for the presidential campaign in 2016 and is an issue that the Trump administration also tried to deal with as well, albeit unsuccessfully.

U.S. RELATIONS WITH OTHER PARTS OF THE WORLD UNDER OBAMA

U.S. Relations with Russia

Relations between the United States and Russia have been difficult, especially following Russia's 2014 invasion of Ukraine and subsequent takeover of Crimea. Despite differences as to the desired outcome in Syria—Russia supports Assad while the United States and other Western countries would like to see him gone—the members of the UN Security Council all agreed that the highest priority is negotiating and implementing a cease-fire. The United States and Russia briefly worked together to achieve that goal. In September 2016, the two countries were able to broker a pause in the fighting, which lasted about seven days before the Syrian military declared it over and resumed attacks on the rebel-held parts of Aleppo. The cease-fire negotiated between the United States and Russia initially was seen as a confidence-building measure between the two countries; instead, it became another source of acrimony.[31]

It seems clear that President Putin was trying to chart an independent path for Russia even though that put it in direct conflict with the countries of the West in general and the United States in particular. In March 2016, facing mounting international pressure, President Putin announced that "the main part" of Russia's forces would leave Syria having accomplished their mission. Although Russia did recall a handful of aircraft, the reality is that it remains a major presence in Syria. According to one analysis, on the ground "Russia seems to be running the show," with Russian and Syrian forces operating "on Russian terms."[32] In addition to bringing discipline to the haphazard Syrian military forces, Russian forces are involved in intelligence and targeting operations, Russian instructors train their Syrian counterparts, and

Russian officers have been involved with brokering cease-fires at the local level. In short, Russia seems to be in Syria for the long haul.[33]

According to a BBC analysis of the situation: "What began as another Arab Spring uprising against an autocratic ruler has mushroomed into a brutal proxy war that has drawn in regional and world powers." Further, "Iran and Russia have propped up the Alawite-led government of President Assad and gradually increased their support. Tehran is believed to be spending billions of dollars a year to bolster Mr. Assad, providing military advisers and subsidized weapons, as well as lines of credit and oil transfers. Russia has meanwhile launched an air campaign against Mr. Assad's opponents."[34] Hence, Syria is another battleground for playing out U.S.-Russian confrontation.

Russia and the 2016 Election

In many ways it appears that relations between the United States and Russia became as tense as at any point since the Cold War. This was played out in the 2016 presidential election campaign with Republican contender Donald Trump saying complimentary things about President Putin, while Democrat Hillary Clinton said that the relationship between the two countries is a complicated one. Like many other areas in the 2016 campaign, how to approach Russia and Putin was one of the major policy differences between the two candidates.

As far back as 2013, when Rex Tillerson, Trump's first secretary of state, was CEO of Exxon-Mobil Oil, he met with Vladimir Putin, who confided that "he detested Obama." Rather, he told Tillerson, "'I've given up on your president. I'll wait for your next president to see if I can get along with him.'"[35] It was obvious that Putin wanted Trump to win, and it has become clear that Russia engaged in a number of activities to further that goal; since that time, information has become readily available that Russia intervened in the election on behalf of Donald Trump. While Russia denied any involvement, there were a number of meetings prior to the election between members of Trump's campaign staff and individuals connected to Russia. Members of the U.S. intelligence community confirmed that there was interference on the part of Russia and as early as fall 2016, before the election. U.S. officials warned Moscow to stop their actions, followed by a statement by Obama warning Putin to stop the activities or face "serious consequences" if he did not. On December 29, 2016, Obama issued an executive order announcing measures to punish Russia for interfering in the elections, including the imposition of sanctions, closing two Russian compounds in the United States, and expelling thirty-five diplomats accused of spying.[36] While this angered the incoming Trump administration, Russian Ambassador Sergey Kislyak had a conversation with incoming director of the National Security Council, Michael Flynn, who "assured the ambassador that the incoming administration would likely resist sanctions and possibly rescind them." In doing so, "Flynn was undermining the current administration and breaking the standards of diplomacy."[37] Flynn lasted only twenty-four days on the job, and when he later lied about this communication, it became the basis for his arrest and subsequent jailing. It should be noted that toward the end of his term, President Trump pardoned Flynn.

The intelligence community and subsequently a Senate investigation concluded that there was overwhelming evidence that the Russian government did interfere in the election, with evidence also suggesting that the goal was to help Trump win. While there is no evidence that its role affected the outcome of the election, it did put the United States on notice about the possibility of foreign interference in our elections, but also contributed to incoming President Trump's suspicion of the intelligence community, which would affect his relationship with that important part of the government throughout his tenure in office.[38]

U.S. Relations with Europe

Relations between the United States and its European allies had been strained severely because of the U.S. decision to go to war with Iraq in 2003. The enmity that many in Europe felt toward the United States was heightened by the onset of the economic crisis in 2008, which, correctly or not, was blamed on the United States.[39] Obama initially met with many European leaders either individually or as part of summits, and he came into office wildly popular in Europe. Nonetheless, the lesson that Obama learned is that Europe is no longer an unquestioning ally, willing to go along with whatever the United States wants or wherever the United States leads. Knowing that, Obama worked hard to reestablish relationships with the European allies.

The results of a Pew Global Attitudes poll show that in 2012, near the end of his first term in office and despite Obama's desire to distance himself from Bush administration policies, concerns remained about the ways in which the United States uses its military power. These concerns were exacerbated by news about the U.S. use of drone strikes to target perceived extremist groups in countries such as Pakistan and Yemen.[40] Also contributing to this was the administration's inability to live up to its promise to close the prison at Guantanamo Bay in Cuba, a promise that Obama was never able to keep during his eight years in office.

There are important lessons to be learned from the U.S. relationship with its European allies and the interaction between and among them. First is the fact that the individual president, in this case Barack Obama, has a direct impact on perceptions that other countries, even allies, have of the United States. We can see this clearly with the change in attitudes toward the United States from the period of the Bush presidency to Obama's and again from Obama to Trump. Second, even though many both at home and abroad disagreed with some of the administration's policies, other countries retained confidence in the United States and in this president to lead. And third, even though there might be a decline in the overall popularity of the president, there is still a belief in the importance of the relationships—political, military, and economic—between the United States and the countries of Europe. That relationship, however, was threatened once again during the 2016 presidential campaign. Where candidate Hillary Clinton spoke of the importance of such relationships, candidate Trump disparaged them, thereby sowing seeds for future mistrust.

The European allies have their own issues to deal with, as they have to determine how to respond to the results of the "Brexit" vote in June 2016 and the British decision to leave the European Union. Although it might appear that this has little to do with the United States, the reality is that the United States is tied to the European Union as a bloc economically; it is the largest trading partner that the United States has. Also the possible breakup of the European Union raises questions about European security and what this might mean for NATO. During the 2016 presidential campaign candidate Trump raised questions about the relevance of NATO in the wake of the Cold War, claiming that the United States is bearing too much of the burden for Europe's security. In contrast, candidate Clinton talked about the importance of NATO, especially in the face of a resurgent Russia. This difference in approach reflects the divergence between the two candidates about Russia in general, with Trump talking about Putin in complimentary terms and hinting that the United States and Russia could (and should) work together to address the crisis in Syria and elsewhere, while Clinton called Putin a "bully." Trump's relationship to Putin is discussed in more detail below.

Prior to the end of her tenure as secretary of state, Clinton warned Obama about Russia, claiming that relations between the two countries (Russia and the United States) were at a low point. This is another example of the difference in perspective between the two candidates and illustrates why the rest of the world watches U.S. elections, especially presidential ones, so closely. Trump's dismissal of NATO during the campaign and his assertions that U.S. support of the NATO allies would be contingent on their willingness to increase their financial contribution to the alliance raised concerns among the European allies. Uncertainty regarding the future of NATO and the strength of the partnership caused consternation on both sides of the Atlantic, further contributing to concerns about a resurgent Russia.

"Pivot to the Pacific"

China's rise as a major regional, if not global, power is perhaps one of the challenges to the United States for any number of reasons. China is highly integrated into the global economy in general, and the U.S. economy in particular, which, to a large extent, constrains the policy options available to the United States. On the one hand, a sound argument can be made that China's integration into and role in the world economy suggest that it is unlikely to engage in any armed conflict that would disturb that balance. On the other hand, China's aggressive actions in Asia, and especially in the South and East China Seas since 2013, have resulted in tensions between China and the United States and its allies in the region, especially Japan, but have also led to the question of whether China's continued ascendency can remain peaceful.

Hence, U.S. relations with China seem to be especially problematic. As the 2010 *Nuclear Posture Review Report* notes, "The United States and China's Asian neighbors remain concerned about China's current modernization efforts, including its qualitative and quantitative modernization of its nuclear arsenal." Moreover, "the lack of transparency surrounding its nuclear programs—their pace and scope, as well as the strategy and doctrine that guide them—raises questions about China's future intentions."[41] It is this uncertainty that is so problematic for the United States, but also for other states in the region that wonder about China's intentions. In fall 2011, President Obama announced a shift in U.S. policy that was known as "the pivot to the Pacific." Obama took the opportunity of a visit to Australia in November 2011 to announce an agreement that would expand military cooperation between the two allies and would enhance U.S. military presence in the region by deploying U.S. marines to a base in Darwin in the northern part of Australia. By framing the increased U.S. presence in the Asia-Pacific region as a cooperative agreement between the United States and Australia, a traditional ally, analysts said that it would appear to be a less-confrontational policy than the United States might otherwise have pursued, although clearly it sends a message to China as well as to other U.S. allies in the region and beyond that the United States will stand by its security agreements.

A Pew Global Attitudes poll in 2014 revealed an interesting, and also problematic, shift in global perceptions about both the United States and China. According to the report, general publics around the world see a shift in the global balance of power, with China's economic might on the rise, and they perceive that China will eventually surpass the United States as the world's dominant superpower. But overall, more people perceive the United States more favorably than they do China, seeing the United States as a better partner and more willing than China to consider other countries' interests.[42]

One of the successes of the Obama administration regarding Asia was the completion of the Trans-Pacific Partnership (TPP) in 2016, a free trade agreement that would link the United States, Canada, and Mexico with nine other countries that border the Pacific Ocean. According to the Office of the Trade Representative, if approved this agreement would result in benefits for the United States, including eliminating a number of taxes and tariffs that work against the United States, incorporating protections for U.S. workers, and adding environmental protections.[43] Nonetheless, pressure from Democratic presidential contender Bernie Sanders resulted in candidate Clinton's pledge not to put the agreement forward for approval, a position shared by Trump. As noted below, Trump actually pulled the United States out of that agreement, thereby paving the way for China to play a major role in the region and even globally. We will return to this theme below.

U.S. Relations with Africa

In addition to dealing with the changing power balance in Asia, the United States has been working hard to establish a role in Africa, a region that has long been neglected by this country. Many countries are starting to recognize the important contributions that Africa can make internationally in a globalized world. However, Sub-Saharan Africa had generally not been a primary area of focus of U.S. foreign policy. Even during periods of civil war and genocide in countries such as Rwanda and Sudan, the United States remained removed from any active policies beyond verbally condemning the acts. Because Africa was seen as outside the U.S. sphere of influence, successive presidents, including Clinton and Bush, could not justify U.S. military intervention. As the first African American president and with a Kenyan father, Obama has stronger ties to Africa than any previous president. His decision to visit Ghana following the G8 summit in July 2009 was seen as an indicator that U.S. policy toward Africa might become more proactive in an Obama administration. And the visit of Michelle Obama to South Africa in June 2011 was also seen as a positive step. But the reality is that little changed regarding U.S. foreign policy toward the continent.

That point became clear when Obama and his family visited three African countries, Senegal, South Africa, and Tanzania, at the end of June 2013. That visit was overshadowed by the illness of Nelson Mandela, who was then hospitalized in critical condition. Throughout his trip, in his various speeches Obama paid homage to Mandela, although he did not make a visit to see the ailing leader. He did take the opportunity to unveil what he called "a new partnership with Africa, one that would help sustain its recent run of tremendous economic growth while broadening the rewards to help as many people as possible."[44] Trade between the United States and Africa has more than doubled in the past decade and Obama used the visit to stress the economic partnership between the United States and the countries of Africa.[45]

By coincidence, former-President George W. Bush was in Tanzania at the same time as the Obama visit, which could not help but create comparisons between the two administrations. While in office, Mr. Bush started the Millennium Challenge Corporation to direct aid to African states that tried to reform corrupt and undemocratic governments. He also initiated the President's Emergency Plan for AIDS Relief, or PEPFAR, which invested tens of billions of dollars to fighting HIV, and later tackled malaria and tuberculosis. Thus, while the policies of the Bush administration continue to remain suspect at home, his work with Africa has been widely applauded. In contrast, Obama's critics claim that Obama has not done enough for and with Africa. In response to that implicit charge, Obama has sought "to demonstrate his own commitment to improving the lives of Africans, announcing plans to bolster trade and investment, improve the delivery of electricity and expand PEPFAR to combat other diseases."[46] And Obama promised to return to the continent before his second term ended, which he did. In addition to his visit in 2013, in 2015 he visited Kenya and Ethiopia. At a time when China has been paying more attention to the countries of Africa, investing in them economically, the United States really has done little to strengthen the relationship with the countries in this rapidly developing continent.

OTHER CHALLENGES TO THE UNITED STATES UNDER OBAMA

As we look at Obama's legacy, it is clear that the idealistic views he put forward at the start of his first term, to "rebuild alliances, partnerships, and institutions," would neither be as easy nor as predictable as he had thought or hoped. Rather, events intervened that deflected the path that he had hoped to take. Making Obama's task even more challenging has been an intransigent House of Representatives with a Republican majority that took power in 2010 and a Republican majority in the Senate. While the country's founders advocated for divided government as a form of protection against tyranny of the government, they could not have anticipated the gridlock in Washington that has made it even more difficult to get legislation passed. The economic crisis that broke just before the November 2008 election had to take priority over all else. Consistent with the terms of the SOFA, Obama ended the war in Iraq, although instability continues in that country. While the U.S. combat role in Afghanistan formally ended in 2014, a small American military presence has remained (although done without congressional authorization) primarily to provide air support for Afghan forces who continue to fight the Taliban and ISIS forces. What Obama could not have imagined or anticipated were the revolutions that swept the Middle East and that continue to cause havoc in Egypt and Syria.

Furthermore, Obama had to confront new threats: cyberterrorism and cybersecurity have become major factors in ensuring the security of the United States in a way that could not have been imagined even in 2008 when Obama was first running for office. Yet now they are a fact of life during an age in which technology is ubiquitous. Similarly, climate change presents an ongoing concern as changing weather patterns have contributed not only to major storms but also to unprecedented heat, drought, and floods in parts of the country. Issues of what feminist authors call "human security"—protecting health and preventing disease, access to clean water, equal educational opportunity, for example—also have been surfacing as more important globally as well as being challenging to deal with.

OBAMA'S LEGACY

The presidential election campaign of 2016 presented very different and conflicting views of the role of the United States and the future of U.S. foreign policy. Republican candidate Donald Trump offered a dark vision of an America under threat, a claim aided by the various terrorist attacks that had taken place earlier in the summer. In contrast, Democratic candidate Hillary Clinton presented a picture of a strong country further strengthened by decisions made by President Obama. The reality is probably a little of each.

In fact, there is little debate that there was a resurgence of apparently terrorist violence, although it still remains unclear whether some of these were "lone wolf" attacks or part of a larger plan perpetrated by ISIS. Going into the 2016 election the Middle East remained in chaos, with the civil war in Syria a critical factor for both security and humanitarian reasons. The Israeli-Palestinian situation was no closer to resolution and the future of both Afghanistan and Iraq remained uncertain. A general election held in South Africa in August 2014 as well as local elections in 2016 raised questions about the stability that followed the end of apartheid and, as one of the continent's largest and most stable countries, there were questions about that country's future. The rise of the terrorist group Boko Haram made the situation in Nigeria, an oil-producing country and member of OPEC, unstable. Refugees fleeing conflict in the Middle East as well as environmental issues in Africa continued to flood into Europe, raising questions about the responsibilities of individual countries as well as the international system toward these people who have fled their homeland. And while many of these issues and problems seem to be removed from the United States, the reality is that countries still looked to the United States to provide guidance and leadership. The challenge for the president coming into office in January 2017 became how to address this range of international challenges without neglecting the many domestic priorities that also needed attention.

Foreign policy is not made in a vacuum. Rather, it is a response to events that have occurred while also trying to anticipate what might take place. As we consider Obama's legacy and what President Trump inherited, we must also be aware that despite the best planning, things happen that cannot be anticipated and that will come to the top of the foreign policy agenda. It is how a president deals with those that shape the legacy and how the president will ultimately be judged.

THE ELECTION OF DONALD TRUMP

"Democratic backsliding today begins at the ballot box."[47] Very few pundits and election prognosticators predicted the election of Donald Trump in 2016. Hillary Clinton, former U.S. senator from New York, secretary of state under popular president Barack Obama, and wife of a former president seemed to have all the political credentials. Further, many seemed to be ready for a woman in the White House. Despite the polls, which indicated that she was leading (and she did win the popular vote by more than three million), it was Donald Trump who won the Electoral College and therefore the presidency.

He came into office with no background in government, the military or security, or public policy. Rather, as a businessman, he claimed he understood how to make a deal. His campaign was all about how to "Make America Great Again," claiming that the United States had been taken advantage of consistently by trade partners and allies as well as by adversaries. As he noted in his acceptance speech at the Republican National Convention in July 2016, "'Nobody knows the system better than me, which is why I alone can fix it.'"[48]

As we have seen throughout the book, historically, the speech made by the incoming president at his inauguration sets a tone for the administration that follows. For example, as noted in chapter 2, Woodrow Wilson's first inaugural address outlined the values that he hoped would guide his administration.[49] And the high-minded rhetoric of John Kennedy's inauguration address set a tone for his brief time in office: "Let every nation know, whether it wishes us well or ill, that we shall pay any price, bear any burden, meet any hardship, support any friend, oppose any foe, in order to assure the survival and the success of liberty. This much we pledge—and more."[50] Donald Trump's inaugural address, on January 20, 2017, in many ways was a harbinger of what his four years in office would be like. Unlike the soaring rhetoric and ties to American values that typically characterize such speeches, Trump's was a dark vision of the United States, both domestically and internationally. It is interesting to contrast it with other more "typical" inaugural addresses.

EXCERPTS FROM DONALD J. TRUMP'S INAUGURAL ADDRESS JANUARY 20, 2017

We, the citizens of America, are now joined in a great national effort to rebuild our country and to restore its promise for all of our people. Together, we will determine the course of America and the world for years to come.

We will face challenges. We will confront hardships. But we will get the job done. . . .

For too long, a small group in our nation's Capital has reaped the rewards of government while the people have borne the cost. Washington flourished—but the people did not share in its wealth. Politicians prospered—but the jobs left, and the factories closed. The establishment protected itself, but not the citizens of our country. Their victories have not been your victories; their triumphs have not been your triumphs; and while they celebrated in our nation's Capital, there was little to celebrate for struggling families all across our land. That all changes—starting right here, and right now, because this moment is your moment: it belongs to you. . . .

But for too many of our citizens, a different reality exists: Mothers and children trapped in poverty in our inner cities; rusted-out factories scattered like tombstones across the landscape of our nation; an education system, flush with cash, but which leaves our young and beautiful students deprived of knowledge; and the crime and gangs and drugs that have stolen too many lives and robbed our country of so much unrealized potential. *This American carnage stops right here and stops right now* [emphasis added]. . .

The oath of office I take today is an oath of allegiance to all Americans. For many decades, we've enriched foreign industry at the expense of American industry; Subsidized the armies of other countries while allowing for the very sad depletion of our military; We've defended other nation's borders while refusing to defend our own; And spent trillions of dollars overseas while America's infrastructure has fallen into disrepair and decay. We've made other countries rich while the wealth, strength, and confidence of our country has disappeared over the horizon. . ..

From this day forward, a new vision will govern our land. From this moment on, it's going to be America First. Every decision on trade, on taxes, on immigration, on foreign affairs, will be made to benefit American workers and American families. We must protect our borders from the ravages of other countries making our products, stealing our companies, and destroying our jobs. Protection will lead to great prosperity and strength. I will fight for you with every breath in my body—and I will never, ever let you down. America will start winning again, winning like never before. . ..

We will seek friendship and goodwill with the nations of the world—*but we do so with the understanding that it is the right of all nations to put their own interests first* [emphasis added]. We do not seek to impose our way of life on anyone, but rather to let it shine as an example for everyone to follow. We will reinforce old alliances and form new ones—and unite the civilized world against Radical Islamic Terrorism, which we will eradicate completely from the face of the Earth. At the bedrock of our politics will be a total allegiance to the United States of America, and through our loyalty to our country, we will rediscover our loyalty to each other.

Available at https://www.whitehouse.gov/briefings-statements/the-inaugural-address/.

An "America First" Foreign Policy

For his administration, Trump painted a picture of "America first," which suggests a return to a unilateralist or even isolationist stance. And while for many of his supporters at home Trump's message was a refreshing change and an acknowledgment that their voices would be heard, it sent a startling message to America's allies, and it raised questions about the policies that this country would adopt. One of the more interesting things to note about

Trump and his approach to foreign policy is that other Republicans before him had said many of the same things: the need for the United States to reexamine its place in the world and the support it had been giving other nations now that the Cold War was over.[51] While those were undercurrents and ideas espoused by potential candidates like Pat Buchanan and H. Ross Perot, who were not seen as part of the mainstream, with the election of Donald Trump, they resurfaced and became part of the U.S. policy structure.

The elements of Trump's "America first" agenda pervaded virtually all of the foreign policy decisions made by his administration at least through January 2020 when the advent of the coronavirus pandemic upended all aspects of the administration's policy. However, by that time the course of U.S. foreign policy was set. While there are some aspects of Trump's policy that could be seen as positive and advantageous to the United States' national interest (e.g., prodding the NATO nations to spend more on defense), some of that came at a price of U.S. prestige globally.

Keeping with his campaign promises, shortly after coming into office, in January 2017 Trump issued a Presidential Memorandum withdrawing the United States from the Trans-Pacific Partnership (TPP). Although this was one of the major multilateral accomplishments of the Obama administration that was designed to foster international trade while keeping China in check, Trump argued that "it is the intention of my Administration to deal directly with individual countries on a one-on-one (or bilateral) basis in negotiating future trade deals." The memorandum continues "I hereby direct you [the U.S. trade representative] to withdraw the United States as a signatory to the Trans-Pacific Partnership (TPP), to permanently withdraw the United States from TPP negotiations, and to begin pursuing, wherever possible, bilateral trade negotiations to promote American industry, protect American workers, and raise American wages."[52] In other words, consistent with his stated America first policy, going forward the United States would not engage in multilateral agreements but only bilateral agreements, all to be negotiated or renegotiated (in the case of NAFTA) by his administration. In June 2017 Trump pulled the United States out of the Paris Climate Agreement, again, justified on the need to negotiate a treaty that would be more favorable to the United States:

> I am fighting every day for the great people of this country. Therefore, in order to fulfill my solemn duty to protect America and its citizens, the United States will withdraw from the Paris Climate Accord . . . but begin negotiations to re-enter either the Paris Accord or a really entirely new transaction on terms that are fair to the United States, its businesses, its workers, its people, its taxpayers. So we're getting out. But we will start to negotiate, and we will see if we can make a deal that's fair. And if we can, that's great. And if we can't, that's fine.[53]

The Paris Climate Agreement was another of the accomplishments of the Obama administration and was an example of U.S. leadership in the area of climate change and global warming. Negotiating a new agreement was never a priority of the Trump administration.

The other major treaty that the United States withdrew from was the Joint Comprehensive Plan of Action (JCPOA) with Iran, more commonly known as the Iran nuclear plan. As noted above, this agreement was negotiated under Obama in coordination with a group known as the P5 +1, the permanent members of the UN Security Council (China, France, Russia, United Kingdom, United States, plus Germany) and was designed to slow Iran's nuclear program. Trump also campaigned on the need to pull the United States from this agreement, which he did in May 2018, claiming that it "failed to protect America's national security interests." Trump was quoted as saying that "The Iran Deal was one of the worst and most one-sided transactions the United States has ever entered into." Some of his top advisors, including Secretaries Mattis and Tillerson and chief of staff McMaster all tried to convince Trump that "a regionally aggressive Iran without nuclear weapons was a much better outcome than a regionally aggressive Iran armed with nukes."[54] The deal limited Iran's ability to build a nuclear weapon until at least 2030, which would leave a lot of time to maneuver until then. Trump, however, not only hated the agreement but he had made this a campaign promise that he felt that he had to honor.

Instead of that agreement, according to the White House fact sheet, "President Trump will work to assemble a broad coalition of nations to deny Iran all paths to a nuclear weapon and to counter the totality of the regime's malign activities. Nations must work together to halt the Iranian regime's destabilizing drive for regional hegemony."[55] The proposed path to doing so would be to reimpose sanctions on Iran, which the United States did unilaterally. The European Union continued to trade with Iran, and the leaders of that country remained intransigent in the face of U.S. sanctions.

These are examples of the new direction that the United States took under Trump: unilateral decisions justified by the need to ensure the best interest of the United States; withdrawing from treaties that not only had the United States agreed to but had taken a lead in accomplishing; and engaging in these policy directions without consulting allies, including those who had been most involved with the original agreements. Other aspects of his foreign policy, such as his relations with Russia and North Korea, were also unconventional and will be discussed in more detail below. Taken together, they illustrate a pattern of unilateralist action designed to further the national interest as defined by the Trump administration.

The Early Outlines for a Trump Foreign Policy

Trump actually has been very consistent in many of his views going back to his days as a New York developer, but they had a profound impact on policy once he became president. For example, on September 2, 1987, Trump took out a full-page ad in the form of an open letter to the public in three major newspapers, the *New York Times, Washington Post,* and *Boston Globe,* in which he outlined his views on foreign and security policy. He titled it "There's nothing wrong with America's Foreign Defense Policy that a little backbone can't cure." Putting this ad in context, it is important to note that this was *before* the Cold War ended and when the United States was the primary security pillar for many of our allies, such as Japan.

The first line of the ad outlines a theme that was to be a constant in his presidential campaign and then in his presidency: "For decades, Japan and other nations have been taking advantage of the United States." He continued: "Why are these nations not paying the United States for the human lives and billions of dollars we are losing to protect *their* interests?" (emphasis in original). And in a theme that would be reprised throughout his administration, Trump wrote "Make Japan, Saudi Arabia, and others pay for the protection we extend as allies." Over time, Trump's emphasis shifted from Japan and Saudi Arabia to China and the NATO nations, but the point was the same.

That ad engendered a great deal of speculation at the time as to what Trump's political intentions were. An article in the *New York Times* on the day that the ad was published stated "Donald J. Trump, one of New York's biggest and certainly one of its most vocal developers, said yesterday that he was not interested in running for political office in New York, but indicated that the Presidency was another matter."[56] What is perhaps most surprising is not that Trump ultimately decided to run for president (and won), but that as far back as 1987 he had outlined his "America first" position and desire to make other countries pay for U.S. support and security.

The Political Emergence of Donald J. Trump

From the time Donald Trump descended the gold escalator in Trump Tower, New York, on June 16, 2015, to declare his candidacy for president it was clear that the campaign and the administration would be different from "the norm." Trump's slogan of "Make America Great Again," the proliferation of MAGA paraphernalia, and the rallies that were more reminiscent of a rock concert than a political event all indicated a different approach to politics. In addition, Trump was a businessman from New York who had no experience in government nor any military training although, as indicated from his 1987

OPEN LETTER FROM DONALD J. TRUMP
PUBLISHED IN *NEW YORK TIMES, WASHINGTON POST,* AND
BOSTON GLOBE
SEPTEMBER 2, 1987

There's nothing wrong with America's Foreign Defense Policy
that a little backbone can't cure

An open letter from Donald J. Trump on why America should stop
paying to defend countries that can afford to defend themselves.

To the American people:

For decades, Japan and other nations have been taking advantage of
the United States.

The saga continues unabated as we defend the Persian Gulf, an area
of only marginal significance to the United States for its oil supplies,
but one upon which Japan and others are almost totally dependent. Why
are these nations not paying the United States for the human lives and
billions of dollars we are losing to protect *their* interests? [emphasis in
original]. Saudi Arabia, a country whose very existence is in the hands
of the United States, last week refused to allow us to use their mine
sweepers (which are, sadly, far more advanced than ours) to police
the Gulf. The world is laughing at America's politicians as we protect
ships we don't own, carrying oil we don't need, destined for allies who
won't help.

Over the years, the Japanese, unimpeded by the huge costs of defending themselves (as long as the United States will do it for free), have
built a strong and vibrant economy with unprecedented surpluses. They
have brilliantly managed to maintain a weak yen against a strong dollar. This, coupled with our monumental spending for their, and others,
defense, have moved Japan to the forefront of world economies.

Now that the tides are turning and the yen is becoming strong against
the dollar, the Japanese are openly complaining and, in typical fashion,
our politicians are reacting to these unjustified complaints.

It's time for us to end *our* vast deficits by making Japan, and others
who can afford it, pay [emphasis in original]. Our world protection is
worth hundreds of billions to those countries, and their stake in *their*
protection is far greater than ours [emphasis in original].

Make Japan, Saudi Arabia, and others pay for the protection we extend as allies. Let's help our farmers, our sick, our homeless by taking

from some of the greatest profit machines ever created—machines created and nurtured by us. Tax these wealthy nations, not America. End our huge deficit, reduce our taxes, and let America's economy grow unencumbered by the costs of defending those who can easily afford to pay us for the defense of their freedoms. Let's not let our country be laughed at anymore.

Sincerely,
Donald J. Trump

ad, he had some very definite opinions. While some, especially many of his supporters, saw the fact that he was an outsider as very positive, others associated with the Washington establishment and the national security arena especially were far less sanguine. With his election, it was apparent that the country would be deeply divided on a range of issues and the question was whether Trump, as president, could unite it, or would want to.

The European allies were especially concerned about what his election would mean for U.S.-European relations, given the rhetoric of the campaign. According to an article in the *New York Times* in November 2016, shortly after the election, "Chancellor Angela Merkel of Germany, whose immigration policies Mr. Trump has dismissed as 'insane,' offered her cooperation but emphasized the importance of human rights, while President François Hollande of France noted that some of Mr. Trump's views might test 'the values and the interests that we share with the United States.' Mexican officials congratulated Mr. Trump but said they would not pay for his proposed border wall, as he has flatly insisted they will." Mexico paying for the border wall had been one of Trump's campaign promises.[57]

What is especially interesting was the reaction of other countries to his election. Again, according to the *New York Times*, "Foreign leaders who have had tense relations with Mr. Obama were particularly welcoming to Mr. Trump. Prime Minister Benjamin Netanyahu of Israel called Mr. Trump 'a true friend' of Israel, while President Vladimir V. Putin of Russia said he hoped to have a 'constructive dialogue' with him."[58] Although Trump and Putin had not yet spoken at that time, it was clear that there was a "special" relationship between the two men, something that would come out as part of the investigations regarding Russia's interference in the 2016 election.

As concerned as some within the United States and abroad were about Trump and the policies that his administration was likely to espouse, they were reassured by the selection of some of the members of his cabinet, paramount among them the decision to name retired Marine Corps General James Mattis as his secretary of defense. Mattis was a well-respected officer who was known for his intellectual approach to understanding military and security policy and warfare. Furthermore, he believed very strongly in the importance of the allies of the United States, especially NATO, which he described at his confirmation hearings as "'the most successful military alliance probably in modern world history and maybe ever.'"[59]

Rex Tillerson, a former chief executive of ExxonMobil, was chosen by Trump to be secretary of state. Although Tillerson had no government experience, through his position with Exxon he had traveled widely, and in those travels, he got to know Vladimir Putin, whom he had first met in the 1990s. Tillerson brought to his position insights that he had gained about Putin, including his desire "to restore Russian greatness and credibility." Tillerson explained to Trump that "The only thing Putin understands is truth and power," and that he is always playing "the long game."[60] Although Trump listened to Tillerson's assessment, he "rejected the notion that Putin would try to take advantage of the United States."[61] Ultimately, Trump came to believe that he understood Putin better than anyone, including Tillerson, which allegedly was part of Tillerson's undoing as secretary of state. He was fired by Trump in March 2018 while on a diplomatic mission to Africa on behalf of the United States and was subsequently replaced by then director of the CIA, Mike Pompeo.

While Trump appointed additional experienced actors to important national security positions in the executive branch (e.g., former congressman Dan Coats as director of national intelligence and retired General John Kelly as secretary of Homeland Security), these were offset by problematic appointments, including Michael Flynn as his national security advisor. Flynn lasted just twenty-four days before he was forced to resign when it was discovered that he had lied to Vice President Pence about the nature of his communication with the Russian ambassador to the United States. Trump also allowed a range of people, including his daughter Ivanka and son-in-law Jared Kushner, to serve as advisors with offices in the White House despite the fact that they had no training or background in the areas they were asked to oversee. Again, while this served as a red flag to some in Washington, to others it was another example of Trump's unconventional way of engaging in foreign and security policy. Trump's mistrust of experts and belief that his gut instinct was the best source of information led him to make some unconventional decisions, such as his series of meetings with North Korean president Kim Jong-un.

Throughout his four years in office he stayed fairly consistent regarding his America-first message. In his address to the UN General Assembly on September 24, 2019, Trump reiterated his views when he said:

> Looking around and all over this large, magnificent planet, the truth is plain to see: If you want freedom, take pride in your country. If you want democracy, hold on to your sovereignty. And if you want peace, love your nation. Wise leaders always put the good of their own people and their own country first.
>
> The future does not belong to globalists. The future belongs to patriots. The future belongs to sovereign and independent nations who protect their citizens, respect their neighbors, and honor the differences that make each country special and unique.[62]

Political journalist Dan Balz says of this speech that "On their face, those words are not particularly discordant. But analysts who have served presidents of both parties come to a different conclusion. They say *Trump's presidency has marked the greatest discontinuity in American foreign policy since World War II*" (emphasis added). To support this assertion, Balz quotes Nicholas Burns, former U.S. ambassador to NATO, who said that while former presidents were engaged with the world, "President Trump isn't. He's almost at war with the world." And Ivo Daalder, also a former U.S. Ambassador to NATO and now president of the Chicago Council on Global Affairs, says that "He [Trump] doesn't believe in alliances, open markets, promotion of freedom and human rights—the three pillars of [American] foreign policy. On the essential concept of the United States as the global leader of the international order, Donald Trump has thrown all that out the window."[63]

Coronavirus Pandemic

It is clear that the United States under President Trump was going to chart its own course and that it was going to be America first. But the onset of the coronavirus pandemic in January 2020 altered the administration's priorities. At a time when countries were looking for leadership, generally the role that the United States had taken on in times of international crisis, it was absent. This raises some important questions for the future role of the United States, but also for international relations in general. While we generally think of security threats as coming from other countries, from potential military attacks or lately cyber warfare, what the pandemic has illustrated clearly is that the United States and all other countries need to be prepared for very different types of threats, something that will be discussed in more detail in chapter 8.

Whatever foreign policy agenda the Trump administration was pursuing came to a halt with the outbreak of the coronavirus pandemic. That dominated all aspects of U.S. foreign and domestic policy through the election in November 2020. In an intelligence briefing in the Oval Office on January 28, 2020, President Trump was warned about the potential threat posed by the coronavirus that was first detected in China. "'This will be the biggest national security threat you face in your presidency,' national security adviser Robert C. O'Brien told Trump," according to a book by *Washington Post* associate editor Bob Woodward. "'This is going to be the roughest thing you face.' Matthew Pottinger, the deputy national security adviser, agreed. He told the president that after reaching contacts in China, it was evident that the world faced a health emergency on par with the flu pandemic of 1918, which killed an estimated fifty million people worldwide."[64]

Although initially Trump publicly downplayed the extent of the virus—he told Woodward that he did so to avoid panic—in less than a year it had spread across the United States, killing almost six hundred thousand people. (The exact number is not final as we go to press as the number of deaths increases daily.) What is clear is that the predictions were correct about this being the "biggest national security threat." The Trump administration, which had been fixated on trying to get a deal with North Korea and limiting Iran's ability to gain a nuclear weapon, seemed unprepared for, or unwilling to deal with this bio-threat that wracked the United States and brought the economy to a grinding halt.

The United States was not the only country to have to confront the devastation caused by the coronavirus pandemic. As the countries in Europe and parts of Asia were hit by the virus, they engaged in a series of often-extreme national measures to get it under control. For example, Italy and Spain both imposed strict lock-down orders, with people only able to leave their homes for necessities such as groceries. While this imposed a severe hardship, it did ensure that there was a nationwide policy that helped bring the virus under control. In contrast, in the United States, while Trump formed a coronavirus task force that put forward recommendations such as the need to wear masks, there was no single national policy, with the administration leaving it up to individual governors to make decisions for their states.[65]

While dealing with the pandemic is primarily a domestic issue—it is up to the national leadership to protect its people—it has had important foreign policy implications. Two recent polls, one by the Pew Research Center and the other by the Chicago Council on Global Affairs, underscore how the Trump administration's inability to address the coronavirus crisis early on has undermined perceptions of the United States. The Pew poll is especially instructive in examining how other countries perceive the ways in which the United States handled the outbreak. The survey was conducted among 13,273 adults in thirteen advanced countries including Canada, the United Kingdom, Japan, and South Korea, all of which are traditionally America's strongest allies. Among the findings are that "Since Donald Trump took office as president, the image of the United States has suffered across many regions of the globe. . . . America's reputation has declined further over the past year among many key allies and partners. In several countries, the share of the public with a favorable view of the U.S. is as low as it has been at any point since the Center began polling on this topic nearly two decades ago."[66] Even the staunchest allies of the United States, Britain, France, and Germany, reflect a serious decline in perceptions of this country. According to the Pew survey, "Part of the decline over the past year is linked to how the U.S. has handled the coronavirus pandemic. Across the 13 nations surveyed, a median of just 15% say the U.S. has done a good job of handling the outbreak." In contrast, perceptions are that the World Health Organization, which the United States has threatened to withdraw from and not support, and the European Union have done a good job. Although few think that China handled the outbreak well, it still was ranked higher than the United States.[67]

So why is this important to U.S. foreign policy, especially as handling the pandemic is largely a domestic issue? First, as the polls showed, it is important because it indicates that other countries, especially our allies, have little faith in the Trump administration's ability to handle a crisis. Compared to other countries that took action quickly and imposed national policies, the United States was far more reluctant to take any action and ultimately did not impose any national policy. And the reactions of individual states has been uneven, with some imposing strict policies regarding masks and gatherings, while others did not. Second, traditionally countries have looked to the United States to lead in the event of any crisis. But what this survey shows is that that is no longer the case. Countries are not now looking to the United States as a global leader, allowing other countries, such as China, to supplant the United States, which has important implications for the future. Third, there seems to be a conflation of Trump as president and perceptions of the United States globally. This is not a surprise, as the president is the chief symbol of the country, and when the assessment of the president is low then the perceptions of the country will plummet as well. In fact, the survey found that the respondents saw Trump more negatively than other world leaders; although ratings for Russia's president Vladimir Putin and China's president Xi Jinping are negative, they are not as negative as those for Trump.[68]

Thus, at the end of four years of a Trump administration, even with some modest successes (discussed below), largely due to the pandemic global perceptions of the United States have diminished, allowing other countries, such as China, to emerge to challenge the role that the United States has had internationally since the end of the Second World War.

U.S. Relations with Russia

Trump's "go-it-alone," America-first rhetoric was translated into policy decisions early in the administration, often to the consternation of its allies. Nowhere can this be seen more clearly than in the warm personal relationship between Trump and Putin, which was developing at the same time that Trump was dismissing the closest allies of the United States.

While campaigning for the presidency, Donald Trump spoke very highly of Russian President Vladimir Putin. Even after U.S. intelligence agencies revealed that Russian hacking was designed to skew the 2016 election in his favor, Trump dismissed the charges and did not appear to take them seriously, although he finally did agree to have an intelligence briefing on the topic. Despite what his own intelligence community said about Russian interference in the election, Trump instead affirmed Putin's denials. At a press conference following a bilateral meeting between Trump and Putin in Helsinki, Finland, in July 2018, Trump observed "that Putin was 'extremely strong in his denial. . . . He just said it's not Russia. . . . I don't see any reason why it would be.' Well, that's settled."[69] This followed a Group of Seven (G7) summit in Canada in June when Trump demanded the reinstatement of Russia to the group, a proposal that was rejected. Further, Trump insulted the G7 host, Canadian Prime Minister Justin Trudeau, accusing him via Twitter of making "false statements" about the U.S.-Canada trade negotiations. At a subsequent NATO meeting in July, Trump criticized Germany as being "totally controlled by Russia," a clearly unsubstantiated claim that alienated another close ally.[70]

In many ways, the Helsinki summit in July 2018 set the tone for the relationship between Trump and Putin. That meeting was held in secrecy, with no top-level aides present, just the two leaders and their translators. At the end of the meeting, each of the two men praised the other. Even more revealing, Putin denied Russian meddling in the U.S. election and Trump supported him, in opposition to the findings of U.S. intelligence sources. Even some members of the president's own party were stunned by what appeared to be Trump's support of Putin as opposed to his own intelligence apparatus. There have been no official notes of that meeting made public. Upon his return to the country, Trump encountered immense pushback from many sides, include some analysts on the usually friendly Fox News, who excoriated Trump for taking the word of a former KGB official over his own intelligence community. Nonetheless, a few days later Trump announced that he had invited Putin to the White House.

U.S. policy toward Russia during the Trump administration emerges as bifurcated. On the one hand, the Trump administration followed a generally hardline policy toward Russia. For example, the United States expelled sixty diplomats after Russia's attempts to assassinate a former Russian spy in the United Kingdom. The Trump administration also approved $40 million in arms sales to the Ukrainian government fighting Russian-backed rebels in that country. However, despite those examples, Trump himself did little that would alienate Putin, including jokingly reminding Putin at a G20 meeting in June 2019 not to meddle in American elections again. Clearly, that did not have an impact, as it appears that Russia continued to do so going into the 2020 presidential elections. According to Peter Bergen, "Putin remained what he always was, an unreconstructed KGB officer committed to maintaining his authoritarian rule and expanding Russian influence whenever he could, in particular, if that would also undermine American interests."[71]

Both the U.S. House of Representatives and the Senate conducted investigations about the extent of Russia's involvement in the 2016 elections. Further, the Department of Justice appointed a special prosecutor, Robert Mueller, to look into that issue as well as related ones. As the investigations started to unfold, it appeared that members of the President's inner circle, including Trump's son-in-law Jared Kushner, had ties to Russia either directly through the government, or indirectly through banks and the oligarchs. Trump's former campaign manager Paul Manafort was indicted and convicted on charges pertaining to his ties to foreign governments, and Trump's lawyer, Michael Cohen, pleaded guilty to charges related to campaign finance irregularities. Both men served time in prison, though both were released early; Trump pardoned Manafort shortly before he left office. And Trump was impeached by the House of Representatives in part due to his behavior regarding Ukraine, which the president was convinced was behind the undermining of the 2016 elections, rather than Russia. However, Trump was not convicted by the Senate.

For reasons that remain unknown, Trump seemed to go out of his way to praise and work with Putin while, at the same time alienating the traditional allies of the United States, including NATO members and Ukraine, which is the critical bulwark against Russia's aggression. After Putin won reelection as president in March 2018, President Trump called to congratulate him, contrary to the advice of members of his staff who urged him not to do that.

These behaviors on the part of the U.S. president serve to reinforce Tillerson's assessment of Putin as a wily operator with a "deep desire to restore Russia's greatness and credibility, or at least give it the sheen of a country to be feared, in part by forging a partnership with a world power such as the United States."[72] Part of that "long game" involved weakening U.S. influence internationally. So while President Trump was developing his relationship with Putin, Russia was extending its role in the Middle East, developing its ties with China, and strengthening the relationship with North Korea's Kim Jong-un.

U.S. Relations with the Western Allies

While President Trump was strengthening his ties with Putin and Russia, he was also alienating many of the U.S. allies in the West, especially the NATO nations. Trump had long made it clear that he thought that the allies were taking advantage of the United States by not doing their part to support NATO, and that he, in turn, had little use for the alliance. For Trump, the allies of Western Europe and Canada were not providing value added to the United States. As Peter Bergen describes it, Trump's policies must be seen within the context of his "complete lack of understanding of the United States' historical role as the leader of a rules-based international order and the unique strategic value of America's alliances. For Trump, every country seemed to be judged only through the narrow lens of its bilateral trade balances with the United States."[73] Hence, despite what cabinet members like Defense Secretary Mattis thought about the importance of multilateral alliances such as NATO it was Trump's view that prevailed.

Despite Trump's underlying suspicion about NATO, he did have some minor successes regarding the alliance. At a NATO meeting in December 2019, the leaders reaffirmed the goal of increasing their defense spending and, by that time, nine of NATO's twenty-nine members had reached the goal of committing 2 percent of GDP to defense. Even Trump stated that "Great progress has been made by NATO over the last three years." And he cited NATO figures that "European allies and Canada will add a cumulative $130 billion in spending by the end of 2020 from 2016."[74] At that same meeting, the leaders "formally recognized the challenge of China's rise for the first time," and they designated land, air, and naval units "that can be ready to fight within a month—a central part of the alliance's response to the threat from Russia."[75] Although there was some agreement at that meeting, that does not erase the underlying suspicion that remains among the alliance members, as well as deep-seated differences about priorities and the role of NATO.

In foreign policy, actions have consequences, and by the end of Trump's time in office, the European allies and members of the G7 were looking to countries other than the United States to lead. A headline in *The New York Times* on October 20, 2020, two weeks before the election, summed up the situation: "Europe Wonders If It Can Rely on U.S. Again, Whoever Wins."[76] The point made here is an important one: after four years of being ignored, dismissed, and undermined, an important trust has been broken between the United States and its closest allies, and that relationship will not easily be repaired even with another president. What is clear at the end of the Trump administration is that the United States is now seen as an unreliable ally for the first time since the end of the Cold War.

As noted in chapter 4, from the time it was created in 1949 NATO served many purposes beyond just an alliance of collective security. It was an affirmation of common values and a commitment to the liberal democratic order that all NATO nations supported. The Trump administration seemed to undermine those values, thereby exacerbating divisions. If one of the bedrock themes of U.S. foreign policy is that it is continuous, with little radical or revolutionary change apart from a major crisis, the Trump administration has upended that idea. Instead, the radical shift in U.S. attitudes about and policy regarding the allies has undermined U.S. credibility, leading the Europeans to think more about "strategic autonomy," that is a Europe that is less dependent on the United States and more about developing its own position and voice in order to address the myriad threats that exist.[77]

U.S. Relations with China under Trump

An article in *The New Yorker* provides a cogent explanation of the ways in which China is taking advantage of the lack of a coherent U.S. foreign policy to establish its own role and power internationally. With President Xi's power firmly established following the Communist Party Congress in October 2017, China was positioned to pursue a larger role internationally at the same that the United States was reducing its commitments abroad under the banner of "America First."[78] This is consistent with Xi's priorities to make China a "major country," a point he has been advocating for many years. Now, with the assistance of the United States, China is in a position to realize that ambitious goal. In many ways, what seems to be emerging is a new Cold War, this time pitting the United States against China.

Like many other countries, China was trying to understand the United States and its policies and priorities under President Trump. In fact, at the start of the Trump administration a foreign ministry spokeswoman said "China like every other country is closely watching the policy direction the

U.S. is going to take. Cooperation is the only right choice for both sides."[79] China's initial concerns about U.S. policies were assuaged during and following Trump's state visit to China in November 2017 as part of a major presidential visit to Asia when Xi feted the president and first lady, including a private tour of the Forbidden City and a special performance of the Beijing Opera. During that visit, the two countries concluded trade deals worth over $200 billion, and reaffirmed the importance of enforcing UN resolutions regarding North Korea. However, any relief in tension between the two countries was short-lived.

By April 2018, a trade war between the United States and China was brewing. Early in April, the United States published a list of about 1,300 Chinese products that it proposed to hit with tariffs of 25 percent. One day later, China produced its own list of 106 categories. America's list "covers Chinese products worth $46 billion in 2017 (9% of that year's total goods exports to America). China's covers American goods worth around $52bn in 2017 (38% of exports)."[80] The imposition of these tariffs by Trump builds on threats that he made during his campaign and reflects the hardline views of some of his advisors. The sector that was hit especially hard in the United States in the brewing trade war was agriculture.

As the Trump administration railed about China's unfair trade practices, in September 2018, the United States imposed tariffs on $250 billion worth of Chinese products, restricted Chinese investments in the United States, and threatened further tariffs. China responded with its own tariffs on American goods leading to the onset of a full-blown trade war. A truce between the two countries was reached on December 1, 2018, at the G20 meeting in Argentina to give the two countries six months to work out a subsequent agreement.

In January 2020, the United States and China signed a trade deal that would commit China to buying more farm goods from the United States. Importantly, however, it did not include a timeline for those imports. The trade between the two countries has been curtailed significantly by the onset of the coronavirus, which closed China's ports.[81]

After the National People's Congress voted to abolish the two-term limit on a president's tenure, in effect making Xi China's "president for life," the real question that many are asking is what China sees as its own position in the world at this point. A corollary to that is how China views conflict between its priorities and what the United States wants. In 2013, a senior Chinese military officer argued that "China should regain its position as the most powerful nation in the world, a position it had held a thousand years before its humiliation."[82] It is clear that China's aggressive foreign policy stance has caused concern for a number of countries, beyond just the United States. As one of five permanent members of the UN Security Council, China is able to wield more power internationally, which can be seen not only with its stance regarding the South China Sea, but also regarding the major role it has been playing regarding North Korea and Iran and, more recently, Syria.

China has been unapologetic in its expansion beyond Asia. In 2015, Xi Jinping visited more countries than President Barack Obama and he made his first trip to the Middle East early in 2016; no Chinese president had been to the region since 2009.[83] While China certainly does not want to be embroiled in the conflicts in the region, it also has a big stake in what goes on there. China is the world's largest oil importer, getting more than half its crude oil from the Middle East.

The "new Silk Road," also known as the Belt and Road Initiative, linking China and Europe, made possible because of Chinese-funded infrastructure, runs across the Middle East. China's desire to create the new Silk Road has led that country to invest in building a high-speed rail network linking the Greek port of Piraeus, the country's largest, to Hungary and eventually Germany. It is funding the creation of a highway in Pakistan as well. In 2016, for example, "more than half of China's overseas contracts were signed with nations along the Silk Road—a first in the country's modern history."[84] In June 2016, Xi visited Serbia and Poland, making deals for other projects in each country. Then Russia's President Putin paid a visit to China and the two leaders promised to link infrastructure plans with the new Silk Road. In addition, finance ministers from about sixty countries held the first meeting in Beijing of the Asian Infrastructure Investment Bank (AIIB) created specifically to finance many of these projects.[85] China clearly is positioning itself to be a major economic and trade powerhouse globally, a position that it will exploit still further with the United States' exit from the Trans-Pacific Partnership (TPP).

The creation of this new Silk Road is an important goal to Xi, who sees this as a critical part of expanding China's commercial interests and soft power internationally. China's dream of global, as opposed to regional, dominance is based both on hard power, the growth of military and Chinese military bases around the world, and soft power, an area that has often been overlooked and is often less noticed. According to one journalist, China has been using its influence, including various corporations, to make inroads in the United States and other developed countries. While Huawei, which the U.S. government blacklisted as a threat to national security, is one example, there are others, such as TikTok, which have access to data about the United States and its citizens. These cases are far more difficult to identify and therefore to address, but they do give China access and therefore power.[86]

Increasingly during his time in office, Trump moved from looking at China as a potential ally to a major threat. This can be seen clearly by the Trump administration's depiction of the coronavirus, referring to it as the "China virus," thereby ascribing negative qualities to the virus and to China. Gradually, the two countries are "dismantling decades of political, economic and social engagement, setting the stage for a new area of confrontation." This is a fight that has been inflamed by both sides, each one thinking that it will provide a political advantage at home. But the end result could be "the entrenchment of a fundamental strategic and ideological confrontation between the world's two largest economies." According to one China-watcher in the United States, "They [the Trump administration] want to reorient the U.S.-China relationship toward an all-encompassing systemic rivalry that cannot be reversed by the outcome of the upcoming U.S. election. They believe this reorientation is needed to put the United States on a competitive footing against its 21st-century geostrategic rival." This is consistent with Trump's desire to change the U.S. relationship with China, starting with trade, but clearly expanding far more broadly.[87]

North Korea

The Trump administration's policy regarding North Korea could best be described as schizophrenic. As president-elect, Trump met in November 2016 with then president Obama, who warned Trump that "North Korea would be the greatest challenge he would confront as president."[88] As he did with Putin and Russia, regarding North Korea Trump based his policies on relationships with the leader, rather than on larger strategic issues.

Tensions escalated in spring and summer 2017 when North Korea engaged in a series of missile tests. Trump's response was to threaten that if North Korea went through with its promise to develop a nuclear weapon capable of reaching the U.S. mainland, "They will be met with fire and fury and, frankly, power, the likes of which this world has never seen before."[89] Then, in fall 2017, Trump taunted North Korean President Kim Jong-un as "little rocket man." As often happens in foreign policy, de-escalation started not because of anything that the United States or North Korea did, but because of a change in policy by South Korea, which clearly had a vested interest in ensuring that the two sides did not go to war. In an example of how sometimes circumstances can change for unforeseen reasons, South Korea was to host the winter Olympics in February 2018. South Korea's President Moon Jae-in invited North Korea to send its athletes to the Olympics and to have them march with their South Korean counterparts. Trump took advantage of this overture to work with South Korea to help facilitate a meeting with the North Korean president. Thus started the process of personal diplomacy between Trump and North Korea's president Kim Jong-un.[90]

By all accounts, the period leading up to that summit was a dangerous one. However, in June 2018, Trump met with Kim in Singapore and later declared, "We fell in love." This was the first of a series of summits between Trump and Kim. The symbolism of the Singapore meeting was important, as it was the first time that a president of the United States met with a leader of North Korea. At that time, both leaders agreed on the need for North Korea's "denuclearization," although it now appears that the term meant different things to each of the two leaders. For the United States, it had been a "longstanding goal of American foreign policy to achieve the 'complete, verifiable, irreversible dismantlement' of the North Korean nuclear program." However, it meant something very different to North Korea, specifically "getting the United States to withdraw any nuclear weapons in the region surrounding North Korea and also to formally end the Korean War." As noted in chapter 4, the Korean War ended in an armistice rather than a formal peace treaty, and resulted in the ongoing deployment of U.S. troops to the Korean Peninsula. Hence, for North Korea the concept of "denuclearization" also meant "the withdrawal of the twenty-eight thousand troops stationed in South Korea."[91]

By the conclusion of the Singapore meeting, North Korea had exacted an important concession from the United States: Trump announced that the United States would be stopping joint U.S.-South Korean military exercises, an announcement that had not been coordinated with the Pentagon or South Korea. Trump also prematurely announced that there was no longer a threat from a nuclear North Korea.

Building on what Trump saw as the special relationship that he had developed with Kim Jong-un, following a G20 meeting in Japan in June 2019, Trump and Kim met at the DMZ for a photo-op, which was primarily symbolic in nature, rather than substantive. The next meeting of the two leaders in Hanoi in March 2019 was supposed to be the one where a major agreement would be signed. Yet, the summit ended abruptly amid "a standoff over Kim's demand that the United States remove economic sanctions against North Korea without a promise to end his nuclear program."[92] According to press coverage of the summit, some of Trump's advisors, including then national security advisor John Bolton and secretary of state Mike Pompeo, questioned the wisdom of the meeting at all, aware of the fact that "the chances of a grand bargain for total nuclear disarmament were virtually zero."[93] However, Trump, who saw himself as the consummate deal maker as well as his belief in the personal relationship between the two men, wanted to move forward, apparently unaware of the fact that this was the same plan that the United States had pushed and North Korea had rejected for decades.

In the area of international relations, we know that an individual can make a difference, especially an individual leader, something that Trump was counting on here.[94] What he was not counting on, however, was the fact that Kim Jong-un had his own agenda and definition of "national interest," and that the two were in conflict.

In a postscript to this aspect of Trump's foreign policy, in October 2020, at a military parade marking the seventy-fifth anniversary of the ruling Worker's Party, North Korea unveiled a new intercontinental ballistic missile (ICBM) that would be one of the world's largest if and/or when it becomes operational.

The Middle East

The Trump administration's policy regarding the Middle East showed mixed results. On the one hand, the United States was able to improve relations with Israel, which had soured considerably under Obama. On the other hand, U.S. troops remained in Afghanistan, despite Trump's promise to pull them out, and a nascent agreement with the Taliban that was supposed to finally bring peace to that country was uncertain. The civil war continues in Syria, and while Trump personally seemed to have good relations with Turkey's president Erdogan, relations between Turkey and its other NATO allies remain strained. The United States remained a strong supporter of Saudi Arabia, in spite of its role in the murder of journalist Jamal Khashoggi.

There is no room in this concise history to address all of these areas, so we are going to focus on two specifically: U.S. relations with Israel and the situation in Afghanistan. Both of these clearly illustrate the unique approach that the Trump administration has taken to foreign policy in that region.

Relations with Israel

One of the highest priorities of the Trump administration was to change U.S. relations with Israel, which admittedly had been strained under Obama. Here, too, the confluence of a number of factors altered the dynamic between the two countries, some of those because of decisions made within the United States, and some because of Israel's leader, Benjamin Netanyahu.

During most of the Trump administration, Netanyahu was himself under scrutiny in Israel for allegations of bribery, fraud, and breach of trust, which led to his indictment in November 2019. While this did not require him to step down as prime minister, the investigations did cloud Israeli elections, leading to the creation of a series of coalition governments. This also made the role of the United States, an important ally to Netanyahu, even more central.

As U.S. ambassador to Israel Trump appointed David Friedman, one of Trump's lawyers and a Zionist. Shortly after the appointment, Friedman announced that one of his first acts would be to move the U.S. embassy from Tel Aviv to Jerusalem, a move that inflamed the Palestinians but enhanced Netanyahu's stature in Israel and pleased many of his supporters. U.S. policy had been to keep the embassy in Tel Aviv while working on a so-called two-state solution to the Palestinian issue; Jerusalem was the home of a number of sites of importance to all three major monotheistic religions and the fear was that moving the embassy would further politicize an already divided city. Nonetheless, on May 15, 2018, Ambassador Friedman, accompanied by Ivanka Trump and her husband Jared Kushner, formally opened the new U.S. embassy in Jerusalem. The move was viewed critically by the international community and in December 2017, when it was initially announced, it was condemned by 128 countries in the UN, with only 8 countries voting in support of the United States. In addition, the United States withdrew its support for the United Nations Relief and Works Agency (UNRWA), "which educated hundreds of thousands of displaced Palestinian kids living as refugees in countries around the Middle East."[95] This further inflamed the Palestinians.

Also in November 2018, Secretary of State Pompeo, in another reversal of U.S. policy, announced that "the State Department is rescinding a 1978 department legal opinion that viewed settlements in the Israeli-occupied West Bank as inconsistent with international law. That legal opinion, known as the Hansell Memorandum and crafted during the Carter administration, said that 'civilian settlements in those territories is inconsistent with international law.'" Pompeo went on to say that the Trump administration "does not view the settlements as inconsistent with international law and leaves the issue of individual settlements up to Israeli courts."[96] While this statement was praised by Netanyahu, it was condemned by much of the international community which adheres to the broadly accepted definition under international law.

One of Trump's goals regarding Israel was to facilitate a peace plan, and he put his son-in-law Jared Kushner in charge of the process. Although the United States had been unable to broker a solution to the Israeli-Palestinian issue in the past, Trump believed that it was still possible and Kushner eventually proposed a two-part solution, one part that would be economic and the other political. However, after the embassy move, Palestinian Authority president Mahmoud Abbas declared that Kushner could no longer be considered an honest broker and stopped meeting with him.

Kushner, with Trump's backing, continued to try to find a solution. To address the economic side of the proposed peace deal, in June 2019 Kushner hosted a "Palestinian investment conference" in Bahrain to try to secure $50 billion to be used as funding for investments for Palestinian projects. The goal was to create a master fund that would be used to manage financial and project support for investments that would "empower the Palestinian people."[97] However, no country, not even the United States, was willing to commit to any funding.

The full peace plan was formally unveiled during a meeting at the White House in January 2020, with Netanyahu present. The political framework was supposed to build on the notion of the two-state solution that has been long advocated as the way to ensure peace in the region. The reality is that the plan proposed did not have any provision for a Palestinian state or for the return of any lands annexed by Israel. The Palestinians would not participate in the negotiations, thereby further undermining any chance of success. In addition, the failure to raise any money to support the economic fund coupled with the inability of Netanyahu to form a coalition government in Israel in April 2019 and then in subsequent elections held in September 2019 ensured that Israel would not be moving forward with any plan, especially one fraught with controversy. In short, this became another failed peace plan between Israel and the Palestinians.

That said, the Trump administration was able to broker agreements between Israel and the Gulf states of the United Arab Emirates (UAE) and also Bahrain. Signed in Washington in September 2020, these bilateral deals set the stage for further economic relationships between Israel and the other nations as well as facilitating greater people-to-people contacts, such as tourism and exchange of workers. Perhaps most important, the agreements further integrated Israel into the region, thereby lessening the possibility of future conflict. This was followed in October 2020 by a similar agreement to normalize relations between Israel and Sudan, also brokered by the United States. The latter also required the United States to remove Sudan from the list of countries condemned as state sponsors of terrorism along with a compensation package from Sudan to the United States for victims of terrorism. A fourth normalization agreement was signed between Israel and Morocco on December 10, 2020, although the price for that agreement was that the United States recognize Western Sahara as part of Morocco, a claim that has been rejected by virtually every international body including the UN, the World Court, and the African Union. From the time that Morocco annexed the territory from Spain in 1975, it was fraught with controversy, which is why no country recognized Morocco's claim, until now. And, similar to the case of the Palestinians, most of the international community has argued that the area should be recognized as a self-governing territory, allowing the people within the territory to determine their own future (self-determination). Once again, the United States' position has run counter to the majority of countries and organizations in the international system.

These agreements were all hailed as important steps forward in stabilizing relationships in the region even if the ultimate goal of reaching peace between Israel and the Palestinians was not achieved.

Afghanistan

One of the stated foreign policy goals of candidate and then President Trump was to withdraw U.S. troops from Afghanistan. As of Election Day 2020, approximately forty-five hundred U.S. troops remained in Afghanistan with another three thousand in Iraq and about one thousand in Syria. Thus, while Trump had long advocated for getting U.S. troops out of the Middle East, some remained as a way to ensure stability in the region and keep ISIS at bay. In December 2018, Trump ordered the withdrawal of about seven thousand troops from Afghanistan, about half the total number deployed, after first ordering that all troops be withdrawn. Withdrawal of all U.S. forces was one of the Taliban's main demands regarding any negotiations, and this seemed to signal that the United States would be willing to meet that condition. However, there was good reason for at least a relatively small number of U.S. troops to remain in order to ensure some stability.

The Trump administration offered its own approach to brokering a peace agreement in Afghanistan, one that it was hoped would result in the withdrawal of U.S. troops and ultimately lead to a peace agreement. In July 2018, the administration opened direct negotiations with the Taliban while excluding the elected government of Afghanistan from the talks. Starting in September 2018, the talks were under the direction of Zalmay Khalilzad, an Afghani-American whom Trump had designated his special representative for Afghanistan. This was not the first time that that the Afghan government and the Taliban had been encouraged to work toward peace. As far back as 2007, then Afghan President Hamid Karzai advocated for talks, but his overtures were rebuffed by the Taliban. Additional attempts were made during the Obama administration, again unsuccessfully.

In February 2020 Washington and the Taliban reached an agreement. Called the "Agreement for Bringing Peace to Afghanistan," the agreement was the result of eighteen months and nine rounds of talks between the United States and the Taliban and was preceded by a seven-day "reduction in violence" "that was seen as a test of the Taliban's ability to control its forces."[98] The agreement outlines four goals, with the last two dependent on the first two: (1) Afghanistan will not be used as a base for attacks against the United States or its allies and specifically, the Taliban will not threaten the United States and it would prevent any armed groups from using Afghanistan to do the same; (2) the United States is committed to withdrawing all its forces and those of its allies as well as all civilian personnel from Afghanistan within fourteen months of signing the agreement, and depending on a show of good faith on the part of the Taliban; (3) negotiations between the Taliban and the Afghan government were to begin, starting with the release of a designated number of prisoners on both sides, leading ultimately to a complete release of all prisoners; and (4) "The agenda for intra-Afghan negotiations will include discussion of how to implement a permanent and comprehensive cease-fire, and a political roadmap for the future of Afghanistan. Pending successful negotiations and an agreed-upon settlement, the United States has agreed to seek economic cooperation from allies and UN member states for Afghan reconstruction efforts and has pledged no further domestic interference in Afghanistan."[99] As part of the February 2020 agreement, the Trump administration committed to a May 2021 withdrawal of U.S. troops, point number 2, assuming other conditions are met.

Going into the talks, each side had a different goal. For the United States, the highest priority was to find a way to withdraw U.S. troops from Afghanistan, finally ending America's longest war. The Taliban's main goal was to make sure that all foreign troops were withdrawn from Afghanistan thereby giving them greater influence, and to advocate for an Afghanistan ruled by Islamic law. For the Afghan government, which was brought into the talks with the Taliban in September 2020 when the negotiations were well underway, the main goal was to reach a cease-fire with the Taliban and to do so in a way that could result in some power-sharing agreement, something that the Taliban also advocated for. The Taliban agreed to begin talks with the Afghan government as long as the United States committed to a timeline for withdrawing troops from the country.

Many Afghani citizens remain concerned about the growing role of the Taliban. Paramount among these are the worry that any compromise with the Taliban will undermine the gains won, especially women's rights and protections of minorities. Since 2001 and the fall of the Taliban, Afghan women have expanded their rights and roles, including greater participation in public life and access to education. The official government delegation does include women, although the Taliban do not have any in their delegation.[100]

By October 2020, it was clear that the agreement was not working as it was supposed to, that is to end the violence, when the Taliban launched an offensive in Helmand province that drove thousands of civilians from their homes. In response, the United States initiated extensive air strikes against the Taliban that resulted in the deaths of approximately eighty Taliban. As a result, Khalilzad said that the two sides had agreed to "reset" adherence to the agreement. This "reset" made it clear that the conditions of the agreement have yet to be met.[101] On October 8, 2020, President Trump announced that he wanted all U.S. troops home by Christmas, something that seemed increasingly unlikely. Later in October, the top U.S. general in Afghanistan told the *Military Times* that they are trying hard to make the peace process work, and stressed that success is based on both sides complying with agreed-upon conditions.[102]

On November 17, 2020, after Trump lost the election, Pentagon officials announced that they would halve the number of U.S. troops in Afghanistan over the next two months from about five thousand to twenty-five hundred, and from three thousand to twenty-five hundred in Iraq. This was after Trump continued to state that he wanted all U.S. forces home by Christmas. But senior U.S. military officials continue to raise concerns about the Taliban's commitment to their part of the agreement. And U.S. members of Congress from both parties expressed concern about withdrawing U.S. forces too quickly, absent an indication of good faith on the part of the Taliban.[103]

Speaking to Voice of America just after the U.S. presidential elections, a spokesman for the Taliban said that "they expect President-elect Joe Biden to stick to a peace agreement the insurgent group sealed with the United States earlier this year to end the war in Afghanistan, America's longest." And he further indicated that he expected that "the ongoing peace process and the agreement with the U.S. government will remain on track."[104] As we go to press, it is too early to know what the Biden administration will do regarding this ongoing and apparently intractable conflict. As the May 1 deadline quickly approaches, it appears that they are weighing the risks of complying with the May deadline against the dangers of breaking an agreement signed by the United States. At this time, there is a review underway of the options, with Secretary of Defense Lloyd Austin stating that "the United States 'will not undertake a hasty or disorderly withdrawal from Afghanistan that puts [its] forces or the alliance's reputation at risk.'"[105] The fear is that a premature withdrawal from the country could lead to civil war, increased danger from terrorist attacks, and human rights abuses, especially directed against women. There are also approximately ten thousand NATO personnel from thirty-six countries deployed to Afghanistan, and the Biden administration must also weigh what will happen to them if and when U.S. forces leave.

There are a number of lessons that can be drawn from the case of Afghanistan. The amount of posturing that was done in public on both sides (U.S. and Taliban) only served to undermine negotiations that are most effective when done in private. The public pronouncements seem to suggest that both sides were also playing to a domestic audience, which was certainly the case when Donald Trump announced in October, going into the November elections, that the troops would be home for Christmas. Another important point that needs to be considered was the decision on the part of the Trump administration to negotiate with the Taliban, rather than the elected government of Afghanistan. Not only did this elevate the position of the Taliban, previously considered a terrorist group, it undermined the legitimacy of the Afghan government, which the United States had been fighting to protect. Finally, the agreement had a number of conditions and preconditions, making success extremely difficult.

Despite the best intentions of the Trump administration to get U.S. troops out of Afghanistan, they remain in place and the situation continues to remain unstable.[106] It is up to the Biden administration now to determine next steps.

Other Noteworthy Foreign Policy Issues

We do not have time to address the full range of other foreign policy issues raised during the four years of the Trump administration beyond saying that the administration leaves behind uncertainty and even chaos that the Biden administration will have to address. Many of those issues reflect Trump's own way of viewing the world. For example, in March 2018, Trump tweeted "When a country (USA) is losing many billions of dollars on trade with virtually every country it does business with, trade wars are good, and easy to win." Trump also tweeted "When we are down $100 billion with a certain country and they get cute, don't trade anymore—we win big. It's easy!"[107] With that, Trump announced he would impose a 25 percent tariff on steel and a 10 percent tariff on aluminum as early as the next week. His claim is that even if these moves by the United States spark a trade war, it is a war that we would win. However, what has become apparent is that trade wars are not easy to win, nor do they bring any advantage to the United States. Rather, they create more chaos and uncertainty within an international trade regime that has been in place since the end of World War II. And, as seen with China, trade wars are not easy to win, and it is often the U.S. consumer who is harmed the most.

Another area that could be explored more fully pertains to Trump's relationship to multilateral international organizations. Trump came into office inherently suspicious of them and his time as president did little to assuage his concerns. This can be seen very clearly regarding the administration's policy toward the World Health Organization (WHO), an organization that became especially critical during the coronavirus pandemic. The WHO is a specialized agency of the UN that is responsible for public health. According to its website, "WHO works worldwide to promote health, keep the world safe, and serve the vulnerable. Our goal is to ensure that a billion more people have universal health coverage, to protect a billion more people from health emergencies, and provide a further billion people with better health and well-being."[108] Hence, it seems logical that this would be the organization that the international community would turn to when the pandemic struck.

However, it was the United States, one of the initial founders of the organization, that turned away from it. In May 2020, the U.S. Ambassador to Switzerland, home of the WHO, delivered a list of seven demands from the United States at the start of discussions between the U.S. and the organization. Just hours after these demands were delivered, President Trump announced that the United States was planning to leave the WHO. According to health officials involved with the process, some of the requests were "reasonable" and could have been negotiated while other were "inappropriate." Rather, the United States reverted to its accusation that there was a lack of independence on the part of the WHO, which, the U.S. claimed, was tied to the Chinese Communist Party. The U.S. claimed that the director general of the WHO, Tedros Adhanom Ghebreyesus, was "too quick to praise China or frame the outbreak in ways favorable to Beijing." And while some European health officials shared some of the Trump administration's concerns, they also saw those as relatively minor in the midst of a pandemic that required international cooperation.[109]

In general, the European allies especially wanted to keep the United States from leaving the WHO. They felt that the organization was backed up by an international treaty and that it would be more effective for the U.S. to remain in it and to try to affect change from within. The WHO had already tried to make some changes, for example, beginning an investigation into the source of the coronavirus outbreak and WHO's handling of it. However, some of the other demands were seen as unreasonable and an infringement of the sovereignty of other nations. For example, the U.S. demanded that the WHO "call on China to provide live virus samples and stop censoring Chinese doctors or journalists," which would have been a break from the WHO policy of not usually criticizing its members.[110] This also would have privileged the United States by allowing it to dictate the organization's position regarding another country. The United States had a number of other demands, including calling for the WHO to prequalify coronavirus drugs and vaccines once they were authorized by major regulators in the United States, Canada, Japan, or Europe. Again, this was seen as allowing the U.S. to dictate drug policy.

In short, the Trump administration was suspicious of the WHO and found ways to make demands that, when they were not met, could become justification for withdrawing from the organization. The reality is that the administration did not even allow for negotiations on these issues to go forward, preferring instead to withdraw. As is the case in so many other areas, it will now be up to the Biden administration to determine next steps.

And there are more examples of ways in which the Trump administration approached multilateral issues and organizations in a nonconventional way. Any of these, plus countless other topics, could be the basis of a book in and of themselves, and are beyond the scope of this short text. However, the main point is that one individual can change the course of U.S. foreign policy and therefore this country's relationships with the rest of the international community.

U.S. FOREIGN POLICY POST-TRUMP

As we look to the future of U.S. foreign policy, and the role of the United States as a global leader, it is clear that there will be another reckoning, perhaps equal to or greater than the changes that followed the end of the Cold War. As Bacevich notes, "The unsettling presidency of Donald Trump suggests that the time might be ripe for introducing into the conversation ideas previously classified as beyond the pale." He then enumerates what these might be: "Reframing the conversation on economic policy, America's role in the world, the meaning of freedom, and, not least of all, the distribution of political power, particularly in Washington, just might point toward a fresh understanding of the nation's purpose."[111] Or, put another way, the United States is at a point where it *needs* to think about its place in the world and how best to achieve its national interest at a time of new and challenging threats. Can the United States continue to "go it alone," or is this the time to really think about and formulate foreign policy and security policy more appropriate to the challenges that lie ahead?

In chapter 8 we will examine some of these new and emerging threats and the role of the United States going forward after Donald Trump, including the challenges that the incoming Biden administration will face.

CHRONOLOGY 2009–PRESENT

2008–2009	Global economic crisis starts
2009	Obama's outreach to the Islamic world
	"Surge" of U.S. troops to Afghanistan
2010–2011	Arab Spring
2011	(March) Start of civil war in Syria
	(May) Death of Osama bin Laden
2014	(March) Russia annexes Crimea
	(December) U.S. and Cuba "normalize" relations

2015	(July) Iran nuclear deal signed
	(December) Paris climate change agreement reached
2016	(February) TPP signed
	(June) Brexit vote in UK
	(November) U.S. presidential elections
2017	Trump announces U.S. withdrawal from the Paris agreement, the TPP and the Iran nuclear deal
2018	(March) U.S. moves Israeli embassy to Jerusalem
	(April) Start of trade war between U.S. and China
	(June) Trump and Kim Jong-un meet in Singapore for the first of their summits
	(July) Trump-Putin meeting in Helsinki
2019	(February) Trump and Kim Jong-un summit in Hanoi
	(June) Trump and Kim Jong-un photo-op at DMZ
	(December) NATO summit affirms goal of 2 percent GDP spending on defense
2020	(January) Outbreak of coronavirus in China; quickly spreads globally
	(September-October) U.S. brokers agreements between Israel and UAE,
	Bahrain and Sudan
2020	(November) U.S. presidential elections

SELECTED PRIMARY SOURCES

Candidate Barack Obama's speech in Berlin, July 2008, http://www.nytimes.com/2008/07/24/us/politics/24text-obama.html?_r=0.

Barack Obama's first inaugural address, January 21, 2009 https://obama whitehouse.archives.gov/blog/2009/01/21/president-barack-obamas-inaugural-address.

"Remarks on a New Strategy for Afghanistan and Pakistan," March 27, 2009, https://obamawhitehouse.archives.gov/the-press-office/remarks-president-a-new-strategy-afghanistan-and-pakistan.

"Remarks on a New Beginning," Cairo, Egypt, June 4, 2009, https://obamawhitehouse.archives.gov/the-press-office/remarks-president-cairo-university-6-04-09.

John F. Kennedy's First Inaugural Address, January 20, 1961, https://avalon.law.yale.edu/20th_century/kennedy.asp.

Woodrow Wilson's First Inaugural Address, March 4, 1913, https://avalon.law.yale.edu/20th_century/wilson1.asp.

Donald J. Trump's Inaugural Address, January 20, 2017, https://www
    .whitehouse.gov/briefings-statements/the-inaugural-address/.

"Remarks by President Trump to the 74th Session of the United Nations
    General Assembly," September 24, 2019, https://www.whitehouse
    .gov/briefings-statements/remarks-president-trump-74th-session-united
    -nations-general-assembly/.

8

Biden and Beyond

The Future of U.S. Foreign Policy

Following a bruising election cycle, on January 20, 2021, Joe Biden became the forty-sixth president of the United States. He brings with him years of experience, first as a senator and then eight years as Barack Obama's vice president. However, he also faces innumerable foreign policy challenges, not least of which will be making important strategic decisions about what role the United States can and should play internationally going forward, and then determining how best to achieve his goals.

On the plus side, his initial cabinet selections reflect a strong and experienced team to help guide him in the area of foreign policy: Antony Blinken as secretary of state, Jake Sullivan as national security advisor, and Linda Thomas-Greenfield as U.S. ambassador to the UN, to name but a few. And in a sign of the importance of climate change for the United States, Biden created a new cabinet-level position, "special presidential envoy for climate," which will be held by John Kerry, former senator, secretary of state, and Democratic candidate for president. The rest of his cabinet, which includes Janet Yellin as secretary of the treasury, is of similar stature and underscores Biden's desire to make sure that his cabinet reflects the United States. Unlike the team initially established by the Trump administration, this group also brings years of experience within government and outside in various policy-making capacities and, more important, is ready to "hit the ground running" in order to address the myriad crises facing the new administration.

Biden has worked with many of these people before, they know him and each other, and, perhaps more important, they know both Washington and the other countries they will be asked to work with. In his formal introduction to the team, Biden sought to send an important signal to U.S. allies and adversaries when he declared that "America is back." He further stated,

> It's a team that will keep our country and our people safe and secure. It's a team that reflects the fact that America is back. Ready to lead the world, not retreat from it. Once again, sit at the head of the table. Ready to confront our adversaries and not reject our allies, ready to stand up for our values.[1]

Even though there was no mention of a secretary of defense in the introduction of his "national security, foreign policy team," a glaring omission to some, the initial announcement of the team members shortly after the election was designed to bring a sense of stability and normalcy after years of chaotic foreign policy–making under Trump. It also sent an important signal domestically to the bureaucrats and members of the diplomatic corps within the country who had been demoralized after years of neglect and abuse, that the administration will "have their backs" and that they are an important part of the structure of U.S. foreign policy–making.

On the negative side, however, even allies have learned that America's promises could quickly be forgotten and that a change in leadership could result in a significant shift in policy. No matter how much reassurance a President Biden can offer, the lessons learned under Trump were that U.S. promises and agreements could be undone or ignored in the face of political change. No longer can the United States be relied on to lead and, absent U.S. leadership, who will fill the void?

Biden and his team took pains to make the point that this would not be a continuation of the Obama administration, despite the reemergence of many who had served earlier, noting that "the dangers his team would confront were starkly different from the ones they dealt with during the Obama presidency." In an interview, Biden explained that "This is not a third Obama term [because] we face a totally different world than we faced in the Obama-Biden administration." And as if he needed to make clear some of the differences, he said that "President Trump has changed the landscape. It's become America first, it's been America alone."[2] The clear implication is that that will no longer be the case in a Biden administration.

Furthermore, as we will discuss in more detail later in this chapter, the United States and the rest of the world are facing new and more dangerous threats not only from other countries and non-state actors, but from microscopic viruses, from a depleted environment, and from some areas of "human security" that were neglected in the previous administration, such as assuring that all people have access to clean water. In many ways, these threats are more insidious than a traditional state adversary which can be met with weapons that need not be used, but simply threatened in order to make a point. A virus does not respond to a military threat, but it can be countered by science, although that can require sacrifices that many are not willing to make, as the coronavirus pandemic made clear. Thus, meeting these new challenges will require different approaches if they are to be addressed.

It is also important to remember, though, that confronting these new challenges does not mitigate the threat posed by traditional ones. A resurgent Russia, an aggressive China, a nuclear North Korea and Iran, the rise of autocratic regimes that do not adhere to the liberal world order, are among the more traditional threats that the new Biden administration will also have to face. History has also shown us that no matter how carefully the Biden administration plans and lays out its foreign policy goals, events could intervene that will upend those plans. Nonetheless, there does need to be a road map that will guide U.S. foreign policy for the next four (or eight) years, not only for the good of the United States but also as a necessity for other countries so that they, too, can determine their own policies.

THE ELECTION OF 2020 AND THE TRANSITION

Going into the presidential election of 2020, the contest was described as one that was for the soul of the country, with both candidates using language that harkened back to the founding of the country as "the city on the hill." Rather than build on his record in office, President Trump ran his reelection campaign in much the same way as he ran his initial campaign in 2016, tied to divisive issues and pitting one part of America and group of Americans against another. In spite of the coronavirus pandemic, he continued to depend on large rallies to mobilize his base, and he raised the specter of an America that would be overrun by immigrants and threatened by socialist policies should his opponent succeed in becoming president. For his part, candidate Biden adhered to the medical strictures imposed by the coronavirus, limiting his events to small gatherings and preferring to speak from the home studio in his basement. In other words, the campaign was a study in contrasts that reflected the personalities and approaches of the two men running for office.

Once the election was called for Biden, who won 306 electoral votes and a popular vote of over 80 million to Trump's 232 electoral votes and almost 74 million popular votes, Trump not only refused to concede but, in a breach of established policy, would not allow the formal transition to begin until almost three weeks after the election and only after pressure from fellow Republicans, including close allies like former governor Chris Christie. In other words, Trump was leaving office in much the same way as he ran the presidency: on his own terms. Because of its own experience in the government, the Biden team was able to move forward anyway, and sought to establish an image of an administration that would return to the established norms of decision-making.

Perhaps the greatest sign of how unusual the transition was came on January 6, 2021, when the Congress was assembled to confirm the Electoral College ballots. At a rally near the White House that morning, President Trump reinforced the refrain that the election was stolen, and appeared to encourage his supporters to go to the Congress to disrupt the proceedings. While the extent of Trump's culpability is under investigation at this time, many of his supporters complied and stormed the Capitol, breaking windows and desecrating the building. Members of Congress were forced to hide or flee, many fearing the violent intent of the mob. The common refrain was "stop the steal," as Trump's supporters continued to believe the lie that the election was stolen from Trump and that Biden and his Vice President, Kamala Harris, were not the legitimate winners. Despite this violent interruption, the review of the ballots finally did continue, affirming what was already known: the election of Joe Biden as president and Kamala Harris as vice president, the first woman and person of Black and Asian descent to be elected to that office. They were inaugurated as planned on January 20, 2021. However, that violence, and the fact that many questioned the legitimacy of the election, sent a signal to other countries about the fragility of the American democratic system. For his part in inciting this insurrection, Trump was again impeached by the House of Representatives although not convicted by the Senate.

We know from chapter 1 that foreign policy is an interactive process; what one country does will affect and, in turn, be affected by another. The more clearly those policy goals are outlined early on in the administration, in theory at least, the better prepared the United States and other countries will be to meet future challenges.

Writing in *Foreign Affairs* in March/April 2020 as he was running for president, Biden chose to lay out for the attentive public his vision for U.S. foreign policy. In this he was following the precedent set by predecessors who either directly, as Barack Obama did for himself, or indirectly, for example when Condoleezza Rice laid out George W. Bush's vision, presented the foreign policy priorities so that the outline was there even before the election was over. While reality often intervened and not all the goals were met or policies even followed, at least there was an early road map and a sense of what would lie ahead.

In this article, Biden made clear that if he were to become president, he would "take immediate steps to renew U.S. democracy and alliances, protect the United States' economic future, and once more have America lead the world."[3] And he stressed that before any changes are possible, it would be necessary to repair and reinvigorate our own democracy." He also claimed the need to prove to the world that *"the United States is prepared to lead again—not just with the example of our power but also with the power of our example"* (emphasis added). This will involve reversing many of the Trump administration's policies, including taking down some of the trade barriers that the Trump administration erected in the name of "America first," strengthening ties with allies, and relying (once again) on diplomacy as the backbone of U.S. foreign policy. He also noted the need to lead on existential challenges, such as climate change, an idea reinforced by bringing the United States back into the Paris climate change agreement. And, perhaps most noteworthy, Biden stated that "the United States cannot be a credible voice while it is abandoning the deals it negotiated." Underlying all these goals is the belief that the United States cannot do this alone but must work in concert with other nations albeit with the United States leading the way.[4] But the question remains: Is this now possible?

Biden reiterated many of these same themes in his address on November 7, after the election was formally called for him. In addition to a plea for unity, which was the hallmark of his campaign, Biden stated, "I sought this office to restore the soul of America, to rebuild the backbone of this nation, the middle class, *and to make America respected around the world again"* (emphasis added). And he used the address to start to lay out the priorities for his administration:

> Now this campaign is over, what is the will of the people? What is our mandate? I believe it's this: Americans have called upon us to marshal the forces of decency, the forces of fairness, to marshal the forces of science and the forces of hope in the great battles of our time. The battle to control the virus. The battle to build prosperity. The battle to secure your family's health care. The battle to achieve racial justice and root out systemic racism in this country. And the battle to save our planet by getting climate under control.[5]

And in another message not only to those in this country but to others, Biden also stated that "Tonight, the whole world is watching America. And I believe at our best, America is a beacon for the globe. . . . I've always believed we can define America in one word: possibilities. . . . I believe in the possibility of this country. We're always looking ahead."[6] This was a message of hope for Americans and for the United States' place in the world. Yet it is also a world full of challenges and threats, many that will not be of their making, that they will have to confront.

Among the clues of what challenges might lie ahead and how they will confront them were some of the public reflections of the new team as they looked back on the Obama years and planned for the future. For example, shortly after he was named as incoming secretary of state, Antony Blinken admitted that it was a mistake for the Obama administration to underreact to the plight of the Syrian people, who were under attack by their own government. To that point he admitted "'Any of us, and I start with myself, who had any responsibility for our Syria policy in the last [Obama] administration has to acknowledge that we failed. We failed to prevent a horrific loss of life. It is something I will take with me for the rest of my days.'" And he also referenced that the Obama administration did little to recognize the scope of Russia's interference "in the 2016 election until it was too late" and also that they moved too slowly "in responding to the China challenge."[7] One of the points that Blinken was making, and it is worth stressing, is that while many of those who will be in office in the Biden administration served in government in the past, they made mistakes and are not afraid to admit and learn from them.

Especially with the U.S. troops still in Syria and Afghanistan, Trump's coddling of Russia's Putin for four years, and an increasingly aggressive China, those issues remain and, in fact, will continue to grow as threats to U.S. security. They will be joined on the list of national security challenges by Iran and North Korea, both of which seem to be moving forward in their plans to develop nuclear weapons. While Biden has indicated a desire to rejoin the Iran nuclear agreement, it is unclear how easy that will be now, or whether Iran will allow the United States back in without renegotiating some of the terms. How the Biden administration deals with these threats and others, and whether he can get other countries to work with us, will determine the direction of U.S. foreign policy and its possible successes—or failures.

THE CHALLENGES AND THREATS

Biden outlined some of the challenges that his administration will be facing, and he offered a brief overview of how he would like to confront some of those threats, specifically, by working with other countries in partnership and leading as necessary. What follows are some of the challenges and threats that the United States is facing and will continue to face. What is important to note is that these represent a mix of threats coming from traditional nation-state adversaries, such as China and Russia, but also those that come from areas that threaten what feminist writers think of as "human security," specifically, those areas that threaten our way of life. These come from a depleted environment and climate change, the spread of disease such as the global pandemic that wracked the world in 2020 and 2021, and the movement of people, as one group flees one country to seek safety and security in another. Note that they do not include all the threats that are now known or might emerge. Rather, the focus here is on a few existing threats coming from other nations and also on more existential threats that the Biden administration knows that it will have to confront relatively quickly. As we have seen, much can happen over the next four years that has not been anticipated and that will have to be addressed perhaps quickly. Our emphasis here, however, is on that which is known or likely, based on the record to date.

At the end of the chapter, we will return to some of the basic principles of American foreign policy as outlined in chapter 1, and see what lessons can be learned about making foreign policy in theory and in practice.

U.S. RELATIONS WITH OTHER NATIONS

U.S. Relations with China

According to an article published right after the election in the *New York Times* about U.S. relations with China, "U.S. relations with China are the worst since the countries normalized ties four decades ago." It continues, "Nothing is more urgent, in the eyes of many experts, than reversing the downward trajectory of relations with China, the economic superpower and geopolitical rival that Mr. Trump has engaged in what many are calling a new Cold War."[8] This article echoes what any number of analysts, journalists, and pundits have been saying for years: that China is on the rise leading to a potential clash with the United States. What is especially disconcerting is that the warning signs were there, and the United States let this happen, for example by withdrawing from the Trans-Pacific Partnership (TPP), which helped pave the way for China's rise.

Graham Allison, who has long studied international conflict, wrote in the preface to his book *Destined for War*, "When a rising power threatens to displace a ruling power, alarm bells should sound: danger ahead. China and the United States are currently on a collision course for war—unless both parties take difficult and painful actions to avert it."[9] Allison takes pains to remind us that *"war between the U.S. and China is not inevitable* (emphasis added)."[10] However, avoiding conflict will require active steps on the part of both nations.

Writing a number of years before Allison, Fareed Zakaria also warned not about the decline of America but, as he put it, "the rise of everyone else"[11] as we move into what he calls a "post-American world." He predicted that this period will be characterized by a number of power centers that bring with them new challenge and threats, including some coming from non-state actors. As he notes, in the next few decades, "three of the world's biggest economies will be non-Western (Japan, China and India). And the fourth, the

United States, will be increasingly shaped by its non-European population."[12] And responding to these changes will require a new and perhaps different approach to foreign policy.

Nowhere can this be seen more clearly than in U.S. relations with China. As noted in chapter 7, it is not a surprise that China has been seeking to reclaim its dominant position regionally if not internationally. The challenge facing the Biden administration will be how to counter that in a way that will not exacerbate conflict. As one commentator noted, "A China that feels strong enough to threaten U.S. allies is a different China than the Obama administration ever faced. Coming to grips with this reality is the largest and most complex task Biden's foreign policy team will face."[13] It is apparent that China has opted to take advantage of the chaos in the United States to flex its muscles both at home and internationally, secure in the belief that the United States will do little to stop it.[14]

In thinking this through, it is important to note that it is not only the United States but its allies who are directly threatened by a resurgent China. This argues for the need for an allied response to formulating policy regarding China, and not just the United States going it alone. China has a long history of appropriating U.S. technology and intellectual property to the detriment of the United States, while extending its global reach militarily and economically. Biden gave a hint as to how he plans to approach the challenges posed by China in his *Foreign Affairs* article when he wrote, "The most effective way to meet that challenge is to build a united front of U.S. allies and partners to confront China's abusive behaviors and human rights violations, even as we seek to cooperate with Beijing on issues where our interests converge, such as climate change, nonproliferation, and global health security."[15] But this, too, will take serious work at a time when the United States is estranged from many of its allies because of Trump administration policies; when the Europeans are dealing with their own set of problems and issues, including Brexit; and when Biden himself, during the election campaign, referred to China's president Xi as a thug.

One of the challenges that the Biden administration will have to face in dealing with Asia in general and China in particular will be how to respond to or deal with the two major trade agreements that were signed *without the United States*. After the United States withdrew from the TPP in 2017, the remaining eleven countries negotiated and signed the Comprehensive and Progressive Agreement for Trans-Pacific Partnership or CPTPP a year later. "More recently, 15 countries including China, Australia, Japan, South Korea as well as Southeast Asian nations, signed the Regional Comprehensive Economic Partnership (RCEP): It is the largest trading bloc globally, covering a market of 2.2 billion people and $26.2 trillion of global output—about 30%

of world GDP."[16] Entering these existing trade agreements carries domestic challenges for the United States and the Biden administration as well as international issues, especially in asking countries that have already signed onto those agreements to rethink them in order to admit the United States, which had earlier walked away from them. In 2016 one of the reasons that then candidate Clinton indicated that she would withdraw from the TPP was because of pressure about the potential impact that it would have at home, especially in agriculture and manufacturing. However, Trump's trade war with China has negatively affected these sectors, and joining or rejoining some of these trade agreements could help ameliorate some of that impact while also balancing out China's influence.

In his *Foreign Affairs* article Biden pledged that "I will not enter into any new trade agreements until we have invested in Americans and equipped them to succeed in the global economy."[17] But he is also facing the reality that if the United States is excluded from these trade agreements, the country will suffer, and so there is a delicate balance that the Biden administration will have to maintain. Further, Biden might have to face the reality that joining these agreements will be blocked by Congress, which has its own protectionist elements. Here Biden could take a page from both Trump and Obama and simply rejoin by executive order if he faces congressional resistance. However, underlying any policy decision must be the desire to ease tensions with China on trade, while still exerting pressure on its myriad human rights abuses.

The United States and the Iran Nuclear Agreement

According to one news report after the election, "Mr. Biden has vowed to reverse what he called the 'dangerous failure' of Mr. Trump's Iran policy, which repudiated the 2015 nuclear agreement and replaced it with tightening sanctions that have caused deep economic damage in Iran and left the United States largely isolated on the issue."[18] Biden has indicated the importance of countering the threat of an Iranian nuclear buildup by rejoining the agreement with that country, albeit under certain conditions, including Iran's commitment to further negotiations. This is a move that no doubt will be supported by the Europeans who helped broker that deal, but will also anger others, including Israel, which was opposed to any agreement with Iran. The assassination of one of Iran's top nuclear scientists, Mohsen Fakhrizadeh, at the end of November 2020 potentially could alter that possibility. Intelligence officials say that "there is little doubt that Israel was behind the killing." Israel's Prime Minister Netanyahu "has long identified Iran as an existential threat" and named the murdered scientist as a national enemy. But even more telling, Netanyahu declared that "'There must be no return to the previous agreement."[19]

While Israel has not assumed responsibility for the assassination of Fakhrizadeh, its involvement will definitely complicate any effort on the part of the United States to reenter the agreement. For example, it could strengthen the hand of hard-line factions in Iran who could argue against a return to diplomacy. It seems likely from statements made by members of the Iranian government that they will respond to this attack somehow at a time and in a way of their choosing.

What happens next will be up to Iran as much as to an incoming Biden administration. Until he is officially in office, all the Biden team can do through their public messages is to encourage Iran to be patient; even after he is inaugurated, it could take a while to put a diplomatic initiative into place, and that would probably require working with the other members of the P5+1 group. This could all take time and will require all countries, the P5+1 and Iran, to trust the United States that it is now bargaining in good faith. How long it will take to rebuild that trust is another question.

It is possible that Israel's actions were designed to limit the options available to the Biden administration to return to negotiations with Iran, something that not only Israel but other Middle Eastern countries, such as Saudi Arabia, opposed from the beginning. Until the Biden administration establishes its own relationship with Israel absent Trump, at best all it can do is signal Israel to stop its covert sabotage. In this regard, it is also important to remember that Netanyahu remains under investigation and following another set of contested elections in Israel in March 2021, his leadership remains uncertain. Dealing with that becomes another unknown that will also affect what happens in this highly charged part of the world.[20]

The lesson here is that while it was relatively easy for Trump to withdraw from the Iran nuclear agreement, it will be much harder and more complicated for the United States to rejoin it.

The United States, Russia, and Arms Control

Even during the height of the Cold War, discussions on arms control agreements between the United States and Russia helped keep the relationship relatively stable. As noted in chapters 4 and 5, regardless of the tensions between the two superpowers, the fact that there were ongoing talks about how to control their nuclear weapons meant that the two sides were engaged with one another for a common purpose. As the Biden administration determines how best to deal with Russia, it also must confront the potential end of a number of agreements between the two countries. As was the case during the Cold War, the two countries are in a period of heightened tension, and affirming the agreements could once again help make the relationships more predictable and stable.

One of the treaties that the Trump administration withdrew from was "Open Skies." This treaty was negotiated during the administration of George H. W. Bush and was signed in March 1992 by the United States, Canada, and twenty-two other countries. Thirty-four countries are now signatories to the treaty, including Russia and Ukraine. The goal of the treaty was "to reduce the risk of war by allowing Russia and the West to carry out unarmed reconnaissance flights over each other's territories."[21] In May 2020, President Trump gave notice that the United States was planning to withdraw on the grounds that Russia had not complied with the terms. And in a move that limited Biden's options to return to the treaty, the United States is disposing of the two specifically equipped aircraft (OC-135B) that were used to carry out Open Skies flights. One senior defense official in the Trump administration said that that planes are being designated as "excess defense articles" that can be sold or given to foreign partners. This official claimed that "'They are really old and cost-prohibitive for us to maintain. We don't have a use for them anymore.'"[22] However, should another country purchase the aircraft, it would make it more difficult—and costly—for the United States to reenter that agreement.

Biden has been critical of the decision to withdraw from the treaty, saying that "the accord had strong allied support and that problems with Russian compliance should be addressed by using the treaty's dispute procedures." He also noted that he had supported the treaty when he was a senator because of the benefits in being part of it.[23] However, going into office, the Biden administration has not made it clear whether the United States will try to re-enter this agreement, noting that a higher priority is extending the New Start nuclear weapons treaty.

New Start

The New Start agreement was signed in April 2010 and is due to expire in February 2021 unless it is specifically extended for another five years or is renegotiated, per the terms of the treaty; if it were allowed to expire, there would be no binding limits on the two countries' nuclear arsenals. New Start superseded earlier arms control treaties by updating and extending the provisions of those treaties, such as START I. The goal of New Start was to build on the arms control process that had been in place for decades. Specifically it includes elements of the 1991 START Treaty and replaces the 2002 Strategic Offensive Reductions Treaty (SORT) by including verification and confidence-building measures. The treaty sets aggregate limits on various warheads and weapon systems and includes provisions for on-site inspections and monitoring using national technical means, that is, various satellites and other means of surveillance. It also sets a limit on the number of strategic warheads each side could have.

In June 2020 Russia and the United States began talks to extend the treaty; the United States also invited China to join the talks, but Beijing refused. Russia has indicated a desire to extend the treaty, while the Trump administration remained noncommittal. The treaty was set to expire shortly after the Biden administration took office, putting additional pressure on it to determine next steps.

Biden has long espoused the importance of arms-control agreements, and in his *Foreign Affairs* article, he made the pledge to "renew our commitment to arms control for a new era." In that article, Biden claimed that "Trump has made the prospect of nuclear proliferation, a new nuclear arms race, and even the use of nuclear weapons more likely."[24] Clearly, one goal of his administration will be to reverse that trend.

However, it also must be remembered that the success of an arms-control or any international agreement is dependent on all parties involved. While Biden has made it clear that he wants to negotiate an extension of that treaty, Vladimir Putin's intentions are unknown. Putin was one of the last international leaders to congratulate Biden on his victory, which some saw as a statement of Putin's loyalty to Trump. Further, Biden tended to take a hard line toward Russia as have the new members of his administration. Despite their obvious preference for Trump, one report notes that "Russia[n] leaders expect Biden, if elected, would be more critical of Russia's geopolitical agenda and potentially may take more punitive actions such as additional sanctions, but felt at least he might usher in a more predictable strategic relationship."[25] And for any political leader, having predictable and stable relations with the United States should make their own policy priorities easier to assign.

In a phone call between Biden and Putin on January 26, 2021, they agreed to extend the New Start treaty for another five years, with each leader directing their staffs to complete all necessary procedures to ensure the continuation of the treaty. Although tensions remain high between the two leaders, the commitment to extending New Start was seen as an important step.

U.S. Relations with Europe

Although Biden has always expressed support for the European allies, on the other side of the Atlantic it might not be as easy to forget or to repair the damage that has been done by the Trump administration. Hence, part of the challenge facing Biden and American foreign policy is not only how to reestablish that trust, but how to put the United States into a leadership position once again. This will be a difficult balancing act, coming at a time when the Europeans will also be dealing with the disruptions caused by Brexit.

One of the most important aspects of the relationship between the United States and its allies has been their common values and views of the world. Although there are many examples of periods of tension between the United States and its European allies (as noted in earlier chapters in this book), the fact that they had similar approaches to and belief in the liberal economic and democratic political order allowed them to transcend those differences. For example, the former prime minister of Norway was quoted as saying about U.S. relations with Europe "'We had differences, but there was never a basic mistrust about having common views of the world.'"[26] While it may take some time to regain trust, and bearing in mind that one of the lessons is that a new president could reverse course once again, it appears that there are many common interests that hold the allies together.

One of the issues that NATO as an alliance will have to face will be the aftermath of a U.S. troop withdrawal from Afghanistan. NATO has about 11,000 troops in that country to train and advise the Afghan national security forces. "But the alliance relies heavily on U.S. armed forces for air support, transport and logistics. . . . President Trump's decision to pull almost half the U.S. troops out by mid-January leaves NATO in a bind."[27] Done with no consultation, the decision to withdraw U.S. troops means that NATO will have to make some decisions. According to NATO Secretary-General Jens Stoltenberg, "'We [NATO] face a difficult dilemma. Whether to leave, and risk that Afghanistan becomes once again a safe haven for international terrorists. Or stay, and risk a longer mission, with renewed violence.'"[28] The peace deal that was negotiated between the United States and Taliban without involvement of the NATO allies or the Afghan government would require all foreign troops to leave Afghanistan by May 2021, assuming certain conditions are met. It is this part of the agreement that is currently under review by the Biden administration. One of the points that Stoltenberg made in talking about this issue is the importance of making a coordinated decision about next steps, something that will be high on the agenda for future NATO meetings. The expectation is that the relations among the allies will change in a Biden administration but the underlying issues that they will be facing will remain critically important, especially in light of increased violence on the part of the Taliban in spite of the terms of the agreement. This is another case where the options facing the Biden administration will be constrained by decisions made by the outgoing Trump administration.

OTHER THREATS

The twenty-first century has ushered in new threats that in many ways are more dangerous and challenging to confront than more "traditional" threats coming from other countries, like the ones posed by China and Russia, noted above. We are going to focus on two here: threats from disease and climate change, which many are calling a significant existential threat. The Biden administration has plans to confront both of these.

Threats from Disease: Pandemics

There is little more that can be said about the threat posed by the spread of disease[29] beyond what we wrote in chapter 7. However, there are certainly lessons that can be learned from the way in which the outbreak was—or was not—handled by the Trump administration and what Biden and other administrations could do going forward.

In spite of Republican allegations that the Obama administration left the United States unprepared for the pandemic that would hit in 2020, the reality is that the Obama administration developed a *Playbook for Early Response to High-Consequence Emerging Infectious Disease Threats and Biological Incidents*. This document, which is now publicly available,[30] offers a comprehensive assessment of possible threats and proposed responses to those threats. The document "is a 69-page National Security Council guidebook developed in 2016 with the goal of assisting leaders 'in coordinating a complex U.S. Government response to a high-consequence emerging disease threat anywhere in the world.' It outlined questions to ask, who should be asked to get the answers and what key decisions should be made."[31] In fact, because of the Obama team's experience fighting Ebola and what it learned, they produced not only this "Playbook" for the NSC, but also similar ones for the CDC and the Department of Health and Human Services. The administration also conducted a series of "tabletop exercises" to simulate the outbreak of a major pandemic, and in 2019, the Trump administration was involved with a similar exercise as well, known as "Crimson Contagion."

With all that attention to the possibility of a threat from disease, why did it appear that the United States was caught off guard? And, a more important question looking forward, perhaps, is what is the Biden administration going to do to address the pandemic, which was going into the third wave in the winter of 2020–2021 just as it was taking office. Although a number of vaccines had been approved for use by the CDC and were being distributed by late December and into January 2021, initially the pace was slower than predicted, meaning that the country was far short of the goal of vaccinating twenty million people by the end of December. The amended government goal was to have one hundred million people vaccinated with either the Pfizer or Moderna vaccine by March 1, 2021.[32] On December 29, 2020, then president-elect Biden gave a speech excoriating the Trump administration for its failure to distribute the vaccine in a timely fashion and outlining his plan to have a hundred million people vaccinated in his first one hundred days in office. While he praised the scientists who developed the vaccines so quickly, and the drug companies for producing them, he also made it clear that the failure was with the Trump administration to have a plan for distributing the vaccine. And he outlined his own plan to accelerate production and distribution of the vaccine, as well as to ensure that people are vaccinated, especially in those communities that have been most resistant to the idea, and which are also of greatest risk. In contrast to the Trump administration, which put the burden on the states to deal with the vaccine, in a Biden administration the federal government will be more involved, including implementing a mask requirement as a simple but effective step.[33] As of this writing, the Biden administration was ahead of its goal to vaccinate one hundred million people by the first one hundred days in office. Further, a vaccine developed by Johnson and Johnson was also approved for use, joining those already approved by Pfizer and Moderna. The Johnson and Johnson vaccine, which only requires one shot, as opposed to the other two vaccines, which require two, means that it will be possible to vaccinate generally hard-to-reach populations, such as the homeless.

As part of the transition, Biden announced the appointment of Vivek Murthy to serve as surgeon general in his administration. Murthy had served as surgeon general during the Obama administration and was willing to return to government to lead a team that would be focused on controlling the pandemic. Working closely with him will be Dr. Anthony Fauci, who has become known as the most trusted man in America, a moniker previously held by CBS anchor Walter Cronkite.

Biden's approach has been to recognize that the economy will not recover unless or until the disease is brought under control. And while the economy can be aided by infusions of cash through various stimulus bills passed by Congress, the reality is that no real recovery will be possible as long as the economy is shut down, people are out of work, and those who can afford to shop are afraid to do so. Addressing this complex and interrelated set of challenges will be the task of the medical team working with the economic group to develop more holistic policies. In addition to trying to bring the virus surge under control, one of the health team's main tasks will be to oversee the distribution of the new coronavirus vaccines approved for use, as noted above, and complementary to that will be developing a strategy to encourage people to take the shots. This task has been made worse by the politicization of the vaccine, coupled with an anti-vaxxer movement.

Dealing with the pandemic is more than a domestic issue, however. After the previous administration pulled the United States out of the World Health Organization (WHO), one of Biden's stated priorities has been to rejoin the organization, which he said he would do early in his administration. WHO director-general Tedros Adhanom Ghebreyesus welcomed Biden's remarks, and acknowledging that the organization needed to make some changes, noted that it was in the process of doing so. In remarks, Tedros recognized the importance of cooperation within the international community and said that "'We need to reimagine leadership, build on mutual trust and mutual accountability to end the pandemic and address the fundamental inequalities that lie at the root of so many of the world's problems.'"[34] Paramount among this is a return of U.S. leadership in this area, as in others. Writing in the noted medical journal *The Lancet*, a group of well-respected authors made the following point: "The COVID-19 pandemic offers rare opportunities for the US President-elect to spearhead long-overdue structural changes and revitalize global health leadership. Building trust among global partners will be challenging, given the USA's withdrawal from, and disruption of, international cooperation under the presidency of Donald Trump. The USA will have to lead in a different, more collaborative way."[35] This will be especially important, as the international community has to grapple with ways to distribute the vaccine globally and ensure that all countries have access to it. It will be up to the United States to take the lead in negotiating the purchase and distribution of the vaccine so that all countries will benefit.

This case makes it clear that dealing with the myriad issues surrounding the pandemic is not just a domestic issue but a global one that will require international leadership.

Climate Change

During the campaign and then after he was officially named president-elect, Biden stressed that one of his first acts will be for the United States to rejoin the Paris Agreement on climate. In fact, in his *Foreign Affairs* piece published while he was a candidate, he stated clearly, "The United States must lead the world to take on the existential threat we face—climate change. If we don't get this right, nothing else will matter." Here, too, he outlined both a domestic and international strategy for meeting that threat. The domestic agenda included making investments at home to move toward a "clean energy economy with net-zero emissions by 2050." Internationally, Biden proposed not only to rejoin the Paris Agreement but to "convene a summit of the world's major carbon emitters, rallying nations to raise their ambitions and push progress further and faster."[36] And to underscore the importance he is giving to this area, he appointed John Kerry to serve in a new cabinet-level position as "special presidential envoy for climate." In his new position, Kerry will also sit as a member of the National Security Council, thereby reinforcing the notion that climate change is a security threat to the United States and the world. After four years in which U.S. credibility on climate change has plummeted, "Mr. Kerry will need to convince skeptical global leaders—burned by the Trump administration's hostility toward climate science and its rejection of the 2015 Paris Agreement—that the United States not only is prepared to resume its leadership role but will also stay the course, regardless of the Biden administration's future."[37] In other words, the burden will be on the United States to prove that this foreign policy priority is greater than any single administration.

Attention to this issue has become especially important in light of a series of environmental catastrophes that are the result of a changing environment. Early in December 2020, the United Nations published a "State of the Climate" report, which UN Secretary-General Guterres said reinforces the fact that "the state of the planet is broken." And to support this assertion, he "cited reductions in biodiversity, the bleaching of coral reefs, the fact that the past decade was the hottest in human history, and other indicators to emphasize that time is running out to limit the harms from global warming by reining in greenhouse gas emissions." He also ticked off extreme weather events seen this past year, including Siberian fires and a record Atlantic hurricane season.[38]

In a 2019 poll, Gallup found that "65 percent of Americans would favor protecting the environment even if it meant curbing economic growth."[39] Biden has outlined a world where it is possible to have *both* clean energy and a cleaner environment as well as economic growth. And while much of this will depend on domestic issues, such as finding ways to move away from coal-fired plants and toward clean energy such as wind and solar, some of it will also require getting international cooperation, including from countries such as China and India. This is an area where John Kerry's stature and persuasive powers can prove to be especially important. But here, too, reestablishing trust in the United States and its political will to take on this issue will be the challenge facing the Biden administration.

THE FUTURE OF U.S. FOREIGN POLICY: RETURNING TO FIRST PRINCIPLES

Chapter 1 posed several questions about U.S. foreign policy, starting with why it is important to learn about the subject. The goal of this part of the chapter is to tie together the themes and ideas raised throughout the book so that you can begin to answer some of those questions for yourself. Remember that in many cases there are no clear-cut answers, nor are there always objective "right" or "wrong" answers. Rather, the main point is that you need to know how to gather and analyze information so that you have the tools to better understand U.S. foreign policy.

It is beyond the scope of this book to try to speculate or predict the future direction of U.S. foreign policy. However, by looking at the past and understanding the ideas that have governed its development, you will be in a better position to understand what *might* happen in the future and why, as well as to evaluate what *did* happen in the past.

THE COLD WAR AS A FRAMEWORK FOR U.S. FOREIGN POLICY

The Cold War provided a clear framework for guiding U.S. foreign policy.[40] According to the realist theorists, power is the ability of one country to influence another to do what it wants or to influence the outcome of events. During the Cold War, "power" was thought of primarily as hard power (i.e., tied to military might), and foreign policy was based on the belief that it was necessary to maintain a balance of power between the United States and the Soviet Union. This did not mean that both sides needed to have exactly the same number of weapons; rather, it meant that there had to be enough weapons to deter a threat and also instill a sense that if one side attacked, the other side had the capability to respond, at least enough so that it would not be worth it for either side to attack first (i.e., capability and credibility).

While it is not often placed in the same category as military might, economic power also has been used to leverage the outcome of events. The decision to "reward" a country by giving it financial aid or other assistance was one economic approach used during and after the Cold War to sway countries to a particular side. Conversely, imposing economic sanctions or tariffs to "punish" countries is an approach that is still used; removing those tariffs is another way to reward a country. For example, agreeing to lift economic sanctions was among the incentives for Iran to agree to the nuclear deal and for Cuba to open diplomatic relations with the United States. Hence, economic tools can be used to influence a country's position. In a world that has become increasingly interdependent, economic power is an important commodity.

Absent the Cold War framework, as we have seen, U.S. foreign policy–making seemed to flounder with no clear direction. In theory, foreign policy decisions should further the national interest and during the Cold War, it was relatively easy to determine what that was. After the Cold War ended, and prior to 9/11, it was much more difficult to identify "national interest." The events of 9/11 offered some clear direction but, as we have also seen, the subsequent emergence of new threats and challenges has made it even more difficult to steer a course for the future.

The Changing Notion of Power

One of the things that has changed most dramatically since the Cold War ended has been the very notion of what "power" is or means, as well as discussions and disagreements about how the United States should wield the power that it has. It still is important to have economic power and enough military power to deter, defend, and protect as necessary, and both are considered examples of "hard power." As noted in chapter 1, the concept of power can be broadened to include "soft power." According to Nye, "Hard power rests on inducements (carrots) or threats (sticks)," whereas "soft power rests on the ability to set a political agenda in a way that shapes the preferences of others."[41] While soft power has always been a component of U.S. foreign policy, it has become more prominent since the end of the Cold War. Walter Russell Mead makes a further distinction when he divides American power in particular into four types: sharp (military), sticky (economic), sweet (culture and ideals), and hegemonic.[42] His point is that power can be looked at in any number of ways; American power is hegemonic because when the various types of power are applied together, as they have been since the end of World War II, they allow the United States to grow in strength and importance in the international arena. In his estimation, the United States has been so effective because of the use of the *full range* of the power that it has and has used.

Applying any form of power carries with it dangers, some of which have become apparent in the wake of September 11, 2001. Where "soft power arises in large part from our values" and from the desire for other countries or for people in other countries to want to emulate the United States,[43] it also carries with it the risks that those values are, or are perceived to be, antithetical to the core values of another country or culture. The imposition of one country's values on another is known as "cultural imperialism," something that the United States has been accused of.

A major foreign policy challenge facing the United States is how to use its hegemonic power—the application of its military, economic and "soft" power of culture, ideals, and values—and to what ends. That is one of the challenges facing the Biden administration. After years of resorting to primarily hard (military and economic) power with little success, should the country rethink its approach to power? And after four years of a Trump administration, where

the United States vacillated between using power unilaterally and withdrawing from global interactions, this is an important question to ponder. This
question becomes especially relevant in the face of an ascendant China, the
rise of non-state actors especially terrorist groups, fraying security relationship with some of our allies, a Middle East in turmoil, and a host of other
issues that the United States is confronting well into the twenty-first century.

U.S. Power and National Interest

By 1991, the Cold War was over. Since that time, the United States has yet
to develop a cohesive foreign policy framework that can guide the country
through the many challenges it faces in the twenty-first century. Much as
George H. W. Bush advocated for a new world order, Bill Clinton shifted the
focus to the economy and globalization, and George W. Bush stressed the
imposition of freedom and democracy, the reality is that U.S. foreign policy
in the twenty-first century has been as much a product of reactions to various
events as the result of proactive decisions. As Meade notes, "Each generation
of Americans must reinvent its country and its foreign policy to meet the demands of a world that, thanks in large part to our own success, is perpetually
more complex and more explosive."[44]

As we look to the future of U.S. foreign policy, it is essential to go back to
first principles and ask what policies are in the national interest and how that
is determined. How should the United States use its power and its superpower
status? Is the goal of U.S. power, as President Bush outlined in his second
inaugural address, "to seek and support the growth of democratic movements
and institutions in every nation and culture, with the ultimate goal of ending
tyranny in our world"?[45] Is the goal, as Mead suggests, that the United States
act as "the chief agent in a global revolutionary process through which liberal
capitalism and liberal democracy are sweeping the world"?[46] Or is the goal
"to join with citizens and governments; community organizations, religious
leaders, and businesses . . . around the world to help our people pursue a
better life," as President Obama stated in his address in Cairo?[47] All of these
represent a liberal/ idealist interpretation of the role of the United States, one
tied to values and cooperation for mutual good. If those are the priorities, then
U.S. foreign policy should be directed toward achieving those goals using
the appropriate type and amount of power to achieve them. These all stand
in marked contrast to the vision of "America first" perpetuated by Trump,
which translated into America alone in a way that this country has not seen
since the interwar period.

Looking forward, on his website Joe Biden laid out his foreign policy
vision for America: "to restore dignified leadership at home and respected

leadership on the world stage." Biden raises the important point that "our policies at home and abroad are deeply connected" and designed to "advance the security, prosperity, and values of the United States by taking immediate steps to renew our own democracy and alliances, protect our economic future, and once more place America at the head of the table, leading the world to address the most urgent global challenges."[48] In other words, the vision he put forward of U.S. foreign policy is that it cannot be removed from domestic issues and challenges, suggesting that the United States, once again, should be a force for good at home and abroad.

The Changing Notion of Threat

A "threat" is anything that endangers or potentially could endanger a country or its people. Since the end of the Cold War, U.S. foreign policy has had to confront the changing perception of threat. Traditionally, threat has been tied to military might, as threats were generally perceived as the dangers from one country attacking another. But in the twenty-first century, a threat could emerge from situations other than military attack or an attack from one country against another. Suffice it to say the attacks of September 11, 2001, were one example of a direct threat coming from a nonstate actor, in this case an Islamic fundamentalist group. As the coronavirus pandemic illustrated clearly, other threats need to be considered as well, for they too pose a threat to the security of the people of the United States and will—or should—influence American foreign policy decisions.

In a globalized world, as American companies such as Starbucks or McDonald's open stores in more countries, they bring with them the perception of American dominance. McDonald's is ubiquitous, and Starbucks has been able to make inroads in China and Japan, both tea-drinking countries.[49] On the one hand, this means that people in those countries are accepting the image that Starbucks is selling, which is tied closely to American culture. On the other hand, that success also represents an assertion of American cultural values that not everyone in those countries likes or accepts. It is also an indirect and very visible assertion of American power and influence, that is, soft power. And, as a result, it has made the United States and its citizens targets for those who oppose our values.

One of the characteristics of the globalized world in which we now live is a breakdown in national borders, as people, products, and ideas are transmitted easily from one country to another—communication between and among countries is virtually seamless. One can travel around the world in less than a day. Ideas and knowledge are shared easily, as scientists collaborate with colleagues in other countries using e-mail and computer technology or as information is published online. A globalized world means that contraband materials, such as weapons and drugs, can be shipped from one place to another virtually undetected. Infectious diseases, such as coronavirus can spread quickly as one person who is unknowingly carrying the disease gets on a plane and spreads it among fellow passengers, who then disperse and spread it still further.[50] Illegal immigrants can move from one country to another, some seeking economic opportunity or to flee conflict, while others might be intent on terrorism or other more dangerous goals. This, too, has brought with it a new set of problems and issues that the United States has had to confront, and no doubt will continue to confront, in a Biden administration.

Unchecked climate change has been identified as one of the greatest existential threats to the world, as global warming has led to an increase in weather-related catastrophes. An increase in the number and severity of hurricanes, long periods of record-breaking heat in parts of the United States as well as other countries, the melting of Arctic ice that has led to a rise in sea levels, not to mention danger to animals such as polar bears, and a lengthening of the wildfire season in the western United States contributed to a greater number of more destructive fires. In addition, some of the issues and threats noted above are interrelated. For example, increased drought has contributed to crop failures in parts of Africa which, in turn has led to an increase in the number of environmental or climate refugees. Rising sea levels have forced inhabitants in low-lying areas to flee to make their homes on higher ground. All of these are examples of the threats to human security that will only get worse if not checked. Furthermore, many of these issues transcend borders and will require international cooperation to address. If the United States does not take the lead in addressing these issues, then who will? Or will the United States be put into a position of having to follow the lead of other countries?

It also should be noted that the traditional approaches to American foreign policy decision-making are not necessarily able to deal with these new and emerging threats; U.S. foreign policy–making is still premised on a threat coming from a country and taking a particular form. However, as the examples above show, the nature of the threat has changed. Although the Bush administration created the Department of Homeland Security in 2002 to try to address terrorist threats (i.e., a threat by a nonstate actor) and restructured the intelligence community in 2008 to be nimbler at tracking potential threats, no administration to date has arrived at a way to create U.S. foreign policy that can anticipate and respond to the full range of potential dangers and threats that this country now faces. The inability to confront these threats and the difficulty in even identifying the sources of such threats are among the foreign policy challenges that the United States and other countries face in the twenty-first century.

Identifying threats from non-state actors does not mean that other nation-states do not also pose a threat to the United States. In his State of the Union address in January 2002, then president Bush identified three countries he called an "axis of evil," Iraq, Iran, and North Korea. "States like these, and their terrorist allies, constitute an axis of evil, arming to threaten the peace of the world. By seeking weapons of mass destruction, these regimes pose a grave and growing danger."[51] Since the time he made that speech, the government in Iraq has changed, although the situation is far from stable. In 2015 Iran and the United States signed an agreement that would limit Iran's ability to build a nuclear weapon for at least the next fifteen years, although President Trump withdrew the United States from that agreement. Since that happened, there are indications that Iran is stockpiling nuclear materials once again. President Biden has indicated the importance of rejoining that agreement in order to stop or reverse that trend.

North Korea continues to remain a threat, if not to the United States directly, then certainly to U.S. allies and potentially the world if it continues to pursue the development of nuclear weapons, which it has given every indication that it intends to do. As U.S. forces withdraw from Afghanistan, there are questions about the future of that country after more than a decade of war. Under the leadership of Vladimir Putin, Russia has become more militant and aggressive in its foreign policy, resulting in growing tensions between the United States and Russia once again. China is another country currently vying for major power status, a perspective that will certainly affect U.S. foreign policy. It has become the second-most-important country in the world economically and militarily and on course to soon overtake the United States, adding a new element to the international system.

What all this suggests is that the United States is confronting more and different types of threats and challenges than it did in the past. This means that the United States needs to develop a foreign policy better suited to the challenges that the country is facing now and likely will continue to face. This might mean injecting more diplomacy, thereby balancing soft with hard power. It may mean more reliance on allies once again. Or it might mean, as Joe Biden has said, that "America is back. Ready to lead the world, not retreat from it. Once again, sit at the head of the table."[52] The critical factor should be to ensure that the foreign policy is appropriate to the situation and existing political and economic realities.

THE ACTORS AND THE DOMESTIC BALANCE OF POWER

In the first chapter, we talked about the actors who make foreign policy and the constitutional framework that was to guide this process. However, in the wake of 9/11 we once again see the emergence of a strong executive. Under George W. Bush Congress was willing to allow the administration to pursue policies that, in retrospect, might be seen as questionable. Among these policies were the circumvention of the Foreign Intelligence Surveillance Act (FISA) and authorization of wiretaps on American citizens by the NSA; the use of torture, such as waterboarding, on terrorism suspects; and the use of extraordinary rendition to send suspects to other countries for extreme forms of interrogation. These policies were all enacted in the name of national security and were justified as essential to safeguarding the security of the United States. What emerged subsequently have been charges and countercharges about what information Congress was given about these policies, how much members of Congress actually knew and when they knew it, and what their role should be. Note that these policies are not confined to one administration. In 2013 it was revealed that the Obama administration had authorized the NSA to monitor phone and data records of U.S. citizens as well as allies, most notably Germany, building on policies put into place under Bush but also raising questions about the range and reach of the government. And as noted in chapter 7, the Obama administration's decision in 2014 to authorize air strikes in Syria and parts of Iraq was made without congressional authorization.

We can look at a more recent and dramatic example with the imposition of tariffs by the Trump administration. While Article 1, Section 8 of the Constitution gives Congress the power "To lay and collect Taxes, Duties, Imposts and Excises," and "To regulate Commerce with foreign Nations,"[53] in reality, Congress abrogated those responsibilities by allowing the Trump administration to get into a trade war with China, as well as with Canada, one of our major trading partners. Hence, the balance of powers set forth in the Constitution is only as strong as the branches are in applying those powers to curtail the power of another branch.

What history has shown is a pendulum swinging between the assertion of presidential authority and congressional prerogatives given in the Constitution if not to oversee that authority, at least to balance presidential power. The last time the perception arose that the pendulum had swung too far and that the president was abusing his power was during the administration of Richard Nixon. This resulted in passage of the War Powers Resolution and a belief in the need to check the power of the president. What followed was a series of fairly weak presidents (Ford and Carter), until Reagan once again started asserting executive power. What we saw subsequently under George W. Bush was an unapologetic assertion of executive power justified by events of the time.

Obama had the advantage of coming into office as a popular president and with a strong Democratic majority in Congress. Like Johnson before him, he also had a robust domestic agenda that he wanted to accomplish, including addressing the economic downturn and the crisis in health care. However, a political shift in 2010 brought to power a Republican majority in the House with a strongly conservative focus. Even the then minority leader of the Senate, Republican Mitch McConnell, noted that his goal was to make Obama a one-term president.[54] Although this did not happen, the partisan politics of Washington made it much harder for Obama to enact the policies that he had hoped to. In addition to affecting his domestic policies, it also made it much more difficult for Obama's foreign policy agenda, although Obama became very effective at using executive action as a way to circumvent the Congress.[55] This led to questions during the 2016 presidential campaign about "overreach," although Obama would contend that that was the only way in which he could ensure the implementation of some of his priority issues. However, this also set a precedent and, as president, Trump became a master at ignoring or circumventing the Congress.

As president, Trump used executive action to accomplish many of his policy goals. Even though he had a Republican majority in the Senate, a Democratic majority in the House served as a check on his power, getting to the point of impeaching him for abusing the power of his office by soliciting the interference of a foreign government (Ukraine) in an election.[56] While the Senate did not convict him, it served as a reminder that under the Constitution, one of the responsibilities of the Congress is to check the power of the president. However, that also assumes that the president will respect the oversight function of the Congress and will comply with its mandates.

Challenges to U.S. Foreign Policy in the Future

As we have seen, the United States is facing a number of foreign policy challenges. As the United States inaugurated another president in January 2021, the challenges remain and, in many ways, are even more difficult because of the range of domestic and international actors involved. As noted above, the very nature of the threat has changed which, in turn, has affected the types of responses available.

One point that has been made throughout this book is that many of the issues that the United States will face are beyond the control of the country or its leaders. For example, few could have anticipated the Brexit vote or what it might mean for the future of the United Kingdom and the other member states of the EU, all important allies as well as trading partners of the United States. Although this will not directly affect NATO or U.S. security ties, the reality is that the exit of the UK from the European Union will have an impact on all countries with which the EU interacts as that bloc struggles to determine its own future. This was completely unexpected and yet will force the United States to reassess its relationship with the countries of Europe both individually and as parts of both the EU and NATO.

The world of the twenty-first century is a difficult and complicated place, and it will be up to present and future decision-makers to determine how to frame foreign policy that will meet those challenges and also serve U.S. national interest.

SELECTED PRIMARY SOURCES

Joseph R. Biden Jr. "Why American Must Lead Again: Rescuing U.S. Foreign Policy after Trump,'" *Foreign Affairs*, March/April 2020, 2, https://www.foreignaffairs.com/articles/united-states/2020-01-23/why-america-must-lead-again.

Full text of Joe Biden's speech after historic election, ABC News, November 7, 2020, https://abcnews.go.com/Politics/read-full-text-joe-bidens-speech-historic-election/story?id=74084462.

George W. Bush, second inaugural address, January 20, 2005, http://www.npr.org/templates/story/story.php?storyId=4460172.

George W. Bush, "State of the Union Address," "Axis of Evil," January 29, 2002, http://georgewbush-whitehouse.archives.gov/news/releases/2002/01/20020129-11.html. A video of the address is available at the same site.

Barack Obama, "Remarks on a New Beginning," Cairo, Egypt, June 4, 2009, https://obamawhitehouse.archives.gov/the-press-office/remarks-president-cairo-university-6-04-09.

Joseph R. Biden, "The Power of America's Example: The Biden Plan for Leading the Democratic Challenges of the 21st Century," https://joebiden.com/americanleadership/#.

Notes

CHAPTER 1: SETTING THE STAGE

1. Fareed Zakaria titles the first chapter of his book, *The Post-American World*, "The Rise of the Rest," and notes that the book is "not about the decline of American but rather about the rise of everyone else." He also makes it clear that "the rest" is not only states but also nonstate actors, which have also come to play a greater role. Fareed Zakaria, *The Post-American World, Release 2.0* (New York: W.W. Norton & Company, 2012), 1.

2. See for example, Tracy Wilkinson, "Global Response Weak as U.S. Retreats," *Los Angeles Times*, April 17, 2020, (https:enewspaper.latimes.com/infinity/article_share.aspx?guid=38dbe-ae68-4f53-ae92-15b651bfcee5); and David M. Shribman, "U.S. Exit from World Stage Is a Global Crisis," *Los Angeles Times,* May 9, 2020 (http://enewspaper.latimes/infinity/article_share.aspx?guid=f724aa25-3cf9-44af-9845-b20e6d8c8862).

3. Nicholas Burns, "How to Lead in a Time of Pandemic: What U.S. Foreign Policy Should be Doing—but Isn't—to Rally the World to Action," *Foreign Affairs*, March 25, 2020, https://www.foreignaffairs.com/articles/2020-03-25/how-lead-time-pandemic.

4. For more detail on accessing specific websites see chapter end notes and also the section on "Selected Primary Sources," especially the reference to specific web pages. Bear in mind that specific URLs can change. However, most of the primary sources are readily available through Google or other search engines.

5. Two excellent relatively recent books that make the case that the conditions that gave rise to Donald Trump and the movement surrounding him are *The Age of Illusions: How America Squandered Its Cold War Victory*, by Andrew Bacevich (New York: Metropolitan Books, 2020) and *Mission Failure: America and the World in the Post–Cold War Era*, by Michael Mandelbaum (New York: Oxford University Press, 2016). Both authors argue to some degree that the United States squandered the ad-

vantages it had at the end of the Cold War through a series of poor choices and also lack of understanding of global economics and politics.

6. Walter Russell Mead, in *Special Providence: American Foreign Policy and How It Changed the World* (New York: Routledge, 2009), notes that "foreign policy and domestic politics were inextricably mixed throughout American history" (26). That said, throughout the book he also condemns Americans, even those in positions of leadership and responsibility, for their "lack of interest in the history of American foreign policy" (7). As Rucker and Leonnig note, that is especially true of Donald Trump. They give the example of the president's visit to Pearl Harbor in November 2017 on his way to Asia. When visiting the memorial, Trump asked his then chief of staff, John Kelly, "What's this all about? What is this a tour of?" According to the story, Trump "appeared to understand that he was visiting the scene of a historic battle, but he did not seem to know much else." Philip Rucker and Carole Leonnig, *A Very Stable Genius: Donald J. Trump's Testing of America* (New York: Penguin Press, 2020), 169.

7. While many political science texts refer to the early period of U.S. foreign policy as "isolationist," diplomatic historians, such as Walter McDougall, make the point that the period is better described as "unilateralist." According to McDougall, "the essence of Unilateralism was to be *at Liberty* to make foreign policy independent of the 'toils of European ambition.' Unilateralism never meant that the United States should, or for that matter could, sequester itself or pursue an ostrich-like policy toward all foreign countries. It simply meant . . . that the self-evident course for the United States was to avoid permanent entangling alliances and to remain neutral in Europe's wars." Walter A. McDougall, *Promised Land, Crusader State* (New York: Houghton Mifflin, 1997), 40. The concept of *unilateralism* describes a foreign policy through which the United States is engaged with the world although steering clear of formal alliances or political obligations.

8. "The National Security Strategy of the United States of America," http://georgewbush-whitehouse.archives.gov/nsc/nssall.html.

9. As we will see in chapter 6, the Bush administration justified the decision to go to war in Iraq based on alleged evidence that Saddam Hussein had weapons of mass destruction, an allegation that was subsequently disproved. A relatively new book, *Bush,* by John Edward Smith makes the case that Bush's decision to invade Iraq was one of the worst foreign policy decisions made by an American president (New York: Simon & Schuster, 2016).

10. John B. Judis makes the case that "the End of the Cold War created the conditions for finally realizing the promise of Wilson's foreign policy" (7). John B. Judis, *The Folly of Empire: What George W. Bush Could Learn from Theodore Roosevelt and Woodrow Wilson* (New York: Scribner, 2004). In many ways, it also set the stage for the policies of George W. Bush, specifically the idealistic desire to spread democracy worldwide, which in many ways harkens back to the idealism of Wilson.

11. For a detailed description of the ways in which an American corporation affects other countries, see the three articles on "the Wal-Mart effect" in the *Los Angeles Times*: Abigail Goldman and Nancy Cleeland, "An Empire Built on Bargains Remakes the Working World," November 23, 2003; Nancy Cleeland, Evelyn Iritani,

and Tyler Marshall, "Scouring the Globe to Give Shoppers an $8.63 Polo Shirt," November 24, 2003; Nancy Cleeland and Abigail Goldman, "Grocery Unions Battle to Stop Invasion of the Giant Stores," November 25, 2003. Although the articles are relatively old, they do a great job of describing the relationship between Wal-Mart and individuals in this country, with other countries, and with a range of other critical actors. The series won a Pulitzer Prize in 2004.

12. Joseph Nye, *The Paradox of American Power: Why the World's Only Superpower Can't Go It Alone* (Oxford: Oxford University Press, 2002), 9.

13. Walter Russell Mead, *Power, Terror, Peace and War: America's Grand Strategy in a World at Risk* (New York: Knopf, 20014).

14. Hans J. Morgenthau, *Politics among Nations: The Struggle for Power and Peace* (Boston: McGraw-Hill, 1993), 5.

15. According to Barry Hughes, core interests "flow from the desire [of the state] to preserve its essence: territorial boundaries, population, government, and sovereignty." Barry Hughes, *Continuity and Change in World Politics: The Clash of Perspectives*, second ed. (Englewood Cliffs, NJ: Prentice Hall, 1994), 79.

16. Cynthia Enloe makes a persuasive argument about the need to take women's experiences in foreign policy and international relations seriously. For example, she writes about why and how "Carmen Miranda's movies helped make Latin America safe for American banana companies at a time when U.S. imperialism was coming under wider regional criticism." This is but one example of the ways in which women's images have been used to shape international business and economics as well as foreign policy. Cynthia Enloe, *Bananas, Beaches, and Bases* (Berkeley: University of California Press, 2000), 124.

17. See J. Ann Tickner, *Gendering World Politics* (Cambridge: Cambridge University Press, 2001).

18. One of the more interesting findings to grow from the COVID-19 pandemic was that women leaders tended to be more successful at addressing the threat within their own countries than men were. Although anecdotal, this was true of Prime Minister Jacinda Ardern of New Zealand, Angele Merkel in Germany, and Tsai Ing-wen, the president of Taiwan, who "has presided over one of the most successful efforts in the world at containing the virus." While there is no definitive answer as to why this is the case, there is a great deal of speculation as to what these women leaders brought to their understanding of the crisis, versus many of their male counterparts. See Amanda Taub, "Why Are Women-Led Nations Doing Better with Covid-19?" *New York Times*, May 15, 2020, https://www.nytimes.com/2020/05/15/world/coronavirus-women-leaders.html.

19. John Shattuck, "Human Rights and Humanitarian Crises: Policy-Making and the Media," in *From Massacres to Genocide: The Media, Public Policy, and Humanitarian Crises*, ed. Robert I. Rotberg and Thomas G. Weiss (Washington, DC: Brookings Institution, 1996), 174.

20. A series of polls released in June 2005 showed that public support for the conflict in Iraq was dropping. One poll found that 37 percent of those polled approved of the president's handling of the situation in Iraq, down from 45 percent in February (Robin Toner and Marjorie Connelly, "Bush's Support on Major Issues Tumbles in

Poll," *New York Times*, June 17, 2005). A *Washington Post*–ABC News poll found that 50 percent of the respondents "now disapprove of the way Bush is handling both the economy and the situation in Iraq." This poll also found that "support for the war is the lowest yet recorded in this poll" (David Broder, "A Growing Public Restlessness," *Washington Post*, June 12, 2005, B9). Also see "Bush's Approval Ratings Stay Low," CBS News poll, http://www.cbsnews.com/news/bushs-approval-ratings-stay-low/.

21. "Less Optimism about Iraq," Pew Research Center for People and the Press, May 1, 2008, http://www.people-press.org/2008/05/01/section-5-less-optimism-about-iraq.

22. Many foreign policy texts refer to the early period of U.S. foreign policy as a period of "isolationism," meaning that the United States was "isolated" (removed) from the rest of the world, preferring to focus within. In fact, I would argue that the United States was involved in a limited way of its own choosing, thereby making the word *unilateralist* more appropriate, consistent with the point made by McDougal (note 7). However, Mearsheimer makes the case that U.S. policy in the period between the two world wars really was isolationist, in that "the United States made no serious move toward a continental commitment when the war [World War II] broke out." In fact, he notes, from the period from 1923 to the summer of 1940, the "United States committed no forces to Europe," suggesting a return to the policy advocated by George Washington of remaining "aloof from" the wars in Europe. John Mearsheimer, *The Tragedy of Great Power Politics* (New York: W. W. Norton, 2001), 254. For purposes of this text, each term will be used to describe policies that are slightly different, as appropriate at various periods in U.S. history.

23. Eugene R. Wittkopf, Charles W. Kegley Jr., and James M. Scott, *American Foreign Policy*, sixth ed. (Belmont, CA: Wadsworth/Thomson Learning, 2003), 27.

24. George Washington's Farewell Address, September 17, 1796, http://avalon.law.yale.edu/18th_century/washing.asp.

25. Charles Francis Adams, *The Works of John Adams, Second President of the United States*, Kindle edition (Amazon Digital Services), 2010.

26. Mead, *Special Providence*, 14.

27. Mead, *Special Providence*, 17.

28. Mearsheimer writes that "the United States achieved great-power status in about 1898" and that "the United States was no ordinary great power by 1900. It had the most powerful economy in the world and it had clearly gained hegemony in the Western Hemisphere." Mearsheimer, *The Tragedy of Great Power Politics*, 234–35.

29. While technically the United States remains engaged internationally through alliances such as NATO and its role in other organizations such as the G7, one could argue that the Trump administration has altered the framework for U.S. foreign policy by moving the United States out of multilateral alliances, such as the Trans-Pacific Partnership and the Paris Climate Change Agreement, in favor of bilateral agreements. This is consistent with Trump's worldview that the United States would be in a better position if it were to renegotiate many of these older agreements in terms that would be more favorable to the United States. This is discussed in more detail in chapter 7.

30. A joint U.S.-Soviet commission was established as part of the 1972 summit, when the two countries also initialed the SALT I agreement. The purpose of this commission was to begin the process for granting most favored nation trade status to the Soviet Union by the United States. The trade patterns between the two countries ebbed and flowed throughout the Cold War.

31. The U.S.-North Korean Agreed Framework of 1994 allowed for the export of U.S. oil to North Korea as well as assistance in dismantling its graphite-moderated nuclear reactors to replace them with water-moderated reactors, which is a safer method of nuclear power production. See "Agreed Framework of 21 October 1994 between the United States of America and the Democratic People's Republic of Korea," https://www.iaea.org/sites/default/files/publications/documents/infcircs/1994/infcirc457.pdf.

32. For a more detailed explanation of the various actors and their relationship to one another and to the "rings" of power, see Roger Hilsman (with Laura Gaughran and Patricia A. Weitsman), *The Politics of Policy Making in Defense and Foreign Affairs: Conceptual Models and Bureaucratic Politics*, third ed. (Englewood Cliffs, NJ: Prentice Hall, 1993).

33. See the Constitution of the United States, which can be found at the following website, among others: http://www.archives.gov/exhibits/charters/constitution_transcript.html.

34. For more detail as to the relationships among the various branches of government specifically regarding war powers, see Donald L. Westerfield, *War Powers: The President, the Congress, and the Question of War* (Westport, CT: Praeger, 1996). Westerfield goes through a number of cases and reviews issues of constitutionality as well as how "the sense of the Congress" plays a role in limiting the power of the president.

35. Article II, Section 2, Clause 2, Constitution of the United States, http://www.archives.gov/exhibits/charters/constitution_transcript.html.

36. Article II, Section 2, Clause 1, Constitution of the United States, http://www.archives.gov/exhibits/charters/constitution_transcript.html.

37. Article I, Section 8, Clause 11, Constitution of the United States, http://www.archives.gov/exhibits/charters/constitution_transcript.html.

38. "Truman's Korean War Statement," June 27, 1950, http://www. presidency.ucsb.edu/ws/?pid=13538.

39. The Tonkin Gulf Resolution is described and explored in more detail in chapter 4, "The Cold War."

40. The Constitution made Congress the branch of government that is closest to the people. This is especially true of the House of Representatives, where all members must stand for election every two years. This means that they are most sensitive to public opinion.

41. Katie Glueck and Thomas Kaplan, "Joe Biden's Vote for War," *New York Times*, January 12, 2020, https://www.nytimes.com/2020/01/12/us/politics/joe-biden-iraq-war.html.

42. See Rucker and Leonnig, *A Very Stable Genius*.

43. Kathryn Dunn Tenpas, "Tracking Turnover in the Trump Administration," Brookings Institution, August 2020, https://www.brookings.edu/research/tracking -turnover-in-the-trump-administration/.

44. The term *military-industrial complex* was coined by President Eisenhower in his farewell address, delivered on January 17, 1961, in which he said, "We must guard against the acquisition of unwarranted influence, whether sought or unsought, by the military industrial complex. The potential for the disastrous rise of misplaced power exists and will persist." http://avalon.law.yale.edu/20th_ century/eisenhower001.asp.

45. Article 5 of the NATO treaty states that "an armed attack against one or more of them [the parties to the treaty] in Europe or North America shall be considered an attack against them all." The full text of the North Atlantic Treaty can be found at the NATO website, http://www.nato.int/cps/en/natolive/official_texts_17120.htm.

46. A report released the UK in July 2016 by an Iraq Inquiry Committee found that "the decision to go to war had been based on flawed intelligence, and that the threat of unconventional weapons used to justify military intervention had been presented with a certainty that was not justified by the evidence," as noted by John Chilcot who led the inquiry. This has opened old wounds in the UK as well as led to a scathing indictment of the then prime minister Tony Blair for his judgment. See Dan Bilefsky, "Chilcot Report Reopens Wounds for Relatives of Fallen British Soldiers, *New York Times*, July 6, 2016, http://www.nytimes.com/2016/07/07/world/europe/chilcot -report-families-british-soldiers.html.

47. Avery Johnson, "Sticker Shock at the Lumberyard," *Wall Street Journal*, August 11, 2004, D1.

48. "Twenty-Sixth Amendment: Reeducation of Voting Age Qualification, http:// www.archives.gov/exhibits/charters/constitution_transcript.html.

49. John B. Judis, *The Folly of Empire: What George W. Bush Could Learn from Theodore Roosevelt and Woodrow Wilson* (New York: Scribner, 2004), 46. What is instructive about this is that these are virtually the same words Vice President Cheney said in an interview he gave to *Meet the Press* on March 16, 2003, just after the U.S. invasion of Iraq. At that time he said: "I think things have gotten so bad inside Iraq, from the standpoint of the Iraqi people, my belief is we will, in fact, be greeted as liberators." https://www.reuters.com/article/us-iraq-war-quotes/factbox-iraq-war-the -notable-quotes-idUSL212762520080311 However, just as the United States remained fighting in the Philippines for thirteen years, as of January 2020, approximately 5,200 American troops remained in Iraq, over the objections of the Iraqi government. There are a number of other cases and examples where it appeared that the United States was repeating earlier mistakes.

CHAPTER 2: UNILATERALISM TO ENGAGEMENT

1. Mark Binelli, "'Hamilton' Creator Lin-Manuel Miranda: The *Rolling Stone* Interview," *Rolling Stone*, June 1, 2016, http://www.rollingstone.com/ music/features/hamilton-creator-lin-manuel-miranda-the-rolling-stone-interview -20160601#ixzz4DwpmWUx1.

2. Walter A. McDougall, *Promised Land, Crusader State* (New York: Houghton Mifflin, 1997), 20.

3. Jean E. Smith, *The Constitution and American Foreign Policy* (St. Paul, MN: West Publishing, 1989), 14.

4. Quoted in Smith, *The Constitution and American Foreign Policy*, 16–17.

5. Charles Tilly makes the point that the evolution of the European state system was tied, in large measure, to war (i.e., the means of coercion), especially at a time when the United States was being created and established. "As European states moved into the phase of nationalization (especially between 1700 and 1850 . . .) dynasties lost much of their ability to make war on their own behalf, and something we call vaguely 'national interest' came to dominate states' involvement or non-involvement in wars. National interest synthesized the interests of the dominant classes, but compounded them with a much stronger drive to control contiguous territories and populations within Europe, as well as a fiercer competition for land outside Europe." It appears that Washington and some of the other founders of the country saw what was going on in Europe and, understanding that drive for competition leading to war, wanted to keep the United States removed from it as much as possible. Charles Tilly, *Coercion, Capital, and European States: AD 990–1990* (Cambridge, MA: Basil Blackwell, 1990), 185.

6. Alexander Hamilton, *The Federalist Papers*, No. 24 (New York: Mentor, 1961), 160–61. Also available at https://www.congress.gov/resources/display/content/The+Federalist+Papers.

7. James Madison, *The Federalist Papers*, No. 41 (New York: Mentor, 1961), 256–57. Also available at https://www.congress.gov/resources/display/content/The+Federalist+Papers.

8. McDougall, *Promised Land, Crusader State,* 31–32.

9. The Farewell Address is well worth reading in its entirety for the way in which Washington perceived the country at that time, as well as for the argument that he made about what U.S. foreign policy should be. See full text of George Washington's Farewell Address, September 17, 1796, text box 2.1, available at http://avalon.law.yale.edu/18th_century/washing.asp.

10. Eugene R. Wittkopf, Charles W. Kegley Jr., and James M. Scott, *American Foreign Policy*, sixth ed. (Belmont, CA: Wadsworth/Thomson Learning, 2003), 28.

11. Mearsheimer makes the point that "the phrase 'Manifest Destiny' was not actually coined until 1845." By that time, the United States was well into its westward expansion and had already acquired the Louisiana Purchase and the Texas territories. John Mearsheimer, *The Tragedy of Great Power Politics* (New York: W. W. Norton, 2001), 487, fn. 11.

12. George C. Herring, *From Colony to Superpower: U.S. Foreign Relations since 1776* (New York: Oxford University Press, 2008), 127.

13. McDougall, *Promised Land, Crusader State*, 36.

14. Quoted in McDougall, *Promised Land, Crusader State*, 92.

15. T. Harry Williams, *The History of American Wars: From Colonial Times to World War I* (New York: Alfred A. Knopf, 1981), 144–45.

16. Herring, *From Colony to Superpower*, 205.

17. Herring, *From Colony to Superpower*, 207.
18. Mearsheimer, *The Tragedy of Great Power Politics*, 244.
19. Walter Russell Mead, *Special Providence: American Foreign Policy and How It Changed the World* (New York: Alfred A. Knopf, 2002), 14. In the first chapter of his book, Mead makes the case that U.S. economic interests were directly tied to other parts of the world through interlinked financial markets. This meant not only that "foreign money dug the canals, built the railroads and settled much of the West" but also that "domestic prosperity was threatened or ruined by financial storms that originated overseas" (15–16). We see many of these same patterns today.
20. Roxanne Dunbar-Ortiz, *An Indigenous People's History of the United States* (Boston: Beacon Press, 2014), 118. The author is grateful to Robert Marks who reminded her of the importance of including the impact of U.S. westward expansion on the native peoples, a point often overlooked in most foreign policy books.
21. Dunbar-Ortiz, *An Indigenous People's History of the United States*, 120–21.
22. National Archives, "American Indian Treaties," https://www.archives.gov/research/native-americans/treaties.
23. Office of the Historian, Department of State, "Indian Treaties and the Removal Act of 1830," https://history.state.gov/milestones/1830-1860/indian-treaties.
24. Herring, *From Colony to Superpower*, 172.
25. Herring, *From Colony to Superpower*, 173.
26. Mead, *Special Providence*, 26.
27. Paul Kennedy, *The Rise and Fall of the Great Powers* (New York: Vintage, 1987), 180.
28. The Treaty of Chemulpo between the United States and Korea begins by stating that "there shall be perpetual peace and friendship between the President of the United States and the King of Chosen [Korea] and the citizens and subjects of their respective Governments." "Treaty of Peace, Amity, Commerce and Navigation Between Korea (Chosen) and the United States of America," https://www.loc.gov/law/help/us-treaties/bevans/b-korea-ust000009-0470.pdf. This treaty also provided for trade on a most-favored-nation basis, established diplomatic relations between the two countries, allowed for the immigration of Koreans to the United States, and established mutual defense in case of foreign invasion. According to George Herring, although this agreement was part of the United States' search for markets, trade between the two countries was "negligible." George C. Herring, *From Colony to Superpower: U.S. Foreign Relations Since 1776* (Oxford: Oxford University Press, 2008), 287.
29. The de Lôme letter can be found at https://www.ourdocuments.gov/print_friendly.php?flash=false&page=transcript&doc=53&title=Transcript+of+De+L%26amp%3Bocirc%3Bme+Letter+%281898%29.
30. Note that there are parallels between the sinking of the USS *Maine*, which contributed to the outbreak of war with Spain, and the Gulf of Tonkin incident, which led to the resolution passed in 1964 that gave Lyndon Johnson the excuse to escalate the war in Vietnam. In that case, the U.S. destroyers *Maddox* and *Turner Joy* allegedly came under attack while patrolling the Gulf of Tonkin. This was seen as an act of war and gave President Johnson the rationale to go to Congress to secure passage of a

resolution authorizing him to take "all necessary measures to repel any armed attacks against the forces of the United States and to prevent further aggression." (See chapter 4 for more detail about this incident.) The commander of the *Maddox* indicated that "freak weather effects" and "overeager" sonar operators might have been to blame, rather than an actual attack. But it was clear that Johnson, who had the resolution already prepared, and Secretary of Defense Robert McNamara were ready to escalate the conflict, and this incident provided the opportunity for them to do so. See George C. Herring, *America's Longest War: The United States and Vietnam, 1950–1975* (New York: McGraw-Hill, 1996), 133–37.

31. "Not for Cuba Only," *New York Times,* July 30, 1891, http://timesmachine. nytimes.com/timesmachine/1898/07/30/105963836.html?pageNumber=6.

32. Russia and Japan did not comply but went to war in 1904–1905 over control of Manchuria and Korea (the Russo-Japanese War).

33. Work on the Panama Canal started in 1907, and it was opened in 1914. Its completion meant that the United States could move warships quickly between the Atlantic Ocean and the Pacific, which "transformed naval strategy" and, in fact, "changed hemisphere policy." But it also meant that "a deep distrust had been sown . . . in the minds of Latin Americans, about the ambitions and lack of scruple of American foreign policy." J. M. Roberts, *Twentieth Century: A History of the World, 1901–2000* (New York: Viking, 1999), 105.

34. Robert B. Marks, *The Origins of the Modern World: A Global and Environmental Narrative from the Fifteenth to the Twenty-First Century,* fourth ed. (Lanham, MD: Rowman & Littlefield, 2020), 135.

35. The First *Lusitania* Note, May 13, 1915, available at http://wwi.lib.byu.edu/ index.php/Wilson's_First_Lusitania_Note_to_Germany.

36. Daniel J. Boorstein and Brooks Mather Kelley, *A History of the United States* (Lexington, MA: Ginn, 1981), 448.

37. "Peace without Victory," address of President Wilson to the U.S. Senate, January 22, 1917, available at http://www-personal.umd.umich.edu/~ppennock/doc -Wilsonpeace.htm.

38. Office of the Historian, U.S. Department of State, "U.S. Entry into World War I, 1917," https://history.state.gov/milestones/1914-1920/wwi.

39. "Wilson's Speech for Declaration of War against Germany," address delivered at joint session of Congress, April 2, 1917, available at http://millercenter.org/ president/speeches/detail/4722. It is also important to note that in this speech, Wilson stated, "We have no quarrel with the German people. We have no feeling toward them but one of sympathy and friendship. It was not upon their impulse that their government acted in entering this war." In this speech, his words are very similar to words George Kennan used in his "Long Telegram," sent from Moscow in 1946, in which he, too, drew a distinction between the outlook of the Russian people, and that of their government. This point is developed in chapter 4.

40. Quoted in House of Representatives, "Historical Highlights: The House Declaration of War Against Germany in 1917," https://history.house.gov/Historical -Highlights/1901-1950/The-House-declaration-of-war-against-Germany-in-1917/.

41. It should be noted that despite Wilson's high-minded moralism, he also was known to be a racist, a point that was made dramatically in spring 2020 during the Black Lives Matter protests following the death of George Floyd. On June 27, 2020, Princeton University's president, Christopher L. Eisgruber, sent an open letter to the Princeton community noting that the Board of Trustees had agreed to remove Wilson's name from the School of Public and International Affairs and Wilson College. He wrote that "the trustees concluded that Woodrow Wilson's racist thinking and policies make him an inappropriate namesake for a school or college whose scholars, students, and alumni must stand firmly against racism in all its forms." Princeton University Office of Communications, "President Eisgruber's message to community on removal of Woodrow Wilson name from public policy school and Wilson College," June 27, 2020, https://www.princeton.edu/news/2020/06/27/president-eisgrubers -message-community-removal-woodrow-wilson-name-public-policy.

42. "The Fourteen Points," Wilson's address to Congress, January 8, 1918, available at http://avalon.law.yale.edu/20th_century/wilson14.asp.

43. According to John B. Judis, "Wilson understood that the war itself [World War I] was rooted not just in Prussian militarism but in a flawed international system that had encouraged and would continue to encourage war." Judis continues: "Wilson also understood that the United States would have to abandon both its isolationist and imperialist approaches to foreign policy. . . For Wilson, America's mission was not to create an empire, but a global democracy of equal and independent nations." To do so, the United States would have to be prepared "to abandon forever Washington and Jefferson's injunctions against 'entangling alliances.'" John B. Judis, *The Folly of Empire: What George W. Bush Could Learn from Theodore Roosevelt and Woodrow Wilson* (New York: Scribner, 2004), 96–97.

44. The Covenant of the League of Nations can be found at http://avalon.law. yale. edu/20th_century/leagcov.asp. This principle of "collective defense" the idea that all are bound together in the event of an attack on any one, is the cornerstone of Article 5 of the North Atlantic Treaty that created NATO (the North Atlantic Treaty Organization) in 1949, after World War II. Article 5 states, "The parties agree that an armed attack against one or more of them in Europe or North America shall be considered an attack against them all and consequently they agree that, if such an armed attack occurs, each of them, in exercise of the right of individual or collective self-defense . . . will assist the Party or Parties attacked." The text of the Treaty is available at the NATO web page, http://www. nato.int/cps/en/natolive/official_texts_17120.htm.

45. Mead, *Special Providence*, 8–9.

46. For example, see Nancy F. Cott, *Public Vows: A History of Marriage and the Nation* (Cambridge, MA: Harvard University Press, 2000); Linda K. Kerber, *No Constitutional Right to Be Ladies* (New York: Hill & Wang, 1998); and Joyce P. Kaufman and Kristen P. Williams, "United States and Derivative Citizenship," in *Women, the State, and War: A Comparative Perspective on Citizenship and Nationalism* (Lanham, MD: Lexington Books, 2007), 41–77.

CHAPTER 3: FROM ISOLATIONISM TO SUPERPOWER

1. Although the early period might be called unilateralist, I concur with Mearsheimer, who makes it clear that "isolationism was the word commonly used to describe American policy during the years between the world wars" (254). In this case, the distinction between unilateralism and isolationism is that during the period from about 1920 to 1940, the United States really did try to stay removed from the political and military events—especially conflicts—outside its borders. Although the United States did have some gunboats patrolling Asia at this time, their role was limited. A further indicator of the policy of isolationism during this period was that the United States chose not to respond militarily in the 1930s when Japan conquered Manchuria, nor when Japan and the Soviet Union clashed later in that decade (258). John Mearsheimer, *The Tragedy of Great Power Politics* (New York: W. W. Norton, 2001).

2. According to Paul Kennedy, by 1917 the United States "produced half of the world's food exports, which could now be sent to France and Italy as well as to its traditional British market." Thus, the United States played an important role in sustaining the Allies' war effort far beyond just military support. Paul Kennedy, *The Rise and Fall of the Great Powers* (New York: Vintage, 1987), 271.

3. Quoted in John B. Judis, *The Folly of Empire: What George W. Bush Could Learn from Theodore Roosevelt and Woodrow Wilson* (New York: Scribner, 2004), 120.

4. J. M. Roberts, *Twentieth Century: The History of the World, 1901 to 2000* (New York: Viking, 1999), 333–34.

5. Immigration had been a major issue for the United States for many decades, as so-called new immigrants came to the United States in the period following the Civil War. They now were coming from eastern and southern Europe and also Asia, a change in the pattern that had existed previously. The presence of this new group of immigrants was a source of tension and even conflict. One of the most extreme examples was the Chinese immigrants, who were lured to this country to work in the mines in the west and on the transcontinental railroad. In 1879, Congress passed a bill limiting the number of Chinese who could enter the United States by ship. While this was vetoed by then president Rutherford B. Hayes, the United States negotiated a treaty with China that allowed U.S. limitations on immigration from China. Congress then passed another bill, suspending Chinese immigration for ten years, "the first such exclusion in U.S. history." And more exclusion laws followed. George C. Herring, *From Colony to Superpower: U.S. Foreign Relations since 1776* (New York: Oxford University Press, 2008), 281–84.

6. The Immigration Act was a direct reaction to the influx of immigrants that had risen to approximately one million per year prior to World War I. Unlike the notion of America as a welcoming "melting pot" that characterized an earlier immigration pattern, the new law tied immigration to country of origin and, according to Ferrell, limited immigration to "3 percent of the number of foreign-born of each nationality residing in the United States in 1910. This reduced European immigrants to a maximum of 355,000 a year. . . . Congress passed it [the act] in the belief that millions of

Europeans . . . were about to descend on the United States. By this time, the notion of a melting pot was in disrepute, and there was talk about 'alien indigestion.'" Although the law restricted the number of people who could enter the country from Europe and parts of Asia, it did not place restrictions on immigration from the Western Hemisphere or the Philippines. As a result, there was an influx of immigrants from Mexico and the Philippines. Robert H. Ferrell, *The Presidency of Calvin Coolidge* (Lawrence: University Press of Kansas, 1998), 113–14.

7. Ponting notes that the act stopped the "very low level of black immigration" by prohibiting "aliens ineligible for citizenship." Since 1790, only whites could become naturalized citizens, thereby precluding nonwhite immigrants from entering the country. Clive Ponting, *The Twentieth Century: A World History* (New York: Henry Holt, 1999), 475.

8. The Washington Conference resulted in a number of treaties. Under the Four Power Treaty, signed in December1921, the United States, Britain, France, and Japan agreed to respect one another's possessions in the Pacific. The Five Power Treaty of February 1922 committed Great Britain, France, Italy, Japan, and the United States to limit the number of their ships with over 10,000 tons displacement. And the countries agreed not to build any more military forts or naval bases on their possessions in the Pacific. "Although the agreement gave Britain and the United States overall superiority, it allowed Japan local dominance in the Pacific." Ponting, *The Twentieth Century*, 256. A Nine Power Treaty was signed in February 1922, protecting Western interests by binding all countries to respect the Open Door in China as well as China's integrity and not to seek land or special privileges there. The result of these treaties was to head off a naval arms race and to stabilize the situation in the Pacific in the short term, although, as Kennedy notes, while Britain and the United States "economized during the 1920s and early 1930s, Japan built right up to the treaty limits—and secretly went far beyond them." Kennedy, *The Rise and Fall of the Great Powers*, 300.

9. See the full text of this agreement for a listing of the many national leaders who signed the pact. *The Kellogg Peace Pact*, August 27, 1928, available at https://avalon.law.yale.edu/20th_century/kbpact.asp.

10. In this phrase, the pact draws on the work of Carl von Clausewitz, who defined war as "a mere continuation of policy by other means." But Clausewitz concludes his treatise *On War* this way: "War is an instrument of policy; it must necessarily bear its character, it must measure its scale: the conduct of War, in its great features, is therefore policy itself, which takes up the sword in place of the pen, but does not on that account cease to think according to its own laws." Carl von Clausewitz, *On War*, ed. Anatol Rapaport (Baltimore: Penguin, 1968), 410. Also available on-line at https://www.usmcu.edu/Portals/218/EWS%20On%20War%20Reading%20Book%201%20Ch%201%20Ch%202.pdf as well as other places.

11. The Kellogg Peace Pact, August 27, 1928, available at https://avalon.law.yale.edu/20th_century/kbpact.asp.

12. It should be noted that technically the pact remains in force today.

13. F. D. Roosevelt's first inaugural address, March 4, 1933, available at http://avalon.law.yale.edu/20th_century/froos1.asp.

14. Roberts, *Twentieth Century*, 367.

15. Roberts, *Twentieth Century*, 367

16. All quotes taken from Roosevelt's first inaugural address.

17. In 1938, Mexico nationalized all foreign oil companies, about 60 percent of which were British and 40 percent American. Needless to say, this directly affected American interests. But by that point, U.S. concerns were elsewhere. Roberts, *Twentieth Century,* 375.

18. Roberts, *Twentieth Century*, 421.

19. Quoted in Herring, *From Colony to Superpower*, 538–39.

20. Roosevelt's address at Charlottesville, Virginia, June 10, 1940, available at https://millercenter.org/the-presidency/presidential-speeches/june-10-1940-stab-back-speech.

21. Roberts, *Twentieth Century*, 421.

22. Roosevelt's "Four Freedoms" speech, January 6, 1941, available at http://www.americanrhetoric.com/speeches/fdrthefourfreedoms.htm.

23. Roosevelt's "Four Freedoms" speech, January 6, 1941, available at http://www.americanrhetoric.com/speeches/fdrthefourfreedoms.htm.

24. Contrary to the way the closeness between Roosevelt and Churchill has popularly been depicted, the two men had an often difficult relationship, which grew even more tense as the war progressed. There seemed to be a personal rivalry between the two, as well as strategic questions and differences, such as when and where Allied forces should land in Europe. For more detail and some interesting insight about the relationship between the two men and between the United States and England in general during this period see Lynne Olson, *Citizens of London: The Americans Who Stood with Britain in Its Finest, Darkest Hour* (New York: Random House, 2010). See also *The Splendid and the Vile: A Saga of Churchill, Family and Defiance during the Blitz*, by Erik Larson (New York: Random House, 2020). The author is especially grateful to Jil Stark for introducing her to these books and a different perspective on the "special" Anglo-American relationship.

25. See the Atlantic Charter, August 14, 1941, available at http://avalon.law.yale.edu/wwii/atlantic.asp.

26. See Kennedy, *The Rise and Fall of the Great Powers*, 202.

27. Executive Order 9066; Resulting in the Relocation of Japanese," http://historymatters.gmu.edu/d/5154.

28. Executive Order 9066: Resulting in the Relocation of Japanese," http://historymatters.gmu.edu/d/5154.

29. Under political pressure, Roosevelt issued Executive Order 8802 affirming the policy of the United States that there shall be "no discrimination of workers in defense industries or government because of race, creed, color or national origin." Available at http://docs.fdrlibrary.marist.edu/odex8802.html. However, members of the military resisted the call for integration of the armed forces out of concern that this change in policy would affect military readiness. President Harry Truman formally ended segregation in the military in 1948 by Executive Order 9981, *On Equality of Treatment and Opportunity in the Armed Forces*, available at https://www.ourdocuments.gov/doc.php?flash=false&doc=84&page=transcript.

30. It is important to note that Japanese cities were constructed largely of wood, so firebombing literally incinerated them. The city of Kyoto, the original capital of Japan (Heian), was spared specifically because of its historical and religious importance.

31. "Einstein's Letter to President Roosevelt, August 2, 1939," *Atomic Archive*, https://www.atomicarchive.com/resources/documents/beginnings/einstein.html.

32. "The Manhattan Project: Making the Atomic Bomb," *Atomic Archive,* http://www. atomicarchive.com/History/mp/introduction.shtml.https://www.atomicarchive .com/history/manhattan-project/introduction.html.

33. See, for example, work done at the Ohio University Contemporary History Institute, a summary of which was published as "The Great Atomic Bomb Debate," by Bryan McNulty, in *Perspectives* (Spring–Summer 1997).

34. White House press release, August 6, in Robert H. Ferrell, ed., *Harry S. Truman and the Bomb: A Documentary History* (Worland, Wyo.: High Plains Publishing, 1996), 48; for the full text of the release, see 47–52. The text can be found online at https://www.trumanlibrary.gov/library/research-files/press-release-white-house.

35. White House press release, August 6, available at https://www.trumanlibrary .gov/library/research-files/press-release-white-house.

36. Paul Kennedy notes that a "mix of motives" pushed the United States "toward the decision to drop the bomb—the wish to save allied casualties, the desire to send a warning to Stalin, the need to justify the vast expenses of the atomic project," all of which are still debated. What is not debated is that dropping the atomic bombs "marked the beginning of a new order in world affairs." Kennedy, *The Rise and Fall of the Great Powers*, 356–57. And Bill Gordon, scholar of Japanese history and culture, writes, "The concerns of top American leaders about the Soviet Union's future actions had the most significant influence on President Truman's deliberations on whether or not to drop the atomic bomb on Japan. If America did not drop the bomb in order to demonstrate its military superiority, American leaders had concerns that the Soviet Union would occupy Manchuria and would share the occupation of Japan with the U.S. . . . In addition, American leaders believed that dropping of the bomb would strengthen their position in future dealings with the Soviet Union concerning their sphere of influence in Eastern Europe." Bill Gordon, "Reflections on Hiroshima," available at http://www.bill-gordon.net/papers/hiroshim.htm

37. Gordon, "Reflections on Hiroshima," available at http://www.bill-gordon.net/ papers/hiroshim.htm.

38. Bryan McNulty, "The Great Atomic Bomb Debate," http://sprintz.weebly .com/uploads/5/1/2/0/5120516/the_great_atomic_bomb_debate_article.pdf.

39. Townsend Hoopes and Douglas Brinkley, *FDR and the Creation of the U.N.* (New Haven, CT: Yale University Press, 1997), 9.

40. Hoopes and Brinkley, *FDR and the Creation of the U.N.*, 9.

41. The Atlantic Charter reaffirms that "all nations of the world, for realistic as well as spiritual reasons must come to the abandonment of the use of force. Since no future peace can be maintained if land, sea or air armaments continue to be employed by nations which threaten, or may threaten, aggression outside of their frontiers, they believe, *pending an establishment of a wider system of general security, that the dis-*

armament of such nations is essential" (emphasis added). Atlantic Charter, August 14, 1941, https://avalon.law.yale.edu/wwii/atlantic.asp.

42. Quoted in Hoopes and Brinkley, *FDR and the Creation of the U.N.*, 40.

43. See "Declaration of the United Nations," https://avalon.law.yale.edu/20th _century/decade03.

44. Chiang Kai-shek was the leader of China at the time. Prior to World War II, Chiang had been fighting a civil war against Mao Tse-tung (Mao Zedong), the leader of the communist forces. The civil war resumed after World War II ended and resulted in Mao's victory over the nationalist forces led by Chiang. In 1949, Chiang Kai-shek and his troops fled mainland China for the island of Taiwan, and on October 1, Mao and the communists declared the creation of the People's Republic of China.

45. Franklin D. Roosevelt, "Fireside Chat 27," December 24, 1943, https://millercenter.org/the-presidency/presidential-speeches/december-24-1943-fireside-chat-27-tehran-and-cairo-conferences.

46. See "Proposals for the Establishment of a General International Organization," Dumbarton Oaks, October 7, 1944, available at https://digital.library.cornell.edu/catalog/ss:21796682.

CHAPTER 4: THE MAKING OF A SUPERPOWER

1. According to Mearsheimer, "When the Third Reich finally collapsed in April 1945, the Soviet Union was left standing as the most powerful state in Europe. Imperial Japan collapsed four months later (August 1945) leaving the Soviet Union also as the most powerful state in Northeast Asia. . . . The United States was the only state powerful enough to contain Soviet expansion." John Mearsheimer, *The Tragedy of Great Power Politics* (New York: W. W. Norton, 2001), 322.

2. On the role of economics as part of the U.S. policy of containment, Mead notes, "The progress toward free trade and the development of an international legal and political system that supported successive waves of expansion and integration across the entire world economy is one of the great (and unheralded) triumphs of American foreign policy in the second half of the twentieth century." He considers this policy "very much an element of the overall grand strategy of containing communism in part through creating a prosperous and integrated noncommunist world." Walter Russell Mead, *Power, Terror, Peace, and War: America's Grand Strategy in a World at Risk* (New York: Alfred A. Knopf, 2004), 33–34.

3. See Roosevelt's "Four Freedoms" speech, January 6, 1941, available at https://www.americanrhetoric.com/speeches/fdrthefourfreedoms.htm.

4. Harry S. Truman, "Address on Foreign Policy at the Navy Day Celebration in New York City," October 27, 1945, https://millercenter.org/the-presidency/presidential-speeches/october-27-1945-navy-day-address.

5. Truman: "Address on Foreign Policy at the Navy Day Celebration in New York City.," October 27, 1945, https://millercenter.org/the-presidency/presidential-speeches/october-27-1945-navy-day-address.

6. Truman: "Address on Foreign Policy at the Navy Day Celebration in New York City," October 27, 1945, https://millercenter.org/the-presidency/presidential-speeches/october-27-1945-navy-day-address.

7. "Speech Delivered by J. V. Stalin at a Meeting of Voters of the Stalin Electoral District, Moscow," February 9, 1946, https://digitalarchive.wilsoncenter.org/document/116179.

8. Referring to Kennan, Gaddis writes, "Rarely in the course of diplomacy does an individual manage to express within a single document, ideas of such force and persuasiveness that they immediately change a nation's foreign policy. That was the effect, though, of the 8,000-word telegram dispatched from Moscow by Kennan on February 22, 1946." John Lewis Gaddis, *Strategies of Containment: A Critical Appraisal of American National Security Policy during the Cold War* (New York: Oxford University Press, 2005), 18–19.

9. All quotes are taken from Kennan, "The Long Telegram," available at. https://digitalarchive.wilsoncenter.org/document/116178.pdf

10. On September 27, 1946, Soviet ambassador to the United States Nikolai Novikov sent a cable back to Moscow in which he described U.S. foreign policy as expansionistic and part of a drive for world hegemony. Although parts of Novikov's analysis were questioned and Novikov apparently also was dissatisfied with the result of the document, as one observer notes, "The general picture of the world they [Novikov and Kennan] painted was essentially the same: a dichotomous cleavage—on one side the powers of good, on the other, evil." Viktor L. Mal'kov, "Commentary," in *Origins of the Cold War: The Novikov, Kennan, and Roberts "Long Telegrams" of 1946*, ed. Kenneth M. Jensen (Washington, D.C.: United States Institute of Peace Press, 1993), 75. It is well worth reading the three telegrams, by Kennan, Novikov, and Frank Roberts (British chargé d'affaires in Moscow) for the picture each paints of the emerging Cold War.

11. All quotes are taken from George Kennan, "The Sources of Soviet Conduct," originally in *Foreign Affairs*, July 1947, found in its entirety at https://www.digitalhistory.uh.edu/disp_textbook.cfm?smtID=3&psid=3629.

12. Kennan, "The Sources of Soviet Conduct."

13. All quotes are taken from Harry S. Truman, "Special Message to the Congress on Greece and Turkey," March 12, 1947, available at http://avalon.law.yale.edu/20th_century/trudoc.asp.

14. The structure of the Department of Homeland Security was outlined by President Bush in June 2002. The legislation formally creating the agency was passed by the U.S. Congress and signed by the president in November 2002. The text of the act (Public Law 107-296) that created the Department of Homeland Security can be found at http://www.dhs.gov/xlibrary/assets/hr_5005_enr.pdf. This change was followed by sweeping changes to the intelligence community with congressional passage of the Intelligence Reform and Terrorism Prevention Act of 2004 (IRTPA). "The IRTPA created the Office of the Director of National Intelligence (ODNI) to oversee a 17-organization Intelligence Community (IC) and improve information sharing, promote a strategic, unified direction, and ensure integration across the

nation's IC." ODNI Fact Sheet, https://www.dni.gov/files/documents/ODNI%20
Fact%20Sheet_2011.pdf.

15. The full text of the *National Security Act of 1947* (Public Law 80-253) with
some supporting documentation can be found at http://global.oup.com/us/companion
.websites/9780195385168/resources/chapter10/nsa/nsa.pdf.

16. The National Security Act of 1947 gave each of the three military branches
(army, navy, and newly created air force) its own civilian service secretary. In 1949,
the National Security Act was amended "to give the Secretary of Defense more power
over the individual services and their secretaries." U.S. Department of State, *National
Security Act of 1947*, http://global.oup.com/us/companion.websites/9780195385168/
resources/chapter10/nsa/nsa.pdf.

17. The text of the "Marshall Plan" speech, given on June 4, 1947, at Harvard
University, is available at https://www.marshallfoundation.org/marshall/the-marshall
-plan/marshall-plan-speech/. There is also an audio version available at that site.

18. North Atlantic Treaty, Article 5. The full text of the North Atlantic Treaty
can be found at the NATO website, http://www.nato.int/cps/en/natolive/official
_texts_17120.htm. When the treaty was drafted, the stipulation of collective security/
defense outlined in Article 5 was assumed to be directed at a Soviet attack from the
east on Western Europe, probably an attack on Germany through the Fulda Gap.
However, the only time in its history that NATO invoked Article 5 was on September
12, 2001, in response to the September 11 attacks on the United States.

19. As noted in chapter 2, Article 10 of the League charter was the focus of much
of the concern by congressional opponents of the League. Their fear was that if the
United States signed the charter, Article 10 could have the effect of drawing the
United States into wars that did not directly involve the country and, therefore, were
not in U.S. national interest.

20. North Atlantic Treaty, Article 2, http://www.nato.int/cps/en/natolive/official
_texts_17120.htm.

21. This is also one of the reasons that the former communist countries of Eastern
Europe, such as Poland, Hungary, the Czech Republic, and others, were so eager to
join NATO when it enlarged initially in the 1990s, and why the countries of Eastern
Europe and the former Soviet Union have wanted to join as NATO continued to
enlarge. To them, this served as a way of formally recognizing that they, too, are
members of that democratic capitalist group of countries tied to the West. It was also
recognition that the old days of Soviet domination had ended.

22. For more background on the creation of the state of Israel and the implication
for the Middle East today, see William Cleveland and Martin Bunton, *A History of the
Modern Middle East*, sixth ed. (New York: Routledge, 2018). Also see Dennis Ross,
The Missing Peace: The Inside Story of the Fight for Middle East Peace (New York:
Farrar, Straus and Giroux, 2004).

23. Soviet communism was based on the idea of a planned economy that had at its
hub centralized state planning with large urban bureaucracies/ministries to manage it.
The central state made the decisions and choices about the allocation of resources. In
contrast, in China, Mao's model relied on the mass mobilization of rural labor as central to his idea of communism. His model was based on the voluntary collectivization

of agriculture and the full employment of peasant labor found in a more rural country. Each of the two versions of communism was designed for the needs of the particular country as envisioned by its leaders. Ultimately, the two versions were seen by each country as being at odds with each other.

24. John B. Judis, *The Folly of Empire: What George W. Bush Could Learn from Theodore Roosevelt and Woodrow Wilson* (New York: Scribner, 2004), 142.

25. The entire document of NSC 68, while quite lengthy, lays out in detail U.S. perceptions of the Soviet Union and its intentions, the goals of the United States, and why the two were in conflict. It also describes Soviet military capabilities as then known and a range of options available to the United States to successfully deter and counter the Soviet Union. While it recognizes the "heavy responsibility" placed on the United States, the document also makes clear the need to "organize and enlist the energies and resources of the free world" in support of this effort. NSC 68 also notes the importance of keeping "the U.S. public fully informed and cognizant of the threats to our national security so that it will be prepared to support the measures which we must accordingly adopt." National Security Council, NSC 68: "United States Objectives and Programs for National Security," April 14, 1950, available at https://fas.org/irp/offdocs/nsc-hst/nsc-68.htm

26. Fred Kaplan, *The Bomb: Presidents, Generals and the Secret History of Nuclear War* (New York: Simon & Schuster, 2020),136.

27. This is an important point because the United States was aware that if the vote had come when the Soviet ambassador was present, he probably would have exercised the veto, thereby killing the motion. It is also important to note that the Security Council seat held by "China" at that time was actually held by the government of Taiwan, not the PRC, which was allied with North Korea. It was not until October 1971 that the UN General Assembly voted to seat the PRC in place of Taiwan, which resulted in removing Taiwan from the UN.

28. "Truman's Statement on the Korean War," June 27, 1950, available at https://digitalarchive.wilsoncenter.org/document/116192.pdf?v=31e383a7e226b441e40fb0527a828da0. According to political scientist Peter Irons, President Truman specifically circumvented the Congress in authorizing U.S. troops into Korea without asking for approval or a formal declaration of war. Irons also makes the case that Truman violated the provisions of the UN charter by taking unilateral action prior to a UN Security Council call for assistance. Thus, Irons concludes, "Truman had no legal or constitutional authority for his actions at the outset of the Korean War. He ordered U.S. forces to undertake acts of war in Korea, despite his claim at a June 29 press conference, that 'we are not at war.'" Peter Irons, *War Powers: How the Imperial Presidency Hijacked the Constitution* (New York: Metropolitan Books, 2005), 171.

29. On April 11, 1951, President Truman called a press conference to announce that General MacArthur had been removed from the command of the forces in Korea. Truman believed that MacArthur had overstepped his bounds when he launched an attack into North Korea that pushed the enemy back toward the Yalu River, bordering China. MacArthur requested support to blockade the Chinese coast and bomb the mainland, which was denied by Washington. MacArthur was then warned to restrict the fighting to the area south of the thirty-eighth parallel, so as not to incite China.

When MacArthur spoke out against what he saw as this strategy of "limited war," Truman saw this as a direct challenge to him as president and commander in chief, and he responded by firing MacArthur. See "Truman Relieves M'Arthur of All His Posts; Finds Him Unable to Back U.S.-U.N. Policies; Ridgway Named to Far Eastern Commands," *New York Times*, April 11, 1951, https://archive.nytimes.com/www .nytimes.com/learning/general/onthisday/big/0411.html.

30. Joseph McCarthy, "Enemies from Within," Speech delivered in Wheeling, West Virginia, February 9, 1950, http://www.digitalhistory.uh.edu/disp_textbook_print.cfm?smtid=3&psid=3633. Different versions of the speech include different numbers of individuals in the State Department who allegedly were members of the Communist Party. The numbers range from 57 to 205, and McCarthy increased the number in speeches he gave on the floor of the Senate.

31. Quoted in Paul Kennedy, *The Rise and Fall of the Great Powers* (New York: Vintage, 1987), 382.

32. According to Roberts, "This was to turn out to be one of the most influential acts by a statesman of any nationality since 1945. It shook the monolithic front communism had hitherto presented." J. M. Roberts, *Twentieth Century: A History of the World, 1901–2000* (New York: Viking, 1999), 649. Excerpts of Khrushchev's speech can be found at https://www.marxists.org/archive/khrushchev/1956/02/24.htm.

33. Kaplan, *The Bomb*, 10

34. All quotes taken from Secretary of State John Foster Dulles, "The Strategy of Massive Retaliation," speech before the Council of Foreign Relations, January 12, 1954, http://msthorarinson.weebly.com/uploads/4/1/4/5/41452777/dulles_address .pdf.

35. In his memoirs, Khrushchev reflected, "For some time the United States lagged behind us. We were exploring space with our Sputniks. People all over the world recognized our success. Most admired us; the Americans were jealous." Nikita Khrushchev, *Khrushchev Remembers: The Last Testament*, trans. Strobe Talbott (Boston: Little, Brown, 1974), 54.

36. Under President Eisenhower's leadership, spy and intelligence technology made great advances in the 1950s. Specifically designed to monitor the Soviet Union and protect the United States from surprise nuclear attack, the U.S. intelligence apparatus came to depend increasingly on reconnaissance aircraft and spy satellites. For the background story of many of these developments, see Philip Taubman, *Secret Empire: Eisenhower, the CIA, and the Hidden Story of America's Space Espionage* (New York: Simon & Schuster, 2003).

37. For a fascinating and detailed account of the U-2 incident, see Michael R. Beschloss, *Mayday: Eisenhower, Khrushchev, and the U-2 Affair* (New York: Harper & Row, 1986).

38. Quoted in James MacGregor Burns, *The Crosswinds of Freedom* (New York: Alfred A. Knopf, 1989), 262.

39. Kaplan writes that in the first few months of the new Kennedy administration, based on findings from the photoreconnaissance satellite "Discoverer," the "missile gap" proved to be a myth. In fact, the Discoverer pictures revealed that the Soviet Union did not have two hundred long-range missiles, which was the Air Force

estimate, or even fifty, as the Army and Navy intelligence had estimated; in fact, it had only four. The results of these findings showed that "There *was* a missile gap—but, they said, the gap was very much in *America's* favor" (emphasis in original). Kaplan, *The Bomb*, 44.

40. Kaplan, *The Bomb*, 64.

41. Full text of "Roswell Gilpatric speech before the Business Council," October 21, 1961, https://archive.org/stream/RoswellGilpatricSpeechBeforeTheBusiness Council/ELS000-010_djvu.txt. All quotes are from that text.

42. Kaplan, *The Bomb*, 65.

43. The news conference of Friday, April 21, 1961, can be found at https://www .jfklibrary.org/asset-viewer/archives/JFKPOF/054/JFKPOF-054-012.

44. Resentment and tensions had been building between the Soviet Union and China. Since the 1950s, China had implemented policies to reduce its dependence on the USSR. The tensions between the two countries grew until the Soviet Union withdrew its economic and technical aid and advisors in 1960. Concurrent with that, the two countries engaged in countercharges about border violations, with shots fired across the border as early as 1963. In 1964, China exploded its first nuclear weapon, becoming the fifth country to acquire this technology (following the United States, Soviet Union, Britain, and France). Subsequently, the two countries pursued very different policies, undermining the notion of monolithic communism.

45. Upon hearing that Soviet ships bearing missiles heading to Cuba had stopped and then turned around at sea, then secretary of state Dean Rusk was quoted as saying, "We're eyeball to eyeball and I think the other fellow just blinked." This statement is quoted in any number of places as indicative of the tensions that existed at this time. This one was taken from an article by Michael Dobbs, "The Price of a Fifty-Year Myth, *New York Times*, October 15, 2012, http://www.nytimes.com/2012/10/16/ opinion/the-eyeball-to-eyeball-myth-and-the-cuban-missile-crisiss-legacy.html. The article itself deals with this as just one example of a foreign policy decision based on misunderstanding.

46. See, for example, Graham T. Allison, *Essence of Decision: Explaining the Cuban Missile Crisis* (Boston: Little, Brown, 1971). This is perhaps the classic book on the missile crisis. Also see Raymond L. Garthoff, *Reflections on the Cuban Missile Crisis* (Washington, DC: Brookings Institution, 1989) and Robert F. Kennedy, *Thirteen Days: A Memoir of the Cuban Missile Crisis* (New York: W. W. Norton, 1969) for a fascinating first-person account of the event by someone intimately involved. For a work that draws on previously secret documents from Russian and U.S. archives to offer further insights into the crisis, see Aleksandr Fursenko and Timothy Naftali, *"One Hell of a Gamble": Khrushchev, Castro, and Kennedy, 1958–1964* (New York: W. W. Norton, 1997). Also see Michael Dobbs, *One Minute to Midnight: Kennedy, Khrushchev, and Castro on the Brink of Nuclear War* (New York: Alfred A. Knopf, 2008) for a detailed account of the crisis that draws on exhaustive and relatively new research.

47. Don Oberdorfer, "Cuban Missile Crisis More Volatile Than Thought," *Washington Post*, January 14, 1992, A1.

48. Quoted in Martin Tolchin, "U.S. Underestimated Soviet Force in Cuba during '62 Missile Crisis," *New York Times*, January 15, 1992.

49. Michael Dobbs, in his 2008 book about the Cuban Missile Crisis, notes that there were many "unintended consequences" of the event, some of which are just being realized. For example, he quotes Clark Clifford, who served as secretary of defense after Robert McNamara, as saying that "the architects of the Vietnam War were 'deeply influenced by the lessons of the Cuban missile crisis.' They thought that concepts like 'flexible response' and 'controlled escalation' had helped Kennedy prevail over Khrushchev—and would work equally as well in Vietnam." Dobbs also asserts that "[a] somewhat different—but equally mistaken—lesson from the Cuban missile crisis was drawn by modern-day neoconservatives. In planning for the war in Iraq, they shared the conceit that the political will of the president of the United States trumps all other considerations." Dobbs, *One Minute to Midnight*, 347.

50. Quoted in George C. Herring, *America's Longest War: The United States and Vietnam, 1950–1975* (New York: McGraw-Hill, 1996), 38.

51. Quoted in Herring, *America's Longest War*, 78.

52. Statement by President Kennedy on the importance of Laos, at a news conference March 23, 1961, available at http://www.mtholyoke.edu/acad/intrel/pentagon2/ps5.htm.

53. For more detail about Laos and its relationship to Vietnam, see Norman B. Hannah, *The Key to Failure: Laos and the Vietnam War* (Lanham, MD: Madison Books, 1987). Hannah makes the argument that not only were the situations in Laos and Vietnam related, which seems apparent, but in chapter 2, "The Bay of Pigs and Indochina," he makes the case that "the pattern of our failure in Indochina was set at the Bay of Pigs" (9).

54. Roberts, *Twentieth Century*, 673.

55. According to Doris Kearns Goodwin, "Johnson did worry about the loss of his domestic programs. As a boy of five, he had heard his Populist grandfather describe the devastating impact of the Spanish-American War on social reform. He had lived through the periods of reaction following World War I and World War II, seen a virtual paralysis of domestic action in the aftermath of Korea. And one cannot doubt the intensity of this concern." Doris Kearns, *Lyndon Johnson and the American Dream* (New York: Harper & Row, 1976), 259.

56. Kearns, *Lyndon Johnson and the American Dream*, 251–52.

57. For a broader discussion of the events in the Gulf of Tonkin during that period in early August, including questions about what really happened on August 4 and references to declassified documents, see John Prados, "Essay: 40th Anniversary of the Gulf of Tonkin Incident," National Security Archive, available at http://nsarchive.gwu.edu/NSAEBB/NSAEBB132/essay.htm.

58. The Southeast Asia Collective Defense Treaty that established the Southeast Asia Treaty Organization (SEATO) was signed in 1954 and entered into force in 1955. It joined the United States and the countries of Australia, France, New Zealand, Pakistan, Philippines, Thailand, and United Kingdom. Article 4 of this treaty is the collective defense provision similar to the one in Article 5 of the NATO treaty. The

goal of the treaty and of SEATO was to oppose communist gains in Southeast Asia after the withdrawal of the French. The organization was divided by the U.S. role in Vietnam and was officially disbanded in 1977.

59. "President Johnson's Message to Congress," August 5, 1964 available at https://www.mtholyoke.edu/acad/intrel/tonkinsp.htm.

60. *Joint Resolution of Congress*, H.J. RES 1145, available at https://avalon.law .yale.edu/20th_century/tonkin-g.asp.

61. Donald L. Westerfield, *War Powers: The President, the Congress, and the Question of War* (Westport, CT: Praeger Press, 1996), 53. Article I, Section 8, of the Constitution explicitly grants to the Congress the power to declare war.

62. Herring, *America's Longest War*, 136.

63. Quoted in Westerfield, *War Powers*, 84.

64. Herring, *America's Longest War*, 167.

65. Herring, *America's Longest War*, 173.

66. Herring, *America's Longest War*, 173.

67. Walter Cronkite, "We Are Mired in Stalemate," broadcast, February 27, 1968, https://www.digitalhistory.uh.edu/active_learning/explorations/vietnam/cronkite. cfm. It can also be seen on YouTube, various postings. Supposedly, when Lyndon Johnson heard Cronkite's commentary on the news that night, he was reported to have said, "If I've lost Cronkite, I've lost the country," https://www.npr.org/templates/ story/story.php?storyId=106775685.

68. Burns, *The Crosswinds of Freedom*, 412.

69. Burns, *The Crosswinds of Freedom*, 413.

70. The full text of Lyndon Johnson's announcement of March 31, 1968, can be found at https://millercenter.org/the-presidency/presidential-speeches/march -31-1968-remarks-decision-not-seek-re-election. The video of the last critical minutes of this announcement can be found at http://abcnews.go.com/Archives/video/ march-31-1968-lbj-seek-election-9626199 and on other YouTube sites.

71. Quoted in Kearns, *Lyndon Johnson and the American Dream*, 343.

72. John Lewis Gaddis, *The Cold War: A New History* (New York: Penguin Press, 2005), 67.

73. Kaplan, *The Bomb*, 99.

CHAPTER 5: THE COLD WAR CONTINUED

1. Quoted in George C. Herring, *America's Longest War: The United States and Vietnam, 1950–1975* (New York: McGraw Hill, 1996), 244.

2. Herring, *America's Longest War*, 245.

3. For more detail about this and other related events during this period see Office of the Historian, "Ending the Vietnam War, 1969–1973," https://history.state.gov/ milestones/1969-1976/ending-vietnam.

4. Richard Nixon, "Address to the Nation on the War in Vietnam," November 3, 1969, available at https://millercenter.org/the-presidency/presidential-speeches/ november-3-1969-address-nation-war-vietnam.

5. Gallup, "Presidential Approval Ratings—Gallup Historical Statistics and Trends," http://www.gallup.com/poll/116677/presidential-approval-ratings-gallup-historical-statistics-trends.aspx.

6. Herring, *America's Longest War*, 262.

7. James P. Sterba, "Last U.S. Troops Leave Cambodia," *New York Times*, July 1, 1970, https://www.nytimes.com/1970/07/01/archives/last-us-troops-leave-cambodia-34000-south-vietnamese-stay-most-near.html.

8. J. M. Roberts, *Twentieth Century: A History of the World, 1901–2000* (New York: Viking, 1999), 675.

9. George C. Herring, *From Colony to Superpower: U.S. Foreign Relations Since 1776* (New York: Oxford University Press, 2008), 770. The full text of the *Pentagon Papers*, officially titled "Report of the Office of the Secretary of Defense Vietnam Task Force," is available online at https://www.archives.gov/research/pentagon-papers.

10. Herring, *From Colony to Superpower*, 770.

11. Herring, *America's Longest War*, 280.

12. Memorandum from the President's Assistant for National Security Affairs (Kissinger) to President Ford, May 12, 1975, available at https://history.state.gov/historicaldocuments/frus1969-76v10/d280.

13. War Powers Resolution, Public Law 93-148, 93rd Congress, H.J. RES. 542, November 7, 1973, "Joint Resolution Concerning the War Powers of Congress and the President," https://avalon.law.yale.edu/20th_century/warpower.asp.

14. War Powers Resolution, Public Law 93-148, Sec. 2. (a).

15. Despite the caveats built into the War Powers Resolution, in October 2002, Congress gave President George W. Bush virtually the same authority regarding the conduct of the war with Iraq. Congress gave the president authorization "to use the Armed Forces of the United States as he determined to be necessary and appropriate in order to (1) defend the national security of the United States against the continuing threat posed by Iraq; and (2) enforce all relevant United Nations Security Council Resolutions regarding Iraq." Like the Tonkin Gulf Resolution, this resolution was premised upon a case that has since been disproved. Joint Resolution to Authorize the Use of United States Armed Forces against Iraq, available at https://www.congress.gov/107/plaws/publ243/PLAW-107publ243.pdf.

16. For a more detailed discussion of the constitutionality of the resolution and these parts in particular, see Donald L. Westerfield, *War Powers: The President, the Congress and the Question of War* (Westport, CT: Praeger Press, 1996), 90–92, and many of the sources that he cites. Irons raises an interesting point when he notes that "rather than limiting the president's war-making powers, as its sponsors intended, the War Powers Resolution of 1973 actually expanded them by failing to include any enforcement provisions." This leads him to state that, therefore, "presidents could—and most often did—ignore the resolution's consulting and reporting provisions, or comply in the most perfunctory manner." Peter Irons, *War Powers: How the Imperial Presidency Hijacked the Constitution* (New York: Metropolitan Books, 2005), 219. However, as desired, the act has forced presidents to report to the Congress. Whether, when, and how Congress responds is a different question.

17. In addition to the United States and Soviet Union, the United Kingdom became a nuclear power in 1956, France in 1960, and China in 1964. India conducted its first nuclear test in 1974, and by the 1980s it was clear that Pakistan had nuclear weapons as well. In addition, Argentina, Brazil, and South Africa all had a nuclear capability but chose not to build nuclear weapons. It is an open secret that Israel has nuclear weapons, and North Korea and Iran have both made it clear that each is pursuing its own nuclear weapons program.

18. Fred Kaplan, *The Bomb: Presidents, Generals and the Secret History of Nuclear War* (New York: Simon & Schuster, 2020), 114.

19. Kaplan, *The Bomb*, 120.

20. Quoted in Eugene R. Wittkopf, Charles W. Kegley Jr., and James M. Scott, *American Foreign Policy*, sixth ed. (Belmont, CA: Wadsworth/ Thomson Learning, 2003), 51.

21. Wittkopf, Kegley and Scott, *American Foreign Policy*, 51.

22. John Lewis Gaddis, *The Cold War: A New History* (New York: The Penguin Press, 2005), 81.

23. Office of the Historian, U.S. Department of State, "Strategic Arms Limitations Talks/Treaty (SALT) I and II," https://history.state.gov/milestones/1969-1976/salt.

24. On December 13, 2001, President George W. Bush announced that the United States would withdraw from the ABM Treaty claiming that "it prevented U.S. development of defenses against possible terrorist or 'rogue-state' ballistic missile attacks." Under the terms of the original treaty, a party was allowed to withdraw if "extraordinary events . . . have jeopardized its supreme interests." The U.S. withdrawal went into effect on June 13, 2002, and the treaty is no longer in effect. Arms Control Association, "The Anti-Ballistic Missile (ABM) Treaty at a Glance," July 2017, https://www.armscontrol.org/factsheets/abmtreaty.

25. Richard Nixon, "Statement on the Forthcoming Visit to Western Europe," February 6, 1969, https://www.nixonfoundation.org/wp-content/uploads/2019/04/2.06.1969-Statement-on-the-Forthcoming-Visit-to-Western-Europe-pdf.io_.pdf.

26. Quoted in Chris Barber, "Why Europe Was Nixon's First Foreign Trip," March 5, 2014, https://www.nixonfoundation.org/2014/03/europe-president-richard-nixon/.

27. For more detail about the end of Bretton Woods and the restructuring of U.S. economic and monetary policy and their impact on the allies see Luke A. Nichter, *Richard Nixon and Europe: The Reshaping of the Postwar Atlantic World* (New York: Cambridge University Press, 2015), especially chapter 2, "Closing the Gold Window," 36–67.

28. Joyce P. Kaufman, "The U.S. Perspective on NATO under Trump: Lessons of the Part and Prospects for the Future," *International Affairs* 93, no. 2 (March 2017): 256.

29. For a fascinating and brief description of Nixon's position on China, including short excerpts of some of his writings on the topic, see "Finding China," in James MacGregor Burns, *The Crossroads of Freedom* (New York: Alfred A. Knopf, 1989), 468–75.

30. Office of the Historian, Department of State, "Joint Statement Following Discussions with Leaders of the People's Republic of China," February 27, 1972, https://history.state.gov/historicaldocuments/frus1969-76v17/d203.

31. Ford's statement about the pardon and his rationale for it can be found in the *New York Times*, "Statement by the President in Connection with his Proclamation Pardoning Nixon, September 9, 1974, http://timesmachine.nytimes.com/timesmachine/1974/09/09/99181264.html?pageNumber=24.

32. U.S/ Department of State, "Address by President Jimmy Carter to the UN General Assembly," March 17, 1977, https://2009-2017.state.gov/p/io/potusunga/207272.htm.

33. U.S/ Department of State, "Address by President Jimmy Carter to the UN General Assembly."

34. Kaplan, *The Bomb*, 128.

35. See Kaplan, *The Bomb*, 134.

36. Kaplan, *The Bomb*, 138.

37. Kaplan, *The Bomb*, 140.

38. For a detailed first-person account of the events leading up to the Iranian hostage crisis, the U.S. attempts at diplomatic solutions, the failed rescue attempts and the implications of the crisis, see Gary Sick, *All Fall Down: America's Tragic Encounter with Iran* (New York: Random House, 1985).

39. What Kennedy meant was that he, too, is a citizen of Berlin. Although most people knew what he was trying to say, the actual translation of this statement is, "I am a jelly-filled donut," since a "Berliner" is a popular type of pastry. This is one example of how language, especially in translation, can confound international relations. This example is cited in Raymond Cohen, *Negotiating across Cultures* (Washington, DC: United States Institute of Peace Press, 1992).

40. President Reagan delivered the speech on June 12, 1987, at the Brandenburg Gate in West Berlin. It is important to note that the speech could be heard on the eastern side of the Berlin Wall and sent an important message. About halfway through the speech, Reagan directed his comments not only to the people of Berlin but to Mikhail Gorbachev in the Soviet Union when he said, "General Secretary Gorbachev, if you seek peace, if you seek prosperity for the Soviet Union and Eastern Europe, if you seek liberalization: Come here to this gate! Mr. Gorbachev, open this gate! Mr. Gorbachev, tear down this wall!" The transcript of the speech with video can be found at http://www.americanrhetoric. com/speeches/ronaldreaganbrandenburggate.htm.

41. Roberts, *Twentieth Century*, 742.

42. For a detailed discussion of "soft" and "hard" power and the role that each has played in American foreign policy, see Joseph S. Nye, Jr., *The Paradox of American Power: Why the World's Only Superpower Can't Go It Alone* (New York: Oxford University Press, 2002). Nye later built on that by adding in the concept of "smart power," which he defines as "the ability to combine hard and soft power resources into effective strategies." Joseph S. Nye, Jr., *The Future of Power* (New York: PublicAffairs, 2011), 22–23.

43. President Reagan delivered the first "evil empire" speech, as it came to be known, to the British House of Commons on June 8, 1982. Although Reagan did

not label the Soviet Union the "evil empire" per se, in speaking to the British people about the contest of democracy versus communism and West versus East, he did say, "Given strong leadership, time, and a little bit of hope, the forces of good ultimately rally and triumph over evil." Available at https://millercenter.org/the-presidency/presidential-speeches/june-8-1982-address-british-parliament. Reagan reprised many of these themes in a speech he gave on March 8, 1983, to the National Association of Evangelicals in Florida. However, he was even more blunt this time, given his audience: "So, in your discussions of the nuclear freeze proposals, I urge you to beware the temptation of pride—the temptation of blithely declaring yourselves above it all and label both sides equally at fault, to ignore the facts of history and the aggressive impulses of an *evil empire*, to simply call the arms race a giant misunderstanding and thereby remove yourself from the struggle between right and wrong and good and evil" (emphasis added). Available at https://www.reaganfoundation.org/library-museum/permanent-exhibitions/berlin-wall/from-the-archives/remarks-at-the-annual-convention-of-the-national-association-of-evangelicals-in-orlando-florida/.

44. Roberts, *Twentieth Century*, 747.

45. The arms control process did continue under Reagan, but unsuccessfully, at least initially. For more detail about the progress of some of the negotiations, see Strobe Talbott, *Deadly Gambits* (New York: Alfred A. Knopf, 1984). Especially instructive is chapter 6, "A Walk in the Woods" (117–51), describing the informal talks that took place between U.S. negotiator Paul Nitze and Soviet negotiator Yuli Kvitsinsky, and why those negotiations were doomed to fail.

46. Kaplan, *The Bomb*, 174.

47. Jack F. Matlock, Jr., *Reagan and Gorbachev: How the Cold War Ended* (New York: Random House, 2004), 302. This is an example of how a powerful individual actor can play an important role in international relations and the direction of a particular nation-state. As a postscript to this, in reflecting on what happened during this period, Brent Scowcroft claims that Gorbachev is "one of the most detested people in Russia . . . because he destroyed the glory of Russia." Zbigniew Brzezinski and Brent Scowcroft, *America and the World: Conversations on the Future of American Foreign Policy,* moderated by David Ignatius (New York: Basic Books, 2008), 162. Some argue now that it is that glory that current Russian President Putin is trying to regain.

48. In Gorbachev's first meeting with a Western leader, Prime Minister Margaret Thatcher reported that she was impressed and described Gorbachev as someone she could work with. Further, Gorbachev articulated his apparently forward-looking ideas about glasnost (openness) and perestroika (economic restructuring away from a command economy) in his book *Perestroika*, which was published in the West. Mikhail Gorbachev, *Perestroika: New Thinking for Our Country and the World* (New York: Harper & Row, 1987).

49. See Matlock, *Reagan and Gorbachev*. One of the more interesting insights that can be seen in this book is the role of both Raisa Gorbachev and Nancy Reagan. In a number of places, Matlock describes the important behind-the-scenes roles that the two wives had in influencing their husbands at this critical point. If one is looking at foreign policy through "gender-sensitive lenses," although the two women had the

traditional role of wife, in both cases they were extremely important in influencing the outcome of events.

50. Kaplan, *The Bomb*, 149.
51. Kaplan, *The Bomb*, 155.
52. Kaplan, *The Bomb*, 156.
53. Kaplan, *The Bomb*, 166.
54. See Howard Zinn, *The Twentieth Century* (New York: HarperCollins, 2003), 355–57. The "Boland Amendment" was the name given to three congressional amendments sponsored by Congressman Edward Boland (D-MA) between 1982 and 1984, all of which dealt with limiting U.S. assistance to the Contras. The first one, passed in 1982, was an amendment to the Defense Appropriations Act. The second one was an amendment to the Intelligence Authorization Act for Fiscal Year 1983 and was passed on November 3, 1983. It was initially introduced as a House resolution "to prohibit United States support for military or paramilitary operations in Nicaragua." It also amended the Intelligence Authorization Act "to prohibit the Central Intelligence Agency or any other agency involving intelligence operations from using FY 1983 or FY 1984 appropriations to support military or paramilitary operations in Nicaragua" (http://www.milnet.com/boland.htm). The third was passed as part of a defense appropriations bill in 1984 for fiscal year 1985, again limiting funding for Nicaragua.

CHAPTER 6: THE PERIOD OF AMERICAN HEGEMONY

I got the title for this chapter from one of the reviewers who looked at my proposed changes to this addition. I love the name, as it refers to a period in time when the United States really was the only superpower. I am indebted to that reviewer.

1. John Updike quoted in Andrew Bacevich, *The Age of Illusions: How America Squandered Its Cold War Victory* (New York: Metropolitan Books, 2020), 1.
2. Bacevich, *The Age of Illusions*, 2.
3. The beginning of the end of the Cold War started in 1989 when "the Soviet Union suddenly reversed course . . . and abandoned its empire in Eastern Europe." John Mearsheimer, *The Tragedy of Great Power Politics* (New York: W. W. Norton, 2001), 201–2. In the most tangible example of the changes taking place, in November 1989 the Berlin Wall came down. Two years later, in 1991, the Soviet Union broke apart and became fifteen separate states. With that, the Cold War ended.
4. Zbigniew Brzezinksi and Brent Scowcroft, *America and the World: Conversations on the Future of American Foreign Policy,* moderated by David Ignatius (New York: Basic Books, 2008), 3.
5. Michael Mandelbaum, *Mission Failure: American and the World in the Post–Cold War Era* (New York: Oxford University Press, 2016), 5.
6. Mandelbaum, *Mission Failure*, 7.
7. Mandelbaum, *Mission Failure*, 9.
8. "Toward a New World Order," President George H. W. Bush's address to a joint session of Congress and the nation, September 11, 1990, https://millercenter

.org/the-presidency/presidential-speeches/september-11-1990-address-joint-session
-congress.

9. Text of UN Security Council Resolution 660, http://unscr.com/en/resolutions/
660.

10. The text of Resolution 678 can be found at http://unscr.com/en/resolutions/
678. Twelve of the fifteen members of the Security Council voted in favor of the
resolution. Two countries, Cuba and Yemen, voted against it; China, one of the permanent members and therefore with veto power, chose to abstain. It is interesting to
note that the resolution referred to "member states" at a time when one of the major
changes in the international system was the emergence and predominance of nonstate
actors. This, too, created a dilemma for U.S. foreign policy, since policy had always
been premised on nation-to-nation interaction. This issue of how to deal with nonstate
actors became especially acute after September 11, 2001, and the attack that was
mounted by Al Qaeda, a terrorist organization.

11. In his memoirs, George H. W. Bush notes that while preparing to go to Congress, he studied the way in which Johnson "had handled Congress at the time of
the Gulf of Tonkin Resolution in 1964." Bush acknowledges that "the Vietnam War
was different, but his effort made a big impression on me, and I began to think about
seeking a similar congressional vote of support." George Bush and Brent Scowcroft,
A World Transformed (New York: Alfred A. Knopf, 1998), 371.

12. See "Authorization for use of military force against Iraq," Public Law 102-1,
Joint Resolution, January 14, 1991, https://www.govinfo.gov/content/pkg/STATUTE
-105/pdf/STATUTE-105-Pg3.pdf#page=1.

13. Bush and Scowcroft, *A World Transformed*, 446.

14. Brzezinski and Scowcroft, *America and the World*, 12–13.

15. J. M. Roberts, *Twentieth Century: A History of the World, 1901–2000* (New
York: Viking, 1999), 775.

16. Leslie H. Gelb, *Power Rules: How Common Sense Can Rescue American
Foreign Policy* (New York: HarperCollins, 2009), 62–63.

17. For an excellent history of Yugoslavia leading up to the breakup, see John R.
Lampe, *Yugoslavia as History: Twice There Was a Country*, second ed. (Cambridge:
Cambridge University Press, 2000). Also see Susan L. Woodward, *Balkan Tragedy:
Chaos and Destruction after the Cold War* (Washington, DC: Brookings Institution,
1995).

18. The country of Yugoslavia was a federation of six republics: Serbia, Croatia,
Bosnia-Herzegovina, Montenegro, Macedonia, and Slovenia. With the exception of
Bosnia, the other five were fairly homogeneous, that is, Serbia was primarily Serb,
Croatia was primarily Croat, and so on. In general, all the groups are ethnically similar. The main difference is religion. Serbs tend to be Eastern Orthodox, Croats are
generally Catholic, and Bosnians are generally Muslim. Prior to the war, intermar-
riage among the groups, especially in Bosnia, was not unusual. (In Bosnia, prior to the
war, as many as 30 percent of marriages were between different groups.) The emergence of leaders such as Slobodan Milosevic in Serbia and Franjo Tudjman in Croatia
fueled the nationalist fervor within each group and led directly to ethnic conflict. The

most destructive and longest war was in Bosnia-Herzegovina, and it involved fighting among the Serbs, Croats, and Bosnian Muslims.

19. Roper Public Opinion Archives, "George H. W. Bush Presidential Approval," https:// presidential.roper.center.

20. Edward Luce, "US Democrats Should Remember, 'It's the economy, stupid,'" *Financial Times*, March 27, 2019, https://www.ft.com/content/b8e4f7c8-5070-11e9 -9c76-bf4a0ce37d49.

21. Mandelbaum, *Mission Failure*, 29.

22. Eugene R. Wittkopf, Charles W. Kegley, Jr., and James M. Scott, *American Foreign Policy*, sixth ed. (Belmont, CA: Wadsworth/Thomson Learning, 2003), 452–53.

23. Elizabeth Drew, *On the Edge: The Clinton Presidency* (New York: Simon & Schuster, 1994), 323.

24. For a harrowing description of the battle in Mogadishu, Somalia, and the issues surrounding it, see Mark Bowden, *Black Hawk Down* (London: Corgi Books, 1999).

25. Drew, *On the Edge*, 318.

26. Quoted in Fraser Cameron, *American Foreign Policy after the Cold War: Global Hegemon or Reluctant Sheriff?* (New York: Routledge, 2002), 22.

27. The fact that the United States chose not to intervene in genocide in various places has been condemned by a number of authors who felt that an important role that the United States could and should play in the post–Cold War world was as a moral leader. For example, one journalist who covered the wars in the Balkans told me that, in her opinion, the lack of action by the Bush administration meant that the United States exercised no "moral authority" regarding policies in Bosnia, and that this lack of action set a precedent that would hamper the Clinton administration's ability to take action. (Interview with the author in December 2000.) For more detail about specific cases, see Samantha Power, *"A Problem from Hell": America and the Age of Genocide* (New York: HarperCollins, 2002).

28. "A Joint Resolution regarding United States Policy toward Haiti," S.J. Res 229, October 6, 1994, https://www.congress.gov/bill/103rd-congress/senate-joint -resolution/229/text.

29. Quoted in Woodward, *Balkan Tragedy*, 6.

30. According to a Pew poll, Clinton's approval rating in September 1994 was 41 percent, and disapproval was at 52 percent. "Americans Unmoved by Prospect of Clinton, Lewinsky Testimony," Pew Research Center for People and the Press, August 4, 1998, http://www. people-press.org/1998/08/04/americans-unmoved-by -prospect-of-clinton-lewinsky-testimony.

31. A number of books deal with the war in Bosnia and the negotiations surrounding the Dayton peace agreement. See, for example, Ivo H. Daalder, *Getting to Dayton: The Making of America's Bosnia Policy* (Washington, DC: Brookings Institution, 2000); Saadia Touval, *Mediation in the Yugoslav War: The Critical Years, 1990–1995* (London: Palgrave, 2002); and Joyce P. Kaufman, *NATO and the Former Yugoslavia: Crisis, Conflict, and the Atlantic Alliance* (Lanham, MD: Rowman & Littlefield, 2002).

32. "National Security Strategy for a New Century," 1997, https://clintonwhite house2.archives.gov/WH/EOP/NSC/Strategy/.

33. In an interview with the author in Washington, D.C., in August 2000, one high-level official in the Clinton administration told me that the United States should not have publicly taken the position that it did about its unwillingness to use ground forces. He claimed that doing so clearly sent the wrong signal to Milosevic, limited negotiating options, and further damaged relations within NATO and between the United States and its NATO allies.

34. Roper Public Opinion Archives, "Bill Clinton Presidential Approval," https://ropercenter.cornell.edu/presidential-approval/.

35. Article 2 states, "The Parties will contribute toward the further development of peaceful and friendly international relations by strengthening their free institutions, by bringing about a better understanding of the principles upon which these institutions are founded, and by promoting conditions of stability and well-being. They will seek to eliminate conflict in their international economic policies and will encourage economic collaboration between any or all of them." The North Atlantic Treaty, April 1949, https://www.nato.int/cps/en/natolive/official_texts_17120.htm.

36. Joyce P. Kaufman, *NATO and the Former Yugoslavia: Crisis, Conflict and the Atlantic Alliance* (Lanham, MD: Rowman & Littlefield Publishers, Inc. 2002), 34.

37. Mandelbaum, *Mission Failure*, 69. It should be noted that Michael Mandelbaum was one of the most outspoken critics of NATO enlargement. He laid out his arguments in his book, *The Dawn of Peace in Europe* (New York: Twentieth Century Press, 1996).

38. Mandelbaum, *Mission Failure*, 39.

39. NAFTA remained in effect into the Trump administration, which renegotiated the agreement to create the U.S.-Mexico-Canada Agreement, which was signed in 2018.

40. When George W. Bush became president in 2001, he defied convention because the first foreign leader he met with was President Vicente Fox of Mexico, rather than one of the leaders of Canada or Europe, which had been the tradition.

41. Some of the material in this section draws on Case 1, "Environmental Protection as a Common Good," in chapter 6, "Pulling It All Together," in Joyce P. Kaufman, *Introduction to International Relations: Theory and Practice*, second ed. (Lanham, MD: Rowman & Littlefield, 2018), 229–38.

42. In 2006, the documentary *An Inconvenient Truth* was released that documents Al Gore's fight on behalf of the environment. The documentary won an Academy Award in 2006 for best documentary feature.

43. UNFCC, "Fact Sheet: The Kyoto Protocol," February 2011, https://unfccc.int/files/press/backgrounders/application/pdf/fact_sheet_the_kyoto_protocol.pdf.

44. In June 2017, President Trump announced that the United States would withdraw from the Paris Agreement claiming that the pact "imposed wildly unfair environmental standards on American businesses and workers." Michael D. Shear, "Trump Will Withdraw U.S. from Paris Climate Agreement," *New York Times*, June 1, 2017, https://www.nytimes.com/2017/06/01/climate/trump-paris-climate

-agreement.html. As will be discussed in chapter 8, one of the first policy changes that President Biden made upon coming into office was to rejoin the agreement.

45. It is important to remember that terrorist attacks against the United States or Americans abroad were not limited to the Clinton administration. The suicide bombing of the U.S. Marine barracks in Beirut, Lebanon, in October 1983, during the Reagan administration resulted in the deaths of 241 marines and other U.S. personnel. In fact, a State Department survey of international terrorist attacks for the period 1981 through 2000 showed a decline in the overall number of attacks, down from a high of 666 in 1987. However, what has changed has been an increase in the intensity of attacks directed specifically at U.S. citizens or interests. While the overall number of attacks might have declined, the loss of life from attacks such as those in Beirut, the USS *Cole* in Yemen (2000), the American embassies in Kenya and Tanzania (1998), the first World Trade Center bombing (1993), and, of course, September 11 all have resulted in a significant increase in the number of American lives lost. Statistics are drawn from Wittkopf, Kegley, and Scott, *American Foreign Policy*, 193.

46. In an op-ed piece in the *New York Times* following the terrorist bombs detonated in London on July 7, 2005, Robert A. Pape makes the point that since 1990, most of the suicide terrorists "came from America's closest allies in the Muslim world—Turkey, Egypt, Pakistan, Indonesia and Morocco—rather than from those the State Department considers 'state sponsors of terrorism,' like Iran, Libya, Sudan and Iraq." Robert A. Pape, "Al Qaeda's Smart Bombs," *New York Times*, July 9, 2005, A29.

47. Gelb, *Power Rules*, 65.

48. "Remarks of President Clinton to the UN General Assembly," September 21, 1998, http://avalon.law.yale.edu/20th_century/t_0026.asp.

49. Wittkopf, Kegley, and Scott, *American Foreign Policy*, 265. The Roper Archives, which compiled a series of polls in December 2000 just before Clinton left office, listed his approval ratings at between 65 and 67 percent. Roper Public Opinion Archives, "Bill Clinton Presidential Approval," https://ropercenter.cornell.edu/presidential-approval/.

50. ISIS is an acronym for the terrorist group, Islamic State of Iraq and Syria. The U.S. government often refers to the group as ISIL, Islamic State of Iraq and the Levant, and it is also referred to by its Arabic language acronym, DAESH. For simplification, we will simply refer to it here as ISIS.

51. There is a great deal of documentation suggesting that there were some in the Bush administration, generally grouped under the heading of the "neocons," as well as Bush himself, who were looking for ways to invade Iraq even before the 9/11 attacks. For example, Godfrey Hodgson notes that "from the very first days of his administration, well before 9/11, George Bush showed an interest in attacking Iraq." Godfrey Hodgson, *The Myth of American Exceptionalism* (New Haven, CT: Yale University Press, 2009), 169. He continues that "Bush had been preoccupied with the danger from Iraq long before 9/11" (170). Hodgson builds a case that for some in the administration, especially Paul Wolfowitz, concern about Iraq goes back to the Cold War, especially concern about control of Iraq's oil fields. Judis also notes that "the

nationalists and neoconservatives had begun to call for Saddam Hussein's ouster in the late 1990s after the UN inspectors left Iraq. In 1998, Rumsfeld joined Wolfowitz and other conservatives in signing the Project for the New American Century's open letter to [President] Clinton calling for Saddam's ouster." John B. Judis, *The Folly of Empire: What George W. Bush Could Learn from Theodore Roosevelt and Woodrow Wilson* (New York: Scribner, 2004), 175. Philip Gordon is another author who also identifies both the individuals and the policies, going back to the 1990s, who made the case for war against Iraq way before 9/11. Philip H. Gordon, *Winning the Right War* (New York: Times Books, 2007).

52. "President Bush Discusses Global Climate Change," press release, June 11, 2001, http:// georgewbush-whitehouse.archives.gov/news/releases/2001/06/20010611-2 .html.

53. According to the terms of the 1994 U.S.-North Korean Agreed Framework, North Korea was required to freeze and eventually dismantle its nuclear facilities that could be used to manufacture fuel for nuclear weapons. In exchange, North Korea was promised light-water reactors (which could not be used for nuclear weapons) and the U.S. promise to send tons of heavy fuel to the country. As a result of these talks, North Korea was encouraged to engage in negotiations with Asian countries as well. One effect has been increased trade between North Korea and South Korea, China, and Japan. "The U.S.-North Korean Agreed Framework at a Glance," https://www .armscontrol.org/factsheets/agreedframework.

54. "Statement by the North Atlantic Council," September 12, 2001, https:// www.nato.int/docu/pr/2001/p01-124e.htm#:~:text=On%20September%2012th %2C%20the%20North,yesterday%20against%20the%20United%20States .&text=Accordingly%2C%20the%20United%20States'%20NATO,of%20these%20 acts%20of%20barbarism.

55. There were some in the Bush administration who had been looking for an excuse to invade Iraq and to get rid of Saddam Hussein since the end of the first Persian Gulf War. Although there was never any proof that Iraq had anything to do with 9/11, that attack became part of the justification for the invasion and subsequent "regime change."

56. Peter Irons, *War Powers: How the Imperial Presidency Hijacked the Constitution* (New York: Metropolitan Books, 2005), 217–18.

57. Irons, *War Powers*, 218.

58. Irons, *War Powers*, 218.

59. *War Powers Resolution*, Public Law 93-148, November 7, 1973, http://avalon .law.yale. edu/20th_century/warpower.asp.

60. The lone "no" vote in the House was cast by Barbara Lee, Democrat of California. For the full text of S.J. Res 23 see, "Authorization for Use of Military Force," http://www.govtrack. us/congress/bills/107/sjres23/text.

61. S.J. Res. 23, passed September 14, 2001, http://www.govtrack.us/congress/ bills/107/ sjres23/text.

62. "President Signs Authorization for Use of Military Force Bill," Statement by the President, September 18, 2001, http://avalon.law.yale.edu/sept11/ president_022 .asp.

63. "September 11, 2001: Attack on America—S.J. Resolution 23 Authorization for Use of Military Force (Enrolled Bill); September 18, 2001," http://avalon.law .yale.edu/sept11/ sjres23_eb.asp.

64. For the actual data see "Presidential Approval Ratings—George W. Bush," http://www. gallup.com/poll/116500/presidential-approval-ratings-george-bush.aspx.

65. Alan Cowell, "A Nation Challenged: Britain; Blair Declares the Airstrikes Are an Act of Self-Defense," *New York Times*, October 8, 2001, http://www.nytimes .com/2001/10/08/world/ nation-challenged-britain-blair-declares-airstrikes-are-act -self-defense.html.

66. As of January 2009, when Obama took office, there were 33,000 U.S. troops in Afghanistan, 15,000 troops with the NATO ISAF mission, and 18,000 fighting insurgents and training the Afghan army and police. By contrast, there were 144,000 U.S. troops in Iraq. The White House, "Facts and Figures on Drawdown in Iraq," August 2, 2010, https://www.whitehouse. gov/the-press-office/facts-and-figures -drawdown-iraq.

67. George W. Bush, "State of the Union Address," January 29, 2002, http:// georgewbush-whitehouse.archives.gov/news/releases/2002/01/20020129-11.html. A video of the address is available at the same site.

68. George W. Bush, "President Thanks World Coalition for Anti-Terrorism Effort: Remarks on the Six-Month Anniversary of the September 11 Attacks," https:// georgewbushwhitehouse.archives.gov/news/releases/2002/03/20020311-1.html.

69. "The National Security Strategy of the United States of America," September 2002, https://georgewbush-whitehouse.archives.gov/nsc/nss/2002/.

70. Todd S. Purdum, *A Time of Our Choosing: America's War in Iraq* (New York: Times Books, 2003), 4.

71. Purdum, *A Time of Our Choosing*, 41–42.

72. The Neoconservatives, or "Neocons," refers to a group of foreign policy analysts, exemplified by a number of high-level decision-makers such as Vice President Dick Cheney, Secretary of State Donald Rumsfeld, and Deputy Secretary of Defense Paul Wolfowitz. This group started with the assumption that America is a great power and needs to be more assertive in promoting its ideals, including using military might as necessary. The Neocons were adamantly opposed to the decision made at the end of the first Persian Gulf War to end hostilities and leave Saddam Hussein in place. According to Peleg, from the time of the election of George W. Bush they were determined to revisit the issue of Iraq. With Cheney as Vice President and other Neocons in high-level positions, it was possible to do so. Ilan Peleg, *The Legacy of George W. Bush's Foreign Policy: Moving Beyond Neoconservatism* (Boulder, CO: Westview Press, 2009), 49–50.

73. See George W. Bush, "President's Remarks at the United Nations General Assembly," September 12, 2002, https://georgewbush-whitehouse.archives.gov/news/ releases/2002/09/20020912-1.html.

74. Purdum, *A Time of Our Choosing*, 52.

75. "H.J.Res. 114 (107th) "Authorization for Use of Military Force Against Iraq Resolution of 2002," https://www.congress.gov/bill/107th-congress/house-joint -resolution/114/text.

76. "H.J.Res. 114 (107th).

77. Public Law 107-40, September 18, 2001, https://www.congress.gov/107/plaws/publ40/PLAW-107publ40.pdf

78. Purdum, *A Time of Our Choosing*, 55.

79. UN Security Council Resolution 1441, adopted November 8, 2002, https://2001-2009.state.gov/p/nea/rls/15016.htm.

80. "President Bush's Address on the Iraqi Invasion," March 19, 2003, https://georgewbush-whitehouse.archives.gov/news/releases/2003/03/20030319-17.html.

81. While some NATO allies, primarily Great Britain, Poland, and Spain, did support the United States and sent troops to fight in Iraq, others, most notably Germany and France, were vocal in their opposition. After a major bombing in Madrid in March 2004, elections brought a socialist government to power in Spain. One of the first acts of newly elected Prime Minister Zapatero was to authorize the withdrawal of Spanish troops from Iraq.

82. Leslie Gelb, a former reporter for the *New York Times* as well as former president of the Council of Foreign Relations, wrote a very insightful piece in the *Wall Street Journal* in which he proposed some solutions to the situation in Iraq. He concluded: "Even the wisest of strategies will confront the odds in making Iraq a better place. . . . A good strategy fashioned with Iraqis, fitted to Iraq's political realities plus a U.S. withdrawal plan, can tap that volcano." Leslie H. Gelb, "Tap the Volcano," *Wall Street Journal*, August 2, 2005.

83. See, for example, Thomas Ricks, *Fiasco: The American Military Adventure in Iraq* (New York: Penguin Press, 2006); Andrew Bacevich, *The Limits of Power: The End of American Exceptionalism* (New York: Metropolitan Books, 2008); and Philip H. Gordon, *Winning the Right War: The Path to Security for America and the World* (New York: Times Books, 2007). Even as I revise this book again, more than seventeen years after the initial invasion, the situation in Iraq remains unstable.

84. See "Bush and Public Opinion: Reviewing the Bush Years and the Public's Final Verdict," Pew Global Attitudes Project, December 18, 2008, https://www.pewresearch.org/politics/2008/12/18/bush-and-public-opinion/. "In 2008, the Pew Global Attitudes Project asked citizens of 24 countries whether they could count on Bush to do the right thing regarding foreign affairs. Majorities in only three (India, Nigeria, and Tanzania) said they had a lot or some confidence." The report continues "On the other side of the ledger, majorities in 19 of the 24 countries in the survey had little or no confidence in the American president. In the four Western European countries surveyed, majorities without much confidence ranged from 81% in Great Britain to 88% in Spain. . . .The survey also found a widespread belief that U.S. foreign policy "will change for the better" after the inauguration of a new American president next year."

85. George W. Bush, "State of the Union Address," January 29, 2002.

86. Amy Belasco, "The Cost of Iraq, Afghanistan, and Other Global War on Terror Operations since 9/11," Congressional Research Service, March 29, 2011, https://fas.org/sgp/crs/natsec/RL33110.pdf.

87. Mike Dorning, "Iraq War Lives on as Second-Costliest U.S. Conflict Fuels Debt," *Bloomberg News*, December 26, 2011, https://www.bloomberg.com/news/

articles/2011-12-27/iraq-war-lives-on-as-u-s-conflict-fuels-debt. The only conflict that has been costlier for the United States is World War II, according to this article.

88. George W. Bush, second inaugural address, January 20, 2005, http://www.npr .org/ templates/story/story.php?storyId=4460172.

89. See chapters 9 and 10 in Judis, *The Folly of Empire*, 165–212.

90. Tyler Marshall, "Bush's Foreign Policy Shifting," *Los Angeles Times*, June 5, 2005, http://articles.latimes.com/2005/jun/05/world/fg-democracy5.

91. Philip H. Gordon, *Winning the Right War: The Path to Security for America and the World* (New York: Times Books, 2007), 96.

92. Steven Lee Myers, "Question of Bush's Legacy Lingers over His Farewell Visits to European Capitals," *New York Times*, June 14, 2008, http://www.nytimes .com/2008/06/14/world/europe/14prexy.html.

93. "Reviewing the Bush Years and the Public's Final Verdict: Bush and Public Opinion," Pew Research Center for the People and the Press, December 18, 2008, http://www.people-press.org/files/legacy-pdf/478.pdf.

94. Peleg, *The Legacy of George W. Bush's Foreign Policy*, 32–33.

95. G. John Ikenberry, Thomas J. Knock, Anne-Marie Slaughter, and Tony Smith, *The Crisis of American Foreign Policy: Wilsonianism in the Twenty-First Century* (Princeton, NJ: Princeton University Press, 2009), 9.

96. Judis, *The Folly of Empire*, 212.

97. "Agreement between the United States of America and the Republic of Iraq on the Withdrawal of United States Forces from Iraq and the Organization of Their Activities during Their Temporary Presence in Iraq," November 17, 2008,http:// www.state.gov/documents/organization/122074. pdf.

98. Steven Lee Myers and Marc Santora, "Premier Casting U.S. Withdrawal as Iraq Victory," *New York Times*, June 25, 2009, https://www.nytimes.com/2009/06/26/ world/middleeast/26maliki.html.

99. Myers and Santora, "Premier Casting U. S. Withdrawal as Iraq Victory."

100. "Agreement between the United States of America and the Republic of Iraq . . ."

101. Gordon and Trainor, *The Endgame*, 694–95.

102. Steven Erlanger and David E. Sanger, "Chilcot Report on Iraq War Offers Devastating Critique of Tony Blair," *New York Times*, July 6, 2016, https://www .nytimes.com/2016/07/07/world/europe/chilcot-report.html.

103. Erlanger and Sanger, "Chilcot Report on Iraq War Offers Devastating Critique of Tony Blair."

CHAPTER 7: OBAMA AND TRUMP

1. Danielle Kurtzleben, "What Kind of 'Jobs President' Has Obama Been—In 8 Charts," NPR, January 7, 2017, https://www.npr.org/2017/01/07/508600239/what -kind-of-jobs-president-has-obama-been-in-8-charts.

2. Mark Landler, "For Obama, an Unexpected Legacy of Two Full Terms at War," *New York Times*, May 14, 2016, https://www.nytimes.com/2016/05/15/us/politics/obama-as-wartime-president-has-wrestled-with-protecting-nation-and-troops.html.

3. "The Historic Deal That Will Prevent Iran from Acquiring a Nuclear Weapon," https:// www.whitehouse.gov/issues/foreign-policy/iran-deal.

4. Barack Obama, "Renewing American Leadership," *Foreign Affairs*, July/August 2007, https://www.foreignaffairs.com/articles/2007-07-01/renewing-american-leadership, 5.

5. "Obama's Speech in Berlin," full script of Obama's speech, July 24, 2008, Berlin, Germany, http://www.nytimes.com/2008/07/24/us/politics/24text-obama.html?_r=0.

6. "Global Public Opinion in the Bush Years (2001–2008)," Pew Global Attitudes Project, http://www.pewglobal.org/2008/12/18/global-public-opinion-in-the-bush-years-2001-2008/, 1.

7. "Barack Obama's Inaugural Address," January 21, 2009, https://obamawhitehouse.archives.gov/blog/2009/01/21/president-barack-obamas-inaugural-address.

8. Philip H. Gordon, *Winning the Right War: The Path to Security for America and the World* (New York: Times Books, 2007), 97.

9. "Global Public Opinion in the Bush Years (2001–2008)," Pew Global Attitudes Project, http://www.pewglobal.org/2008/12/18/global-public-opinion-in-the-bush-years-2001-2008/, 1.

10. "Remarks by the President on a New Strategy for Afghanistan and Pakistan," March 27, 2009, https://obamawhitehouse.archives.gov/the-press-office/remarks-president-a-new-strategy-afghanistan-and-pakistan.

11. Landler, "For Obama, an Unexpected Legacy of Two Full Terms at War."

12. David E. Sanger, *The Inheritance: The World Obama Confronts and the Challenges to America's Power* (New York: Three Rivers Press, 2009), 455.

13. All references here are from Leslie H. Gelb, *Power Rules: How Common Sense Can Rescue American Foreign Policy* (New York: HarperCollins, 2009), 156–57.

14. Michael R. Gordon, "In U.S. Exit from Iraq, Failed Efforts and Challenges," *New York Times*, September 22, 2012, http://www.nytimes.com/2012/09/23/world/middleast/failed-efforts-of-americas-last-months-in-iraq.html?pagewanted=all. https://www.nytimes.com/2012/09/23/world/middleeast/failed-efforts-of-americas-last-months-in-iraq.html. For a more detailed account of the end of U.S. involvement in Iraq as well as the war itself, see Michael R. Gordon and General Bernard E. Trainor, *The Endgame: The Inside Story of the Struggle for Iraq, From George W. Bush to Barack Obama* (New York: Vintage Books, 2012); Michael Mandelbaum, *Mission Failure: America and the World in the Post–Cold War Era* (New York: Oxford University Press, 2016).

15. Remarks of Senator Barack Obama: "The War We Need to Win," delivered at the Woodrow Wilson Center, Washington, DC, August 1, 2007, online at Gerhard Peters and John T. Woolley, *The American Presidency Project*, http://www.presidency.ucsb.edu/ws/?pid= 77040.https://www.americanrhetoric.com/speeches/barackobamawilsoncenter.htm. Audio available as well as the transcript of the speech.

16. "Obama's Speech on the Death of Osama bin Laden," May 1, 2011, https://obamawhitehouse.archives.gov/blog/2011/05/02/osama-bin-laden-dead.

17. In his earlier speech in Ankara, President Obama said, "The United States is not, and never will be, at war with Islam. In fact, our partnership with the Muslim world is critical not just in rolling back the violent ideologues that people of all faiths reject, but also to strengthen opportunity for all its people." "Remarks by President Obama to the Turkish Parliament," Ankara, Turkey, April 6, 2009, https://obamawhitehouse.archives.gov/the-press-office/remarks-president-obama-turkish-parliament.

18. "Remarks by the President on a New Beginning," Cairo University, Cairo, Egypt, June 4, 2009, https://obamawhitehouse.archives.gov/the-press-office/remarks-president-cairo-university-6-04-09.

19. Fred Kaplan, *The Bomb: Presidents, Generals and the Secret History of Nuclear War* (New York: Simon and Schuster, 2020), 244.

20. Mandelbaum, *Mission Failure*, 338.

21. Kaplan, *The Bomb*, 245.

22. For more about these negotiations and what Mitchell hoped to achieve see George J. Mitchell and Alon Sacher, *A Path to Peace: A Brief History of Israeli-Palestinian Negotiations and a Way Forward in the Middle East* (New York: Simon & Schuster, 2016).

23. Steven Lee Myers, "Amid Impasse in Peace Negotiations, America's Chief Middle East Envoy Resigns," *New York Times*, May 13, 2011, https://www.nytimes.com/2011/05/14/world/middleeast/14mitchell.htm.

24. Remarks by President Trump and President Abdel Fattah Al-Sisi of the Arab Republic of Egypt Before Bilateral Meeting, April 9, 2019, https://www.whitehouse.gov/briefings-statements/remarks-president-trump-president-abdel-fattah-al-sisi-arab-republic-egypt-bilateral-meeting/.

25. For a very detailed account of some of the discussions going on in the White House about how to respond to Syria see Mark Landler, *Alter Egos: Hillary Clinton, Barack Obama, and the Twilight Struggle over American Power* (New York: Random House, 2016), especially pages 204–30.

26. "Syria death toll tops 380,000 in almost nine-year war: monitor," France24, April 1, 2020, https://www.france24.com/en/20200104-syria-death-toll-tops-380-000-in-almost-nine-year-war-monitor.

27. United Nations High Commissioner for Refugees, "Syria Emergency," http://www.Unhcr.org/en-us/syria-emergency.html.

28. Karen DeYoung, "Congressional Panels Approve Arms Aid to Syrian Opposition," *Washington Post*, July 22, 2013, http://www.washingtonpost.com/world/national-security/ congressional-panels-approve-arms-aid-to-syrian-opposition/2013 /07/22/393035ce-f31a-11e28505-bf6f231e77b4_story.html.

29. In October 2019, with about one thousand U.S. forces remaining in Syria to help its Kurdish partners and to continue to fight ISIS forces, President Trump abruptly announced that U.S. military forces would be withdrawn. This basically would cede control of the area to the Syrian government forces and Russia. Further, it raised the dangers of a resurgent Islamic state. This resulted in intense criticism

from members of Congress on both sides of the aisle and a reversal of the decision, with the administration saying that a smaller number of forces would remain. But this did little to help the ongoing confusion about U.S. policy regarding Syria, nor did it address the ongoing conflict in that country.

30. Gerald F. Seib, "Few Good Choices for U.S. in Mideast," *Wall Street Journal*, July 30, 2012, A4.

31. Anne Barnard and Michael R. Gordon, "Aid Convoy Is Hit in Syria as Cease-Fire Falters and Bombings Resume." *New York Times*, September 19, 2016, http:// www.nytimes. com/2016/09/20/world/middleeast/syria-aid-john-kerry.html.

32. "Russia and Syria: The Withdrawal That Wasn't," *The Economist*, May 14, 2016, 43.

33. "Russia and Syria: The Withdrawal That Wasn't," 43.

34. "Syria: The Story of the Conflict," BBC News, March 11, 2016, http://www .bbc.com/ news/world-middle-east-26116868.

35. Quoted in Philip Rucker and Carol Leonnig, *A Very Stable Genius: Donald J. Trump's Testing of America* (New York: Penguin Press, 2020), 112.

36. See "Executive Order—Taking Additional Steps to Address the National Emergency with Respect to Significant Malicious Cyber-Enabled Activities," December 29, 2016, https://obamawhitehouse.archives.gov/the-press-office/2016/12/29/ executive-order-taking-additional-steps-address-national-emergency.

37. Rucker and Leonnig, *A Very Stable Genius*, 22.

38. Roll Call, "Senate Report Outlines 'Grave' Russian Threat in 2016 Election Interference Probe," August 18, 2020, https://www.rollcall.com/2020/08/18/senate -intelligence-committee-russian-interference-2016-election-report/. The various reports are available on-line, as are the volumes of the Mueller Report, which also looked into Russian interference.

39. See "Global Public Opinion in the Bush Years (2001–2008)," Pew Global Attitudes Project, December 18, 2008, http://www.pewglobal.org/2008/12/18/global -public-opinion-in- the-bush-years-2001-2008.

40. "Global Opinion of Obama Slips, International Policies Faulted," Pew Global Attitudes Project, June 13, 2012, http://www.pewglobal.org/2012/06/13/global-opinion -of-obama-slips- international-policies-faulted.

41. "Nuclear Posture Review Report," Department of Defense, April 2010, http:// www.defense.gov/Portals/1/features/defenseReviews/NPR/2010_Nuclear_Posture_ Review_Report. pdf.

42. "Chapter 3: Balance of Power: U.S. vs. China," Pew Global Attitudes Project, July 14, 2014, http://www.pewglobal.org/2014/07/14/chapter-3-balance-of-power-u -s-vs-china/. For a very interesting take on the relationship between the United States and China and what it might mean for the future see Graham Allison, *Destined for War: Can America and China Escape Thucydides's Trap?* (New York: Houghton Mifflin Harcourt Publishing Company, 2017).

43. "The Trans-Pacific Partnership: Leveling the Playing Field for American Workers and American Businesses," Office of the United States Trade Representative, https://ustr.gov/tpp/#overall-us-benefits.

44. Nicholas Kulish and Michael D. Shear, "In Tanzania, Obama Calls for a Partnership with Africa to Aid Its Economy," *New York Times*, July 1, 2013, http://www.nytimes.com/ 2013/07/02/world/africa/obama-tanzania-visit.html.

45. Kulish and Shear, "In Tanzania, Obama Calls for a Partnership.".

46. Peter Baker, "Bush a Fond Presence in Africa for Work during and since His Presidency," *New York Times*, July 2, 2013, http://www.nytimes.com/2013/07/03/world/africa/bush-a-fond-presence-in-africa-for-work-during-and-since-his-presidency.html.

47. Steven Levitsky and Daniel Ziblatt, *How Democracies Die* (New York: Broadway Books, 2018), 5.

48. David Jackson, "Donald Trump accepts GOP nomination, says 'I alone can fix' system," *USA Today*, July 21, 2016, https://www.usatoday.com/story/news/politics/elections/2016/07/21/donald-trump-republican-convention-acceptance-speech/87385658/.

49. See Woodrow Wilson's First Inaugural Address, March 4, 1913, https://avalon.law.yale.edu/20th_century/wilson1.asp.

50. Inaugural Address of John F. Kennedy, January 20, 1961, January 20, 1961, https://avalon.law.yale.edu/20th_century/kennedy.asp.

51. See, for example, Andrew Bacevich, *The Age of Illusions: How America Squandered Its Cold War Victory* (New York: Metropolitan Books, 2020), especially chapter 3, "Kicking It to the Club," 44–57.

52. "Presidential Memorandum Regarding Withdrawal of the United States from the Trans-Pacific Partnership Negotiations and Agreement," January 23, 2017, https://www.whitehouse.gov/presidential-actions/presidential-memorandum-regarding-withdrawal-united-states-trans-pacific-partnership-negotiations-agreement/.

53. "Statement by President Trump on the Paris Climate Accord," June 1, 2017, https://www.whitehouse.gov/briefings-statements/statement-president-trump-paris-climate-accord/.

54. Peter Bergen, *Trump and His Generals: The Cost of Chaos* (New York: Penguin Press, 2019), 185.

55. White House fact sheet, "President Donald J. Trump Is Ending United States Participation in an Unacceptable Iran Deal," May 8, 2018, https://www.whitehouse.gov/briefings-statements/president-donald-j-trump-ending-united-states-participation-unacceptable-iran-deal/.

56. Michael Oreskes, "Trump Gives a Vague Hint of Candidacy," *New York Times*, September 2, 1987, https://www.nytimes.com/1987/09/02/nyregion/trump-gives-a-vague-hint-of-candidacy.html.

57. Patrick Healy and Jeremy W. Peters, "Donald Trump's Victory Is Met with Shock across a Wide Political Divide," *New York Times*, November 9, 2016, https://www.nytimes.com/2016/11/10/us/politics/donald-trump-election-reaction.html.

58. Healy and Peters, "Donald Trump's Victory Is Met with Shock across a Wide Political Divide."

59. Quoted in Peter Bergen, *Trump and His Generals*, 245.

60. Quoted in Rucker and Leonnig, *A Very Stable Genius*, 113.

61. Rucker and Leonnig, *A Very Stable Genius*, 114.

62. "Remarks by President Trump to the 74th Session of the United Nations General Assembly," September 24, 2019, https://www.whitehouse.gov/briefings-statements/remarks-president-trump-74th-session-united-nations-general-assembly/.

63. Dan Balz, "America's Global Standing Is at a Low Point. The Pandemic Made It Worse." *Washington Post*, July 26, 2020, https://www.washingtonpost.com/graphics/2020/politics/reckoning-america-world-standing-low-point/.

64. Robert Costa and Philip Rucker, "Woodward Book: Trump Says He Knew Coronavirus Was 'Deadly' and Worse Than the Flu while Intentionally Misleading Americans," *Washington Post*, September 9, 2020, https://www.washingtonpost.com/politics/bob-woodward-rage-book-trump/2020/09/09/0368fe3c-efd2-11ea-b4bc-3a2098fc73d4_story.html.

65. Even as we draft this, another surge of the virus has started to explode in the countries of Europe as well as parts of the United States, along with the identification of new variants of the virus. This latest spread has been attributed in part to the onset of colder winter weather, which has brought people inside and in close proximity to one another, as well as "pandemic fatigue." Many of the European leaders are responding to this latest surge with increasing lockdowns and more mandates to protect people. In the meantime, the approval of a number of vaccines has changed the focus of fighting the disease to ensuring as many people as possible are vaccinated.

66. Richard Wike, Jannell Fetterolf, and Maria Mordecai, "U.S. Image Plummets Internationally as Most Say Country Has Handled Coronavirus Badly," Pew Global Attitudes and Trends, September 15, 2020, 2, https://www.pewresearch.org/global/2020/09/15/us-image-plummets-internationally-as-most-say-country-has-handled-coronavirus-badly/.

67. Wike, Fetterolf and Mordecai, "U.S. Image Plummets Internationally as Most Say Country Has Handled Coronavirus Badly," 3.

68. Wike, Fetterolf and Mordecai, "U.S. Image Plummets Internationally as Most Say Country Has Handled Coronavirus Badly," 5.

69. Bergen, *Trump and His Generals*, 229. One of the points that Bergen makes, as do other accounts of this summit meeting, was that no officials were present to take notes or to report on what was actually said between the two men. As Bergen also notes, "Trump's performance in Helsinki was a sobering reminder to the CIA rank and file that Trump was prepared to take the word of a former KGB officer over the careful work of his own intelligence agencies" (230). This further fueled speculation about what was underlying the relationship between the two men.

70. Bergen, *Trump and His Generals*, 228.

71. Bergen, *Trump and His Generals*, 233.

72. Rucker and Leonnig, *A Very Stable Genius*, 113.

73. Bergen, *Trump and His Generals*, 62.

74. James Marson, "NATO Finds Unity on Some Goals," *Wall Street Journal*, December 5, 2019, A7.

75. Marson, , "NATO Finds Unity on Some Goals," A7.

76. Steven Erlanger, "Europe Wonders If It Can Rely on U.S. Again, Whoever Wins," *New York Times*, October 22, 2020, https://www.nytimes.com/2020/10/22/world/europe/europe-biden-trump-diplomacy.html?referringSource=articleShare.

77. See Erlanger, "Europe Wonders If It Can Rely on U.S. Again, Whoever Wins."

78. Evan Osnos, "Making China Great Again," *The New Yorker,* January 8, 2018, https://www.newyorker.com/magazine/2018/01/08,making-china-great-again.

79. Quoted in Mark Magnier, "China Weighs Approach to Trump," *The Wall Street Journal,* December 23, 2016, A8.

80. "A Trade War between America and China Takes Shape," *The Economist,* April 7, 2018, 59.

81. P. J. Huffstutter, Mark Weinraub, "U.S. Farmers Still Dependent on Trade Aid after China Deal," Reuters, March 11, 2020, https://www.reuters.com/article/us-usa -farmers-subsidies-analysis/u-s-farmers-still-dependent-on-trade-aid-after-china -deal-idUSKBN20Y1B7. In order to assuage the concerns of farmers, especially going into a difficult election, the Trump administration subsidized farmers giving $16 billion in trade aid in 2019 with more promised through 2020.

82. "Chasing the Chinese Dream," *The Economist*, May 4, 2013, 25.

83. "China's Foreign Policy: Well-Wishing," *The Economist*, January 23, 2016, 38.

84. "Foreign Policy: Our Bulldozers, Our Rules," *The Economist,* July 2, 2016, 37.

85. "Foreign Policy: Our Bulldozers, Our Rules,", 37.

86. See Yi-Zheng Lian, "Trump Is Wrong about TikTok. China's Plans Are Much More Sinister," *New York Times*, September 17, 2020, https://www.nytimes .com/2020/09/17/opinion/tiktok-china-strategy.html.

87. Edward Wong and Steven Lee Myers, "Officials Push U.S.-China Relations toward Point of No Return," *New York Times,* July 25, 2020, https://www .nytimes.com/2020/07/25/world/asia/us-china-trump-xi.htm.

88. Rucker and Leonnig, *A Very Stable Genius*, 152.

89. Quoted in Rucker and Leonnig, *A Very Stable Genius*, 153.

90. See Bergen, chapter 10, "From 'Fire and Fury' to 'Love,'" in *Trump and His Generals*, 214–21. It is also important to note that as this was all unfolding, there were significant changes in the Trump cabinet, with Tillerson being replaced by Mike Pompeo as secretary of state, and John Bolton now serving as National Security advisor. This made it even more apparent that it was Trump himself who was making the decisions about North Korea.

91. All quotes taken from Bergen, *Trump and His Generals*, 219.

92. Rucker and Leonnig, *A Very Stable Genius,* 373.

93. David E. Sanger and Edward Wong, "How the Trump-Kim Summit Failed: Big Threats, Big Egos, Bad Bets," *New York Times*, March 2, 2019, https://www .nytimes.com/2019/03/02/world/asia/trump-kim-jong-un-summit.html.

94. See, for example, Joyce P. Kaufman, *Introduction to International Relations: Theory and Practice*, second ed. (Lanham, MD: Rowman & Littlefield, 2018), especially 153–61. I write that "an individual can play an important role in the direction of a country's policy. . . . However, that individual can be helped considerably by other factors, especially the structures within which the leader acts" p. 155). In this case, Trump saw himself as the individual who could change the relationship between the United States and North Korea.

95. Bergen, *Trump and His Generals*, 195.

96. Richard Gonzales, "State Department Loosens U.S. Policy on Israeli Settlements in West Bank," NPR, November 18, 2019, https://www.npr.org/2019/11/18/780587255/state-department-loosens-u-s-policy-on-israeli-settlements-in-west-bank.

97. Drawn from the White House, "Peace to Prosperity: A Vision to Improve the Lives of the Palestinian and Israeli People," https://www.whitehouse.gov/peacetoprosperity/.

98. "What to Know about the Afghan Peace Negotiations," Council on Foreign Relations, September 11, 2020, https://www.cfr.org/article/what-know-about-afghan-peace-negotiations.

99. "What to Know about the Afghan Peace Negotiations.".

100. Much of this information was drawn from Sune Engel Rasmussen, "Afghan Peace Talks: What You Need to Know," *Wall Street Journal*, October 22, 2020, https://www.wsj.com/articles/afghan-peace-talks-what-you-need-to-know-11599922157.

101. Tucker Reals and Ahmad Mukhtar, "U.S. and Taliban Agree to "Re-set" as Afghanistan Peace Deal Marred by Spiraling Carnage," CBS News, October 15, 2020, https://www.cbsnews.com/news/us-and-taliban-agree-reset-on-afghanistan-peace-deal-marred-by-spiralling-carnage-2020-10-15/.

102. See Meghann Myers, "Top US General in Afghanistan Says He's Holding Back to Give Taliban Peace Deal a Chance," *Military Times*, October 21, 2020, https://www.militarytimes.com/news/your-military/2020/10/21/top-us-general-in-afghanistan-says-hes-holding-back-to-give-taliban-peace-deal-a-chance/.

103. Dan Lamothe and Missy Ryan, "As Trump's Term Nears Close, Administration Announces Troop Level Cuts in Afghanistan and Iraq," *Washington Post*, November 17, 2020, https://www.washingtonpost.com/national-security/trump-troop-cut-afghanistan-iraq/2020/11/17/ed6f3f80-28fa-11eb-b847-66c66ace1afb_story.html.

104. Ayaz Cul, "Taliban Expect Biden to Stick to Afghan Peace Deal without 'Significant Change,'" VOA, November 8, 2020, https://www.voanews.com/south-central-asia/taliban-expect-biden-stick-afghan-peace-deal-without-significant-change. As of November 9, the Biden team had not made any statements about their position regarding Afghanistan.

105. Missy Ryan, Karen deYoung and Susannah George, "With Clock Ticking before Exit Deadline, U.S. Appears Poised to Postpone Troop Withdrawal from Afghanistan," *Washington Post*, Mach 12, 2021, https://www.washingtonpost.com/national-security/us-afghanistan-troop-withdrawal-postponed/2021/03/12/cf92d51c-8296-11eb-bb5a-ad9a91faa4ef_story.html.

106. For more details surrounding the background of these negotiations see chapter 13, "Withdrawal," in Bergen, *Trump and His Generals*, 259–68.

107. Thomas Franck, "U.S. Economy: Trump Doubles Down: 'Trade Wars Are Good, and Easy to Win,'" CNBC, March 2, 2018, https://www.cnbc.com/2018/03/02/trump-trade-wars-are-good-and-easy-to-win.html.

108. World Health Organization, "What We Do," https://www.who.int/about/what-we-do.

109. Matt Apuzzo, Noah Weiland, and Selam Gebrekidan, "Trump Gave W.H.O. a List of Demands. Hours Later, He Walked Away," *New York Times*, November 27, 2020, https://www.nytimes.com/2020/11/27/world/europe/trump-who-tedros-china -virus.html?referringSource=articleShare.

110. Apuzzo, Weiland, and Gebrekidan, "Trump Gave W.H.O. a List of Demands."

111. Bacevich, *The Age of Illusions*, 198.

CHAPTER 8: BIDEN AND BEYOND

1. Allan Smith, Nicole Via y Rada, Dareh Gregorian, and Marianna Sotomayor, "'America Is Back': Biden Formally Introduces National Security, Foreign Policy Team," NBC News, November 4, 2020, https://www.nbcnews.com/politics/2020 -election-biden-hold-event-national-security-team-n1248770.

2. Annie Karni and David E. Sanger, "Biden's National Security Team Offers a Sharp Turn. But in Which Direction?" *New York Times*, November 24, 2020, https://www.nytimes.com/2020/11/24/us/politics/biden-nominees-national-security .html?searchResultPosition=1.

3. Joseph R. Biden Jr., "Why American Must Lead Again: Rescuing U.S. Foreign Policy after Trump," *Foreign Affairs*, March/April 2020, 2, https://www.foreignaf fairs.com/articles/united-states/2020-01-23/why-america-must-lead-again.

4. All quotes drawn from Biden, "Why America Must Lead Again."

5. Full text of Joe Biden's speech after historic election, ABC News, November 7, 2020, https://abcnews.go.com/Politics/read-full-text-joe-bidens-speech-historic -election/story?id=74084462.

6. Full text of Joe Biden's speech after historic election."

7. Quoted in Karni and Sanger, "Biden's National Security Team Offers a Sharp Turn."

8. Rick Gladstone, "Biden to Face Long List of Foreign Challenges, with China No. 1," *New York Times*, November 7, 2020, https://www.nytimes.com/2020/11/07/ world/americas/Biden-foreign-policy.html.

9. Graham Allison, *Destined for War: Can America and China Escape Thucydides's Trap?* (New York: Houghton Mifflin Harcourt Publishing Company, 2017), vii.

10. Allison, *Destined for War*, viii.

11. Fareed Zakaria, *The Post-American World, Release 2.0* (New York: W.W. Norton & Company, 2012), 1.

12. Zakaria, *The Post-American World, Release 2.0*, 86–87.

13. Henry Olsen, "Joe Biden Is Going to Need a New China Strategy," *Washington Post*, November 25, 20202, https://www.washingtonpost.com/opinions/2020/11/25/ joe-biden-is-going-need-new-china-strategy/.

14. See David Crawshaw and Miriam Berger, "China Beat Back COVID-19 in 2020. Then It Really Flexed Its Muscles at Home and Abroad," *Washington*

Post, December 28, 2020, https://www.washingtonpost.com/world/2020/12/28/china
-2020-major-stories/.

15. Biden, "Why America Must Lead Again."

16. Saheli Roy Choudhury, "Biden Will Likely Have to Reimagine the Future of U.S. Economic Leadership in Asia, Says Expert," CNBC, November 24, 2020, https://www.cnbc.com/2020/11/24/joe-biden-us-presence-in-asia-pacific-after-tpp
-rcep.html.

17. Biden, "Why America Must Lead Again."

18. Gladstone, "Biden to Face Long List of Foreign Challenges,"

19. David E. Sanger, "Assassination in Iran Could Limit Biden's Options. Was That the Goal?" *New York Times*, November 28, 2020, https://www.nytimes
.com/2020/11/28/world/middleeast/israel-iran-nuclear-deal.html?campaign_id=
2&emc=edit_th_20201129&instance_id=24552&nl=todaysheadlines&regi_id=
45825615&segment_id=45618&user_id=781a9998b2f5d94d4a242914e8a97851.

20. Dealing with the Israel-Palestinian issue will be something else that the Biden administration will likely want to return to, although it appears to be a less immediate priority than dealing with Iran. The Biden administration has indicated that it will not reverse the decision to move the U.S. embassy from Tel Aviv to Jerusalem, nor have they indicated, at least as of this writing, what their approach will be to the settlements and a possible two-state solution. We are not going to speculate here about the role that the United States might take regarding future negotiations beyond indicating that this is another area of foreign policy that the Biden administration will have to address at some point.

21. Michael R. Gordon, "U.S. Withdraws from Open Skies Treaty," *Wall Street Journal*, November 23, 2020, A4 (print).

22. Gordon, "U.S. Withdraws from Open Skies Treaty."

23. Gordon, "U.S. Withdraws from Open Skies Treaty."

24. Biden, "Why America Must Lead Again."

25. Robyn Dixon, "For Russia, Biden Is the Foe They Know. The Kremlin Is Studying Old Playbooks," *Washington Post*, November 1, 2020, https://www.washing
tonpost.com/world/europe/russia-biden-trump-election/2020/10/31/1186305c-184f
-11eb-8bda-814ca56e138b_story.html.

26. Quoted in Gladstone, "Biden to Face Long List of Foreign Challenges."

27. "NATO Mulls Afghan Dilemma as U.S. Draws Down, Attacks Mount," *Los Angeles Times*, November 30, 2020, https://www.latimes.com/world-nation/
story/2020-11-30/nato-mulls-afghan-dilemma-as-us-draws-down-attacks-mount.

28. Quoted in "NATO Mulls Afghan Dilemma as U.S. Draws Down, Attacks Mount."

29. For a comprehensive history of infectious disease and pandemics, see chapter 7, "Infectious Disease and Health Insecurity," in Dan Caldwell and Robert E. Williams Jr. *Seeking Security in an Insecure World*, third ed. (Lanham, MD: Rowman & Littlefield, 2016), 121–38. The author is indebted to Dan Caldwell for sharing this chapter with her and for offering his comments.

30. *Playbook for Early Response to High Consequence Emerging Infectious Disease Threats and Biological Incidents,* Executive Office of the President, https://
assets.documentcloud.org/documents/6819268/Pandemic-Playbook.pdf.

31. "Obama Team Left Pandemic Playbook for Trump Administration, Officials Confirm," *PBS Newshour*, May 15, 2020, https://www.pbs.org/newshour/nation/obama-team-left-pandemic-playbook-for-trump-administration-officials-confirm.

32. Rebecca Spalding and Carl O'Donnell, "Millions of U.S. Vaccine Doses Sit on Ice, Putting 2020 Goal in Doubt," Reuters, December 23, 2020, https://www.reuters.com/article/health-coronavirus-vaccines-distribution/millions-of-u-s-vaccine-doses-sit-on-ice-putting-2020-goal-in-doubt-idINL1N2J30XN.

33. "Joe Biden Speech Transcript on COVID-19 Vaccination Efforts: 'Falling Far Behind,'" *Rev*, December 29, 2020, https://www.rev.com/blog/transcripts/joe-biden-speech-transcript-on-covid-19-vaccination-efforts-falling-far-behind.

34. Stephanie Nebehay and Emma Farge, "WHO Chief Looks Forward to Working 'Very Closely' with Biden Team," Reuters, November 9, 2020, https://www.reuters.com/article/us-health-coronavirus-who/who-chief-looks-forward-to-working-very-closely-with-biden-team-idUSKBN27P14F.

35. Lawrence O. Gostin et al., "A Global Health Action Agenda for the Biden Administration," *The Lancet*, December 1, 2020, https://www.thelancet.com/journals/lancet/article/PIIS0140-6736(20)32585-X/fulltext.

36. Biden, "Why America Must Lead Again."

37. Lisa Friedman, "With John Kerry Pick, Biden Selects a 'Climate Envoy' with Stature," *New York Times*, November 23, 2020, https://www.nytimes.com/2020/11/23/climate/john-kerry-climate-change.html.

38. Quoted in Andrew Freedman, "Pace of Climate Change Shown in New Report Has Humanity on 'Suicidal' Path, U.N. Leader Warns," *Washington Post*, December 2, 2020, https://www.washingtonpost.com/weather/2020/12/02/un-climate-report-2020-warmest-year/.

39. Quoted in Eugene Robinson, "A Climate Catastrophe Is Upon Us. Biden Can Still Make a Difference," *Washington Post*, December 3, 2020, https://www.washingtonpost.com/opinions/a-climate-catastrophe-is-upon-us-biden-can-still-make-a-difference/2020/12/03/cd05b75a-35a3-11eb-b59c-adb7153d10c2_story.html.

40. For example, see John Lewis Gaddis, "Toward the Post–Cold War World," in *The Future of American Foreign Policy*, ed. Charles W. Kegley Jr., and Eugene R. Wittkopf (New York: St. Martin's Press, 1992), 16–32; and John J. Mearsheimer, "Why We Will Soon Miss the Cold War," in Kegley and Wittkopf, *The Future of American Foreign Policy*, 48–62. Also see Gaddis, *Strategies of Containment: A Critical Appraisal of American National Security Policy during the Cold War* (New York: Oxford University Press, 2005); and Gaddis, *The Cold War: A New History* (New York: Penguin, 2005).

41. Joseph S. Nye Jr., *The Paradox of American Power: Why the World's Only Superpower Can't Go It Alone* (New York: Oxford University Press, 2002), 8–9.

42. Walter Russell Mead, *Power, Terror, Peace, and War: America's Grand Strategy in a World at Risk* (New York: Alfred A. Knopf, 2004), 42.

43. Nye, *The Paradox of American Power*, 9.

44. Mead, *Power, Terror, Peace, and War*, 62.

45. George W. Bush, second inaugural address, January 20, 2005, http://www.nytimes.com/2005/01/20/politics/20BUSH-TEXT.html.

46. Mead, *Power, Terror, Peace, and War*, 60.

47. "Remarks by the President on a New Beginning," Cairo University, Cairo, Egypt, June 4, 2009, http://www.whitehouse.gov/the_press_office/Remarks-by-the-President-at-Cairo-University-6-04-09.

48. "The Power of America's Example: The Biden Plan for Leading the Democratic Challenges of the 21st Century," https://joebiden.com/americanleadership/#.

49. Geoffrey A. Fowler, "Converting the Masses: Starbucks in China," *Far Eastern Economic Review*, July 17, 2003, 34–36; and Jason Singer and Martin Fackler, "Japan's Starbooze," *Far Eastern Economic Review*, July 17, 2003, 36. I was in Guangzhou, China, in 1993 when the first McDonald's was opening in that city. There were major traffic jams and huge lines as everyone wanted to experience this phenomenon.

50. In an example of how quickly disease can spread prior to the coronavirus pandemic, SARS (Severe Acute Respiratory Syndrome) is believed to have originated in the city of Guangzhou, in southern China, in late 2002 or early 2003. From there, it was spread unknowingly by a doctor to Hong Kong, where it spread globally as people who were unaware that they were contaminated started to travel, infecting others. Cases were diagnosed as far away as Canada, and tourism to and within Asia came to a virtual halt. It took months to bring the situation under control, although no new cases of the disease have been diagnosed since. But in order to control the situation, governments quarantined anyone who appeared to have the disease; responses included stopping air flights coming from areas that were known to have outbreaks of SARS and examining passengers who appeared to be ill. While some saw this as an infringement on basic human rights and freedoms, few objected if it meant stopping the spread of the disease.

51. George W. Bush, "The President's State of the Union Address," January 29, 2002, https://georgewbush-whitehouse.archives.gov/news/releases/2002/01/20020129-11.html.

52. Smith, et al., "'American Is Back': Biden Formally Introduces National Security, Foreign Policy Team."

53. Constitution of the United States, http://www.archives.gov/exhibits/charters/constitution_transcript.html.

54. In an interview with *National Journal* in October 2010, Mitch McConnell was quoted as saying, "The single most important thing we want to achieve is for President Obama to be a one-term president." Quoted in David M. Herszenhorn, "Hold on to Your Seat: McConnell Wants Obama Out," *New York Times*, October 26, 2010, http://thecaucus.blogs.nytimes.com/2010/10/26/hold-on-to-your-seat-mcconnell-wants-obama-out/?_r=0.

55. For a detailed analysis of how Obama has used executive authority to circumvent a recalcitrant Congress see Binyamin Applebaum and Michael D. Shear, "Once Skeptical of Executive Power, Obama Has Come to Embrace It," *New York Times*, August 13, 2016, http://www.nytimes.com/2016/08/14/us/politics/obama-era-legacy-regulation.html?_r=0.

56. See "Articles of Impeachment against Donald John Trump, December 18, 2019, https://www.congress.gov/116/bills/hres755/BILLS-116hres755enr.pdf.

Index

About the Author

Joyce P. Kaufman is professor emerita of political science and founding director of the Center for Engagement with Communities at Whittier College. She is the author of *NATO and the Former Yugoslavia: Crisis, Conflict, and the Atlantic Alliance* (2002) and numerous articles and papers on U.S. foreign and security policy. She is also the author of *Introduction to International Relations: Theory and Practice*, (second edition, 2018). With Kristen Williams, she is coauthor of *Women at War, Women Building Peace: Challenging Gender Norms* (2013), *Women and War: Gender Identity and Activism in Times of Conflict* (2010), and *Women, the State, and War: A Comparative Perspective on Citizenship and Nationalism* (2007). When she was a faculty member at Whittier College, an institution that focuses on undergraduate education, she regularly taught a political science class on American foreign policy. Joyce P. Kaufman received her BA and MA from New York University and her PhD from the University of Maryland.